The

Privatization

of Hope

SIC stands for psychoanalytic interpretation at its most elementary: no discovery of deep, hidden meaning, just the act of drawing attention to the litterality [*sic!*] of what precedes it. A sic reminds us that what was said, inclusive of its blunders, was effectively said and cannot be undone. The series SIC thus explores different connections to the Freudian field. Each volume provides a bundle of Lacanian interventions into a specific domain of ongoing theoretical, cultural, and ideological-political battles. It is neither "pluralist" nor "socially sensitive": unabashedly avowing its exclusive Lacanian orientation, it disregards any form of correctness but the inherent correctness of theory itself.

SIC

A

series

edited

by

Slavoj

Žižek

Ernst Bloch and
the Future of Utopia

THE PRIVATIZATION OF HOPE

Peter Thompson
and Slavoj Žižek,
editors

sic **8**

DUKE UNIVERSITY PRESS   Durham and London 2013

© 2013 Duke University Press. All rights reserved.
Printed in the United States of America on acid-free paper ∞
Typeset in Sabon by Tseng Information Systems, Inc.
Library of Congress Cataloging-in-Publication Data
The privatization of hope : Ernst Bloch and the future of Utopia /
Peter Thompson and Slavoj Žižek, eds.
pages cm—(SIC ; 8)
Includes bibliographical references and index.
ISBN 978-0-8223-5575-5 (cloth : alk. paper)
ISBN 978-0-8223-5589-2 (pbk. : alk. paper)
1. Bloch, Ernst, 1885–1977—Political and social views.
2. Utopias. I. Thompson, Peter, 1960 July 22– II. Žižek,
Slavoj. III. Series: SIC (Durham, N.C.) ; 8.
B3209.B754P75 2013
193—dc23
2013025251

In memoriam
Jan Robert Bloch
1937–2010

Contents

Acknowledgments

I would first like to thank the contributors to this volume for their patience and for their promptness in responding to queries about their individual chapters. I would also like to thank Creston Davis for his support in the early stages of this project and throughout and for suggesting that I publish this volume in Slavoj Žižek's SIC series at Duke University Press. Thanks are also due to the British Academy for the three-year Research Development Award made in 2008 which allowed me to start my research on Ernst Bloch and which gave rise to this volume. I would also like to thank Nick Hodgin for his translation work, never an easy job when dealing with Blochian language. I would like to thank my colleagues in the Department of Germanic Studies at the University of Sheffield for their support through difficult times and for the intellectual stimulation provided both by graduate students as well as the research culture in the department.

Above all though, my gratitude is due to Karen Leeder, whose editorial work has been without parallel and indeed has rescued the project at several points. Without her this volume would probably never have appeared.

Note on Editions and Translations

Quotations are generally given only in English, except where a particular linguistic or formal point is being made or when a reader who reads German might particularly benefit from having reference to the original. There is no standard edition of Bloch in English. Contributors have therefore used a range of the different English translations of his works available in order to best represent the particular point being made. These, and any adaptations to them, are all acknowledged in the notes to the individual contributions. Some contributors have provided new translations. Unless otherwise specified, all other translations are by the author of the contribution.

The following abbreviations have been used throughout this volume to refer to frequently cited works by Bloch in English.

Atheism	Ernst Bloch, *Atheism in Christianity: The Religion of the Exodus and the Kingdom*, trans. J. T. Swann (New York: Herder and Herder, 1972)
Essays	Ernst Bloch, *Essays on the Philosophy of Music*, trans. Peter Palmer (Cambridge: Cambridge University Press, 1985)
Heritage	Ernst Bloch, *Heritage of Our Times*, trans. Neville and Stephen Plaice (Berkeley: University of California Press, 1990)

Literary Essays   Ernst Bloch, *Literary Essays*, trans. Andrew Joron et al. (Palo Alto, CA: Stanford University Press, 1998)

POH   Ernst Bloch, *The Principle of Hope*, 3 vols., trans. Neville Plaice, Stephen Plaice, and Paul Knight (Cambridge, MA: MIT Press, [1986] 1995)

Spirit   Ernst Bloch, *The Spirit of Utopia*, trans. Anthony A. Nassar (Palo Alto, CA: Stanford University Press, 2000)

Traces   Ernst Bloch, *Traces*, trans. Anthony A. Nassar (Palo Alto, CA: Stanford University Press, 2006)

A good deal of Bloch's work has not been translated. In this case contributors reference the German edition and supply their own translations. Bloch's work is generally cited from the standard sixteen-volume edition of his works by individual volume title:

Ernst Bloch, *Gesamtausgabe in 16 Bänden, St-Werkausgabe, mit einem Ergänzungsband* (Frankfurt: Suhrkamp, Insel, 1959–85).

The following abbreviation has been used for the most frequently cited work.

PH   Ernst Bloch, *Das Prinzip Hoffnung* (Frankfurt: Suhrkamp, 1985)

Slavoj Žižek

Preface:

Bloch's Ontology

of Not-Yet-Being

In his *Arcades Project*, Walter Benjamin quotes the French historian André Monglond: "The past has left images of itself in literary texts, images comparable to those which are imprinted by light on a photosensitive plate. The future alone possesses developers active enough to scan such surfaces perfectly."[1] Far from being just a neutral observation about the complex interdependence of literary texts, this notion of past texts pointing toward future texts is grounded in Benjamin's basic notion of a revolutionary act as the retroactive redemption of the past failed attempts: "The past carries with it a temporal index by which it is referred to redemption. There is a secret agreement between past generations and the present one. Our coming was expected on earth. Like every generation that preceded us, we have been endowed with a weak Messianic power, a power to which the past has a claim."[2]

The question here is: how far should we go along this way? Do we limit the logic of retroactive redemption to human history, or are we ready to take the risk of applying this logic to nature itself, which calls for humanity, human speech, to redeem it from its mute suffering? Here is Heidegger's ambiguous formulation of this obscure point: "I often ask myself—this has for a long time been a fundamental question for me—what nature would be without man—must it not resonate through him in order to attain its own most potency?"[3] Note that this passage is from the time immediately after Heidegger's lectures on *The Fundamental*

Concepts of Metaphysics in 1929–30, where he also formulated a Schellingian hypothesis that perhaps animals are, in a hitherto unknown way, aware of their lack, of the "poorness" of their relating to the world—perhaps there is an infinite pain pervading the entire living nature: "If deprivation in certain forms is a kind of suffering, and poverty and deprivation of world belong to the animal's being, then a kind of pain and suffering would have to permeate the whole animal realm and the realm of life in general."[4]

Heidegger here refers to an old motif of German Romanticism and Schelling taken over also by Benjamin, the motif of the "great sorrow of nature": "It is in the hope of requiting that/sorrow/, of redemption from that suffering, that humans live and speak in nature."[5] Derrida rejects this Schellingian-Benjaminian-Heideggerian motif of the sadness of nature, the idea that nature's numbness and muteness signal an infinite pain, as teleologically logo-centric: language becomes a *telos* of nature, nature strives toward the Word to release its sadness, to reach its redemption. However, one can give to this logic of retroactive redemption also a decisively non-teleological twist: it means that reality is "unfinished," not fully ontologically constituted, and as such open to retroactive restructuring.

And it is here that the unique figure of Ernst Bloch enters, with his ontology of not-yet-being, of reality not yet fully ontologically constituted, immanently pointing toward its future. What comes to my mind here is the countryside in extreme places like Iceland or the Land of Fire at the utmost south of Latin America: patches of grass and wild hedges are intersected by the barren raw earth or gravel with cracks from which sulphuric steam and fire gush out, as if the pre-ontological primordial Chaos is still able to penetrate the cracks of the imperfectly constituted/ formed reality. In cinema, this medium of the "undead" image, this uncanny in-between dimension is clearly discernible in what is arguably the most effective scene in *Alien 4: Resurrection*. The cloned Ripley (Sigourney Weaver) enters the laboratory room in which the previous seven aborted attempts to clone her are on display. Here she encounters the ontologically failed, defective versions of herself, up to the almost successful version with her own face, but with some of her limbs distorted so that they resemble the limbs of the Alien Thing. This creature asks Ripley to kill her, and in an outburst of violent rage, Ripley destroys the entire horror exhibition.

But why shouldn't we risk even a further step back and evoke the "open" ontology of quantum mechanics? That is to say, how are we to interpret its so-called principle of uncertainty, which prohibits us from attaining full knowledge of particles at the quantum level (to determine the velocity *and* the position of a particle)? For Einstein, this principle of uncertainty proves that quantum physics does not provide a full description of reality, that there must be some unknown features missed by its conceptual apparatus. Heisenberg, Bohr, and others, on the contrary, insisted that this incompleteness of our knowledge of quantum reality points to a strange incompleteness of quantum reality itself, a claim that leads to a weird ontology. When we want to simulate reality within an artificial (virtual, digital) medium, we do not have to go to the end; we just have to reproduce features that make the image realistic from the spectator's point of view. Say, if there is a house in the background, we do not have to construct the house's interior, since we expect that the participant will not want to enter the house, or the construction of a virtual person in this space can be limited to his exterior—no need to bother with inner organs, bones, etc. We just need to install a program that will promptly fill in this gap if the participant's activity will necessitate it (say, if he will cut with a knife deep into the virtual person's body). It is like when we scroll down a long text on a computer screen: earlier and later pages do not preexist our viewing them; in the same way, when we simulate a virtual universe, the microscopic structure of objects can be left blank, and if stars on the horizon appear hazy, we need not bother to construct the way they would appear to a closer look, since nobody will go up there to take such a look at them. The truly interesting idea here is that the quantum indeterminacy which we encounter when we inquire into the tiniest components of our universe can read in exactly the same way, as a feature of the limited resolution of our simulated world, that is, as the sign of the ontological incompleteness of (what we experience as) reality itself. That is to say, let us imagine a God who is creating the world for us, its human inhabitants, to dwell in. His task "could be made easier by furnishing it only with those parts that its inhabitants need to know about. For example, the microscopic structure of the Earth's interior could be left blank, at least until someone decides to dig down deep enough, in which case the details could be hastily filled in as required. If the most distant stars are hazy, no one is ever going to get close enough to them to notice that something is amiss."[6]

The idea is that God who created our universe was too lazy (or, rather, he underestimated our intelligence): he thought that we would not succeed in probing into the structure of nature beyond the level of atoms, so he programmed the Matrix of our universe only to the level of its atomic structure—beyond it, he simply left things fuzzy, like a house whose interior is not programmed in a PC game.[7] Is, however, the theologico-digital way the only way to read this paradox? We can read it as a sign that we already live in a simulated universe, but also as a signal of the ontological incompleteness of reality itself. In the first case, the ontological incompleteness is transposed into an epistemological one, that is, the incompleteness is perceived as the effect of the fact that another (secret, but fully real) agency constructed our reality as a simulated universe. The truly difficult thing is to accept the second choice, the ontological incompleteness of reality itself. That is to say, what immediately arises is a massive commonsense reproach. But how can this ontological incompleteness hold for reality itself? Is not reality *defined* by its ontological completeness? If reality "really exists out there," it has to be complete "all the way down." Otherwise, we are dealing with a fiction that just "hangs in the air," like appearances that are not appearances of a substantial Something. Here, precisely, quantum physics enters, offering a model of how to think (or imagine, at least) such "open" ontology.

And the consequences of this radical shift are breathtaking—they reach up to how we conceive the interaction of politics and ideology. The wager of a dialectical approach is not to adopt toward the present the "point of view of finality," viewing it as if it were already past, but precisely to *reintroduce the openness of future into the past*, to *grasp that-what-was in its process of becoming*, to see the contingent process that generated existing necessity. In contrast to the idea that every possibility strives to fully actualize itself, one should conceive of "progress" as a move of restoring the dimension of potentiality to mere actuality, of unearthing, in the very heart of actuality, a secret striving toward potentiality. Apropos the French Revolution, the task of a true Marxist historiography is not to describe the events the way they really were (and to explain how these events generated the ideological illusions that accompanied them). The task is rather to unearth the hidden potentiality (the utopian emancipatory potentials) that were betrayed in the actuality of revolution and in its final outcome (the rise of utilitarian market capitalism). In his ironic comments on the French Revolution, Marx opposes the revolutionary enthusiasm to the sobering effect of the "morning after": the actual result of the sublime revolutionary explosion, of the Event of freedom, equality, and brotherhood, is the miserable utilitarian-egotistic universe of market calculations. (And, incidentally, isn't this gap even wider in the case of the October Revolution?) However, the point of Marx is not primarily to make fun of the wild hopes of the Jacobins' revolutionary enthusiasm and to point out how their high emancipatory rhetoric was just a means used by the historical "cunning of reason" to establish the vulgar commercial capitalist reality. It is to explain how these betrayed radical-emancipatory potentials continue to "insist" as a kind of historical specter and to haunt the revolutionary memory, demanding their enactment, so that the later proletarian revolution should also redeem (put to rest) all these past ghosts. One should thus leave behind the rather commonsensical insight into how the vulgar reality of commerce is the "truth" of the theater of revolutionary enthusiasm, "what all the fuss really was about." In the revolutionary explosion as an Event, another utopian dimension shines through, the dimension of universal emancipation, which is the excess betrayed by the market reality that takes over "the day after." As such, this excess is not simply abolished, dismissed as irrelevant, but, as it were, *transposed into the virtual state*, continuing to haunt the emancipatory imaginary as a dream waiting to be realized.

In his extraordinary opus, Ernst Bloch provided a detailed and systematic account of such an open universe—opened up toward its future, sustained by the hope of redemption, joy, and justice to come. He analyzed this dimension of hope in all its scope, from "low" kitsch romances through political and economic liberation up to religious extasis. In our "postmodern" cynical constellation, he reminds us that denunciation of ideology is not enough: every ideology, even the most horrifying Nazism, exploits and relies on authentic dreams, and to combat false liberation one should learn to discern in it the authentic utopian core.

This approach reaches its climax in Bloch's insight that "only an atheist can be a good Christian and only a Christian can be a good atheist." One should take this insight quite literally: in order to be a true atheist, one has to go through the Christian experience of the death of God—of God as the transcendent Master who steers and regulates the universe—and of resurrection in the Holy Spirit—in the collective of those who fight for emancipation. We may disagree with many points made by Bloch, say, with his critique of Freud, but he is one of the rare figures of whom we can say: fundamentally, with regard to what really matters, he was right, he remains our contemporary, and maybe he belongs even more to our time than to his own.

Notes

1   Walter Benjamin, *The Arcades Project* (Cambridge, MA: Belknap Press, 1999), 482.

2   Walter Benjamin, *Illuminations* (New York: Schocken Books, 2007), 254.

3   Letter from October 11, 1931, *Martin Heidegger—Elisabeth Blochmann: . Briefwechsel, 1918-1969* (Marbach: Deutsches Literatur-Archiv, 1990), 44.

4   Martin Heidegger, *The Fundamental Concepts of Metaphysics* (Bloomington: Indiana University Press, 1995), 271.

5   Jacques Derrida, *The Animal That Therefore I Am* (New York: Fordham University Press, 2008), 19.

6   See Nicholas Fearn, *Philosophy: The Latest Answers to the Oldest Questions* (London: Atlantic Books, 2005), 77.

7   Fearn, *Philosophy*, 77-78.

Peter Thompson

Introduction: The Privatization of Hope and the Crisis of Negation

When this volume was first conceived shortly before the onset of the Second Great Crash in 2007–8, the title *The Privatization of Hope* was intended as a way of showing what had changed since the publication of Bloch's *The Principle of Hope* some fifty years earlier. I wanted to take a look at the way in which concepts of hope, utopia, liberation, fulfillment, transcendence, and all of the other things which contribute to what Bloch called the "warm stream" of human history had become subsumed under the "cold stream" of economic reductionism in its consumer-capitalist form. Happiness and optimism were now counted in cold hard cash and commodities. People were feeling happy about their ability to spend on the basis of their constantly rising house prices and low interest rates. Bingeing had become the international pursuit of pleasure by the wealthy West, encouraged by an economic system which saw it as the only way to maintain itself against the tendency of profit rates to fall in a capitalist economy. Expansion and growth at no cost to people or planet were the totems of the giant noughties Ponzi scheme and concerns about the "externalities"—from global environmental considerations to the Dickensian working conditions in India and China—were either denied *in toto* or pushed to one side as insoluble or, in any case, considered part of the price which had to be paid for economic advance. Living for the day had become the motto of society, and any sense that we were involved in any kind of process or dynamic that would lead to something different, something new, something better had all but disappeared. Francis Fukuyama had proclaimed the end of history in 1989, and despite our objections to it on various grounds, usually ideological, everyone largely accepted that he was right. And for some fifteen years he was right. That particular end of history itself ended in 2008, however, but we have not yet found a new beginning. We are in a Gramscian interregnum in which the old world of the absolute hegemony of capitalism and its ideology is dying, but a new world, or even the semblance of a new world, has not yet emerged to replace it. What is important with Bloch's work now has therefore changed since the first conception of this book. Whereas once it was conceived as a counterblast to the shimmering illusions of the bright satanic malls, now it has become a way of maintaining the "principle of hope" against a growing darkness and uncertainty.

As the crisis has advanced, it has become clear that what was at stake was not only fundamental economic stability but also the political and ideological hegemony of the postwar social settlement itself. Class reappeared on the scene as a political determinant, and the cynical response to David Cameron's contention that "we are all in this together" was boosted by the almost daily revelations about corruption, manipulation, and distortion in the leading echelons of the state apparatus and ruling social groups. Politicians were seen to be feathering their own nests as much as the leading bankers; the press and wider media were seen to be in cahoots with the police and security services; and social inequality and disparity of wealth distribution became clear for all to see. In other words, there had come about an unmasking of the whole political and economic system of ideological control that had prevailed since 1945. The year 2008 was late capitalism's Berlin Wall moment.

As clear as it always was that capitalism is essentially a system of labor exploitation and generalized commodity production—even its more intelligent supporters are aware of that—it also became increasingly impossible to imagine anything beyond the confines of a capitalist order, even one in serious decline. Alain Badiou calls this a "crisis of negation," in which many of the apparent certainties about the way in which the breakdown of social order almost automatically leads to new social alternatives have become severely dislocated. Of course it can be argued that this belief was always naive, unfounded, or—as Henk de Berg argues in this volume—downright dangerous, but in the context of the work of Ernst Bloch, the apparent loss of hope for change or improvement seems to have become a self-fulfilling and debilitating condition. As is so often said these days, it is easier to imagine the end of the world than it is to imagine the end of capitalism. Our thoughts now tend toward the apocalyptic not as the first breath of something new, as Bloch posited it, but as the final gasp of something old.

And yet when Ernst Bloch wrote his *Principle of Hope* he was, as a Jew, Marxist, and atheist intellectual in exile from Nazi Germany, able to maintain a commitment to hope in the darkest of hours. Indeed the first version of *The Principle of Hope* was entitled *Dreams of a Better Life*. It was only the publishers who prevented the use of that title. In many ways it was probably a good thing that they did so, because the title Bloch actually arrived at shows quite clearly that what is at stake is not simply the daydream of how things could be better but the underlying *principle* of how things could be made better and how hope functions in the world as a real latent force. Hope as a principle demonstrates that it is something linked not just to optimism but to the tendencies present in a material world that is constantly in flux.

The chapters in this book demonstrate quite clearly how Bloch saw the world as an experiment. Indeed, his last book was called *Experimentum Mundi* (1975). It begins: "I am. But I do not have myself as yet. We still do not know in any way what we are and too much is full of something that is missing."[1] Bloch was a Marxist process philosopher. For him, there could be no end to history because history itself is the process of the arrival at an autopoietically constructed truth of what it is to be human in the world.

Hope, for Bloch, was the way in which our desire to fill in the gaps and to find something that is missing took shape. But this sense of something missing, of desire, and of hope was not something which had a quasimystical character. For Bloch it started with simple physical material hunger, and yet he maintained a commitment to a dialectical understanding of the unfolding of human interaction with these material forces that give rise to desire and consequently to hope. Thus, while a materialist, he also saw that the route from hunger to hope had taken humanity on a series of ideological and theological byways. These byways were not always, however, blind alleys or dead ends. Instead he searched in them for what was valuable and productive within them.

The gamut of his interests ran from Hegel to Karl May (everything else is just an impure mixture of the two, he once said)[2] via religion, myth, fairy tales, and ideology. The whole of *The Principle of Hope* is thus not just a listing of the ways in which we exercise hope but an analysis of the ways in which hope can be achieved in the real, material world so that our hunger can lead us back home via hope and belief. In this sense he borrowed his categories not only from Marx but also from Aristotle, Hegel, Avicenna, Kant, Spinoza, Schelling, and indeed all those philosophers dealing with the complex and dialectical relationship between the human being and the material world. For him the human being and matter were one and the same thing. That we had not found the way home yet was down to the continuing disjuncture between what he called the *kata to dynaton* and *dynámei on*, between what is possible and what might become possible. Bloch is therefore in that group of philosophers who believe that a genuine and authentic humanity has not yet emerged.

The watchword of much of his thought can therefore also be encapsulated in the idea of the "Not Yet."[3] The process that would take us from a static concept of being to one of becoming and of coming to possess ourselves was at base a material one, but it was also one in which our desires, ideas, hopes, and dreams fulfilled a fundamentally important material function in overcoming the "ontology of the Not Yet."[4] Bloch constantly distinguished between two forms of hope, namely, the objective possibility of hope on the one hand and the always present hope and aspirations of the *noch-nicht-gewordene Mensch* [the human becoming] on the other. As he puts it in his Tübingen lectures: "Matter can be defined in the following way: According to Aristotle's definition it is at one and the same time that which is possible [*das Nach-Möglichkeit-Seiende* (*kata to dynaton*)], in other words that which can appear in history as determined by historical-materialist conditions, as well as that which may become possible [*das In-Möglichkeit-Seiende* (*dynámei on*)], or the correlate of the objectively real possibility of that which is. Matter is the substrata of possibility within the dialectical process."[5]

His attempt to marry the objective and the subjective carried within it both a sober recognition of real-existing possibility as well as the eternal drive of a quasitranscendental vitalism, an innate and irrepressible hope seeking constantly to replicate itself and drive the individual, and thus—in dialectical interpenetration—economy and society, forward. His philosophical efforts were wedded to the human drive, and he was clearly convinced that simply being able to recite the whole of Marx's *Capital* would never move anyone to anything. He was a philosopher who took the Marxist interpretation of the objective development of the economy toward socialization and thus socialism/communism as read and yet wanted to inject the warm stream of human-centered life force into the cold stream of that objective trend and analysis.

The Principle of Hope

The question now—half a century after the first full publication of *The Principle of Hope* and long after the apparent death of the grand narrative of progress—is whether hope can still exist in anything other than an atomized, desocialized, and privatized form. Is the tragedy of late capitalism actually that culturally it has prevented itself from becoming "late," precisely because it has reduced human hope to the lowest common denominator, whilst leaving those of us who would rebel against this apparently denuded and degraded world sighing the powerless quasireligious sigh of the unoppressed creature in a nonhostile world? Have we reached a stage of pure *kata to dynaton* with a *dynámei on* that has lost its driving power? In other words, what has happened to Bloch's "invariant of direction": that drive toward human freedom which, though often suppressed, he claimed was always present? It could be argued that hope generally resides now in individual liberation through money or fame or both. The dreams of a better world are dreams of a better world for oneself or one's family. It is not just socialism which appears to have died but the very concept of the social itself.

In the past few years, and in step with the economic crisis, we have seen more traditional hopeful movements toward the overthrowing of despotic regimes which at least appear to give some hope for a revival of the chance of fundamental change. The Arab Spring, which started in Tunisia and spread throughout the Middle East and is still in its early stages, reminded us of the euphoria of 1989 and the fall of the Berlin Wall. But, just as in 1989, the long-term outcome is open to question and, as with all revolutions, at the moment it appears to have been hijacked by forces that the original revolutionaries would not have sup-ported. Equally, those who overthrow their old leaders today may well find that the new ones are not quite as magnanimous and liberal in victory as they thought they might be.

Despite an apparent turn to a pragmatic accommodation with real existing capitalism, it will be argued here that in philosophical terms Bloch's time might now have finally arrived. As Johan Siebers puts it here in his chapter, this is because "firstly, the idea of truth is recovering from its anesthetic; secondly, religion is back in philosophical discourse, as well as in the workings of geopolitics; and thirdly, questions surrounding the relation of human beings to the rest of nature are urgent." All of these were of central concern to Bloch and, as Loren Goldner claimed in a very perspicacious review of the English version of *The Principle of Hope*, published in 1986, "he [Bloch] still remains more a contemporary of the 21st century."[6]

Bloch was above all a Marxist philosopher who based himself in a Hegelian understanding of Marxism but who sought to reinvigorate a Hegelianism which did not simply present his thought as a dualistic teleology of spirit and nature. To put it in very current terms, he prefigures some of the thinking around contemporary continental thinkers in that he sees philosophy not as something separate from "the Real," or the "*an-sich*," but as a contingent part of it, with necessity playing only a secondary and indeed contingent role. Indeed I would argue that Bloch presents what might be called a *Metaphysics of Contingency*, that is, a philosophy that, though based in contingent materialism, sees matter itself as an unfinished category and carries within it a nonreal drive which contributes to and, as Catherine Moir argues here, creates its own entelechy. Quentin Meillassoux, to take the most prominent contemporary example of "speculative materialism," attempts to create an understanding of the absolute which is both nonmetaphysical and nontranscendental: a "*speculative form of the rational* that would no longer be a *metaphysical reason*."[7] In other words it is an attempt to create a justification for facticity that does not rely on an *in-itself* beyond that which is. Again, Bloch already attempted to do this by talking of "transcending without transcendence."[8]

We might explain this link between contingency and speculative process by paraphrasing Marx's statement in the *Eighteenth Brumaire* to say that "*contingent events* make history, but they do not make it just as they please; they do not make it under self-selected circumstances, but under circumstances existing already, given and transmitted from the past."[9] By stating that every contingent point in history is its own telos, but one conditioned both by its own making as well as its determining circumstances, rather than being a part of some preexisting plan (religious or political-philosophical), Bloch sought to rescue agency and human desire from the dogmatists of determinism whilst defending Marxism against the dogmatists of idealist relativism. Things are neither fully determined nor fully contingent but a dialectical mixture of the two.

We might therefore say that he was a speculative materialist long before the term became adopted in current continental thinking. Indeed, Habermas called Bloch a speculative materialist and attached the label "the Marxist Schelling" to him as early as 1960.[10] Catherine Moir sets out the ways in which Bloch approached the question of matter and the problem of materialism and speculation throughout his work, in particular in his *Das Materialismusproblem, seine Geschichte und Substanz*, and draws some very useful parallels between the work Bloch undertook in the 1930s and that which is going on now. For him, building on Hegel, contingent reality may well be the starting point, but it soon falls away and becomes necessary to the process of the emergence of new possibilities. In Bloch's system of the Not Yet, contingency represents a *kata to dynaton* that carries with it its own *dynámei on*. By arguing for an understanding of history as process in this way, Bloch attempted to rescue both Marx and Hegel from the accusation of teleological thinking.

The only thing that is truly transcendent about humanity, Bloch says, is our desire to transcend. This can take many forms but, as Rainer Zimmermann sets out in his chapter, hope has to be learned as well. It does not just come about automatically, but is the product of experience, failure, and resistance to an everyday acceptance of reality. Bloch called this *docta spes* or educated hope. Hope therefore learns, but it also teaches as well as constitutes its own conditions. It is also the means by which we reach beyond pessimistic nihilism to give purpose to an existence which is objectively purposeless in any transcendental sense. As Bloch puts it, our nature as *homo faber* is what transforms "nature perceived as utterly purpose-free" (*PoH*, 1130–31) to create a sort of optimistic nihilism in which hope is the wave and particle that carries us forward. Nietzsche contended that existence is fundamentally based in the recognition (conscious or not) that "in some remote corner of the universe, poured out and glittering in innumerable solar systems, there once was a star on which clever animals invented knowledge. That was the highest and most mendacious minute of "world history"—yet only a minute. After nature had drawn a few breaths the star grew cold, and the clever animals had to die (amended)."[11] However, it is this very pessimistic bleakness which also gives rise to hope. Hope is not happiness and bland optimism. Hope is what gives us strength in the face of the knowledge of entropy and death, both of the individual—what Bloch calls the greatest of all antiutopias—and of the universe as a whole. It is for this reason that hope plays such an important role in religious belief, of course. Any visit to a religious ceremony will remind one that it is there to hold a light against the darkness. Bloch tried to bridge the gap between the external, nonnecessary facticity of our existence and the internal importance which we give it in the process of dealing with our presence in the world. As he puts it: *True genesis is not at the beginning but at the end*, and it starts to begin only when society and existence become radical, i.e., grasp their roots. But the root of history is the working, creating human being who reshapes and overhauls the given facts" (*POH*, 1376). The point of both philosophy and social action is to overcome dualisms of all kinds so that we might attain the "naturalization of man and the humanization of nature." All this means that in *The Principle of Hope* consciousness comes to the fore not as something secondary to being but as a fundamental part of it. As Loren Goldner highlights, *The Principle of Hope* "exists as a long footnote to Marx's remark that 'humanity has long possessed a dream which it must only possess in consciousness to possess it in reality.'"[12] This would be achieved, as Bloch saw it, only by human activity in harnessing the power of nature around us.

In Vincent Geoghegan's chapter we are shown how mastery of nature—rather than its exploitation—was at the center of Bloch's concerns, placing him firmly on the side of modernity and the development of technology in order to overcome our physical limitations. In this, Geoghegan argues, Bloch must be differentiated from Adorno and Horkheimer who, in the *Dialectic of Enlightenment*, saw technological utopias as the dark side of the human drive to exploitation.[13] Hope married to class struggle and scientific progress were the means by which we could transcend our material roots and speculate about what might be beyond the finitude of both our awareness as a species, as well as our given natural circumstances. In their contribution Francesca Vidal and Welf Schröter show how Bloch's ideas on the ways in which technology can be harnessed for humanity are prevented from becoming real by the ways in which capitalism takes the work that is liberated and turns it into more exploitation for those in work and a greater number out of work. For those in work, at least in the advanced economies, technology has not necessarily liberated them to become more creative but has meant rather that work as unwelcome rather than productive labor has spread into the private sphere so that the boundaries between work, pleasure, and leisure have become eroded.

In the knowledge that, for a great many people in the world, the fetters of being merely a factor of production in whatever economic system prevailed would never be enough to satisfy their desires, Bloch realized that class struggle was not something that could be rejected in favor of some sort of idealistic adherence to an abstract and antipolitical concept of progress, freedom, and liberty. Technology could only liberate in harness with a political struggle to take social control over the labor process. As Bloch puts it in *Atheism in Christianity*, "One should not muzzle the ox that treads the corn, however necessary the drivers may find it to do so, both inwardly and outwardly. Especially when the ox has ceased to be an ox" (2). There are shades of George Orwell's *Animal Farm* here, but there is also the same understanding of the power of class struggle within historical change. Even if people were not aware of their desires or understood them in religious or consumerist terms, with dreams of heaven or a lottery win in the place of social change, the sublimated desire could not help but rear its beautiful head in various preilluminations [*Vorscheine*] and daydreams. Vidal and Schröter show that this is still the case in the most advanced of computerized workplaces.

Caitríona Ní Dhúill argues in her chapter that you don't have to be a Lacanian (although it may help) to realize that desire is born of a sense of lack as well as the lack of a lack. Her chapter deals with an aspect of utopia that is often neglected, namely, that of the position of women. She deals centrally with the way in which traditional patriarchal philosophy sees woman as a vessel for reproduction and often extends this biological fact into a social metaphor. She does not exempt Bloch from this critique, but she does point out that his dialectical understanding of utopia also has implications for feminism and the role of women in a future society which he saw as "eternally female" (*POH*, 1375). For example, when advising an artist friend on how to paint the possibility of revolution under fascism, Brecht said, "Paint a pregnant woman."[14] The trope that the present is always pregnant with the future has, of course, been a commonplace since at least Plato. In this interregnum period, however, we are living with a kind of phantom pregnancy. It is increasingly difficult to see what this historical period will give birth to, hence the sense of a lack of direction and the feeling that the future of humanity has gone missing. Hence also the concentration on one's own private happiness or one's own private paranoia.[15]

As both Bloch and Brecht claim, however, for most human becomings the sense that "something's missing" is both constitutive and provocative. This is why many of the contributions here deal not primarily with political questions but those of hope, faith, negation, negativity, and the void. Bloch was a philosopher firmly rooted in the continental and German idealist tradition, in which speculation about ontological questions plays a primary role and in which epistemological questions about precisely what we can know about our being and becoming are subordinated or, indeed, integrated into our being itself. This helps to explain why Bloch is virtually unknown today—particularly in the Anglo-Saxon world—despite the fact that many of his concepts have found their way into everyday German language. Phrases like *der aufrechte Gang* [the upright gait], concrete utopia, the darkness of the lived moment, the spirit of utopia, and, above all, the principle of hope appear frequently in journalistic articles without any hint of where they might come from or what their explosive content might actually be. Another reason is that much of Bloch's more complex philosophical work, particularly on materialism, has not been translated into English (more exists in Spanish because of his influence in the 1960s and 1970s on liberation theology). In turn this is partly because Bloch's writing style is very difficult terrain at times. David Miller maintains that rather than being frustrated at the way Bloch writes, it is necessary to recognize that his style is itself one of experimentation, both with his own ideas and with those of his readers. Bloch adhered to the idea that thinking was about transgressing, and in order to convey that transgression it was necessary to write in a way that did not fit in with the traditional academic disciplines and that certainly doesn't lend itself to the analytic tradition. We might also say that Bloch's central interest in music as the birthplace of hope—rather than tragedy—means that to read Bloch, one has to read it with a musical ear. Just as it is necessary to give oneself over to music, then it is sometimes necessary to give oneself over to Bloch's writing. Over the coming years translations of Bloch's remaining works not yet available in English will be published by Peter Thompson, Cat Moir, and Johan Siebers with Brill publishers.[16] Moreover, it is to be hoped that this volume will contribute to increased interest in a philosopher who has until now been largely neglected in the English-speaking world but who has substantial contributions to make in the twenty-first century.

The purpose of this book is therefore to make a contribution to rectifying Bloch's anonymity. There are essays here from some of the leading thinkers in Bloch studies both from Germany and the "Anglo-Saxon" world. Although these chapters deal with various areas of Ernst Bloch's work, there are red threads that run through the contributions and, I hope, add up to a more or less complete picture of what he is trying to address in his work. In fact, the subtitle of this book could well have been "something's missing." It appears in many of the chapters here, not only because it was one of Bloch's favorite phrases but also because it contains within its apparent simplicity a philosophical depth to do with presence through absence and the lack of a lack which allows an investigation of the question of what is possible and what might become possible in today's world.

Brecht's 1930 play *Mahagonny* presented a fictional world that bears an uncanny resemblance to the real world in which we find ourselves today. The worship of money has replaced the worship of gods, and it is not always clear whether this is a step forward or a step back. As a good dialectician, of course, Bloch would have said that it is both and that the apparent darkness surrounding us is a necessary precondition for the sparks of hope and the preilluminations of utopia to glow more brightly in the future. As Frances Daly says in her contribution here: "[And] whilst we might no longer face the same type of hegemony in which a dismal disbelief in another world than this gained easy traction, what a present dissatisfaction might mean is not in any sense straightforward." She traces the way in which, for Bloch, the "something's missing," or presence of utopia through its absence, means that nothing-ness and negativity are the very things which are a precondition for the positive realization of our dreams of a better world even when the dark-ness seems darker than ever.

The Spirit of Utopia

Adorno said of Bloch that he had restored honor to the word *utopia*, but Bloch's concept of utopia is far from a straightforward one. Just as he talks about the *principle* of hope, so he also talks about the *spirit* of utopia. Furthermore, he is also famous for having described his utopia as *concrete*. And he uses the term *concrete* here in its Hegelian sense, where it should not be misunderstood to imply some sort of blueprint for the future. Rainer Zimmermann argues in his contribution: "con-crete utopia in the Blochian terminology means thus what can be ap-proached by reflexion and action such that eventually it would become reality, contrary to what is purely utopian and therefore impossible." Bloch takes his understanding of concrete here from Hegel's 1817 En-cyclopaedia, in the section on logic setting a processual—we might say autopoietic—utopia against a preformed and programmatic one. The programmatic version is thus one abstracted from process. Linguisti-cally, the nominalized form *abstract* is actually a solidified form of the verbal phrase *to abstract* or *abstrahieren*. The concrete, on the other hand, is derived from the past participle, *concretus*, of the Latin *concrescere* (to grow together, condense). In other words, the term *concrete* describes an ongoing process of growing together and condensation, whereas the term *abstract* means the extraction of a moment from that ongoing pro-cess. The abstract is, therefore, what Bloch calls a reified processual mo-ment, crucial in its contingent role within history but meaningless in its own right. The truth of an abstraction or a fact can be discerned only on the basis of understanding it within the nonsimultaneity of past, present, and future as we experience and anticipate them.

The problem with an abstract(ed) fact, therefore, is that its truth is limited to itself. It is merely a paradigmatic screen grab from an ongoing film, valid for the moment in which it was taken but limited to that mo-ment and the bubble surrounding it. It is for this reason that Bloch was extremely fond of quoting Fichte and Hegel, who, on being alerted to the fact that their philosophy did not accord with reality, said: "Too bad for the facts!" The vast majority of utopian thinking could be said to rest in abstract utopias, in abstractions from the process in which the utopia becomes something really existing, whereas the concrete utopia is one which exists and does not exist at the same time because it is in the process of its own creation. Little abstracted sparks of utopia exist all around us in everyday life, but they cannot yet add up to a utopian process until and unless they become radicalized, grasped at their roots. The truth of history is, therefore, not an abstraction but the ongoing process of the emergence of the concrete and the growing together of contingency into necessity. History for Hegel and Bloch is thus a tendential process in which the abstracted moments of which we are aware coalesce and condense into a historical truth that has only a retrospective and nonteleological telos. In that sense all history is counterfactual and the future is one of endlessly open possibilities conditioned only by the real and rational outcome of the process to date.

What this in turn means is that a concrete utopia is one that has existence only as a possible outcome of an autopoietic process but that it contains within it shards of past and present utopian images—abstractions—that we carry forward with us on the journey but that also carry us forward, giving us the will to keep pushing forward and to become what we might be. To put this in Lacanian terms, the shards of utopia which we tend to carry with us are the fetishized *objet petit a*, which stand in for, but at the same time are part of, an as yet impossible absolute. Our hopes and desires and utopian impulses become fetishized into abstractions precisely because the process that will fulfill our desires is one that remains by necessity entirely invisible to us.

The Darkness of the Lived Moment

The fundamental opacity of the historical process means we live in what Bloch calls "the darkness of the lived moment" so that we are surrounded both by failure and success, utopia and dystopia, freedom and oppression. The crisis we face today, in contradistinction to Bloch's ultimately optimistic position, is that, as Wayne Hudson puts it in his chapter, "The odds against a boom in utopia are high." In her chapter Frances Daly concentrates on the idea, central to Bloch, of a "darkness of the lived moment," in which we are unable to really appreciate what is too close to us and are therefore thrown into hope as a mediated mood predicated on basic need and transmitted via pure desire.

It is the very absence of any light in the hollowed out spaces of modernity which provides hope in the form of the negation of negativity. Ruth Levitas points out in her chapter on the function of music in Bloch's work—and in particular in *The Principle of Hope*—that he was constantly trying to show that even in the darkest darkness the trumpet call of liberation calls out to us. Bloch repeatedly used the trumpet call from Beethoven's *Fidelio* to illustrate this. Darkness and negativity are prerequisites for their own negation in a mode of eternal hope, an "invariant of direction" as Bloch calls it. However, Daly also alerts us to how much Nietzsche there is in Bloch. But where Nietzsche saw himself as the philosopher with a hammer, determined to smash up all certainties and dogmas, Bloch perhaps becomes a philosopher with a hammer and sickle, determined to transgress but also to create.

What he adds to a consideration of being is a sense of becoming as a social rather than an egotistical goal. In this sense he is firmly in the post-1918 camp of Nietzschean gnostic revolutionaries committed to the overcoming of human limitations through social revolution.[17] Daly reflects, however, that this processual optimism about humanity and the world and our ability to hope has not only been privatized but also brought down to a lowest common level. In other words we have become happy with very limited hopes located within a pragmatic and realistic nearness. The grand dreams have crumbled along with the grand narrative, and both of those were central to Bloch's understanding of human liberation and fulfillment.

What also becomes clear in reading Frances Daly's piece is that most of the time, in most historical epochs, it is the long hours of darkness and negativity that prevail over the sublime moments of hope, over what Alain Badiou might call "irruptions of hope." Henk de Berg, on the other hand, raises the possibility that what has happened is actually all for the best in the best of all possible worlds. That desire for change has ended because there is no real sense of lack in modern capitalism and that this is a good thing; that the end of history is something to be embraced and defended rather than mourned and denied. Reports of the death of utopia have, for him, been far too few on the ground.

Against this, though, we also notice that our times are characterized by a sense of restlessness and apocalypse. Cultural production, especially film, is obsessed with the apocalypse. From the ecological dangers of global warming in *The Day after Tomorrow* to the apocalyptic visions of *2012*, we are bombarded with images of destruction wrought either by ourselves or by external forces or gods. We are also experiencing a form of paralysis brought on by the recognition that, in response to this crisis, there appears to be no alternative to the wrong path, not least because the chances of finding a way of smashing out of the beautiful snow globe of capitalist triumph appear smaller than ever. This means that where before we worked with the concept of the Hegelian negation, which was a precondition for the negation of the negation and thus in turn for the transcendence or *Aufhebung* of the existing, we now work with a Freudian concept of negation, in other words, *Verneinung*, in which we repress the possibility of negating the negation and arrive at pragmatic accommodation. However, that which exists also contains within it repositories of past failures and future dreams that function as driving forces in a "noncontemporaneous" way.

Ungleichzeitigkeit: Noncontemporaneity or Nonsychronicity

Bloch's concept of *Ungleichzeitigkeit* functions in two different and contradictory ways in two of his texts: *Thomas Münzer als Theologe der Revolution* (1922) and *Erbschaft dieser Zeit* (1934) [*Heritage of Our Times*, 2009]. In the first he lays out the ways in which the "invariant of direction" of the desire for human liberation can crop up at inappropriate times and in inappropriate ways. The peasants uprising in 1525 and Münzer's role in it are seen as early attempts to achieve communism based in collectivized property relations and social egalitarianism but whose time came far too soon, before the conditions could be considered correct. In Blochian/Aristotelian terms the *dynámei on* of what might become possible had rushed on ahead of its own *kata to dynaton*. But the revolutionary impulse rather than its failure was the important factor in that episode, and here one is very much reminded of the Beckettian adage that the lesson of history is that one must fail again and fail better until the conditions are right and one can succeed. Aspects of the past that may have gone awry or can be seen as failures can continue to inform present-day events and their future. Rather than reject the failures of the past, we need to build on them.

The second example of noncontemporaneity is Bloch's early attempt to understand the rise of fascism not simply as the armed wing of the bourgeoisie (as the orthodox economistic Left argued in the early 1930s) but as a cultural and quasireligious movement that managed to mobilize and captivate people in a way the Communist Party and the wider Left were not able to. By latching onto golden visions of a nonexistent past, fascism too represented an attempt to fill the void where something was missing. For that reason Bloch got into a lot of trouble with his fellow Marxists in the 1930s for taking fascism seriously, rather than dismissing it as a simple capitalist aberration or a delusion. His reason for this was partly that he saw it as a religious movement, and that all religious movements have their roots in human desire, for him the most powerful of all motivating forces. Fascism attempted to do this by mobilizing forces whose time had long passed but whose perverse utopian shadows projected into the future—a true conservative revolution that harked back and harked forward at the same time. However, while Bloch criticizes the romantic, the nostalgic, and the backward-looking, he does not criticize their impulses.

This attitude toward the rise of fascism therefore mirrored and was a part of Bloch's analysis of religion. Many of the chapters here deal with this central concern of the role that religious faith plays in human history and the way in which it is the carrier not just of delusions, as Richard Dawkins would have it, but also of allusions to a realization of human desires. The utopian drive is held in religion as a sense of light against the darkness of the lived moment. His support for religious impetus and messianic belief as a self-misunderstood revolutionary fervor was accompanied by an absolute opposition to the hijacking and reification of that fervor by churches and organized religions. As he says, the best thing about religion is that it creates heretics.[18] In this field, too, Bloch anticipates much of the contemporary debate about faith, religion, and the relationship between theology and theory undertaken by Slavoj Žižek and Alain Badiou.[19] The fidelity to an event, as Badiou called it, is pursued by Bloch, too, in his fidelity—despite all of his own personal doubts and experiences—to the Bolshevik revolution. For him, just as religion carried the utopian spark in a perverted idealist form, so the Russian Revolution carried it in a perverted materialist form.

Religion, Messianism, and Atheism

Jürgen Moltmann has claimed that Bloch essentially stands in the tradition of Jewish Messianism and was influenced by members of the Weber Group and by Gershom Scholem and Walter Benjamin in particular rather than by Marxism. In his *Redemption and Utopia* Michael Löwy maintains that Jewish Messianic thought embodies five elements:

1. Restoration of a Golden Age;
2. Revolutionary cataclysm and apocalypse;
3. *Et Ketz* or creation of a totally new world rather than reform of the old one;
4. Theocratic anarchy in which there is no gap between the people and God;
5. Anarchistic freedom in which there are no laws because there is no need for law.[20]

It is true that all of these are to be found in Bloch, and as Roland Boer highlights in his contribution to this volume, eschatology and myth play a central role in his thought. David Miller also calls attention to the fact that "Habermas also hints at a role for Lurianic ideas such as *Sheviret ha Kelim* (Shattering of the Vessels) in Bloch's writings." But Bloch's theology is, in the end, essentially Christian in nature but materialist in form. It is this commitment to the violence of the revolutionary eschaton and the ability to love thy neighbor thereafter—Bloch equates loving thy neighbor with the withering away of the state under communism[21]—that gives rise to his famous saying from *Atheism in Christianity* that "only an atheist can be a good Christian; only a Christian can be a good atheist" (viii). In *The Spirit of Utopia* Bloch talks of the need for a new church that will help steer a people who have been made selfish by capitalism to a new fraternalism dedicated to achieving this on earth rather than in heaven. Bloch's presentation of the revolutionary universalism that early Christianity represented—before it degenerated into Constantinian imperialism (*Atheism*, 43)—and the role of St. Paul in promoting the idea of a sudden irruption of faith and change are highly reminiscent of Badiou's work.

The Alpha-Way-Omega structure of his historical model, in which, as he says at the end of *The Principle of Hope*, the true genesis comes at the end and not the beginning, is part of Bloch's Marxism, too, operating as it does with a tripartite and tendentially quasimetaphysical concept of the transition from primitive communism on to historical society through to posthistorical society or communism on a higher plane. Bloch's problem with Marxism as it had developed, though, was the way in which it had reduced the problem of human alienation down to its economic determinants. However, rather than being what Rorty calls another "whacked-out triadomaniac"[22] looking for codes or a key to unlocking a pregiven mystery, Bloch maintained that there were no keys to a preexisting Platonic ideal but only tools by which man could build his own future. Bloch saw it in the same way as Marx puts it in the *Grundrisse*:

> When the narrow bourgeois form has been peeled away, what is wealth, if not the universality of needs, capacities, enjoyments, productive powers, etc., of individuals, produced in universal exchange? What, if not the full development of human control over the forces of nature—those of his own nature as well as those of so-called "nature"? What, if not the absolute elaboration of his creative dispositions, without any preconditions other than antecedent historical evolution which makes the totality of this evolution—i.e., the evolution of all human powers as such, unmeasured by any previously established yardstick, an end in itself? What is this, if not a situation where man does not produce himself in any determined form, but produces his totality? Where he does not seek to remain something formed by the past, but is in the absolute movement of becoming?[23]

Faith, belief, a confidence and certainty in the future of the totality of human becoming against all the pessimism of really existing conditions was also necessary and had to be based in the possibility of transcendence, if not the transcendental. Where William James maintains that the transcendent breaks in on us from some external realm, Bloch maintained, with Marx, that it in fact breaks out of us from the material realm and is the product of the creating, laboring human be(com)ing. What moves Bloch is the way that people do this, the way they hope for, but also misunderstand, what is being done, place hope in things which can never bring exodus and liberation to fruition but which, within the totality, represent the invariant of direction which is the utopian desire for home.

Notes

1   Ernst Bloch, *Experimentum Mundi: Frage, Kategorien des Herausbringens, Praxis* (Frankfurt: Suhrkamp, 1975), 11.

2   Ernst Bloch, *Tendenz — Latenz — Utopie* (Frankfurt: Suhrkamp, 1978), 373.

3   Jamie Owen Daniel and Tom Moylan, eds., *Not Yet: Reconsidering Ernst Bloch* (London: Verso, 1997).

4   Ernst Bloch, *Philosophische Grundfragen I: Zur Ontologie des Noch-Nicht-Seins* (Frankfurt: Suhrkamp, 1961).

5   Ernst Bloch, *Tübinger Einleitung in die Philosophie* (Frankfurt: Suhrkamp, 1970), 233.

6   Loren Goldner, review of Ernst Bloch, *The Principle of Hope*, trans. Neville Plaice, Stephen Plaice, and Paul Knight (Cambridge, MA: MIT Press, 1986), available at http://home.earthlink.net/~lrgoldner/bloch.html.

7   Quentin Meillassoux, *After Finitude: An Essay on the Necessity of Contingency* (London: Continuum, 2008), 77.

8   Ernst Bloch, *Atheism in Christianity: The Religion of the Exodus and the Kingdom* (London: Verso, 2009), viii.

9   See http://www.marxists.org/archive/marx/works/1852/18th-brumaire/index.htm.

10   Jürgen Habermas, *Philosophical-Political Profiles* (Cambridge, MA: MIT Press, 1983), 61.

11   Friedrich Nietzsche, *On Truth and Lies in an Extra-Moral Sense*, quoted in Bloch, *POH*, 1331.

12   See Bloch, *POH*, 1363, for the original.

13   See Theodor Adorno and Max Horkheimer, *Dialectic of Enlightenment*, trans. Edmund Jephcott (Palo Alto, CA: Stanford University Press, 2002).

14   Bertolt Brecht, *Me-ti, Buch der Wendungen* (Frankfurt: Suhrkamp, 1965), no. 5, 164.

15   Anders Breivik even managed to privatize his fascist pogrom and invent his own fantasy international Knights Templar movement.

16   See http://www.brill.nl/.

17   Jean Juarès, for example, is reported to have said that the proletariat is the *Übermensch*. In 1924 Trotsky maintained that communism would allow the generality of man to become a socialized "superman." He would become "immeasurably stronger, wiser, and subtler; his body will become more harmonized, his movements more rhythmic, his voice more musical. The forms of life will become dynamically dramatic. The average human type will rise to the heights of an Aristotle, a Goethe, or a Marx. And above this ridge new peaks will rise." Leon Trotsky, *Literature and Revolution* (Chicago: Haymarket, 2005), 207.

18   See also François Laruelle, *Future Christ: A Lesson in Heresy* (London: Continuum, 2010).

19   See Alain Badiou, *Saint Paul: The Foundation of Universalism* (Palo Alto, CA: Stanford University Press, 2003), and Slavoj Žižek and John Milbank, *The Monstrosity of Christ: Paradox or Dialectic?* (Cambridge, MA: MIT Press, 2009).

20   Michael Löwy, *Redemption and Utopia: Jewish Libertarian Thought in Central Europe* (Palo Alto, CA: Stanford University Press, 1992), 19.

21   Rainer Traub and Harald Wieser, eds., *Gespräche mit Ernst Bloch* (Frankfurt: Suhrkamp, 1977), 166.

22   Richard Rorty, *Philosophy and Social Hope* (London: Penguin, 1999), 134.

23   Karl Marx, *Grundrisse: Introduction to the Critique of Political Economy* (Harmondsworth, UK: Penguin, 1973), 488.

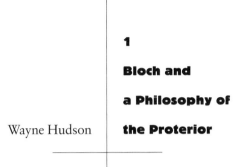

1

Bloch and

a Philosophy of

Wayne Hudson | **the Proterior**

The odds against a boom in utopia are high.
—Jürgen Habermas

Utopia has aged. No one believes anymore in a perfect society or in a perfect humanity. On the other hand, the need to imagine a better future remains. Ernst Bloch was the most original thinker to defend the continuing significance of utopia in the twentieth century, yet he remains relatively little understood in the English-speaking world. When I began to study in Oxford almost forty years ago, I was only allowed to work on Bloch because Leszek Kołakowski agreed to supervise. In the early 1970s Gillian Rose and I were among the very few at Oxford trying to rethink Marxism in the light of classical German philosophy. When I wrote *The Marxist Philosophy of Ernst Bloch* (1982), I had to establish his intellectual credentials and to demonstrate his importance for the Marxist tradition at a time when Althusser and Gramsci were more fashionable figures. In the 1980s German classical philosophy was mainly available in caricature in English, and I did not know enough about Schelling to appreciate Bloch's subtlety at some points. Moreover, although I talked at length with Bloch himself,[1] I was too young to entirely appreciate the dialectical complexity of his thinking, as he noted with a mixture of astonishment and bemusement in our interchanges. Today, as a result of new translations and exceptionally fine studies, classical German philosophy is being received in English as the major philosophical achievement of the West after the Greeks. Now, as then, however, Bloch's extraordinary legacy has still not been adequately received in the Anglo-Saxon world, despite the labors of many.

In this chapter I draw attention to aspects of Bloch's still largely unrealized legacy and propose that it may be possible to inherit this legacy in the context of a philosophy of the proterior.

I

At his death on 4 August 1977 Bloch was known as a utopian Marxist and as the philosopher of hope, characteristics of declining appeal in the decades that followed. In the English-speaking world, no clear view of Bloch's importance has emerged. Both Anglo-Saxon good sense and the arcane nature of his German texts make it hard for us to know what to make of him. Nonetheless, Bloch's legacy is astonishingly rich, and the volumes of his collected works contain model ideas of outstanding contemporary importance.[2] Today, however, there is a need to release Bloch's legacy from the political as well as the philosophical contexts in which it arose.

In political terms, the hope that Marxism can be salvaged along the lines that Bloch and Lukács proposed has passed away. It is now widely agreed that a reconstruction of Marxism must be more severe than Bloch realized and may have to conform to intellectual canons to which Bloch himself was not sympathetic. Bloch then easily appears as a utopian who failed to grasp why utopias have to be given up and as a Marxist who lacked the detailed history and economics to provide a powerful framework for Marxist theory. There are those who argue, plausibly within limits, that Bloch belongs to a phase of German Jewish cultural history that is now irretrievably behind us, that Bloch was at best a Marxist Schelling (Habermas), at worst the philosopher of German Expressionism who failed to develop. Equally, there are those who seek to locate Bloch within a typology of western Marxism as a religious leftist who never freed himself from metapolitical satisfactions and who remained politically deluded for most of his career. This is a reading which vulgarizes the complexity of Bloch's political analyses, including his endorsements of Lenin and Stalin, the hard political judgments which he made about the socialist East, and the degree to which he was prepared to tailor his intellectual activities to the attempt to "build socialism." It is also a reading which fails to account for the shrewdness of Bloch's analysis of the Nazis, his evaluations of the political potential of a green politics, or *Naturpolitik*, and his commitment to an alliance of socialist and progressive Christian forces, as well as to the cause of women's liberation and to work for peace.

Because Bloch's work does not conform to the expectations of philosophers of an epistemological bent, he is sometimes presented as a forerunner of postmodernism without the necessary qualifications.[3] However, once it is established that Bloch was not a postmodernist but an advocate of a new edition of the Enlightenment, the relevance of his work on multi-temporalism, non-contemporaneity, and the need to work outside and below tertiary cultures can be discussed.

What is needed is an interpretation of Bloch that refuses safe houses. Bloch was extra muros. He stood outside the university culture of his time and its Neokantian obsessions with epistemological and intra-systematic concerns. He did so as a rebel against the subjection of rational thought to methodologically controlled discourses. The scandalous character of Bloch's work is essential to it, and it is a fundamental mistake to join those who seek to domesticate Bloch posthumously, as though, cleaned up, he could take his rightful place in the German philosophical pantheon alongside Walter Benjamin and Adorno. Like Jakob Boehme or Johann Georg Hamann, Bloch was an irregular, and the importance of his contributions becomes more evident as the limitations of the modern disciplinary organizations of knowledge are recognized.

Against such domestication, it is necessary to insist on *the unavailability of Bloch's work*, and the fact that there is *a continuing delay* in the course of its reception as only some aspects of Bloch's work are really taken up.[4] An abnormal time structure is fundamental to Bloch: a time structure linking anticipatory insights to later developments and this time structure applies to his own work. It explains why even today his study of the problem of materialism awaits an adequate reception.[5]

Bloch's work demands an effort because it is designed to subvert premature conceptions of rationality and the discourses dependent on them. Bloch used a form of abnormal writing as a way of highlighting questions and perspectives that had been missed. He can be seen as a pioneer of a transdisciplinary writing that runs across the disciplines to uncover issues and themes that they repress, avoid, or render illegitimate.[6] Here, understandably, the French have proved best equipped to appreciate his importance (Gérard Raulet, Jean-François Lyotard, Louis Marin, and Emmanuel Levinas).[7] In the Anglophone world, however, those who deny that Nietzsche's contribution to a philosophy of the future has been adequately assimilated by either Heidegger or Derrida will find Bloch contemporary reading. Bloch's work is recondite and full of postponements. To ask, "Has the Emperor any clothes?" misses its temporal distribution and invites a premature reconstruction of Bloch's ideas. There is no futuristic gnosis (Leszek Kolakowski). Prophecy and predictions are wholly lacking. Nor is occultism the key, Pythagorean or otherwise (George Steiner). Marxist Romantic will not do (Jürgen Habermas). Nor will Jewish messianist suffice (Jürgen Moltmann).

One of Bloch's major insights was that working temporally with the *utopian surplus* found throughout human cultural history and nature was essential to contemporary enlightenment.[8] Bloch grasped the connection between reduced expectations about our ability to find an unassailable foundation for the good and the need to learn to pursue realizable goals by rectifying hope in the light of actual historical outcomes. No doubt such temporally sophisticated hope requires concrete methodological innovations and rational procedural controls that Bloch failed to provide. Nonetheless, Bloch was not wrong to think that corrected hope can lead to knowledge. Nor was he mistaken to think that hope can play a part in rationality intent upon a world in which millions of people will not starve. A reevaluation of hope as an element of rationality would be no mean legacy for Bloch. Finally, at a time when utopia is in disrepute and is widely used as a term of abuse, Bloch can help us to realize that the case for utopia does not fall with utopian illusions.

Bloch was not a social utopian of any standard sort. He devised no ideal society. Instead, he was attracted by many different strands of counterfactual culture. As a result, his work slips through the perspicacious distinctions between utopia, Arcadia and Cockayne, to which historians of utopian thought resort. Bloch was closest perhaps to utopians of the chiliastic variety, above all Thomas Münzer. His utopian expectations related to personal experience of the presence of the end is the now of the moment. On the basis of this experience, he was irrepressibly hopeful. Existing reality restricted his daydreaming less than it constrained his contemporaries. He was invincibly convinced, for both philosophical and psychological reasons, that maximal, if currently counterfactual, good was possible. And for him there was also an anticipatory element in cognition. Where the rest of us tend to judge our success in thinking by its relation to current modes of discourse, Bloch believed that he could think beyond such modes in ways that would bear fruit. This Jules Verne quality went with an eschatological orientation, in part gnostic, in part biblical, and a radical openness to a possible future transformation of nature.

Nonetheless, Bloch was no naive utopian. He believed that what manifested as utopian fantasy in European thought from the Renaissance onward was a socially and economically conditioned expression of a human capacity to reject existing states of affairs and to daydream of states of affairs in which what should be would be the case. What is at stake, then, in Bloch's work is utopia as presemblance that can be harnessed and set to work. Bloch held that manifestations of this reality could be found throughout the human world and that the neglect of it led to a lack of insightful models for political, social, legal, and cultural change. Nonetheless, the manifestations of this psychotemporal reality were not merely subjective. Rather they could involve anticipatory knowledge and be related to developing possibilities.

Taking up Bloch's legacy here requires a willingness to admit both *a constructive function for philosophy* at the level of method and *the irreducible role of normative postulates in philosophical rationalism*. Bloch saw that getting it right in terms of existing conditions was often too conservative, that hazarding what the good required often meant taking leave of epistemological guarantees. He was acutely aware that at least some philosophers needed to take account of the causality of their own work in the context of the future of people and their societies. Here Michel Foucault was among his heirs.

Any attempt to engage with Bloch's legacy and set it to work encounters the problem of what he meant by "utopian philosophy." Given that Bloch wrote so much, it is amazing that he devoted so little space to clear answers to central questions. The answers are there, but they are implicit, and it is often only developments after Bloch's death which help the reader to get past his arcane terminology to a thought that assumes knowledge of Kant's work on practical reason and the sublime,

Schelling on the blind spot of the moment, and the theory of the unconscious found (before Freud) in the works of the now largely forgotten philosopher Eduard von Hartmann (1842–1906). In each case the philosophical background is well known to experts in German philosophy, but not well known to English-speaking intellectuals without such professional expertise. Even in Germany many who are expert on Kant are not *aficionados* of Schelling, let alone of von Hartmann. Hence they tend not to be able to follow Bloch's movement beyond school philosophy and its logics to *a different type of philosophy altogether*. Instead they ask, predictably, what in Bloch is really new?

Bloch contributed a new idea to the history of utopian thought. This was the idea that utopia was not "no place," but existed in the darkness of the lived moment and its transcending dynamic.[9] In contrast to Adorno's negative dialectics or Marcuse's libidinal sophistications, Bloch theorized utopia in terms of Schelling's critique of transparent accounts of consciousness. Utopia was not in the manifest field but in the nontransparent darkness of the lived moment. Our daily experience of the world was traversed by a wonderful, unconstruable *excess*. Hence Bloch could assert that there was no dualism possible between utopia and actuality, since utopia pervaded experienced actuality as a nonavailable *incognito*.[10] Just as there is no way to talk adequately in tertiary terms about the erotic experiences that we all have, and the vocabularies used tend to be scatological or euphemistic, so Bloch held that utopia was given experientially as a daily reality but repressed in discourse. Consistent with the critical pessimist side of his thought, Bloch did not pretend that utopia could be demystified and translated into school philosophy terms. On the contrary, no one could know what utopia corresponded to. But this did not eliminate the problem of utopia because the humanly experienced world was pervaded by a wonderful *incognito*, which could be normatively glossed, even though it could not be identified in ontic terms.

Here Bloch's conception struck at the mundanity and accessibility of much modern philosophy, and it has parallels in French Surrealist discussions of an atopical void or abyss which destroys the possibility of traditional ontology, a prominent theme in the work of Maurice Blanchot. Nonetheless, what Bloch meant by "utopian philosophy" needs to be extended from its historical location in the early Lukács-Bloch collaboration and the turn to utopia by many central European Jewish intellectuals after 1914. The need for philosophical utopias has long been recognized by historians of philosophy. Indeed, historians of philosophy have concluded that without such surplus, the great "ruins" of the history of philosophy would arguably never arise in the first place. The role of utopia in philosophy itself, however, is little investigated, despite the remarkable work of Michèle Le Doeuff.[11]

Bloch sought to pioneer *a utopian philosophy with a constructive historical function*. He held that at least some philosophers should concern themselves with human affairs and the state of the world and with how people understand themselves and their society. Here he influenced Adorno and, through him, some of the subsequent work of the Frankfurt School. It remains a vexed question how far such concerns should be regarded as proper to philosophers qua philosophers, as opposed to concerns which philosophers may take up as citizens or as interdisciplinary writers. Bloch opted for the first alternative.

By utopian philosophy Bloch meant philosophy that took utopia as its central concern, where utopia meant the a-topical *mysterium* in the darkness of the lived moment.[12] Bloch was not suggesting that philosophy should become abstract social utopianism or that philosophers should write accounts of perfect societies. His point was a post-Nietzschean one and based on his own readings of Kant, Hegel, and Schelling. Given that human beings had no access to any supra-historical absolute truth, the human need to project a vision of highest good could not be met by certain established claims of knowledge. On the contrary, there was a clear tension between the restricted and moderate strong knowledges that could be constructed and the unconstruable wonder [*thaumazein*] that human beings experienced but for which they could find no adequate cognitive place. In the contemporary period, Bloch suggested, this wonder and the irrepressible hope to which it gave rise could only be adequately responded to by an assertion of its content which remained without epistemological guarantees. Utopia, in this sense, was all that was available to contemporary humanity by way of transcendence.

This realistic, even pessimistic, side of Bloch's thought has been widely overlooked. Bloch's notion of utopia was a sociohistorically sophisticated one that can be located in early twentieth-century German social philosophy, including the work of the German sociologist Georg

Simmel. In Bloch's account, utopian philosophy would operate in a uto-pian manner, and it lacks a rigorous methodology in the period in which it achieved its initial indications. Utopian philosophy in Bloch's sense would seek to criticize existing discourses, practices, and conditions by reference to utopian postulates and seek to direct attention to concrete possibilities developing in the world, whether social or natural. It would seek to keep the culture open to new possibilities and to provide it with a sense of "where to" in a normative rather than a futurological sense.

Bloch's working out of his idea of utopian philosophy, however, was imbricated with his *persona* as a great German stylist rather than being immediately portable. Accordingly, his monumental cultural synthesis of chiliasm, Kabbalistic Romanticism, German Expressionism, and pro-cess philosophy lent itself to exegesis rather than reconstruction. Today, however, the "ontological path" pursued by Bloch deserves to be reex-amined in the context of a ranked integration of the categories of social and natural being. That some progress can be made in this direction is clear from the work of Roy Bhaskar and Rom Harré.[13] It is also sup-ported by intellectual changes since Bloch's death, including the recogni-tion that recent developments in both French philosophy and analytical philosophy lead back to problematics in Fichte, Hegel, and Schelling and a growing appreciation of process philosophy as a framework with a long history in nonwestern philosophy worldwide, which is also proving powerful in contemporary biology and physics.

Given a better reception of Fichte, Hegel, and Schelling, it is becoming easier to understand why Bloch was convinced that the real world of na-ture and the changing world of the historical process are more impor-tant for philosophy than Kant believed and also why he thought that Schelling's distinction between positive and negative philosophy opened the way for a philosophy of Open System oriented toward productivity. Likewise, Bloch's relation to process philosophy becomes easier to grasp in light of the work of Bergson and Deleuze, with their emphasis on real temporal becoming. Those who miss this dimension of his work make him out to be more of a poetical, existentialist thinker than he was.

Bloch's utopian process philosophy, however, remains too technical for many of his admirers, and as I argued in *The Marxist Philosophy of Ernst Bloch* (1982), there are logical difficulties associated with Bloch's modernist, some allege postmodernist, refunctioning of features of the process philosophy tradition, which in any event is open to multiple subtle and sophisticated interpretations. Such difficulties are not central for those who locate Bloch in the context of the secular theology of utopia embraced by central European Jewish intellectuals in the twentieth century. But such a reading, with all respect to Leo Löwenthal's famous essay "The Utopian Motif Is Suspended," does not do justice to the originality of Bloch's philosophy, which relates objective imagination to the development of possibility in complex ways.[14] Nor does it take account of Bloch's profound anti-rationalist psychology prefigured in his 1930 work *Spuren* [*Traces*].[15]

In Bloch's process philosophy, the exact nature of the process, including its "where to," is not known and must be experimented for in natural and social history. Here Bloch's contribution is to insist that philosophical speculations can be metaphysically constitutive of how reality becomes, and that objective imagination [*objektive Phantasie*] can and should play a crucial causal role. Bloch also provides a process interpretation of the phenomenology of the moment, a phenomenology also detailed by Buddhist and Shankya philosophical systems. The basic datum—the experience of anti-mundane processuality—is relatively uncontroversial. Reference to processuality of which human beings cannot maintain conscious awareness but which may be experienced phenomenologically in the darkness of the lived moment is traditional enough. Bloch, however, characterizes this processuality in terminology taken from Schelling and Eduard von Hartmann as a processuality in which the That of existence drives toward the What of essence, an interpretation which relates the standard phenomenology to an ontology of not-yet-being.

Bloch's radicalism here is to relate the anti-mundane phenomenology of the moment to Schelling's conception of a process in which the order of things itself comes into being and is not presupposed from the start. Bloch's process philosophy can be compared with the process philosophies of Bergson and Whitehead, even though his technical apparatus is difficult to reconstruct in contemporary terms.[16] Nevertheless, criticism of Bloch's interpretation of the moment, including his notion of a process which has not yet "clicked in," does not mean that Bloch was necessarily wrong to reassert an ontological perspective against Neokantian agnosticism or that he was mistaken to relate human experience to the processual nature of reality. The crucial issue is not Bloch's own system but the project of a historically and socially mediated *process realism*.

Bloch rejected the relativism and also the linguistic turn often associated in Anglophone texts with continental philosophy, but he was not a precritical or dogmatic metaphysician. On the contrary, his utopian philosophy rested on a response to, and with, Kant, just as he brought a sophisticated philosophical psychology, indebted to Schelling, to the interpretation of experience. Here Bloch's *Traces* remains a neglected text which now needs to be reread in the context of post-Lacanian debates in France.

Throughout his vast *opus* Bloch pioneered a postrationalism which articulated a more complex understanding of rationality based on taking *the world-informed character of human subjective experience* seriously. It is now widely recognized that over-homogenized conceptions of "reason" have delayed the recognition of various rationalities and impeded the understanding of the "irrational" in restricted contexts. As analytical philosophers grow more sensitive to the limitations of a narrow rationalism, whether in the form of the reduction of all knowledge to different bodies of scientific knowledge or in the form of the reduction of all rationality to what is rational *now*, they are becoming more aware of the need for *a more differentiated account of rationality* that is central to Bloch's work,[17] just as philosophers have now grasped that the allegedly "irrational" needs careful analysis and should not be prematurely rejected out of hand.

Bloch challenges us to envisage a wider conception of rationality, able to take account of various sorts of cultural symbolism, and also the complexly distributed, impure materials of the real world. He argues for *a wider version of practical reason*, which admits that practical reason itself has an irreducible utopian component. Bloch also challenges us to recognize that contents are not simply rational or irrational *now* and that rational contents develop for long periods in a still not fully rational form. For Bloch, following Schelling, an adequate account of rationality takes positive account of "the irrational" and includes strategies for rationalizing instead of eliminating it. Moreover, following Marx in his letter to his father of 1837, he attempts to remain faithful to the *ratio* developing in the thing,[18] while construing the tendency for reason to go beyond its proper limits in key cases as an operation of utopian reason.

In the same way, Bloch reorients us toward the realist potential of the apparently irrational. He rejects the false intellectual superiority that seeks to criticize and repress intellectual approaches characterized by error and illusion, instead of investigating their world-informed character. Against those who make too much of a dualism between reason and imagination, Bloch argues for productive objective imagination that involves pre-semblance of objective real possibility both in nature and in works of art. Today his rehabilitation of supra-empirical imagination against the denigrations of those who worship the actual is becoming more intelligible as analytical philosophers explore virtual reality, science fiction, and counterfactual fantasy in the context of cognitive science.[19] In contrast to modern social utopianism, Bloch argued that utopia extended to every human activity and was endemic to the human historico-social world, including the human experience of nature.

The ubiquity of utopia, however, was linked to the human experience of time. In an argument more comprehensible after the writings of Paul Ricoeur on time and narrative,[20] Bloch held that the dynamic structure of the now of the moment (analyzed by St. Augustine and later Meister Eckhart) shaped the whole of human cultural experience. Hence utopia was not to be collapsed to a literary genre or to so-called social utopias. Instead, it related to the dream of fulfillment, of happiness, of homecoming, which structured the human cultural world because it was given in the dynamic structure of the moment.

However, the quest for a more differentiated conception of rationality and a more complex theory of time could not be divorced from the nature of reality as a whole. Here Bloch's philosophical realism is a major challenge to the relativism and voluntarism of many who identify with the New Left. Moreover, in Bloch's case, rationality and time were related in an account of reality for which the real includes developing possibility content. Those who cannot imagine how such ontological concerns can be defended might read more deeply in the contemporary philosophy of physics with which Bloch, the student of physics, engaged throughout his life. They might also note the rehabilitation of metaphysics in Timothy Williamson's *Philosophy of Philosophy* (2007), the assimilation of Hegel into analytical philosophy in Paul Redding's study *Analytical Philosophy and the Return of Hegelian Thought* (2007), and the significant, although technically problematic, revival of ontology in the work of the contemporary French philosopher Alain Badiou. Of course, Blochian "ontology" and "metaphysics" have a praxis-oriented work character and do not imply either pre-sociological ontological theorizing or a covert reintroduction of transcendence. But this work character is based on tendencies and latencies in a changing and changeable reality; it is not voluntaristic or decisionistic.

The features of Bloch's legacy to which I have drawn attention warrant research programs, most of which are not in place. But there is more. Given that Bloch's work on the ubiquity of utopia, time, and rationality, the phenomenology of the moment, and process realism all need greater theoretical development, especially given the current critique of "Theory" as an aesthetically overdetermined falling away from the highest standards of western rationalism,[21] in all these areas Bloch's work has implications for new political, social, economic, and cultural institutions and practices open to postrationalist formative concerns. Moreover, this is even more the case if Bloch's work is read in the light of developments in French philosophy in Foucault and the later Derrida. Bloch's friends, however, have been slow to develop his ideas and almost reluctant to provide alternative frameworks with the capacity to bring his insights to realization. These frameworks will form part of pluralist dialogical constellations: they will not amount to a single methodologism. At this point, however, they are largely lacking.

II

To give some indication of what is needed, I propose, by way of conclusion, that Bloch's ontology of not-yet-being could be developed in new directions as an ontologically oriented philosophy of the proterior. The term *proterior* captures Bloch's insight that reality is not finished behind us and signals the possibility of an ontology that is not organized around the anterior. It implies that recursive modernism is not enough and that a realist reinterpretation of German Idealism,[22] above all, the work of Hegel, Fichte, and Schelling, is needed which integrates ontological radicalism with the results of the natural as well as the social sciences. A philosophy of the proterior would attempt to resolve the problem of how to be realist and utopian at the same time in a different way to Bloch. Granted that Bloch himself took inadequate account of the dangerous, totalist, and adolescent quality of many forms of utopianism, he was still able to engage profoundly with problems of social structure and economic change, but he was not able to adequately interpret actual political regimes, not only in Russia but in China as well.

A new edition of Bloch's philosophy would need to be less prone to totalist illusions and more carefully integrated with a contemporary philosophy of nature. It would involve a bio-historical naturalism driven by formative concerns for the future of human beings and the worlds of nature. Indeed, it would take the historical formation of both human beings and natural environs as central to a new social and economic thought. A philosophy of the proterior would further elaborate Bloch's insight into an unfinished world, but it would do so with less sympathy for Romanticism and other forms of culture-driven activism. Rather, by conceiving the proterior as basic to an ontology of historical time, it would reconceive utopia in ways that critique and transcend the limited trajectories of Western European utopian thought and open up global dialogues with India, with China, and with Islam. Utopia need no longer be conceived of as an ungraspable totality in which various utopian orientations are allegedly reconciled. It need not remain "the glance from nowhere" or be associated with the metaphysical idea that the true is the whole. Utopia does not reduce to a transcendentalism of the placeless infinite. Nor are Germans and Jews necessarily the key to global culture. Utopianism is a much greater tradition in global thought than students of modernist sublime utopianism suggest. A more global utopianism with a revised ontology could renew the force of Bloch's work without its limiting and distorting conditions of emergence. It could generate concrete proposals for reform in all areas that are not perfect arrangements: it could propose that utopian influences be taken into account at the level of institutional form. To this end, it lays out proposals for new arrangements, practices, and institutions as a contribution to rational discussion and debate, with the aim of testing and extending the public mind. Such a utopianism would be *less religious* than the utopian philosophy proposed by Bloch, partly because it accepts the continuing legitimacy of religious and postreligious concerns in specific domains. It would also involve a different assay upon the problem of how to manage perfection in contemporary political and social orders. Without some element of perfection, political and social orders arguably corrupt. Today, however, in a conscious break with most modern European utopianism, distinctions need to be made between *different types of perfection* and the contexts in which they are appropriate. In particular, it is important to distinguish between sublime perfection, which is always postponed or put off, and vocative perfection, or the call to be perfect, in so far as it inspires real-world reform.[23] Contrary to popular belief, there is no contradiction between utopianism and the effective administration of actual affairs.

A philosophy of the proterior would have no single totalizing ethical vision. It would be decentered rather than totalizing and aporetical rather than monistic. It would also assume pluralism and value conflict. Further, it would generate a new engagement with "theology" and the spiritual histories of humanity and so inherit Bloch's outstanding insight into the productivity of "religion" without relying upon his dated atheism or his hermeneutical studies of religious figures and texts. Here there are dangers but also a chance of moving beyond the agnosticism of contemporary attempts to shrink the real to the onta of discursive reason.

Such indications are no more than *Vorscheine*, to use Bloch's signature term, signaling arguments to be elaborated elsewhere and in the context of the technical discussion of specific domains and their problems.[24] Nonetheless, at a time when global capitalism is without a coherent vision and structure, a renewal of Bloch's legacy has much to commend it, provided it is free from metapolitical illusions. Various attempts to achieve this result may be needed before an adequate framework is found, but Ernst Bloch would have greeted the audacity implied by such efforts with critical sympathy.

Notes

1   See Wayne Hudson, "Two Interviews with Ernst Bloch," in *Bloch Almanach* 9 (1989): 116–21.

2   See Ernst Bloch, *Gesamtausgabe in 16 Bänden, St-Werkausgabe, mit einem Ergänzungsband* (Frankfurt: Suhrkamp, Insel, 1959–85), and his two-volume *Briefe, 1903–1975*. For analysis see my study, *The Marxist Philosophy of Ernst Bloch* (London: Macmillan; New York: St Martin's Press, 1982).

3   For early evaluations of postmodern philosophy, see my "Social Anthropology and

Post-Modernist Philosophical Anthropology," in *Journal of the Anthropological Society of Oxford* 11, no. 1 (1980): 31–38, and "Zur Frage der postmodernen Philosophie," in *Die Unvollendete Vernunft*, ed. Dietmar Kamper and Willem van Reijen (Frankfurt: Suhrkamp, 1987), 122–56.

4   Thus there is almost no reception of Bloch's major work on logic, *Logos der Materie*, even though it has been available in German since 2000. Nor has Bloch's masterpiece, *Experimentum Mundi* (1975), in which he set out a historical *Kategorienlehre* designed to take account of the constitutive nature of category formation for the human historical world, been adequately discussed.

5   See Bloch's *Das Materialismusproblem, seine Geschichte und Substanz* (Frankfurt: Suhrkamp, 1972).

6   Here it is useful to compare Bloch with Russian thinkers such as Berdyaev and Shestov. See Fuad Nucho, *Berdyaev's Philosophy: The Existentialist Paradox of Freedom as Necessity* (London: Gollancz, 1967) and Lev Shestov, *All Things Are Possible and Penultimate Words and Other Essays*, ed. Bernard Martin (Athens: Ohio University Press, 1977).

7   For Lyotard's debt to Bloch, see Jean-François Lyotard, "Puissance des Traces, ou Contribution de Bloch à 'une historie païenne,'" in Gérard Raulet, *Utopie-Marxisme selon Ernst Bloch: un Système de l'Incontructible* (Hommages à Ernst Bloch pour son 90ᵉ anniversaire) (Paris: Payot, 1976), 57–67. In the same volume see Louis Marin, "La pratique-fiction Utopie: À propos de la cinquième promenade des Rêveries du Promeneur solitaire de J.-J. Rousseau," 241–64.

8   The need to defend the Enlightenment while radically modifying older interpretations of it remains. See here Jonathan Israel's *Radical Enlightenment: Philosophy and the Making of Modernity, 1650-1750* (Oxford: Oxford University Press, 2001) and *Enlightenment Contested* (Oxford: Oxford University Press, 2006). For a different but also revisionist perspective, see my *English Deists: Studies in Early Enlightenment* (London: Pickering and Chatto, 2009) and *The Enlightenment and Modernity: The English Deists and Reform* (London: Pickering and Chatto, 2009).

9   See the correspondence between Bloch and Arnold Metzger in *"Wir arbeiten im gleichen Bergwerk": Briefwechsel, 1942-1972*, ed. Karola Bloch et al. (Frankfurt: Suhrkamp, 1987), 83–101.

10 Ernst Bloch, *Philosophische Aufsätze zur objektiven Phantasie* (Frankfurt: Suhrkamp, 1977), 598–621.

11 See Michèle Le Doeuff, *The Philosophical Imaginary* (London: Athlone, 1989) and the discussion in M. Deutscher, ed., *Michèle Le Doeuff: Operative Philosophy and Imaginative Practice* (Amherst, NY: Humanity Books, 2000).

12 Hudson, *The Marxist Philosophy of Ernst Bloch*, chap. 3.

13 Bhaskar's Critical Realism has attracted international attention, and Rom Harré's realist ontology is now belatedly recognized as a major contribution to both the philosophy of science and a possible integration of natural and social philosophy. Not enough attention has been paid to the dialogue that may be possible between Bloch,

Harré, and Bhaskar on issues such as natural necessity, real dispositions, and causal powers. See Roy Bhaskar, *Dialectic: The Pulse of Freedom* (London: Verso, 1993) and Rom Harré and Edward H. Madden, *Causal Powers* (Oxford: Blackwell, 1975).

14   Martin Lüdtke, "'The Utopian Motif Is Suspended': Leo Löwenthal," *New German Critique* 38 (spring–summer 1986): 105–11.

15   Ernst Bloch, *Traces*, trans. by Anthony A. Nassar (Palo Alto, CA: Stanford University Press, 2006).

16   For example, Bloch's work assumes background knowledge of Husserl's phenomenology of internal time consciousness as well as Eduard von Hartmann's spheres of the unconscious, including an "objective-real" sphere beyond the level of conscious awareness.

17   Emphasizing the importance of a distributed account of reason is not to deny that there is a role for the function of myth in the formation of public social meaning. See Catherine Pickstock, *After Writing: The Liturgical Consummation of Philosophy* (Oxford: Blackwell, 1998). For discussion of more recent German debates about reconceiving rationality, see Dieter Freundlieb and Wayne Hudson, eds., *Reason and Its Other: Rationality in Modern German Philosophy and Culture* (Oxford: Berg, 1993). For criticisms of the work of Jürgen Habermas, including translations of essays in German, see Dieter Freundlieb, Wayne Hudson, and John Rundell, eds., *Critical Theory after Habermas: Encounters and Departures* (Leiden: Brill, 2004).

18   Karl Marx, "Letter to His Father," in L. D. Easton and K. H. Guddat, eds., *Writings of the Young Marx on Philosophy and Society* (New York: Doubleday, 1966), 40–50 (43).

19   Kumar recognizes Bloch's importance but excludes him from sustained consideration, claiming that he was mainly influenced by Judaeo-Christian messianism rather than by the utopian tradition. See Krishan Kumar, "Apocalypse, Millennium, and Utopia Today," in Malcolm Bull, *Apocalypse Theory and the End of the World* (Oxford: Blackwell, 1995) and *From Poststructural to Post-Modern Society: New Theories of the Contemporary World* (Oxford: Blackwell, 1995), 223n25.

20   Paul Ricoeur, *Time and Narrative*, 3 vols., trans. Kathleen McLaughlin and David Pellauer (Chicago: University of Chicago Press, [1984]1990).

21   See, for example, Ian Hunter, "The History of Theory," *Critical Inquiry* 33 (autumn 2006): 78–112, and my "Religion and Theory," *Culture, Theory, and Critique* 49, no. 1 (2008): 35–48.

22   Dieter Henrich's reinterpretation of German Idealism is masterful. See his *Der Grund im Bewußtsein: Untersuchungen zu Hölderlins Denken* (1794–95) (Stuttgart: Klett-Cotta, 1992). For a discerning and widely praised critical study of Henrich, see Dieter Freundlieb, *Dieter Henrich and Contemporary Philosophy: The Return of Subjectivity* (Aldershot, UK: Ashgate, 2003).

23   Wayne Hudson, *The Reform of Utopia* (Aldershot, UK: Ashgate, 2003), chap. 4.

24   For a first attempt, see my *Reform of Utopia*. I am now working on a series of books that further develop these ideas.

2

Vincent Geoghegan | **An Anti-humanist Utopia?**

A history of hedgehogs, even of cows in fifteen volumes,
would really not be very interesting.
—Ernst Bloch, *The Spirit of Utopia*

So fair a fancy few would weave
In these years! Yet, I feel,
If someone said on Christmas Eve,
"Come; see the oxen kneel

In the lonely barton by yonder coomb
Our childhood used to know,"
I should go with him in the gloom,
Hoping it might be so.
—Thomas Hardy, "The Oxen"

Can there be a utopia without humans? To explore this question, or
rather set of questions, this chapter looks at the emergence and development of the humanist utopia and considers the possibility of an anti-
humanist utopia. The starting point is Francis Bacon's use of the myth
of Prometheus in his utopian vision of humanity's "empire" over nature.
This leads to the consideration of a modern attempt to refurbish the
humanist utopia in the work of Ernst Bloch, using his reflections on Prometheus and on Bacon as a focus. John Gray's anti-humanism is then
considered, with its ringing indictment of both Prometheus and Bacon.
Finally there is an attempt to work through the implications of a conception of the good place in which we humans have gone.

Christian Humanism

The choice of Francis Bacon (1561–1626) rather than Thomas More might seem an odd starting point. More's work is sufficiently well known and admired to require no further advocacy here, yet of these two lord chancellors of England it is the later, Bacon, who directly or indirectly feeds into epochal tendencies in modernity in a way that More does not. Notably, Bacon's attempt to differentiate the appropriate response of humanity to the natural and the divine generated a fractured legacy that was to open up theoretical space for both a liberal secular humanism and a radical naturalism, as well as, at first sight less obviously, a conservative fideism and anti-humanism.

In 1609 Bacon published *De Sapientia Veterum* (Of the wisdom of the ancients), a collection of ancient myths which Bacon used as a platform for his own speculations. One of the chapters was entitled "Prometheus, or The State of Man," which contains a succinct exploration of the major themes of Bacon's thought, found in more conventional form in *The Advancement of Learning* (1605) and *The New Organum* (1620), which, in turn, provide the intellectual basis for his fragment of a utopia *New Atlantis* (1627). Bacon's version of the myth does not derive directly from the archaic Greek texts of Hesiod *Works and Days* and *Theogony* (eighth century BCE) but from a variety of classical, medieval, and renaissance Latin sources[1] (and differs significantly from the Hesiodic stories).[2] From the perspective of Bacon's commentary, the salient points of the myth are as follows:

> 1. *Prometheus creates humanity out of clay mixed with the particles of diverse animals*. Bacon identifies Prometheus with "Providence" to provide a religious grounding for his humanism, for the providential provision of reason and intellect in humanity attests to a greater reason behind the creation. In Bacon, therefore, we can see the religious roots of the Enlightenment. As he was to put it elsewhere: "our work, because of the supreme element of good in it, is manifestly from God,"[3] for God speaks to humanity in two volumes, scripture and nature, and both speak the truth.[4] Whilst Bacon was always at pains to stress his Christianity, one can detect in this conception of the rational creator the germs of later eighteenth-century deist

notions of God the architect or God the watchmaker. He affirms the God of Israel but provides the weapons for later attempts at his dethronement. The space is opened up for both secularism and naturalism. Bacon's non-interventionist God, uninvolved with his creation, as transmitted and developed through seventeenth-century British science and eighteenth-century Anglo-American liberalism, transmuted into the modern secular conception of a separation of church and state with an essentially privatized religion.[5] Furthermore, the possibility existed of an entirely naturalistic conception, where the universe was deemed to need no divine grounding whatsoever. These developments have not been lost on some contemporary evangelical Christians who in their search for the intellectual origins of modern secularism and naturalism have alighted on Bacon's separation of the natural and the divine.[6]

The subtitle of the chapter "the state of man" hints at the fundamental claim of the piece, one that flows from the fact of rational creation—the world as an arena for human purpose and action: "The chief aim of the parable appears to be, that Man . . . may be regarded as the centre of the world; insomuch that if man were taken away from the world, the rest would seem to be all astray, without aim or purpose. . . . For the whole world works together in the service of man, and there is nothing from which he does not derive use and fruit."[7]

The myth's contention that humanity was composed of clay and animal particles is used by Bacon to symbolize the unsurpassed complexity of humanity in the world and their consequent natural superiority over other organisms whose necessary servility is inscribed in nature.[8] In *The Advancement of Learning* he makes the point that the Fall, that perennial Christian corrective to humanism, did not come about through humanity's knowledge of its own natural suzerainty over nature—instanced in the naming of the creatures in Eden—but in its search for the knowledge of good and evil, which was a denial of the divine foundation of morality.[9] The Fall made life a burden; it did not displace humanity from its central location.

2. *To sustain and promote his human creation Prometheus gives them fire, which he has stolen from heaven by igniting fennel stalks from the chariot of the sun.* A number of Bacon's key concerns can be discerned in his

treatment of this episode. There is a recognition of the vital material dimension in human vulnerability; recall here Marx and Engels's claim that Bacon was the founder of modern materialism.[10] Prometheus knows that humans need sustenance of various sorts and therefore provides fire, which for Bacon isn't simply a metaphor for material assistance but is the actual historical and physical basis of human technology and science—"the help of helps, and the mean of means."[11] It also came about by a physical act, applying the stalks to the chariot, perfectly illustrating for Bacon the need for active intervention in nature. From Bacon's perspective, the images of violence and theft involved in Prometheus's acquisition of fire are appropriate, for nature does not willingly give up its secrets. Hence the meeting of fennel stalks with the chariot of the sun consists of "violent percussions and collisions."[12] A much older translation deploys a more graphic image where the fennel stalks are described as twigs, and "twigs are used in giving blows or stripes"—literally beating material out of nature.[13] Likewise the imagery of larceny, for Prometheus acquired fire "by clandestine processes, as by an act of theft,"[14] for nature is so inscrutable, such a trickster, that it cannot be trusted at face value, and therefore extraordinary procedures are required. The tone is one of struggle, forcing a reluctant nature to submit, with the ultimate goal of what he describes elsewhere as "the victory of art over nature."[15]

3. *Humanity, unimpressed with both its own nature and with fire, complains about Prometheus to Jupiter. Jupiter is delighted with humanity's indictment of Prometheus and rewards it with the gift of perpetual youth, which they place on the back of an ass. Returning home the ass is tricked by a serpent into handing over the gift in return for a drink of water.* Bacon has humanity seeking to surpass Prometheus. This mythic humanity displays for Bacon an admirable combination of modesty and ambition. Humanity decries Prometheus's gifts because to celebrate them would be to equate the mundane condition with divine perfection and to ignore or deny the chasm between the two. Such modesty, to be efficacious, needs to be a springboard for human striving lest it issue forth in an enervating complacency; they must "arraign and accuse nature and the arts, and abound with complainings" and so progress.[16] Bacon uses this aspect of the story to indict

humanity's failure fully to acquire this gift by foolishly placing it on an ass. This allows him to ventilate one of the key themes of his life—the inadequacy of past philosophical and scientific methodology and the need for a new one. The ass is seen as a symbol of the "empirical" (slow and experience-based) and is contrasted with the swift bird—the "dogmatic"—the province of abstract philosophy; and the plea is for the unity of the best of these faculties, which have been historically sundered, with experience becoming the basis for sound principles, which can then be used in further empirical work—though the temptations of snakes to abandon this project have to be resisted. This is Bacon's hugely influential inductive theory of science, which led Marx and Engels again to call him "the real progenitor of . . . all modern experimental science."[17] With this new method, humanity would be able to enjoy the bounty that divine providence had prepared for them.

At this point we can usefully leave the myth and move to the utopia *New Atlantis*. More accurately, one should say a *part* of a utopia, for according to the testimony of his secretary, Rawley, Bacon abandoned the project in favor of work on natural history, "which he preferred many degrees before it."[18] The remaining fragment is a dull, scrappy, and badly constructed thing, almost totally devoid of any literary merit, and yet it is the nearest we get to Bacon's principal ideas made flesh, so to speak. The distinction between the divine and the natural is affirmed in the midst of its fictional breach, necessitated by the need to explain why the utopians are Christians. The religion is brought to the island utopia, Bensalem, via a miraculous cross of light shortly after the death and resurrection of Jesus, but the exceptional nature of this phenomenon is stressed, for God prefers natural processes and laws to work without divine intervention. As one of the indigenous priestly scientists says in his prayer of response: "we learn in our books that Thou never workest miracles but to a divine and excellent end (for the laws of nature are Thine own laws, and Thou exceedest them not but upon great cause)."[19] At the social heart of the community are the high officials of Bacon's ideal scientific institution—Salomon's House. In *The Advancement of Learning* Bacon had bewailed the lack of an institutional basis for the new learning, citing the deficiencies of existing colleges and uni-

versities; here in Bensalem the solution is found—a multifaceted institution, based on inductive science, dedicated to the extraction from nature of its knowledge and products for the benefit of humanity (and, of
course, the glory of God). The institution we are told is named after that
Old Testament exemplar of wisdom, Salomon, one of whose sayings, in
Proverbs 25:2, appears repeatedly in Bacon's works: "the glory of God
is to conceal a thing; the glory of a king is to find out a thing."[20] Its alternative name, "the College of the Six Days' Work," is designed to give a
divine imprimatur to productive work. Humanity's position at the apex
of nature, under God, is illustrated time and again by the positive col-
oration given to a thoroughly instrumental approach to nature: animals
should be dissected to give an insight into human biology, poisons and
new medicines should be tested on them, their shapes and sizes should
be altered as needed, their fertility increased or destroyed, and so on
and so forth. Nature in general is one great resource for human exploitation. In a sense nature has two dimensions here—God's work, and the
stuff of human development—summed up in the account of the founding
of Salomon's House, which was instituted "for the finding out of the
true nature of all things (whereby God might have the more glory in the
workmanship of them, and men the more fruit in the use of them)," or
as he put it in *The New Organon*, "one does not have empire over nature
except by obeying her."[21]

Natura Naturans: Hume to Bloch

The year 1779 saw the posthumous publication of Hume's *Dialogues
Concerning Natural Religion*. The "dialogue" was between contemporary advocates of three positions on religion: deism, fideism, and a skepticism that entertained the possibility of naturalism. There is a sense in
which the direct or indirect legacy of Bacon helped create the theoretical
space in which these options could operate. Bacon's influence is explicitly acknowledged in Hume's first great work of philosophy, *A Treatise
of Human Nature*, where "experience and observation" are deemed to be
the necessary foundation for an authentic "science of man," and a telling
Greek parallel is invoked: "reckoning from Thales to Socrates, the space
of time is nearly equal to that betwixt my Lord Bacon and some late philosophers in England, who have begun to put the science of man on a

new footing."[22] The resulting skeptical empiricism when utilized in *Dialogues Concerning Natural Religion* was devastating for deism, which although deemed to be nearest the truth at the end of the *Dialogues* in fact gets the greatest mauling in Hume's book, and in its discomfiture can be glimpsed the possibility of a naturalism. He wickedly pokes fun at the deists' designer God, raising the possibility that the world might be "the first rude essay of some infant deity" or "the work only of some dependent, inferior deity . . . the object of derision to his superiors" or possibly "the production of old age and dotage in some superannuated deity."[23] Crucially, the text implicitly responds to Bacon's claim, in the Prometheus chapter, that "to derive mind and reason from principles brutal and irrational would be harsh and incredible."[24] Hence the need for a providential Prometheus with a "why not?" A materialist explanation is at least as plausible as supernatural design: "The beginning of motion in matter itself is as conceivable *a priori* as its communication from mind and intelligence."[25] Indeed when Hume himself reflected elsewhere on the Prometheus myth (in Hesiod's archaic account), the thing that struck him was that the gods and humanity had jointly emerged out of chaos, which spoke of "generation" not "creation," and the only being to be created by the gods in the whole story was the divine cat's-paw, the scourge of humanity, Pandora.[26]

In the nineteenth century when Feuerbach read Hesiod's version of the Prometheus myth, he echoed Hume on the emergence of the human and the divine: these early tales "looked upon nature as the source not only of men but also of the gods." His conclusion hints at the radical direction his naturalism had taken: "clear proof that the gods and men are one, that the gods stand and fall with mankind."[27] The impact of this approach on the young Marx, out of whose critique of religion the concepts of alienation and ideology emerged, need not be rehearsed here. Fast forward instead to Ernst Bloch and his attempt to develop a dynamic Marxist naturalism. In *The Principle of Hope* Bloch's most extensive discussion of Bacon occurs in the section on technological utopias. Bacon's technological prescience in *New Atlantis* is extolled; its "amazing anticipation" is evidenced in its account of the technological achievement of Salomon's House, which "more or less contains modern technology in wishful outline" and actually "goes beyond it" (*POH*, 654–55). This, in Bloch's estimation, makes *New Atlantis* "the only utopia of classical status which gives decisive status to the technological productive forces of the better life" (POH, 655). Bloch recognizes that Bacon's project was "the mastery of nature," not "the transfiguration of nature" (POH, 650), but is heartened by what he calls Bacon's "great maxim" that "nature is conquered by obedience" (POH, 657), which he takes to be Bacon's recognition of the active autonomy of nature, of "natura naturans" (nature naturing) (ibid.). Mastery of nature is not the same as the "exploitation of nature," which denies the dignity of nature and which was attendant on the advanced development of a capitalist economy. Bacon is situated in the honest hopes of early capitalism that liberated productive power would banish human want—a vision deemed to be informing *New Atlantis*. These characterizations of Bacon are in marked contrast to those developed in the same era by Horkheimer and Adorno in *Dialectic of Enlightenment*, where Bacon is cast as the formulator of the dark agenda of the Enlightenment premised on "a disenchanted nature," where "what men want to learn from nature is how to use it in order wholly to dominate it and other men. That is the only aim."[28] Bacon's penning of a utopia colors Bloch's approach to him and puts him on the lookout for utopian impulses and traces in the rest of Bacon's writing. He argues that Bacon thought that knowledge of past "inventive dreams" could be used "to emphasize that which seemed daring or impossible to men and which was nevertheless to be found in their technological dreams. The record of realized, and particularly unrealized, plans also gave useful hints for inventive ideas" (POH, 650). Bloch is keen to acquit Bacon of the charge that he is a mere bare-arsed empiricist (the "trial and error method . . . of the philistines" [POH, 653]); stressing, first, that the inductive method involves ascending to axioms before a further descent to work, thus creating a necessary balance between the active and the contemplative and, second, that the method of necessity explores, in Bacon's words, "the basic form of things" and therefore penetrates into the objective structure of nature (ibid.). For Bloch, Bacon's objective historical position at the beginning of a new economic order registered itself in his subjectivity as a "powerful preconscious" sense of a dawning newness—"Not-Yet-Consciousness as conscious premonition" (POH, 118)—which drew its sustenance from "his sense . . . for the objective tendency, objectively real possibility of his age" (POH, 144). Aware of Bacon's Prometheus chapter, Bloch sees the portrayal of the titan in that text as the beginnings of a revolutionary humanism that was to gain further development in literary form in Goethe and Shelley and in political form in the French Revolution: "Prometheus, says Bacon, with a tone never heard before, is the inventive human spirit who establishes human control, intensifies human power to a limitless degree and raises it against the gods" (*PoH*, 1215).

Bloch's outline of a possible new relationship between humanity and nature draws upon a critique of the existing relationship in capitalism and a personal canon of historical conceptions—mythological, religious, philosophical, artistic—of a natural subject. The metaphors he deploys to convey the character of the capitalist technological interaction with nature invoke coercion, violence, and exploitation and are contrasted with an alternative relationship metaphorically expressed in images of affinity and friendship; this technology is thus "more of the slave-driver and the East India Company than the bosom of a friend" (*PoH*, 670) and "nature has not . . . become good friends with its caning master" (*PoH*, 694). Nature from this abstract mechanical perspective is conceived as mere inert stuff, passive material lacking inherent value—there simply to be manipulated by its human sovereigns. Bloch counters with a concept of "creative matter," of *natura naturans*, whose philosophical conception he attributes to the Arab Aristotelian Averroes (*PoH*, 674) and traces through Renaissance intellectual magic, into German idealism, and to its modern apotheosis in the work of Marx and Engels. The historical figure of a natural "subject" is deemed to be both a semi-mythologized expression of this dynamic materialism and a prefiguring of an authentic natural subjectivity lying in the future. As we saw, Bloch acquits Bacon of the charge of seeking to exploit nature, but notes that his desire to master nature fell short of a loftier conception of the relationship between humanity and nature. Such a conception Bloch sees in "co-productivity" (*PoH*, 686). In his explication of this concept Bloch reveals his continuing linkage to the tradition of *humanist* utopianism. True, his humanity is thoroughly natural, and the temporal and spatial immensity of nature is celebrated, yet at the terrestrial scale human mediation is a necessary part of the process of natural transfiguration, and "a subject of nature . . . remains problematic as long as no concrete mediation by man, as the youngest son of nature, has succeeded with it" (*PoH*, 693). He dreams of a "technology without violation" (*PoH*,

691) but firmly in the context of human priorities, and although he satirizes conceptions that make humanity the telos of universal history, humanity's right to be a major participant in the further adventures of nature is an unquestioned assumption.

A Critique of Humanism: John Gray

In the past two decades, in works such as *Enlightenment's Wake*, *Straw Dogs*, and *Black Mass*, John Gray has developed a combative critique of humanism, linked to a long-standing theme in his work—a passionate opposition to utopianism. Going against the grain of Gray's anti-utopianism, it is possible to use his work to explore the possibility of an anti-humanist utopianism and then to consider the challenges to, and opportunities for, utopian thinking presented by this possibility.

Prometheus and Bacon are evident in Gray's indictment of humanism— Prometheus as a symbol of humanity's vaunting and predatory ambitions; Bacon as the modern intellectual source of the human project of subjecting nature to the purposes of humanity. In contrast to Bacon, Gray looks to the archaic Hesiodic characterization of Prometheus as a violator of the natural order and champion of the hubris of humanity. "The punishment of Prometheus," Gray avers, "chained to a rock for stealing fire from the gods, was not unjust."[29] Elsewhere he refers to the "Promethean spirit," citing as a "spectacular display" of this spirit the wholesale killing of sparrows during the Great Leap Forward in China, where the result was, with the removal of their natural predators, a quasi-biblical increase in the insect population.[30] Prometheus flatters humanity, telling them that they can have the knowledge of the gods and thereby claim their rightful place at the center of creation, suzerains of nature; in reality it is the royal road to perdition. The Promethean spirit is not universal but hegemonic—an Occidental product whose reach has become global, and this "Western Promethean conception of human relations with the earth" has "wrought irreversible damage to the environment on a vast scale," part of "the world revolution of Westernization."[31]

Whilst Prometheus is a symbol or metaphor for Gray, Bacon features in his work as the first modern and hugely influential formulator of the repressive Promethean approach to nature: "The conception of the natural world as an object of human exploitation, and of humankind as the master of nature, which informs Bacon's writings, is one of the most vital and enduring elements of the modern world-view, and the one which Westernization has most lastingly and destructively transmitted to non-Western cultures."[32]

For Gray, Bacon draws upon the pervasive humanism of Christianity with its focus on "personality," human and divine: "a conception of the unique status of human beings as loci of infinite worth, immortal souls in a perishable world created by God for human use."[33] Bacon thus represents a step in the process whereby this Christian concept becomes increasingly secularized in modern thought.

Gray considers alternatives to this state of affairs—all of which seem to him to be possible. There is what one might term the ecological option where Baconian and Nietzschean conceptions of the "will to power" over nature is replaced with one in which "human beings seek to find harmony with the earth." There is also the possibility of a non-Western renewal of human thought and practice, where there is the recognition that Western traditions are simply exhausted, beyond rehabilitation.[34] Most striking of all, however, is his consideration of the possibility, one he traces in Gaia thinking that "the mortal earth may shake off the human species so as to gain for itself another lease on life."[35] In *Straw Dogs* we get a pithy conjectural history of the future in this vein: "*Homo rapiens* is only one of very many species, and not obviously worth preserving. Later or sooner, it will become extinct. When it is gone the Earth will recover. Long after the traces of the human animal have disappeared, many of the species it is bent on destroying will still be around, along with others that have yet to spring up. The Earth will forget mankind. The play of life will go on."[36]

There is something distinctly cheerful in Gray's contemplation of the extinction of humanity. He, of course, would say that he is merely projecting from known scientific facts and is not saying that the new dispensation is actually better than the present, but if one dare say so to this scourge of utopianism, his vision of this possible future has shades of the utopian about it—a world well rid of *Homo rapiens*. At the very least his projection can provide a starting point, to those sympathetic to utopianism, for a discussion of the nature of anti-humanist utopianism.

Anti-humanist Utopianism: Utopia without Humans?

"*Theoretical* anti-humanism,"[37] to use Althusser's terminology, as deployed here, wishes to both continue and deepen the process of naturalizing humanity and to displace continuing attempts to privilege humanity's place in nature. Thus whilst it acknowledges Bloch's significant advance beyond Bacon's conception of human empire over nature, with his conception of co-production, it still detects anthropocentrism in Bloch's notion of the human subject liberating nature. It is sympathetic to Foucault's historical claim that "man is an invention of recent date" and, understood as a theoretical ambition, "one perhaps nearing its end."[38] But as Dominique Janicaud argues, the Althusserian and Foucauldian projects, as with Lévi-Strauss, wish at the scientific/theoretical level to dissolve "man as epistemological object," and then at the philosophical level "re-introduce . . . him" (in Janicaud's ambiguous formulation "as unity, value and sensitivity"), and at the practical level support the various emancipatory struggles historically conceived in humanist terms.[39] Perhaps the term *humane* might be used here, retaining the materialist grounding (simultaneously both humbling and ennobling) of the etymology of the human in the "soil" or "earth" (Latin, *Humus*; likewise in Hebrew; *adam*—man, *adamah*—ground),[40] and hence indicative of the ethical values of kindness, care, and the avoidance of inflicting pain. As Heidegger noted in the *Letter on Humanism*, "anti-humanism" did not take sides "against what is human and advocated what is inhumane, defended inhumanity and debased the dignity of man. Opposition to humanism is thought to be because it does not locate the humanity of man high enough."[41] (An admittedly dark provenance given Heidegger's association with Nazi barbarism—but the sense is sound.)

An anti-humanist utopian conception of a universe without humans can take a number of directions. The humane can be explicitly validated through a form of modified survival—as cyborg or through incorporation into some extraterrestrial life form, and modern science fiction has examples of both. Tom Moylan has usefully deployed the term "critical dystopia" to explicate the critical utopian resistance embedded in dystopian horror where, as for example in the context of global war, traces of human hope remain.[42] In this vein Naomi Jacobs characterizes Octavia Butler's trilogy of novels *Lilith's Brood* as a critical dystopia where, out of the devastating predations of global conflict, a posthuman hybrid of humanity and the "alien" species—the Oankali—emerges.[43]

An alternative tack is not to approach the utopian through the dystopian but to go directly to the utopian and ponder the end of humanity as the good place. A distinction (admittedly polemical) can be made, whereby a *self-critical* can be distinguished from a *self-loathing* utopian anti-humanism. In specific thinkers or writers elements of both stances are frequently found, and they should be thought of as moods or dispositions rather than as taxonomic categories. The self-loathing perspective delights in the idea of extinction and, at an abstract level, craves it. Humanity is viewed as largely malignant and pestilential, and its annihilation is deemed to be the natural order cleansing itself. The utopia is not of humanity absent but humanity *crushed*. For all its disdain for Bacon this approach persists with his humanity/nature dualism, transferring the rights and privileges of the human to a supposed natural agency, along with allegiance, in what is still construed as a terrain of struggle— nature as a possessive individualist. These misanthropic utopias of extinction are seldom linked to a utopian praxis—the task of hastening the death of the species—though as John Barry documents, the radical ecological group Earth First! welcomed AIDS, viewing it as they said "not as a problem, but a necessary solution."[44] Fringe groups such as the Church of Euthanasia ("Save the Planet Kill Yourself") and the Gaia Liberation Front ("AIDS, which once offered so much hope, has proved to be just too easy to avoid") have speculated about ways in which humanity could be eradicated.[45] In much of this, as the AIDS references suggest, the culling of humanity is distanced on to others—human self-loathing does not (initially?) extend to certain selves. More usually the end of humanity is predicated on systemic catastrophes, external or internal, some friendly meteorite perhaps, or the floods and fires of global warming. Politics shrinks to containment and mitigation, and personal cultivation and contemplation amidst the ruins become the objective of the wise. Gray's recent work, notably *Straw Dogs*, is inclined to such musings.

The function of an anti-human utopia is going to be different in a self-critical perspective than it is a self-loathing perspective. The self-loathers have a goal but no plausible or morally acceptable means of *humanly* bringing this about—it is in this sense a species of impotent rage. Extinction for the self-critical is a possibility, but it is not a goal. It is a utopia in a different sense, namely, a form of mental play that stimulates the critical and anticipatory functions. Akin to Hobbes's construction of a pre-political and pre-social world in *Leviathan* to illustrate the necessity for certain social and political practices, reflection on the abstraction of humanity, or more accurately the passing of humanity can stimulate important insights into the trajectory currently traveled by humanity. But since extinction *is* a possibility it is a deeply serious form of play. It is also utopian in the sense that its ultimate purpose is to uncover fuller and richer forms of being.

One can glimpse elements of such an anti-humanist utopianism in a number of recent pieces of speculative popular science such as Alan Weisman's *The World without Us* (2008), and David de Vries's television film *Life after People* (2008).[46] They avoid the catastrophic mayhem of the dystopia, critical or regular, with its dead or dying billions, its ravaged earth, and its brutal social relationships, by positing the abrupt exit of humanity from the scene, leaving all other species and the environment intact. Again, the methodology of Hobbes comes to mind, where the state of nature is not a historic reconstruction but a thought-out experiment in which *contemporary* humans are deprived of the state and society. The new question is what will happen to the earth and its life forms when we humans disappear: "What would happen," asks de Vries, "if every human being on the earth were suddenly to vanish?"[47] Likewise, Weisman suggests a "creative experiment" where the controlling variable is that "human extinction is a fait accompli."[48] These are not self-consciously utopian documents, but they have within them utopian moments:

1. The new dispensation critiques the former practices of humanity both through the refreshing absence of certain ways (active pollution, for example), and the continuing traces of the past order (toxic waste that will take tens of thousands of years to degrade, if ever).
2. The transitoriness of the present is evoked and its pretensions are rebuked in powerful images of drowned cities and fallen monuments: "one year after we disappear" the Hoover Dam's "17 massive and seemingly indestructible generators are about to be brought down by an organism the size of a thumbnail" (de Vries).

3. The exhilarating-and-the-disturbing (which we will later discuss in terms of the sublime) is invoked. In *Life after People*, the Ukrainian town of Pripyat, abandoned in a day following the Chernobyl explosion, is visited. A head to camera explains that she is sitting in the former soccer stadium; slowly the camera pans round to reveal a stunning deciduous wood filling the whole of the former pitch. And in the same film the biologist Ray Coppinger envisages New York 150 years after we have gone: "I can picture New York City with all the buildings covered with vines, you know, hawks sailing around. It would be lovely. It would be absolutely lovely" (de Vries).

4. An attempt is made to move beyond the articulation of basic principles, as in a manifesto, to the actual depiction of a new functioning order—that holistic concreteness to be found in the best of earlier utopias. Thus in Weisman's book the massive and the systemic—climate, geology, biological adaptation and evolution—frame the specific: "fire hydrants sprouting amidst cacti,"[49] and in de Vries's film a chronology of change is attempted, from the first day—"Welcome to earth, population zero"—on beyond 5, 10, 100, 1000, 10,000 years.

5. David Brin, an astrophysicist, muses in *Life after People*: "We're tantalized by our myths about our own destruction—but also tantalized by the notion, hey, maybe it's the turn of someone else. What will they do when we're gone? What will the earth do when I am gone? It's the most natural question in the world?" (de Vries). In our two texts there is, in the answers to the above question, a predictive dimension which seeks to establish the relative relationships between the surviving flora and fauna, and which, in the process, draws out the continuing link between the human and the non-human eras. Thus small dogs bred for human wants will probably perish quickly in the face of predators, and our symbionts (such as follicle mites) will necessarily go with us.[50] But utopian energy cannot resist favoring certain outcomes or wishing certain species well, where certain human values are clearly evident. Thus Weisman waxes lyrical on one of our closest primate relatives—the bonobos, which "don't seem very aggressive at all. Although they defend territory, no intergroup killing has ever been observed. Their peaceful nature, predilection for playful sex with multiple partners, and apparent matriarchal social

organization with all the attendant nurturing have practically become mythologized among those who insistently hope that the meek might yet inherit the Earth."[51]

Alas, Weisman concedes that they would stand little chance against the much more numerous and aggressive chimpanzees.

The Sublime

Here we move from anti-humanist utopianism as mental play to another of its functions—the provision of a space for the creative use of astonishment. The concept of the sublime—briefly trailed in the discussion on *Life after People*—might be usefully employed here; starting with that hammer of the utopian, Edmund Burke, in *A Philosophical Enquiry into the Sublime and Beautiful* (1757).[52] The influence of Baconian empiricism is evident in Burke's philosophical reluctance definitively to decide the abiding question in earlier work on the sublime as to whether the sublime inhered in actual objects (the natural sublime) or was a product of human linguistics and emotions (the rhetorical sublime).[53] As Philip Shaw puts it: "The *Enquiry* is thus best described as a work of experimental psychology, a treatise that eschews the metaphysical in favour of patient delineations of the emotional states aroused by any particular experience of the sublime."[54] In contrast, that other great analysis of the sublime in the eighteenth century—Kant's—which locates the sublime in the mind, ends up with a deeply humanist assertion of the independence of humanity from nature, indeed its primacy in the relationship; here the encounter with the sublime generates a "might enabling us to assert our independence as against the influences of nature, to degrade what is great in respect of the latter to the level of what is little, and thus to locate the absolutely great only in the proper vocation of the subject."[55]

For Burke the sublime excites "the ideas of pain and danger" (PES, 39). It is truly *terrible* in its linkage to terror and the terrifying, but also to the sense of the awesome: "The passion caused by the great and sublime in *nature* . . . is Astonishment; and Astonishment is that state of the soul, in which all its motions are suspended, with some degree of horror. In this case the mind is so entirely filled with its object, that it cannot entertain any other. . . . [T]he inferior effects are admiration, reverence and respect" (*PES*, 57).

Burke, however, acknowledges the pleasurable in the sublime which comes from contemplating a distant danger rather than a proximate peril, for "when danger or pain press too nearly, they are incapable of giving any delight, and are simply terrible, but at certain distances, and with certain modifications, they may be, and they are delightful" (*PES*, 40); the sublime therefore facilitates fruitful contemplation, not debilitating fear. Burke is clearly worried on a number of occasions that readers might find the word "delight" inappropriate in this context, and therefore either gives a nominalist explanation of the word (he is using it, he says, in an unusual way), uses another expression to convey his meaning—as in "relative pleasure" (*PES*, 36), or implicitly contrasts it as *negative* with what he calls "positive pleasure" (*PES*, 132).

Crucially, Burke identifies the *independence* of those objects experienced as sublime, specifically their independence from humanity, which is experienced as a form of humbling terror. Using the book of Job, one of the greatest sources of the sublime in the Bible, Burke meditates on why certain animals are experienced as sublime and others are not. He concludes that it comes down to the possession of independent power. Dogs, he says, are loved by us, but this is embedded in a sense of their dependency upon us, for "love approaches much nearer to contempt than is commonly imagined" (*PES*, 67). It is those animals that we cannot control and which are independent of us whose autonomous behavior we find sublime. His first example is a passage on the wild ass in Job: "Who hath loosed . . . the bands of the wild ass? Whose house I have made the wilderness, and the barren land his dwellings. He scorneth the multitude of the city, neither regardeth he the voice of the driver. The range of the mountains is his pasture."

Burke comments that "the description of the wild ass . . . is worked up into no small sublimity, merely by insisting on his freedom, and his setting mankind at defiance" (*PES*, 66); likewise, "the magnificent description of the unicorn and of leviathan in the same book": "Will the unicorn be willing to serve thee? Canst thou bind the unicorn with his band in the furrow? Wilt thou trust him because his threat is great?—Canst thou draw out leviathan with a hook? Will he make a covenant with thee? Wilt thou take him for a servant forever? Shall not one be cast down even at the sight of him?" (*PES*, 66).

Burke picks these passages from the section in Job where God wishes to impress on Job the awesome distance between himself and humanity and the sheer scale of the immensity of the divine nature when set against the human.

An important recent work by Charles Taylor—*A Secular Age*—provides a compelling account of the emergence of the concept of the sublime in the eighteenth and nineteenth centuries, bringing out the critical and constructive functions of this concept and evoking both the historical specificities of its emergence and its relevance as a still living mode of experience. The larger historical picture for Taylor is two crucial and interrelated shifts in imagination that began in early modern Europe. There is a shift from the notion of "cosmos" to that of "universe," from a conception that the overarching reality is grounded in, and limited by, the divine to one without such grounding—just seemingly limitless expanses of space and time, where "there is no longer a clear and obvious sense that this vastness is shaped and limited by an antecedent plan."[56] The second shift concerns the conception of the individual—a shift from the "porous" to the "buffered" self. The porous self involves a premodern notion of being open to, for good and bad, the agencies and processes of the cosmos. This gives way to the "buffered" individual who has a strong sense of a boundary between himself and the world. This for Taylor is a move toward anthropocentrism, where the individual feels a sense of sovereignty over themselves and a degree of autonomous distance from the world. For a period the two processes were in harmony: deist notions of a universe designed for the benefit of humanity sat well with notions of humans as lords of terrestrial creation. But since for Taylor the buffered self involved loss as well as gain—human rights, on the one hand, but also a narrowing—a yearning for that which had been lost surfaced, which, with the increasing marginalization of the deist ordered universe, began to take sustenance from the new perception of the astonishing nature of the universe. This was the historical moment of the sublime.

What is particularly striking about Taylor's characterization of the sublime is his emphasis on the role of goals in the experience. In the sublime, in the experience of terror, awe, and astonishment, we are wrenched out of our concern with the quotidian goals of our normal lives and glimpse far greater purposes, purposes which may carry a religious charge or may not. Either way, a powerful alternative to the narrowness of life is viscerally apprehended: "We are tempted to draw the limits of our life too narrowly, to be concerned exclusively with a narrow range of internally generated goals. In doing this we are closing ourselves to other greater goals. These might be seen as originating outside of us, from God, or from the whole of nature, or from humanity; or they might be seen as goals which arise within, but which push us to greatness, heroism, dedication, devotion to our fellow human beings, and which are now being suppressed and denied."[57]

The sublime can have this effect precisely because it forces us to consider a non-anthropocentric world, a world where, in a sense, humans are absent or are there as external spectators. This, for Taylor, is why in the eighteenth and nineteenth centuries people found the sublime in the wilderness—a place devoid of humanity, but precisely for that reason, a place where true humanity could be inculcated: "Part of the sublimity of the wilderness consisted in its otherness, its inhospitality to humans; in the fact that you couldn't really live there. But opening to it makes it possible for you to live properly outside of it . . . This is the meaning of Thoreau's dictum: 'In Wildness is the Preservation of the World.'"[58]

When Bloch considers the sublime he views it as the meeting point of the objective and the subjective. In a small essay of 1934, "Astonishment at the Rhine Falls," he seeks to understand his own response to visiting and viewing the famous falls at Schaffhausen. The words he uses to register his subjective impressions recall the typical vocabulary of the sublime—"awe," "astonishment," "wonderment"—but he insists that these reactions are more than simply subjective, for they are the tentative apprehensions of a natural creature of objective processes in nature itself: "The non-subjective content of the experience of awe relevant here is still often imprecise, sometimes even fantastically imprecise; yet it is certainly never empty, never meaningless."[59] This perception of the sublime is a form of overcoming the mechanistic exploitative conception of nature characteristic of capitalist modernity. We sense the terrible creative power of nature which, though in one sense is humbling, is also ennobling: "The relatively modest Rhine Falls leads us toward something in regard to which it may be said: not constructed for us, but pertaining to us in the end. In all such natural 'places of interest,' something mysteriously looks back at us, which is not at all articulated in the cities."[60]

The sublime's important role in modern aesthetic theory, as an aestheticized mode of experiencing the disturbing and comforting otherness of nature, can perhaps be seen as an attempt to retain that sense of the radical otherness of the divine in the context of the marginalization or rejection of the divine of the post-Baconian world of modern secularism and naturalism. As Terry Eagleton has argued: "As we enter the epoch of modernity, the sublime is one name for [an] annihilating, regenerating power. . . . As such, like so many modern aesthetic concepts, it is among other things a secularized version of God. In modern times, art has been often enough forced to stand in for the Almighty."[61] In the sublime, as in the religious, the threat of extinction, of annihilation, is not crushing, but cleansing, invigorating. Again, Eagleton puts this well:

> Like the divine and the Dionysian, [the sublime] . . . is enrapturing as well as devastating. . . . To experience our destruction in art rather than reality is to live out a kind of virtual death, a sort of death-in-life. Confronted with the vista of raging oceans which cannot drown us . . . we can know the delirious pleasures of defeating death (so that death itself comes cravenly to die), at the very moment that we can also feel free to embrace our own mortality. . . . As such, it is both self-affirmative and self-destructive.[62]

The human is thus validated but is purged of fantasies of a human *imperium* over nature or of a privileged partnership with the natural.

Religion and Anti-humanism

At first sight, one of the oddest intellectual debts to Hume, and behind him, Bacon, was to be found in the work of the so-called counter-Enlightenment thinker Johann Georg Hamann (1730–88).[63] In fact, orthodox piety in Hume's *Dialogues* emerges, if not unscathed, then not annihilated, for in Hume's uncertain universe the traditional God is not an inherently absurd idea. Hamann, who translated Hume's *Dialogues* into German, described them as "not dangerous at all" and used Hume's project to justify a renovated Lutheranism.[64] From Hamann's perspective, Hume had dispatched rationalist atheism and deism with their own weapon, reason. Hamann is happy to invoke Bacon himself in this project, taunting hubristic philosophy with Bacon's defense of nature against the empty distinctions of metaphysicians: "Your lying, murderous philosophy has cleared nature out of the way. . . . Bacon accuses you of injuring her with your abstractions."[65] Ernst Bloch, discussing utopian elements of "dawning" in the *Sturm und Drang* movement, refers to Hamann as the "magus of this whispering Enlightenment" (*POH*, 134).

The resilience and richness of religion formed the focus of the radical naturalism of Feuerbach and others of the left-Hegelian tradition, to which Bloch owed such a debt. In Bloch's hands religion's capacity to embody the "Utterly Different" (*POH*, 1195) is stressed, and he is drawn, like Burke, to those passages in the Bible which dramatize sublime examples of difference between humanity and the non-human. Thus in two passages from Isaiah, Bloch rejects the view that this difference attests to the worthlessness of humanity. Thus "Behold, ye are of nothing, and your work of nought" (41: 24) "is certainly not being misanthropic" (*POH*, 1194), whilst the words "For my thoughts are not your thoughts, neither are your ways my ways, saith the Lord" (55: 8) are not those of a God "portrayed as a demon" (*POH*, 1194). Rather, drawing on the work of Rudolf Otto and Karl Barth, the remoteness of the divine from the human provokes a life-enhancing "astonishment"—Otto's "shuddering-numinous" (ibid.). This dimension is admittedly *theoretically* embedded in the Feuerbach/early Marx privileging, among religions, of biblical humanism with its apotheosis, the divine human, Jesus—but the dark-bright material of astonishment strains against this domestication and speaks of something which is more modest than humanism but also infinitely greater.

Contemplating a world without us can generate a positive sense of "estrangement"—a term Bloch himself uses [*Verfremdung*] in his analysis of the strength of religious consciousness in the *Principle of Hope* (1197).[66] The vast out-there, which in Bloch's naturalism is clearly not an actual god, in which we are absent, gone, lifts humanity out of itself. Here the universe minus humanity is not itself the utopia. The utopian moment flows from the space created for thought, emotion, and choice: much of it critical in the form of the absence of many systemic features of contemporary reality, some creatively anticipatory, richly novel. The critical betokens modesty; the positive anticipatory betokens a rejection of the genocidal praxis, or passive hope for the end, of the self-loathing mood; in sum a validation of the humaneness of the anti-humanist.

Notes

1   Charles W. Lemni, *The Classic Deities in Bacon: A Study in Mythological Symbolism* (Baltimore: Johns Hopkins University Press, 1933), 128–41.

2   Vincent Geoghegan, "Pandora's Box: Reflections on a Myth," *Critical Horizons* 9, no. 1 (2008): 24–41 (25–27).

3   Francis Bacon, *The New Organon* (Cambridge: Cambridge University Press, 2000), 77.

4   Francis Bacon, *The Advancement of Learning* (London: Dent, 1915), 41–42.

5   See William T. Lynch, *Solomon's Child: Method in the Early Royal Society of London* (Palo Alto, CA: Stanford University Press, 2001) and Thomas Jefferson, *Political Writings*, ed. J. Appleby and T. Ball (Cambridge: Cambridge University Press, 1999), 427 on Bacon.

6   John C. Hutchison, "The Design Argument in Scientific Discourse: Historical-Theological Perspective from the Seventeenth Century," *Journal of the Evangelical Theological Society* 41, no. 1 (March 1998): 85–105.

7   Francis Bacon, *Essays* (London: Penguin, 1985), 270.

8   Bacon, *Essays*, 270–71.

9   Bacon, *Advancement of Learning*, 37.

10   Karl Marx and Frederick Engels, "The Holy Family," in Marx and Engels, *Collected Works*, trans. Richard Dixon et al. (London: Lawrence and Wishart, 1975–2005), vol. 4 (1975), 7–211 (128).

11   Bacon, *Essays*, 271.

12   Bacon, *Essays*, 271.

13   Francis Bacon, *The Essays of Francis Bacon* (London: Odhams Press, c. 1935), 271.

14   Bacon, *The Essays of Francis Bacon*, 271.

15   Bacon, *The New Organon*, 91.

16   Bacon, *Essays*, 272.

17   Marx and Engels, *Collected Works*, 4:128.

18   Francis Bacon, *Major Works* (Oxford: Oxford University Press, 2002), 785.

19   Bacon, *Major Works*, 464.

20   Bacon, *New Organon*, 100.

21   Bacon, *Major Works*, 471; Bacon, *New Organon*, 100.

22   David Hume, *A Treatise of Human Nature* (Harmondsworth, UK: Penguin, 1969), 43, 44.

23   David Hume, *Dialogues and Natural History of Religion* (Oxford: Oxford University Press, 1990), 79.

24   Bacon, *Essays*, 270.

25   Hume, *Dialogues*, 93.

26   Hume, *Dialogues*, 147.

27 Ludwig Feuerbach, *Lectures on the Essence of Religion*, trans. Ralph Manheim (New York: Harper and Row, 1967), 86.

28 Max Horkheimer and Theodor W. Adorno, *Dialectic of Enlightenment*, trans. John Cumming (London: Allen Lane, 1973), 4.

29 John Gray, *Straw Dogs* (London: Granta Books, 2002), xiv.

30 John Gray, *Black Mass* (London: Allen Lane, 2007), 50.

31 John Gray, *Enlightenment's Wake* (London: Routledge, 1995), 267.

32 Gray, *Enlightenment's Wake*, 236.

33 Gray, *Enlightenment's Wake*, 236.

34 Gray, *Enlightenment's Wake*, 273.

35 Gray, *Enlightenment's Wake*, 274.

36 Gray, *Straw Dogs*, 151.

37 Louis Althusser, *For Marx*, trans. Ben Brewster (Harmondsworth, UK: Penguin, 1969), 229.

38 Michel Foucault, *The Order of Things: An Archaeology of the Human Sciences* (New York: Vintage, 1973), 387.

39 Dominique Janicaud, *On the Human Condition*, trans. Eileen Brennan (London: Routledge, 2005), 13.

40 See Tony Davies, *Humanism* (London: Routledge, 2008), 126.

41 Martin Heidegger, *Letter on Humanism*, [n.d.] trans. Miles Groth. Available at http://wagner.wpengine.netdna-cdn.com/psychology/files/2013/01/Heidegger-Letter-On-Humanism-Translation-GROTH.pdf.

42 Raffaella Baccolini and Tom Moylan, eds., introduction to *Dark Horizons: Science Fiction and the Dystopian Imagination* (New York: Routledge, 2003), 1–12 (4–7); Tom Moylan, *Scraps of the Untainted Sky: Science Fiction, Utopia, Dystopia* (Boulder, CO: Westview, 2000).

43 Naomi Jacobs, "Posthuman Bodies and Agency in Octavia Butler's *Xenogenesis*," in *Dark Horizons*, ed. Baccolini and Moylan, 91–111 (91–92).

44 John Barry, "Straw Dogs, Blind Horses, and Post-Humanism: The Greening of Gray?" in *The Political Theory of John Gray*, ed. J. Horton and G. Newey (London: Routledge, 2007), 131–50 (139).

45 See http://www.churchofeuthanasia.org/resources/resources.html, accessed 21 October 2008; Gaia Liberation Front Statement of Purpose. Link on Church of Euthanasia, accessed 21 October 2008; see also Alan Weisman, *The World without Us* (London: Virgin, 2008), 241–44.

46 After this chapter was completed, an article was published that deals with a number of the issues discussed in this work—notably the utopian aspects of envisaging the passing of humanity. The author discusses the work of de Vries and Weisman as well as a wide range of films and literature dealing with concepts of the posthuman world. See Mark S. Jendrysik, "Back to the Garden: New Visions of Posthuman Futures," *Utopian Studies* 22, no. 1 (2011): 34–51.

47 David de Vries, *Life after People*, Flight 33 Productions for History Television Network Productions, 2008.

48 Weisman, *World without Us*, 3.

49 Weisman, *World without Us*, 18.

50 Weisman, *World without Us*, 235.

51 Weisman, *World without Us*, 50.

52 Edmund Burke, *A Philosophical Enquiry into the Sublime and Beautiful* (London: Routledge, 2008). Henceforth PES in parentheses in the text.

53 Philip Shaw, *The Sublime* (Oxford: Routledge, 2006), 27–28.

54 Shaw, *The Sublime*, 53.

55 Immanuel Kant, *Critique of Judgement*, trans. James Creed Meredith, rev. Nicholas Walker (Oxford: Oxford University Press, 2007), 99. See also Shaw, *The Sublime*, 82.

56 Charles Taylor, *A Secular Age* (Cambridge, MA: Harvard University Press, 2007), 325.

57 Taylor, *A Secular Age*, 338.

58 Taylor, *A Secular Age*, 341.

59 Ernst Bloch, *Literary Essays*, trans. Andrew Joron et al. (Palo Alto, CA: Stanford University Press, 2008), 383.

60 Ernst Bloch, *Literary Essays*, 383.

61 Terry Eagleton, *Holy Terror* (Oxford: Oxford University Press, 2005), 44.

62 Eagleton, *Holy Terror*, 44–45.

63 See Sven-Aage Jorgensen, "Hamann, Bacon, and Tradition," *Orbis Litterarum*, 16, nos. 1–2 (1961): 48–73.

64 Isaiah Berlin, *The Magus of the North: J. G. Hamann and the Origins of Modern Irrationalism* (London: Fontana, 1994), 32–33.

65 Johann Georg Hamann, *Writings on Philosophy and Language*, trans. Kenneth Haynes (Cambridge: Cambridge University Press, 2007), 77.

66 Compare Ernst Bloch, *Das Prinzip Hoffnung* (Frankfurt: Suhrkamp, 1990), 1409.

3

Ernst Bloch's Dialectical

Johan Siebers | **Anthropology**

Amid the philosophers of the twentieth century, especially those of the latter half, Ernst Bloch occupies a somewhat isolated position. His philosophy of hope sits as uncomfortably with the scientism of analytical thought as it does with the discourses of the end of philosophy and the end of overarching political and social narratives that have characterized much of continental thought of the past decades. While his work has had considerable influence on several other philosophers, of which Adorno and Benjamin may be the best known, his thought has not led to the formation of a school of thought, and while his thought was especially important in wider discussions in society in the 1960s, since 1989 his work, placed as it is in Marxian currents, has been eclipsed further and further. In addition to the metaphysical and cultural discontemporaneity of his thinking, which was mitigated somewhat by his—never simple— allegiance to Marxism, a writing style that uses and progresses the full potential of the German language and its classical texts, and thus is difficult or vexing at times, even for native speakers, further complicates the reception of this thought. So there are three reasons for the marginal position Bloch's work has come to occupy in philosophy.

First, the idea of truth is recovering from its anesthetic; second, religion is back in philosophical discourse as well as in the workings of geopolitics; and third, questions surrounding the relation of human beings to the rest of nature are urgent. As the life sciences develop further and

further, it appears more and more necessary to ask anew the philosophical question of what life is and more specifically of what human
life is. Bloch's thought, though a voice from the past, speaks to all these
concerns and highlights aspects of them that may not be found so clearly
in other philosophical theories.

Metaphysics and the view of philosophy as a search for, or creation
of, truth was seen in twentieth-century philosophy as broadly something that had been, or had to be, *overcome* (Wittgenstein, Heidegger).
The absolute claim of reason was seen as either invalid or as the cause
for the instrumentalization of reason and the dominance of technology.
In existentialist thought, metaphysics was seen as the denial of human
freedom, and in that sense it was allied to the dominance of technology.
For Bloch, on the contrary, the relation to the philosophy of the past is
one of *heritage*. But heritage is never the simple passing on and receiving
of what went before in order to use it for one's own purposes. Heritage
is only possible to the extent that an unfinished, unrealized kernel in the
past is understood and taken up in light of a possible fulfillment or redemption. That fulfillment can be localized—secular—or it can be seen
in the light of a *totality* of realization. The past carries a desire, and this
desire is what is inherited and, to the extent possible, brought to its own
truth. Tradition and utopia cannot be disconnected.

Bloch is occupied in large parts of his writing with the nature of the
totality of realization. Although the very idea of totality has been criticized severely in philosophy in the recent past, it is for Bloch the anti-
dote to totalitarianisms of all sorts, and it is here that we find one of
the valuable insights for the contemporary context. As a preliminary indication of what is at issue here, we can refer to the relation between
history and eschaton as seen by Jürgen Moltmann, whose *Theologie der
Hoffnung* (1965) was crucially influenced by Bloch's philosophy. Moltmann writes: "It is neither that history swallows up eschatology . . . nor
does eschatology swallow up history. . . . The logos of the eschaton is
promise of that which is not yet, and for that reason it makes history.
The promise which announces the eschaton, and in which the eschaton
announces itself, is the motive power, the mainspring, the driving force,
and the torture of history."[1]

In the form of promise, hope, anticipation, or expectation, an eschaton that is in the end an "all in all" is seen to pervade and constitute

history as the interrelation of temporal modes. What is called "history" here is not the one disjunct in the opposition between historical time and the event of realization or *nunc stans*, nor the one disjunct in the opposition between a mathematico-physical container-time and the modes of past, present, and future. Rather, history itself is made in and by the promise of the eschaton. History is the new as the mode of realization of the not-yet.[2] This is at bottom a Hegelian view of the relation between processual realization and that which is thus realized, a totality of the for-itself. For Bloch, the movement of history is dialectical. Yet the eschaton is not already there, waiting to be realized. It is so much at one with the movement of history that we can say it is that which is not yet: the new and its structural features make up what the eschaton is. The eschaton is not what awaits at the end of time; history is its realization. Yet again, this does not mean that eschatology becomes the science of progress or even a procedural recipe for the construction of the new Jerusalem. At all points, human activity and utopian expectation—*vita activa* and *vita contemplativa*—are two dimensions of the same reality. The revolutionary character of Bloch philosophy lies partly in that it suggests that that distinction is not original but a reified interpretation of what is a living unity in human existence. The basic idea that novelty and ultimacy belong together will turn out to have far-reaching consequences in all fields of philosophy.

Dialectic, Drama, Essay

A philosophy worthy of the name has to be able to motivate. It has to make an existential appeal, or it must involve an attempt at articulating the dimensions of significance in human life and the world in a way that goes beyond their mere intellectual analysis. Bloch likes to use the phrases *tua res agitur* [your cause is being dealt with here] and *de te fabula narratur* [this story is being told about you].[3] In his work it is more than an appendix of extra-academic relevance; it is the air his writing breathes, that which sustains it. In philosophy itself, something has to become right: there is a pleasure or happiness—or as the case may be, sadness or ire—of thought and of the text which is more than the satisfaction or appropriateness of a correct analysis. Thought becomes a medium for life—as we think, we live. Philosophy, in this respect, is like art or religion. Without this aspect, the truth-dimension of philosophy withers away, as does its potential to grow and change. Kant's formulation of the question of philosophy, "What is man?" receives a mostly implicit answer in a philosophy considered as a whole. For Kant, that question refracted in the questions as to what is to be done, what can be known, and what may be hoped for—we are not far off from the basic structure of Bloch's philosophy if we arrange it according to these questions. Upright gait; S is not yet P; identity: these would be the captions of the answers to these questions.

The upright gait is, in Bloch's philosophy, the principle of practical reason and functions as a criterion for action. The basic form of the proposition "S is not yet P" expresses both the structure of the process of knowledge as well as the process of being and in a general way indicates what can be known. Identity, the *unum necessarium* in human and natural striving, builds the horizon of hope. On the other side of the discursive question "what is man?" lies the ontological question that we are, that the world is—the "inconstruable question" as Bloch called it.[4] The fact that there is a relation to be made between the inconstruable question existence poses and the discursiveness of philosophy—and this is what positivism denies, of course—is the retrospective realization of philosophy, the moment philosophy comes to realize that it was possible already and all along. If we take a Wittgensteinian concept out of its context, we can say that that fact is the fact of forms of life: that a relation exists between life and form.[5] Bloch formulates it as follows: "The forms of existence are those of the shaped, shape-taking condition, moving out of itself, as one of relative definiteness. But *that* a relation between 'that' and 'what' can be drawn at all: this relation is itself the basic category, and all others merely perform it, all others are the continued illumination, by a road network, of the what-multiple originating from the 'that.'"[6]

Freed from its essentialist interpretation, we have here the metaphysical problem of the relation between form and existence. It returned in post-metaphysical philosophy in the form of its annihilation—hence the irrationalism of philosophies who place their bets on existence, and hence the formalism of those philosophies who sided with form. The expulsion of the copula from conceptual thought as the "mere positioning of the object" (Kant) lies at the basis of both. But philosophy sentences itself to silence with that expulsion, even if it assumes it has to pass that verdict out of loyalty to its original aims, and it can only be said that it inflicts that expulsion on itself: in the name of truth, philosophy ends in the prohibition to think. The wayfaring [*Wegnetz*], instead of essentialist, interpretation of the relation between "that" and "what" not only saves us from this predicament but it can also help us understand how the Kantian temptation came about, as a resentful recognition of the not-yet of redemption in which its anticipation turns into its refusal.

The Kantian "blockade" (Adorno) of transcendence is allied to the inability to tolerate delay or uncertainty of salvation: the totalization of the Protestant work ethic and its psychopathology. Its notion of dignity necessarily decays into the animalistic.[7] An economy of desire is at work in the basic constellations of philosophical options and choices. This does not mean that philosophy can be reduced to psychology—far from it— but it does mean that the fundamental critique of philosophy has to appropriate a language in which desire can be expressed and discussed as a living reality rather than as an object already formed and categorized by particular epistemological interests and decisions. On the basis of a language of desire, it will also become possible to understand the movement of thought of Bloch's philosophy and how it is a philosophy of desire, inheriting the formations of desire from previous Greek and German idealist dispensations against its own utopian backdrop. The role of the language of desire in philosophy has been stated—we cannot deny a certain irony to the occasion—by Luther, in a passage quoted by Moltmann in his *Theology of Hope*, for its methodological relevance to a discourse of hope. For Moltmann, the context is theological, but I think that its relevance is even greater to philosophy and certainly to the attempt to understand the language of Bloch:

> The Apostle [Paul, when he speaks of the "earnest expectation of the creature," Rom. 8:19] philosophizes and thinks about things in a different way from the philosophers and metaphysicians. For the philosophers fix their eyes on the presence of things and reflect only on their qualities and quiddities. But the apostle drags our gaze away from contemplating the present state of things, away from their essence and attributes, and directs it towards their future. He does not speak of the essence or the workings of the creature, of actio, passio, or movement, but employs a new,

strange, theological term and speaks of the expectation of the creature [*exspectatio creaturae*].[8]

It is ironic that Luther has to be the one who sets philosophy straight here. Bloch always complained about the fact that his ideas had more influence in theology than in philosophy. But this is an unfounded complaint. In the Blochian inheritance of Hegel, theology becomes philosophy, or rather the master-slave relation between theology and philosophy is reversed, and the philosopher can start to use theology, now stripped of its theistic nature, as a mediator that connects it to the layers of the real it tries to understand and articulate. It seems that the theologians understood this decades before the philosophers. It is Paul who "philosophizes," but in a language and manner different from the metaphysicians and the philosophers concerned with present actuality. Paul breaks the fixation of philosophy and opens our eyes to the future things have, to an ontological meaning of expectation that concerns them, that concerns what they are—*tua res agitur*. We are reminded of Leibniz's remark that the present moment is pregnant with, is expecting, the future.[9] Where in Leibniz there might be a sense in which that pregnancy is to be understood as a containment of a future state in the present, in an as yet underdeveloped form (Leibniz uses the metaphor of elasticity in this context, which does, of course, have a basis in the very materiality of the state of pregnancy),[10] with Bloch we can see that the expectation of the creature is precisely that: an expectation, a being-as-expectation, and that it is the openness of that expectation that makes for the "new," that allows the new to be made instead of received. We have to somewhat qualify the normal pattern of substance and quality, and hence also the normal pattern of the S-P structure of propositions, to articulate this point, which bears structural resemblances to the speculative proposition in Hegel as a unity of opposites. The new does not lie outside of the entity as in a synthetic proposition, nor does it lie inside the concept as in an analytic proposition (Leibniz), for it is the new of that entity, and yet it is "really" new—it means, for the entity, a moving beyond [*überschreiten*]. The new is, as Bloch says, at the front, which in its turn is oriented toward an as yet only tendentially latent ultimate of identity, an ultimate that does not exist yet but may realize itself in the process of realization, the stages along which are "symbolic intentions" of this ultimate.[11] These are the three structural moments of the real as process. The dialectical relation between present and future that is articulated in the dialectic of the new, the front, and the ultimate conforms to the structure of desire, and it conceptualizes, articulates, and—in the medium of thought—manifests it as well (philosophy is desire). The work of this materialist dialectic is not that of being-in-and-for-itself as the remembrance of alienation, as it is in Hegel's notion of the absolute idea, nor the understanding of that work of remembrance as an infinite labor of *jouissance*, as it appears in Žižek's Lacanian reading of the Hegelian dialectic. It is the concrete working out or production of the in-and-for-itself in and through, but not exclusively by, history, understood in the terms explained above: Hegel denied the future, but the future will not renounce Hegel.[12]

In contemporary interpretations of Hegel, the point is sometimes made that, contrary to Hegel's intentions, his philosophy warrants the conclusion that the bridge from dialectic discursiveness to the absolute idea cannot be made, that it remains always in abeyance. If we concede that, it becomes possible to see Hegel as the realization that philosophy as such is impossible (it has "come to an end" in Hegel), as the philosophical wisdom of realizing the incompleteness of all discursive dispositions or formations. The abeyance of finality, of identity, then remains as the point at which desire hooks on to realization—a point that can be incorporated into a life in the acceptance of the impossibility of redemption and the embracing of one's own defining eternal desire, which is redeemed once its futility is realized: *encore une fois!* Hegel becomes Lacan; any discursive disposition is as good as any other—there is no possibility of distinguishing between them in terms of their orientation toward "identity," or correspondence with the real, and yet that orientation is not immaterial to them but constitutes discursiveness as such. This would be a realization from within, so to speak; the discursive formation turns out to be haunted by something that escapes it. But it is incomprehensible how there could even be a recognition of that ghost, if there was not some preliminary extension or reaching out toward identity—not as itself a discursive formation, but as drive, orientation, premonition. The incommunicable is just that—incommunicable—and yet it communicates.

Lacan is in no other position than the formalism of positivism, and in the end that formalism collapses under its own lightness and arbitrariness. Bloch does not place a cut-and-dried discourse of identity over against it, but does speak of identity in the language of hope. This is a language that looks to find words for what remains extraterritorial to the process of realization, in order to keep discursive formations from collapsing. It finds these words not in conceptual relations or argumentative structures, but in the language commensurate to the *exspectatio creaturae*. At this point, philosophical discourse becomes dramatic enactment. Expectation or hope can be shown but not said. In Plato we find it in the form of the dialogue, in which the interminability of the process of identification becomes the indication of identity. Benjamin articulates it for Goethe, and we can safely generalize it to include Bloch's writing: "The mystery is, on the dramatic level, that moment in which it juts out of the domain of language proper to it into a higher one unattainable for it. Therefore, this moment can never be expressed in words but is expressible solely in representation: it is the 'dramatic' in the strictest sense."[13]

The implication is that mystery can be made manifest only in the dramatic. The performative enactment of philosophy is part of its truth-content. Here we have reached a point at which thought touches upon a mysticism of the text and at which the discipline of philosophy comes to incorporate as an essential part of it its articulation in texts that are never simply scientific, classificatory, analytical, or even literary, but dramatic in a way that is appropriate to philosophy. Like all realization or taking shape, philosophical writing happens vis-à-vis the inarticulate darkness of the "that," of existence, which remains the black light in which its significance as writing becomes manifest. Philosophy cannot capture that which it aims at, but it can make it visible: "What urges there, comes admittedly always entirely first, but it is not there, no more than Not. As such it is situated, as far as enactment is concerned, even before the first sentence which, for the time being, can be written philosophically at all."[14]

Philosophical texts symbolize, in the precise sense in which Bloch uses that term, the inconstruable origin of discursiveness. That origin does not stand behind us as something receded into the background of past events, but before us as the identity to come that is not yet. We have to take this quite literally; the origin as end is inconstruable. That means it cannot be captured as yet in any conceptualization, any what-category, mediation, or question-answer tandem, and yet it is only accessible, it is only there, in and by conceptualization or mediation. But this means that all writing, all realization, is utopian. Bloch, in a manner not unlike Plato, often takes recourse to stories when he reaches this essential moment of ineffability. One of the earliest can be found in *Geist der Utopie* (1918), where he places it in the context of the wonder in which traditionally philosophy is said to begin and which in Bloch's thought is the moment in which the inconstruable question is experienced.[15] This is a fragment that deals with the dramatic in the sense in which I have used that term here, and that, at the same time, uses a dramatic structure to express its content. Bloch was aware, I think, of the central place this passage occupies in a "systematic" rendition of his philosophy because he refers to it much later in *Das Prinzip Hoffnung* (PH, 337). The text is preceded by a remark about the fleeting nature of the experience of being with oneself [*bei sich sein*]. That experience is contrasted with a more steadfast, solid one:

> Yet there is also something else, more solid, in us, questioning, easily affected, an inner, deepest wonder. It is often ignited quite arbitrarily, indeed inappropriately. Nevertheless with it we know better where we are at, because it shows itself more seldom, even though it is casual enough. . . . A drop falls and there it is; . . . outside wind, heath, and evening in autumn, and there it is again, exactly, the same . . . and we suspect that it could be found here; "Little rat, rustle as long as you like; / Oh, if there were only a crumb!" and upon hearing this small, harsh, strange line from Goethe's *Wedding Song* we sense that in this direction lies the unsayable, what the boy left lying there as he came out of the mountain, "Don't forget the best thing of all!" the old man had told him but no one could ever have come across something so inconspicuous, deeply hidden, uncanny, within the concept.[16]

What triggers this experience can be different for everyone, and different on different occasions, but it is always the same, invariant experience of that which cannot be discovered in concepts but, as Bloch suggests, is yet not without a relation to the conceptual: it can be grasped even better in concepts than more localized moments of identity, which are fleeting at best, because of its invariance, and it is the "best" of the process of conceptualization, of mining in the mountains. We cannot hope to understand the philosophy of Bloch if we do not have access to a similar experience (of which Bloch would say that it is the same experience). If there is such a thing as a starting point for the philosophy of hope (which after all has no difficulty acknowledging its always-already mediated nature), it is this. As the beginning of thought, it is at the same time also its end point, the anchor of hope in history; it is the eschaton as it "makes history" as Moltmann says, and as such it is as much a premonition of future as a source. For Bloch, the true beginning comes at the end, when the totality of identity is realized. That totality is prefigured in the nonconceptual, open totality of the absolute question, and history is suspended between the two.

The totality of the end is latent in the historical tendency, but without it we could only form a distorted view of history or of the relation between history and eschaton, between desire and transformative fulfillment. That distortion would consist in programmatic, truncated views of utopia or in the fetishization of historical epochs or moments of realization in the lives of individual human beings or communities. The function of Marxism in Bloch's work lies largely here, as it provides Bloch with the conceptuality necessary to develop a historical materialist idea of alienation. Capitalism is simply part of dialectical history, for Bloch as much as for Marx, but within the metaphysical economy of desire it constitutes the moment when the web of desire that constitutes the life-world, so to speak, can be detached from its invariant orientation. That produces the preconditions of a salutary, purified, understanding of metaphysical desire and its place in human existence (the "critique of religion"), but it also produces the danger of the development of reductionist cultures of desire and the perversion of religion as simply a cult of desire. Again, no form of pragmatism or communicative rationality, but only a philosophy of hope that does not shun the question of how to articulate the *exspectatio creaturae* and how to relate it to praxis and practices can provide the critical resources necessary to understand what is happening here and to offer an alternative:

> So—I am not shunning the word—another form of preaching is necessary, in the place where up until now the Church has stood. The word *pastoral care* has not been discredited by the Church and the ideological content which has, for a part, been sold in it. So, a road map is necessary,

a system of relating, even to an absolute, to a "what for" of the whole. A thinking through of a humane teleology (. . .). So, therefore, we also need a new aesthetic; also a new philosophy of religion; also a new ethics. An ethics without acquisition; an aesthetics without illusion; a dogmatic without superstition.[17]

The sermon is the rhetorical form of the language of hope. We can see very clearly in many of Bloch's writings the tendency to preach—and this is one of the characteristics that some find unpalatable.[18] But it is an almost necessary concomitant of any attempt to understand hope, one that can be secularized or purified, but not abandoned.

These remarks have served to lay out an understanding of some of the basic motivations and figures of thought of the philosophy of Bloch. They are by no means intended to be exhaustive, but merely indicative. They have not yet addressed any critical concerns we may have, except for the acknowledgment that without personal access to the type of experience of an absolute question Bloch starts with, it will be difficult to gain access to his thought. I think philosophy can have this sensitizing as its task sometimes, even if at first more questions are raised than answered. In making my remarks, I have assumed, implicitly, that we can treat his work more or less as a unity. While this is certainly not self-evident, I will continue to use that assumption. Bloch never developed a systematic exposition of his ideas, although he was not averse to the idea of a system in philosophy and experimented in his youth with the idea of reviving the summa as a form of open system. Mostly his writings have an essayistic form. They span a long period of creative activity—from the early years of the twentieth century to 1977—and Bloch makes remarks that are relevant to a particular topic in many different places. The collected works consist of seventeen volumes. His works have not been published with a subject index or register. This means the serious student of this work has the difficult task of bringing together texts and fragments from a, to a certain extent systematically undisclosed, vast corpus. What help one can get, one will gladly accept. One of these helping factors is the fact that Bloch carried out the publication of his collected works himself: as did Goethe and Schopenhauer, he prepared a final version [*Ausgabe aus letzter Hand*] of all his works. If we want to reconstruct the changes he made at certain points in the texts, we would, again, face an immense task, but for the purpose of systematically re-constructing and critically examining his philosophy, we can be grateful for Bloch's editorial preferences. It remains the case, however, and this is important when considering what Bloch's thought has to say to us today, that there can be no substitute for thorough analysis and reconstruction and that is a task that has only just begun, despite a time of popularity and despite the considerable reception, especially in German-speaking countries, and one that needs to be carried out, in the first instance at least, on the terms and conditions this philosophy sets itself, if it is not to result in distortions or facile adaptations to other schools of thought. We must resist the temptation of wanting to reach a judgment, prove relevance or irrelevance for "contemporary discussions" too quickly. The philosophical questions and concerns we find here may well be quite different from what we find elsewhere.

The form of the essay is a natural medium for the absolute question because it gives space to the drama of discursiveness and ineffability. This drama is the field of hope, and it is that in which the philosophy of hope unmasks and dismantles instrumentality, in the name of "humane teleology." The essay is concerned with experiences that are already mediated: it takes as its object a cultural mediation and tries to find, express, or indicate its truth. As such it starts with an experience, and it denies right from the start any absolute distinction between individual experience and the experience of mankind, of history as a whole.[19] It claims a universality in the making of experience and historical mediation, not of systematic theoretical reduction of one concept to another. As Adorno says, truth and history are not incommensurable in the essay. Its work of sensitizing is made possible by its procedure, which ties the essay always more or less to a concrete occasion, and by its goal, which is to show the concrete occasion as, in one way or another, in communication with an ultimate, in which its truth is to be found. The form of the essay does not start from a norm of systematicity or methodology, which it knows is not to be found in or at least maintained throughout meaningful experience, but neither does it restrict itself to a mere classification or description of reality as it is given. It seeks to understand the individual reality and in general those things which discursive dispositives exclude, as a way of attempting totality. The essay's concern is expression, and it proceeds in an expressionist manner. The principle at the heart of the essay, in Adorno's words, is that of "heresy."[20] And Bloch is, and wants to be, heretical. If there is any way in which the central experience of the absolute question could be communicated and salvaged in a time that relies on its exclusion from discursive dispositives by instrumentally closing these off, it would have to be its essayistic tracing in mediations of past and present, and the pointing out of those places where it is precisely that experience, that reality, that would dislocate and thus put right these dispositives. The critique of ideology is nothing else than the tracing of the absolute as the utopian light which the discursiveness of the essay catches, and it can only release its potential in the essay. System itself becomes essay, and again we see the internally related moments of passing over, front, the new and the ultimate. But the realities the essayistic style aims to understand as well as the substantive truth about them at which it aims are both alien to the abstractions of theory: a remark that shows the genius of Adorno asserts the proximity between the form of the essay and Hegel's Logic, the speculative concept. In Bloch's philosophy the ontology of the not-yet consists entirely of speculative propositions, and the most systematic of his books, *Experimentum Mundi*, stands at the end of the collected works, as much a groundwork that allows us to place the essayistic thinking that comes before it in a context as a movement of concepts which can only be understood with what came before in mind: true beginning comes at the end. The ground work does not close off, nor does it present finality of statement, but shows the whole of the work in its own orientation on the invariant of direction, an orientation which, again, is finite and located. In indicating the substance of the philosophy, it immediately virtuously ricochets, as it were, to the occasions that gave rise to it and expresses the not-yet of identity in that way.

Humanity

With these caveats in mind, which all have to do with the question of how to read Bloch, I now want to return to the Kantian question "What is man?" We are not defining by genus and specific difference; in fact, we are not defining at all. We are not looking for an essence of the concept of "man," but neither are we looking for a family of resembling concepts. We have already established the relation between "that" and "what" as core of the ontological situation and the preliminary, unfinished nature of it. If there were no relation between the two, the "that" of existence would be locked up in an in-itself from which there is no escape, and the "what" of essence would be strictly inconceivable. But it is not inconceivable that there would be an identity between the two. Its full implications would be difficult to lay out as the identity of in-itself and for-itself, if not taken in an idealist fashion, would mean nothing less than the New Jerusalem and as such it is an index or measure only, of falsehood but not directly of truth.[21] Its locus in experience is the fulfilled moment — or rather, the fulfilled moment in experience can be interpreted against the background of a resolution of the "that-what connection." For Bloch the fulfilled moment stands in contrast to two other aspects of the momentary: the darkness of the lived moment and the unbearable moment.

The darkness of the lived moment is a concept that captures the tension between the need for mediation within the for-itself and the impossibility of mediation in the immediacy of lived experience, which after all is immediate. All experience comes to light before us, so to speak, and that is a process of objectification [*Vergegenständlichung* not *Verdinglichung*]: it is the origin of discursiveness we have discussed before. But the adequacy of this process of externalization to the core of the lived moment remains open or unrealized: a *coincidentia oppositorum* remains at bay. The lived moment is dark, it has to go out of itself to become aware of itself, but in that movement immediacy is lost. The category of identity signifies the resolution of this tension. The desire for expression fuels the desire of identity and vice versa.[22] In the section on wonder and the absolute question in *Das Prinzip Hoffnung*, entitled "Source and Outflow" [*Quell und Mündung*], Bloch discusses the darkness of the lived moment and its goal: "If something is properly realized, life comes to the place where it has never been, that is, it comes home. In this possible realization of something still possible, however, two moments *ultimately* constitute source and outflow. The source is characterized by the *darkness of the Now*, in which realization rises, the outflow by the *openness of the object-based background*, towards which hope goes" (*POH*, 288–89; *PH*, 336).

Life, understood in terms of a river with a source and outflow, is a process of realization in which the darkness of the now gives rise to its ex-

ternalization in open objectivity and this movement outwards is hope—
the hope and possibility of an adequacy (PH, 336) of source and outflow.
(What for Bloch remains a hope and a possibility becomes a promise in
the theology of hope; a promise does not relinquish the hope of its fulfillment.) That adequacy in its finally intended form is given in the experience of wonder: an arrest of process, a "lighting up" (PH, 337) of utopian
finality, a symbolic intention of an *Überhaupt*. The absolute or inconstruable question opens up for experience and thought the depth of the darkness of the *jetzt*, but at the same time, in its immediacy, the premonition
of what it would mean if all that is in that darkness of the lived moment
would have been brought out, of adequacy, is vicariously given: "If the
content of what is driving in the Now, what is touched in the Here, were
extracted positively, a 'Stay awhile, you are so fair,' then conceived hope,
hoped-for world would have reached their goal" (PoH, 290; PH, 338).

The experience in which the utopian state, substance as subject, in-
stantly flares up is contrasted with an equally short-lived experience in
which the extent of the gap between source and outflow is felt in a nau-
seating experience of a sudden rift in the fabric of life: a tear through
which we slide into free fall. Bloch speaks of "the unbearable moment,"
and he describes it in several places. Small, insignificant, idiosyncratic
occurrences can trigger it: "In this way already a plate of soup, overflowing, sure enough also too cosy a contentment in the wrong place."[23]
Whatever the psychology of such experiences may be, the philosophical
significance lies in the experience of free fall, of impotence in the face
of complete annihilation, of fear as the counterpart of hope. The fact
that fulfillment is not guaranteed, and that if it occurs, it has to span the
whole of being and not only some portions of it seems to be indicated in
this experience of being lost along the way to realization.

The darkness of the lived moment, the utopian arrest of process (also
a moment), and the unbearable moment all highlight aspects of mediation, and taken together they make up the anatomy of human experience. They already form quite a departure from some current theories
of (human) life, and that is augmented by the conclusion Bloch draws:
we do not even know whether we are humans or not.[24] Man is hidden
to himself, but man is also the place where the incompleteness of being
comes to itself and as a consequence manifests itself most strongly. We

do not know if we are human, or what that means, but we know that we are "the unfinished as such" [*das Unfertige schlechthin*].[25] That realization can provide us with a negative indication of what humanity means, in the form of a standard for inhumanity. Even if we do not know exactly what it means to be human, we do know what it means to be inhuman, and it appears that at least a significant part of what it means to be human consists in keeping the openness of the question "What is human?" alive, at the level of the individual as well as of the community. Humanity as a concept of utopian proportions—not in terms of a wish list of laudable characteristics but as a fundamental openness to an identity that is not yet graspable and yet that provides a standard, at least for inhumanity, and an ultimate goal of the human teleology that is at least as wide as the universe—is accessible only to a form of thought that has learned what it means to hope. That form of thought expresses itself in politics, pedagogy, aesthetics, ethics, and metaphysics. It answers the questions about what is to be done, what can be known, and what may be hoped for.

To some, this will be yet another example of human domination, of the misguided idea that the human being occupies a special place in nature, or in reality as such, here even one that makes the human being the placeholder for the whole of being to come to itself. It might be argued that if this is true, then it is even worse than Hegel, who at least had a godlike understanding of the subject at the end of history. In Bloch, it is humans, you and me, who finally will have their tears wiped away and their faces revealed to one another, and this will be the coming home into the world at the same time. It is, as Bloch often says quoting Marx, the naturalization of man and the humanization of nature. But we must not forget the true extent of this vision. There is a difference of quality between the speculations regarding the *homo absconditus* and the concrete praxis that, certainly, only acquires its meaning against the background of ultimate identity, but that nevertheless remains a historically concrete, material praxis—social, political, cultural, religious, environmental, existential.

In the philosophy of Bloch, philosophical anthropology is ontology. Access to ontological categories always passes through the pathos these categories attract in human existence: desire, not-yet, passing over, darkness of the lived moment, hunger for realization. We understand all these ontological constants first and foremost in relation to ourselves and our concrete experience of them. But that does not mean the human being, as a species next to others, is elevated to living at a status beyond its means. It means that in the most intimate sphere of conscious awareness, the key to the structure of the world, existing independently of us, is to be found, and that that most intimate sphere plunges us outwardly into the open of the world and into the fullness of a moral, creative, intellectual orientation in the world. That is a classical idea of philosophy, one that requires and fosters attentiveness and concentration and one that locates the value of philosophy in the search for truth, regardless of its appropriation or use in other contexts. Philosophy cannot live without truth: "It would be no philosophy anymore, if truth would not be the main point and center for it." But there are different forms of truth. There is the truth of facts, which can be ascertained empirically even though the establishment of facts, for Bloch, requires a carving up of process with the use of abstractions. Facts are therefore never concrete, let alone concrete-utopian. But there is also an ontological understanding of truth, one that we find expressed in phrases such as "a true friend" or "true love." There "truth" denotes a degree of being in which, as we might put it, mediation and being-in-itself come together in the unity of "that" and "what," or mediation and immediacy, that is the formal goal of all desire. That form of truth is concrete; it is localized in expectations, hopes, and dreams that are not free-floating but grounded in concrete possibilities that lead the way; and it is a premonition, a movement, or a tendency. Because of that it escapes positivism, for whose gaze nothing like it could ever exist: "This second truth captures therefore something in reality, which is least graspable by the mere apprehension of what is the case. Because of its relation to reality, it is by no means without empirical evidence, but it turns against the empiricist reification of the moments of process and meets reality accurately only because of that."[26] With great consistency Bloch draws the consequences of the processual nature of this "second truth," and has done so from the start of his thinking in the days of German expressionism. His work, the style of writing and thinking, is an example of what it enunciates. There is a congruity between form and content that is itself an essential component in the truth process of this philosophy, which, in the sense of that second form of truth, can therefore be said to be "true philosophy." Philosophical truth requires creativity.

I have highlighted some of the structural features at the heart of Bloch's philosophy. Against the background of a situation in philosophy, and in the world that invites a renewed orientation on ideas of truth, universality, purpose in history, and the method (or lack of it) of philosophy, the example of Bloch can help us see better what is at stake. There is much in his thinking that stands the test of time and that even only now is becoming clear. I have not been able to do justice to the full richness of much of his work, the concrete embedding, the often brilliant combination of topicality and philosophical profundity, a characteristic of the dialectical and speculative materialism that pervades Bloch's writing. I have also not been able here to engage in a more critical examination of some aspects of his thought. The circle of immanent critique eventually gets around to doing that, but at first its concern has to be to lend a voice to the thought once more so the ground of that critique can be laid bare within the parameters of the work and critique becomes an integral part of the illuminating movement that is the movement of philosophical thought itself. Such a notion of critique would be in line with Bloch's philosophy, with the idea of expression as the creative and transgressive elucidation of the darkness of the lived moment. All great philosophy is a struggle with itself, in that struggle being as utopia becomes livable, becomes a part of what Bloch meant by the term *humanum*, and philosophy appears as an integral dimension of human existence. Bloch's philosophical anthropology and anthropological philosophy outlines the place of human existence in reality anew—in a realist and materialist manner which sees idealism as a distortion of realism, materialism, not their truth. Philosophy is no longer merely contemplative. It is performative or, as it has been called here, dramatic. It is the praxis of hope, with yet uncharted possibilities, which Bloch, the essay-writing heretical philosopher, expressed in 1921 in a way that is as unorthodox, unsettling, and agitating today as when it was written: "And the creatively informing, finally—in the liminal ideal—identifying force of philosophy is so great, that even the completely revealed Now, the complete realization of our lived present, that even yet the "revealed countenance," of which the work of the Apocalyptic speaks, constitutes a philosophical work."[27]

Notes

1   Jürgen Moltmann, *Theology of Hope*, trans. James Leitch (London: SCM Press, 2002), 151.

2   "The nerve of the right historical concept is and remains the new" [Der Nerv des rechten historischen Begriffs ist und bleibt das Novum] (*PH*, 1626).

3   *Nam tua res agitur, paries cum proximus ardet* [For it is your concern, when the wall of your neighbor is burning; Horace, *Epistulae*, I.xviii.84]; *Mutato nomine, de te fabula narratur* [With a changed name, the story is about you (i.e., the joke is on you); Horace, *Sermones*, 1.1.69–70].

4   Ernst Bloch, *Geist der Utopie* (Frankfurt: Suhrkamp, 1971), 343 ff.

5   Wittgenstein, *Philosophical Investigations*, trans. G. E. M. Anscombe (Oxford: Black-well, 1984), 226e: "What has to be accepted, the given—so one could say—is forms of life."

6   Ernst Bloch, *Experimentum Mundi* (Frankfurt: Suhrkamp, 1975), 71. Note that the relation between *that* and *what* is not arbitrary for Bloch, but also not already worked out yet. This contrasts in a marked way with the existential phenomenology of Sartre, in which the same fundamental distinction is used, but the freedom of man appears as the arbitrariness of the relation between *that* and *what*. The difference is a difference within the economy of desire and the result is that for Bloch, hope becomes an ontologically fundamental concept (and only fully understandable as an ontological concept), whereas for Sartre, man becomes a pointless passion. The positivist undercurrent in Sartre's view of the relation between *that* and *what* was noted early on by Herbert Marcuse. See "Existentialism: Remarks on Jean-Paul Sartre's L'Être et le Néant," in *Philosophy and Phenomenological Research* 8, no. 3 (1948): 336. The translation of Bloch's texts presents almost insurmountable problems. Bloch writes in a brilliant but highly idiomatic German and at the same time pushes the boundaries of the expressive power of the language in different ways, sometimes by consciously ignoring grammatical conventions. It is not going too far to say that the *not-yet* is reflected also in the style of writing that Bloch uses. He writes a not-yet German that, however, uses all semantic possibilities of German to make its point in transcending them. This makes translation difficult. In this fragment we have the nominalization of the conjunction *that* and the interrogative pronoun *what*, the semantic field of form, shape and quality/condition/state (*Form, Gestalt, Beschaffenheit*) and the term *etwas-Vielheit*, which Bloch uses elsewhere as well. I have translated the latter term here as "what-multiple," rather than "something-multiple," to retain the link to the "what"-pole of the basic categorical relation, although in German *etwas* activates both the meaning "something" as well as the "what" of it. The alternative "somewhat-multiple" is unavailable in English for obvious reasons.

7   Theodor W. Adorno, *Jargon der Eigentlichkeit* (Frankfurt: Surhkamp, 1970), 523.

8   Luther (1516) as quoted in Moltmann, *Theology of Hope*, 20.

9   *Monadology* 22: "Every present state of a simple substance is a natural consequence of its previous one, so that the present is big with the future." G. W. Leibniz, *Philo-*

sophical Texts, trans. R. S. Woodhouse and R. Francks (Oxford: Oxford University Press, 1998), 271.

10   The topos "pregnancy" is relevant at many other junctions of Bloch's thought. A pregnant woman is said to be "of good hope" [*guter Hoffnung*] in German; the word *matter, materia*, derives from *mother, mater*; the expectation of the child is a desire running parallel to the desire of the thinker for an articulated, discursive thought, in which something, someone, can be recognized. Just as for Bloch (who ontologizes the point), for Socrates philosophy was a state of pregnancy (and Socrates himself only a midwife for the ideas of others). Here we see inheritance as work; inheritance itself requires and to a certain extent is pregnancy. In a late interview Bloch explicitly refers to his work in the context of Socratic maieutics: "Midwifery is the tenor in all books I have written," in *Gespräche mit Ernst Bloch*, ed. Rainer Traub and Harald Wieser (Frankfurt: Suhrkamp, 1975), 235 (my translation).

11   Bloch, *Geist der Utopie*, 365.

12   Ernst Bloch, *Subjekt-Objekt: Erläuterungen zu Hegel* (Frankfurt: Suhrkamp, 1971), 16. For Bloch, being-in-and-for-itself cannot be achieved exclusively along the lines of historical development. History relates in a complex and incommensurable way to its messianic or apocalyptic fulfillment. I cannot discuss this crucially important topic here. For a further exploration, see my entry "*Ultimum*," in *Ernst Bloch Wörterbuch*, ed. Beat Dietschy, Doris Zeilinger, and Rainer Zimmerman (Berlin: de Gruyter, 2012).

13   Walter Benjamin, "Goethes Wahlverwandtschaften," in *Illuminationen: Ausgewählte Schriften I* (Frankfurt: Suhrkamp, 1977), 135. Translation quoted after Marcus Bullock and Michael Jennings, eds., *Walter Benjamin: Selected Writings, vol. 1, 1913–1926* (Cambridge, MA: Harvard University Press, 1996), 355.

14   Ernst Bloch, *Tübinger Einleitung in die Philosophie* (Frankfurt: Suhrkamp, 1970), 210.

15   The fact that Bloch maintains philosophy starts with wonder, a wonder which only properly starts at the end of thought, is another example of the practice of inheritance, but also of the discrepancy between his thought and that of some of his contemporaries. Heidegger famously held that wonder is no longer accessible for us.

16   Bloch, *Geist der Utopie*, 364. Cf. PH, 337. The English translation is adapted from Ernst Bloch, *The Spirit of Utopia*, trans. Anthony A. Nassar (Palo Alto, CA: Stanford University Press, 2000), 192–93.

17   Ernst Bloch, *Tendenz-Latenz-Utopie* (Frankfurt: Suhrkamp, 1978), 202–203.

18   If we wanted to defend Bloch, we could point out that that tendency is indeed suppressed in some other styles of philosophy, but always only until the penultimate paragraph, when it usually can no longer contain itself and comes out with all the cropped-up rancor of the "balanced judgment." It is better to preach and be corrected than to paint yourself into a corner where nothing matters—that is an invariant of direction quite opposite to the one aimed at in preaching. It is difficult to see, at any rate, how a philosophy could come off the ground that did not have some form of positive commitment (Bloch speaks of the partisanship of truth) already in it; we should be open about it.

19   See Adorno, "Der Essay als Form," in *Noten zur Literatur* (Frankfurt: Suhrkamp, 1958), 9–49. English translation in Brian O'Connor, *The Adorno Reader* (Oxford: Blackwell, 2000), 91–111.

20   Adorno, "Der Essay als Form," 49.

21   Bloch expresses this point by adapting Spinoza's statement, "Truth is the index of itself as well as of falsehood": "*Verum nondum index sui, sed sufficienter iam index falsi*" [Truth is not yet an index of itself, but it is already enough of an index of the false], in Ernst Bloch, *Literarische Aufsätze* (Frankfurt: Suhrkamp, 1965), 389.

22   It does indeed lie at the basis of Bloch's expressionist aesthetics and its avowed personalism: "In this way . . . every blow against personalism and enthusiasm over form and letter, consequently against expressionism as a principle, strikes at the same time that spiritualism, which is steadily impending, which emerged most deeply in the iconoclasm, in the insistence on personality and solely animating spirituality, superior to form, to letter, in the chiliasm of Anabaptism and which constitutes the truth of expressionism." Ernst Bloch, *Politische Messungen, Pestzeit, Vormärz* (Frankfurt: Suhrkamp, 1976), 81.

23   Bloch, *Literarische Aufsätze*, 221.

24   Bloch, *Experimentum Mundi*, 173.

25   Bloch, *Experimentum Mundi*, 172.

26   Bloch, *Tendenz-Latenz-Utopie*, 244.

27   From "Die Landesgrenze des Nihilismus" [The Country Border of Nihilism], 1921, in Bloch, *Philosophische Aufsätze zur objektiven Phantasie* (Frankfurt: Suhrkamp, 1977), 219.

Bloch, as an atheist and a Marxist, deduced from the fact that many millions of people continued to believe in religious explanations of the world—despite the growing scientific and rational evidence to the contrary—that it must represent more than just a simple form of false consciousness or delusion. For him religion not only tapped into something deeply significant and suprahistorical about the human psyche and the forces that drive it, but it was also a contradictory and [self-]misunderstood carrier for the concept of hope.

Bloch's major contribution to postwar philosophy was his three-volume set, *The Principle of Hope*, in which he argued that a desire to move forward out of necessity and into freedom was an essential human characteristic, the "invariant of direction," as he called it, underlying the various material expressions of human history. His key point, however, was to emphasize the dialectical relationship between this invariant of direction and the concrete and partial expressions of the invariant. It is this that led to him being described as a left-wing Heidegger, one who posited a Hegelian Marxist processual and dialectical interaction between the ontological and the ontic, between the universal and the particular, between the human being as *Gattungswesen* [species being] and the expression of this essence in history. For many of his friends and comrades—he was close to Adorno, Benjamin, Scholem, Brecht, and Eisler—this tended to put him beyond the metaphysical pale. They saw in his thought a transcendentalist element that shaded back into a religious understanding of the world, an allegation which is sometimes leveled at contemporary communist thinkers such as Alain Badiou and Slavoj Žižek today.

And yet, I would argue, Bloch was engaging in a form of speculative or transcendental materialism that attempted to create a materialist understanding of an as yet nonexistent future, an "ontology of the not yet," which could be used as a means of understanding and decoding the opaque nature of human existence and the way to move toward a self-created utopia. If we could only look beyond the limitations of what actually is possible, he argued, to what might be possible in the future, then we could restore to the concept of utopia a processual and auto-poietic dimension that would not go as far as, but therefore also simultaneously went beyond, the limitations of any reified and programmatic blueprint. Adorno maintained that for all his faults, Bloch thereby restored honor to the word "utopia," seeing it as the outcome of an as yet incomplete process of its own attainment rather than the programmatic attainment of a preexisting telos.

As Bloch once put it, the desire to transcend the given was "the only true characteristic of all humans" (PoH, 45). He was convinced that the very act of hanging on to faith in the future—precisely in the face of evidence to the contrary—represented a commitment to something which, while of fundamental importance to human progress, we were unable to fully grasp. It was this very incomprehensibility which led people, precisely in times of crisis, like the one we are living through at present, to reach for obscurantist and fundamentalist metaphysical explanations. He applied this approach to an understanding of fundamentalism to religion but also to the politics of fascism, seeing National Socialism as an essentially religious movement, but he also described that aspect of it as its major strength rather than a weakness and something that the orthodox and reductionist Marxist Left had disastrously failed to understand.

As a result he searched in the Abrahamic religions, but particularly within Christianity, for clues to the durability of human hope and the desire for a better world. Before he came to Marx, Bloch worked his way through a historical tradition of rebellion that stretched from the book of Job, Gnosticism, early Christian apocalyptics, and early medieval heretics, such as Thomas Münzer, via Kabbalistic thought, on to Meister Eckhart, Jakob Böhme, Hegel, and Schelling. Within his Marxism, though, there was always a heretic trying to get out. Just as he believed that the human being is not yet complete, so he maintained that Marxism was an approach that was not yet complete as, for all its insights, the objective conditions which would allow it to flourish were not yet complete. This combination of the subjective and the objective conditions which puts neither above the other, but combines them into a Hegelian dialectical unity of opposites, is central to his thought and (sets him apart from but also) places him within both subjectivist idealism and objectivist Marxism without needing to abandon either.

Bloch was also a rationalist who, however, castigated rationalism for its apparent inability to account for the remainder or surplus of human existence, that is, for the motoristic drive of hope, imagination, belief, faith, myth, instinct, ciphers, symbols, daydreams, psychology, spirit, religion, the irrational, and the transcendental. Religion was thus for him not something to be dismissed as merely surplus to human logic but to be prioritized precisely because of its surplus nature. He documented our fascination with the remainder and not the given, with what we don't and, indeed, cannot understand, rather than with what we can. The inexplicable was always of greater importance to Bloch than the rationally comprehensible, precisely because it revealed the *not yet* completed nature of both man and the world, which could not yet be apprehended with thought, as thought itself was also not yet complete. In a way we can say that Bloch's emphasis on "not yetness" wiped away the strict division between ontology and epistemology as, within his thinking at least, neither being nor thought were yet fixed.

Along with Walter Benjamin he also took from the Lurianic Kabbalah the idea of the daily manifestations of hope as surplus "shards of light," left over from the creation of the world as negativity, and translated them into the concept of *Vorscheine* [pre-illuminations] of a better world. These *Vorscheine* function in religion as the dispersed symbols of the divine which emerged from the negative creation of the world into a void of un-beingness, but also in the world as pre-illuminations of something not yet possible due to the absence of the necessary conditions for their realization. Existing ideo-theological elements of previous forms of human (pre)history and culture, rather than holding us back, Bloch therefore maintained, can provide us with ways of understanding what might be possible if they could be liberated and returned, as Benjamin describes it in his use of the Kabbalah's *tikkun olam*, to the service of the light. The redemption of these cultural (epi)phenomenal pre-illuminations is thus part of the process of the (material) negation of a (metaphysical) negation through the future re-creation of the unity between myth and reality.[1]

To put it in Žižekian terms, the negative creation of the Real means that though the shards of light are imprisoned on the "other side," the otherness of the other side is in fact "this side." We are, in that sense, always-already the Other to ourselves—as Rimbaud put it, "Je est un autre"—but an Other in process of becoming itself, a coming-to-itself [*zu-sich-werden*] through the process of becoming Other; that Other being the potentially unbarred subject, the ideal self as part of an ideal society. What appear to be negative manifestations of the void in traditional Kabbalistic thought thus become in Bloch, through this negation of the negation, positive indications of the latent possibilities in the content of the Real.

For Bloch, therefore, ideology critique was not simply a case of the discovery [*entlarven*] of a fundamental antagonism between the objectively real and its ideological apprehension, but also one of an unveiling [*entschleiern*] of the ideological veil itself as a distorted and yet essential (mis)apprehension of the Real. For him, however, "the Real [*das Eigentliche*] is a not-yet predicated reality [*Wirklichkeit*]."[2] Objects of ideology, so often taken in orthodox Marxist accounts to be surplus to requirements, thus actually become in Bloch an *essential* surplus of human development which act not *only* to create a barrier to subjectivity but also simultaneously to provide a bridge between what is known and what could be: between Subject and Predicate. For Bloch it is the very imperfections in the veil of ideology and the human struggle to overcome them which are of greatest interest. Bloch's ideology critique is therefore actually a critique of ideology critique, a progressive negation of the negation in which failure, mistake, perversion, and distortion are essential to the human project but which also carry within them the seeds of their own sublation.

In this sense Bloch was an early western Marxist out of philosophical conviction and commitment to the communist cause rather than (or, with Žižek and Badiou, precisely because of) disillusionment with the social and historical reality of communism. His was a conviction that a proper understanding of ideology, theology, and culture had more to say to us about what and who we are and where we might be heading than any supposedly static scientific socioeconomic analysis of the world. Many of his books start with statements about both the contingent facticity as well as the open latency of human existence. *Experimentum Mundi* of 1975, for example, starts with the words "What's happening? I am. But I do not yet possess myself. As a result we have no idea what we are. Too much is full of something that is missing."[3] Through this process of becoming, and above all the acceptance that the process of change and becoming is the only unchanging constant in the world, we overcome both the objective social and economic barriers to a return to something new but also—and perhaps more importantly—whatever psychological traumas may be preventing us from letting go of our foundationally static concepts of human existence. Thus what Heiko Feldner, positing a particularly Lacanian/Žižekian dilemma, calls the "traumatic, non-symbolizable kernel of historical change"[4] is in Bloch, neither traumatic nor non-symbolizable due to the fact that, on the one hand, change itself is an omnipresent reality that simply needs to be apprehended as hope rather than trauma and, on the other, because the symbolization of change is all around us and, again, simply needs to be seen for what it really is rather than what it claims to be. It has to be "unveiled" but with as much, if not more, attention paid to the veil as to the face which it covered.[5]

The reason that the traumatic fear of change and becoming is so powerful, Bloch maintains, is because of the way in which our concept of the future is informed almost entirely by an anamnetic repetition of our emergence out of nothingness, an obsession with an almost eternal repetition of what has already happened—which we falsely then call the future—culminating in death, which Bloch called the ultimate anti-utopia. But, Bloch asks, does this transcendental and supra-historical anamnetic repetition and death-trauma supposedly at the heart of the human *Gattungswesen* really exist in this form? His basic objection to the Freudian *Urtrauma* and psychologization of the political and philosophical debate was that the Socratic idea that all thought is simply anamnesis, that is, constant remembering and repetition of past events, does not take into account the fact that most people actually spend most of their time projecting forward. Of course, they do so on the basis of past experience, but they are not simply caught up in the eternal recurrence of the same but actually *desire* the [eternal] occurrence of the new. Thus religion and philosophy become different routes to the same goal, an invariant of direction in a return to somewhere completely new. Bloch gives his view of the context of the origins and emergence of religion in an interview from 1975 in which he states:

> Death, of course, is not only a purely individual fact, whose individuality is based in the recognition that after my death many other people will live on and yet others will be born. It is not only an individual but also a collective fate in the form of "Nothing(ness)." This Nothingness is not identical with the Not. The Not exists in the darkness of the lived moment: that something "is not" means something is not yet there, not yet brought out, not yet materialized. The Nothing, however, is the frustration of all emergence; the condition in which all human activity, everything which happens in the world, is frustrated, comes to a standstill, like that of entropy in astronomy: the idea that the whole carousel of the planets orbiting the sun comes to a halt, that the sun itself will stop its orbit and that, as a result, the whole universe will collapse, in which case all of our actions become pointless, as if they had never happened. Very early on we developed dreams against this nightmarish idea, the best known of which is that which is spread across all religions, of the dream of the apocalypse, the dream of a "heavenly Jerusalem"; the idea that Jesus "adorned like a bride"[6] will come down to earth and that the only sun which will then shine, when the sun and the moon have disappeared, will be the "lamb of God": Jesus Christ. What an immense and wonderful phantasmagoria against entropy![7]

Here then Christ, properly understood, is not a mediator between man and God, not the rope between ape and the *Übermensch*, but a barrier to entropy, the ultimate unbarred subject who himself becomes a barrier against the future as immanent void. This is what Pauline Christianity means when it states its certainty in the resurrection. Bloch maintains that it is only through this understanding of the origins of religion combined with the Hegelian dialectic and a transcendental element going by the name of hope that it is possible to perceive a way forward in which the subject can become its predicate against the void of the lived moment and through the negation of the negation. Hope in Bloch therefore performs the role of the ahistorical motor in history much as recognition plays in Hegel and Kojève. This represents, then, a concrete *dialectical* positivization of the world spirit; a Deleuzian transcendental empiricism or, as Bloch maintained of his own position, a desire to "transcend without transcendence." In that sense Bloch also anticipates Badiou, when the latter says that "truth is a process, not an illumination" and that the Greek term "*elpis* should be more appropriately rendered as 'certainty.'"[8] This is the ahistorical dimension, the transcendental materialism in the tradition of Avicenna and Averroes which we find in Bloch; that human hope is more than simply the sum of its optimistic parts, but rather a commitment to a certainty contained within but also subtracted from the totality. For Bloch, therefore, hope is equable with Badiou's "Set of no Set" and means that he was already trying to answer Badiou's challenge of understanding the existence of an inexistent. When Badiou says, quoting St. Paul, "One must not argue about opinions. A truth is a concentrated and serious procedure which must never come into competition with established opinions,"[9] one is also reminded that Bloch often quoted Fichte. When told that his philosophy did not accord with the facts, he simply responded: "Too bad for the facts!" Hope is, in this model, the carrier of the factually inexistent and a means toward the completion of a not yet totalized totality.

Truth is beyond comprehension because it contains within it the void that drives us on, but truth also bars the way to comprehension. To achieve comprehension would be to nullify the void, to negate the negation and remove all drive. Thus, though in Bloch's world the daydream is one of harmony, reconciliation, overcoming, transcending, and sublating, regardless of the apparent impossibility of the task, the reality today seems to be one in which we can no longer even imagine a different and better world. Indeed we even take pleasure in thoughts of the apocalyptical end of the world as the only way to achieve a true negation of the negation. For Bloch we experience only the darkness of the lived moment as a step on the way to the totality. For Slavoj Žižek, on the other hand, we experience only the *jouissance* of that darkness. What we do, Žižek maintains, is skip from one desire to another, incessantly dissatisfied because we can never satisfy the drive simply through the satisfaction of desire. In Žižek the *objet petit a* of desire is, after all, merely a plaything found along a road that is unmapped and unmappable, whereas in Bloch desire plays the role of transcendental constant underpinning a logical sequence of human desire and drive that starts, as Schumacher and Schindler point out, with the bare beingness of *Dass*, the "that," and moves on through *Drang* [impulse], *Streben* [striving], *Sucht* [mania], *Trieb* [drive], *Affekt* [affect], *Wünsch* [wish], and finally *Wille* [will].[10]

Thus what sets Bloch apart from Lacan and Žižek, but brings him closer to Badiou, is the sense that in the process of implementing utopia we will not simply find our way toward something but will actually construct that something in the process of attaining it. It is this sense of finding our way home to somewhere which we have never yet been but which represents the nonconcrete materialization of hope as surplus. In the Lurianic tradition, for example, it could be said that these fetishes are the *qlipoth* [shells or husks] which are erected around the shards of divine light and which prevent us from seeing it. Žižek would maintain, of course, that what motivates us is the fear that they are essentially empty vessels, within which there is not light but simply a void. Bloch, on the other hand, believed that the *qlipoth* were neither full nor empty. In Erwin Schrödinger's famous experiment, we can say that Bloch's wager would have been that the light inside the *qlipoth* is in a mixture of states similar to that of the famous cat, in that the *qlipoth* are both full and empty at the same time. After all, is this not the meaning that Franz Kafka gives the protagonist in his story "Vor dem Gesetz," condemned to waiting for eternity outside a gate that was intended only for him? The law, and thus, by extension, God in particular, is both full and empty, full in that it is all there for him but empty in that he has no access to it. There can be no entry and no return, no Benjaminian *tikkun*. But in Bloch, as in Kafka, there is at least the desire to gain access and to push past the guardians of uncertainty.

And this is what gets Bloch out of the stasis of this potential void of eternal uncertain circularity, namely, the intervention of his constant philosophical operator: the *not yet*. That is the "Left-Aristotelian"[11] conviction that all is not yet as it will be, that not only is history not complete but that matter itself, the concrete Real in a Hegelian/Lacanian sense, is not a fixed void but only a latent and mutable potentiality. In contradistinction to Freud, Bloch therefore sees the *Urtrauma* of the Real, the law before which we all have to wait, as something which itself is subject to change and historicization rather than as a finished block. One man's trauma is the same man's meat after all, and in *Subjekt-Objekt: Er-läuterung zu Hegel*, Bloch, in a chapter entitled "Hegel and Anamnesis: Against the Spell of Anamnesis,"[12] is at pains to point out that in Hegel the concept of forward movement is always toward something which, though always-already present in the totality is *not yet* fully formed. However, he states, "the basis/reason [*Grund*] for something only becomes clear in the movement away from it toward its justification [*Be-gründung*]."[13] This essentially psychoanalytical approach in which the trauma is only unearthed through its justification also means that the trauma itself is actually (re)constituted through the cure. As he goes on to say, "in itself it [the *Grund*] appears to be closed off to memory and is at this point far from being the original point of illumination [*Urlicht*]. From this point of view a 'move forward as a regression to the *Grund*' (Hegel) as its 'reflection' would be more radical, i.e., by pulling up the roots, than regressive."[14]

The trauma of the Real thus functions in Bloch not simply as a void that cannot be overcome but as a motoristic source of progress. His Hegelianism thus goes beyond Hegel and returns to Aristotle to maintain that all that exists is not always-already present within totality but that the totality contains within it the possibility that the always-already can be transcended and indeed is always-already in the process of being transcended. The only point of analyzing a trauma, he therefore maintains, is not to be caught up in a circular trap of the eternal recurrence of the same but to use the *approximation* of the trauma in order to move forward and beyond it. In that sense the trauma as void provides the drive, but the drive has to be forward, not backward, and in making that leap forward one also changes the nature of the trauma or the Real. Just as Heinrich von Kleist maintains in a different context: "one's thoughts are only completed in the process of talking about them,"[15] so in Bloch's open system the Real is only constituted through the process of reality creation. Through the processual development of thought through speech, the *Grund* of those thoughts is itself changed, the trauma becomes the cure, and the cure becomes the path forward out of a *temporary* totality. In Bloch this becomes, in terms of his ideology critique, an application of the operator *not yet* to both his own thought and the world as it was developing. He therefore developed what he called an "open system" of theoretical analysis that was entirely focused on an optimistic and quasi-vitalistic approach to the world that looked for the Dionysian radicalism in world change rather than the Apollonian reflection upon it.

The oft-quoted Nietzschean imperative aphorism "Werde, der du bist" [Become who you are!][16] is thus transformed in Bloch from one in which you simply have to fulfill your preexisting creativity (the search for the hero inside yourself, as Heather Small sang) into one in which what you are is only present at the end and as a result of the process of becoming it. Thus in Nietzsche, too, the genesis is at the end and not the beginning. The *not yet* in the form of possibility, tendency, and latency is thus Bloch's fundamental operator.

Bloch's attitude toward the Bolshevik revolution and the Soviet Union, for example, was informed by this same openness of the *not yet* in that it was informed by a sort of Left-Nietzschean vitalism which saw the revolution as the outbreak of the Dionysian spirit necessary to break with the Apollonian structures and strictures of German Social Democracy. This early sense of Dionysian vitalistic possibility over Apollonian economistic inevitablism continued to inform his later philosophy, too. He was determined to inject a "warm stream" of utopian desire into what he considered to be the cold stream of the established and static praxis of orthodox Marxist socioeconomic analysis (which he nevertheless also saw as essential). But the utopian Marxism he envisaged was again processual rather than programmatic. In *Freiheit und Ordnung*, for example, he states that "Marxism therefore is not a non-utopia, but the genuine, concretely mediated and processually open one."[17] This means that in temporal terms, for Bloch, Marxism itself is a *not yet*, an open system of critique and analysis.

All of this added up to an absolutely optimistic belief in opportunity and change emerging from abstract but certain human hope. As Bloch confirmed, "a Marxist does not have the right to be pessimistic."[18] For Bloch, hope was the driving force behind the human endeavor to reach for something better, something universal in which, to use Hegel's categories, substance and subject would coincide. Bloch stated in this context (also referring to Schelling's relationship to Kant) that "Kant's question is: How does the subject come to its object? If one indeed sees transcendental philosophy as the first part of philosophy then the opposite question arises: How does the object come to its subject and thereby to itself?"[19]

In this sense, substance and subject, substance and object, substance and predicate were unfinished and potentially—though *not yet*—interpenetrable. As Bloch put it: "S has *not yet* become P; Subject has not yet become Predicate."[20] In other words, everything is, as Bloch put it, a "noch-nicht-Gewordenes" [a not-yet-having-become] which is, however, coterminous with an Aristotelian *dynámei on* (that which might become possible), simultaneously constrained and enabled by a *kata to dynaton* (that which is possible). Already at the age of seventeen Bloch had recognized this, again in Kantian form, when he stated: "Das Ding *an sich* ist die objektive Phantasie."[21] This apparently oxymoronic formulation—"objective fantasy"—is a perfect example of the optimistic operation of his dialectical analysis of the relationship between subject and object: their essential interpenetration in which hope, fantasy, and possibility are predicated on what is objectively possible as the existence of the inexistent. But at the same time, what is objectively possible is changed by the way in which hope and fantasy are mobilized. This means that in the not-yetness of his philosophy, the utopia and the utopian are always-already present and visible if we can just shift our perspective and look at them awry, as Žižek would put it. Bloch goes beyond perception though and says that within possibility and impossibility there is always a tendency and latency toward the new and that matter itself is not a complete *Klotz* or block, but in development, not yet complete.

But religion, Bloch maintains, represents the maintenance of hope in the face of the repressed recognition of the radically contingent nature of existence and the fact that there is neither objective reason nor necessity for why we are what we are. Bloch's analysis of religion is therefore the key to understanding how it is that humans go about making a necessity out of contingency. The utopian dimension in Bloch is an attempt to claim back for humanity that which they have ceded to the Holy Spirit without denying the value of the spiritual. If you like, Bloch was grateful to religion for having acted as a safe house for utopia for as long as the conditions were not right for its real implementation. Of course, this period is not yet over. But, as Žižek points out, it was also always-already over: in St. Thomas's Gospel, when Jesus was asked when the new world would come, he answered that it was already here but that we have just not noticed it.[22] Similarly, one of Bloch's favorite quotations from Marx (also quoted by Lukács in *History and Class Consciousness*) is taken from a letter written to Arnold Ruge: "We will see . . . that the world has long since dreamt of a thing which it must simply become conscious of in order to possess it in reality. Then we will also see that there is no great conceptual break between past and future but rather the *completion* of the dreams of the past" (*POH*, 1613).[23]

The most important concepts in Bloch, therefore, are a Hegelian sense of becoming, a Schellingian sense of hope, an Aristotelian sense of possibility, a Nietzschean sense of desire all married up with a Marxist sense of historical agency. With all of these concepts in operation, then, the promise and possibility of the birth of utopia can become real for the first time not at the beginning but at the end of a process. But as Bloch and Žižek agree, using both Hegel and Schelling, the *not yet* should not be seen as a linear temporality. This is where Bloch's concept of *Ungleichzeitigkeit*, or noncontemporaneity, comes in, in which, again like Schrödinger's experiment, time itself is in a mixed rather than a linear state. Past, present, and future were for Bloch mixed up inside a box marked "darkness of the lived moment."[24] Though Bloch was critical of Hegel for his concept of the end of history, seeing this as a self-serving accommodation to Prussian autocracy, he also maintained that immanent in Hegel is the concept of the immanence of the future in all past activities which takes totality beyond itself.

As Davie Maclean points out, "with Hegel it is not the past that makes the present but the present that makes the past that makes the present."[25] However, there is a tendency, linked to his apparently orthodox Hegelianism, to see Bloch as someone eternally seeking this future as existing somewhere out there at the end of a telos which is always-already present. This view is, I think, a misunderstanding, in that his concept of *Ungleichzeitigkeit* is predicated on the recognition that the Third is not at the end of the dialectic but is contained within it only as potentiality. The third element is thus not a separate entity but a part of the entity which is the whole and yet, most importantly, non-identical with and surplus to it. It is both an immanent remainder and an incorporated surplus, and it appears only as a glimpse of not just an *Other* world but a better one. It is these glimpses or pre-illuminations which give us clues to what might be possible. They may take distorted and even perverted form (such as Stalinism and even fascism, he argued), but they remain nevertheless efforts to achieve the Third within the First and Second. They are distorted by the not-yetness of Aristotle's *kata to dynaton* (that which is possible) to allow the subject to become substance, for S to become P. But they are, in a sense, concrete aspects of an as yet impossible utopia in that they all represent attempts to overcome the subject through substance. This amounts to a tendency toward the universal grounded in *docta spe* or educated hope: the subject is indeed barred, but it will not always be thus. So Bloch's concept of the "concrete" utopia (concrete in the Hegelian meaning of the term as the *concrescere*, or growing together of an unfinished process) is related to his *Principle of Hope* in a way similar to that in which Žižek/Lacan's concept of the *objet petit a*, the fetishized object of desire, is related to that of the drive provided by "The Real" or the "Big Other." In Bloch the utopia we will create at the end of an as yet inexistent process paradoxically retains elements of a return to an as yet nonexistent homeland, a *Heimat*, in which nobody has yet set foot.

Bloch's openly proleptic concept of "coming home" must, however, be distinguished from the anamnetic version, which sees it simply as a teleological return to a preexisting form either in the past or in the future (or both). For Bloch it is actually the process of historical becoming, rather than a future state of being, which will constitute utopia. It is therefore its very nonexistence, its *not-yetness* as being, which makes it *concrete*. Graham Harman points out that Quentin Meillassoux's work on messianism now comes to similar conclusions when he states that the idea of a Fourth World, truly novel and beyond what can be imagined, is that "lives are charged with the singular *past* of their preceding existences, surmounting the incompleteness and the dehumanizing misery sustained by each of them in the Third World, and capable as such of being the field of new inventions of thought, since they recommence without returning to their point of departure."[26] To paraphrase Plato's notion, we are all pregnant with our own future, and we just have to choose when to give birth to our utopia. In that sense, we are already on the other side. Our substance has already coincided with our subject. However, it is not necessarily us as subject but largely substance which chooses when we give birth. The *Vorscheine* can therefore be seen as Platonic Braxton Hicks contractions; false alarms brought on by the very process of becoming what we already are.

In many ways, however, the pregnancy is also a phantom. The outward signifier is of someone carrying the new within, but actually the Real, the signified, is not there; it is a void. In Žižekian terms it is a void which is the absence of void but which does not yet connote presence: "Surely anchored in the real as a lack of being, a truth procedure is that which gives being to this very lack. Pinpointing the absent cause or constitutive outside of a situation, in other words, remains a dialectical yet idealist tactic, unless this evanescent point of the real is forced, distorted, and extended, in order to give consistency to the real as a new generic truth."[27]

The new generic truth, however, is only a potential truth, a truth *in becoming*. The reference here is to the anamnetic procedures of Freudian analysis of the Sophoclean Oedipal. Žižek then poses the question as to whether the process of sublimation actually is the thing by which we "give being to the lack." But this leads us back into the Nietzschean circularity of eternal recurrence, an entrapment in a being which cannot but seek its own recurrence in order to justify its own decisions and contingencies. This process works not only on the private level but also on the collective level of the sublimation of the desire for utopia into utopian moments, into a reality which sublimates the Real. In the shift from desire to drive, we pass from the lost object to loss itself as an object. As Brecht and Bloch have it, there is a general feeling of *etwas fehlt*, or "something's missing." But if something is missing in our eternally recurring lives, then we have to have the option of filling the lack rather than living with the void. The simple phrase *etwas fehlt* is a perfect example of what Žižek means by giving being to the lack in that it connotes presence through absence; that is, it—something—exists precisely because it doesn't exist. Thus the very lack of that something—the void which is not a void—actually becomes the motor which drives us forward. In the words of Jakob Böhme, "the nothing hungers for the something."[28] Böhme, too, speaks of a void, an *Ungrund* which, however, cannot remain a void: "The Nothing loves to make itself manifest from out of freedom in the deathly darkness, for then the Nothing wills not to be the Nothing, and cannot be the Nothing."[29]

For Bloch, as an essentially Hegelian Marxist with roots in both Schelling and Böhme,[30] there is, therefore, no ontology of being, only of becoming and fulfillment, which means there is no ontology as such, merely an epistemologically limited appreciation of what is doable in the future. What we live with for now is merely the not-ness of the yet and the promise of better to come not as a transcendental Real but as a real transcendental process. But we cannot live eternally in the future, and for that reason we continue to see little glimpses of a better world in everything around us. The conscious ape has to construct his own utopia using the glimpses he has already picked up along the way. In that sense Bloch embraces an eschatological dimension in that the Third he seeks is not a harking back but a harking forward to an eschatological and even messianic Reich, as outlined in Joachim of Fiore, as a new generic. The only way to escape the gravitational pull of the abyss of the eternal recurrence of the same is through the marshalling of progressive political activity based on an optimistic and hopeful outlook, which is in turn informed by a conscious apprehension of those *Vorscheine*. Žižek, arguing against N. Katherine Hales in this vein, says that "the very difference between the (self-enclosed) symbolic system and its outside must itself be inscribed within the system, in the guise of a paradoxical supplementary signifier which, within the system, functions as a stand-in for what the system excludes: for what eludes the system's grasp."[31] This, I would contend, is a Lacanian equivalent of the *Vorschein* and the "Something" of utopia for which the Nothing hungers, something which stands in for what the system excludes, something which is missing. Thus the opacity of what we dream, both anamnetically and proleptically, is inherent in all historical situations because all historical situations are noncontemporaneous. There is no pure Real or Platonic ideal of democracy that is separate from the lived moment but merely the not-yetness of the possibility as a latent tendency. In that sense it is not a question of the past, the present, and the future being made up of a *sequence* of events, which implies a realness of an event, but rather that all three exist as a unified and yet open process of indeterminacy within the dialectic of *becoming*. We are not human beings within a sequence of events but human *becomings* within a total process of event-generation. However, the event does not exist per se but merely as product and producer of a process. Just as the Higgs particle acts to lend mass to what would otherwise be massless particles, so the concept of utopia is concrete because it lends mass to abstract hope. We already live out our own forms of utopia in everyday contingency not because they are present but precisely because they are absent but to be found in all contingent events in past, present, and future.

However, as with Bloch's comments on Hegel and anamnesis, it is only retrospectively that we impose a pattern on this contingency.[32] We interpret the contents of the snapshot only after it has been taken. In order to have arrived at the point where we can take the snapshot, everything that has happened before has been necessary. In Leibniz's terms, there was sufficient reason for it. But there was no necessity for things to have ended up as they have. Necessity is a purely retrospective teleology. We force ourselves to impose the pattern which emerged out of contingency onto the future and believe that we have discovered a means of predicting and thus creating it on the basis of our retrospective teleology. We then call that model utopia (in the programmatic sense) when it actually just reifies a coincidence of past and current events into a dogmatically determined future in which what was process becomes programme and is then projected forward in necessitarian fashion.

This is where the metaphysics of contingency emerges: as the pattern—to use the Platonic model—must preexist or be in some way external and "other" to contingent being. With the decentering of the subject since the nineteenth century, there has been a shift from a metaphysics of preexisting desire and will (*Weltgeist*, God, whatever) to a situation where desire itself has been made marginal and contingent upon events. The desire to construct an event therefore becomes a desire to create a metaphysics of pure contingency in which a thing or an event can be anything it wants to be. This new poststructural metaphysics is also posthistorical in that it robs the event and the desire to shape and control it of any context and removes any truth claim from it. The understandable desire to try to rescue contingency from both dogmatic determinism and dogmatic relativism seems to have ended in a quasi-anarchistic elevation of the event into a nondetermined meaninglessness in which things happen in an inexplicably miraculous way out of nothing.

This is what Badiou means by a "crisis of negation."[33] The tumultuous events that have emerged in world society and economy in the past five years are stuck in a limbo world of pure negation. As has so often been said, it now seems much easier to imagine the end of the world than the end of capitalism. It would seem that we have been cut adrift from the old certainties of the precapitalist world without yet having caught a glimpse of a new one. Bloch's solution to this problem is, with Aristotle and Hegel of course, *werden*—process, becoming—in which the tendency and latency within matter changes matter itself and with it the contingency of existence. The event in Bloch then is merely a contingent stage in a process which cannot be appreciated at the moment of its eventuation, in the "darkness of the lived moment." This is a vision of Benjamin's Angel of History twisted round and forced to maintain his commitment to the future as process, stepping bravely away from the pile of debris cast behind him by history. A Blochian metaphysics of contingency is therefore one in which the layering of contingent events creates a desire for ever-newer levels. Contingencies are built upon and go to create an ever-emerging telos of their own.

As Žižek says, for example, "when something truly New emerges, we cannot go on as if it has not happened, since the very fact of this New changes all the co-ordinates."[34] But this in turn is merely a reification of a moment within the dialectic of quantity into quality. It seems to me that Žižek is right to demand of Badiou here that we engage in at least a minimum of historicity around the event and not just after it. The truth of an event may emerge after the event itself, but that truth goes on to inform coming truths in a processual chain of events which adds up to an ongoing but as yet incomplete totality. There is nothing truly New in that sense, as the new emerges from the womb of the old and is quickly complicit in the conception of a new New. Everything is in flux, including the event itself. The New may well change the coordinates, but it is not separate from those coordinates and indeed was produced from that same set of coordinates. To paraphrase the *Eighteenth Brumaire*: the event makes history, but not just as it pleases, not in conditions of its own making. An event does not just emerge *ex nihilo*. Hegel puts it thus: "When the might of union vanishes from the life of men and the antitheses lose their living connection and reciprocity and gain independence, the need for philosophy arises. From this point of view the need is contingent. But with respect to the given dichotomy the need is the necessary attempt to suspend [sublate] the rigidified opposition between subjectivity and objectivity; to comprehend the achieved existence [the "being-as-having-become," *das Gewordenseyn*] of the intellectual and real world as a becoming."[35]

So utopia is concrete because it always-already exists in those interstices between event and apprehension, in which the apprehension of the event in turn creates a new event, a spiral of being and consciousness out of which *werden* is constituted. Žižek maintains, for example, that after Schoenberg it is no longer possible to go on composing in the old Romantic mode of Beethoven; after Kandinsky and Picasso it is no longer possible to go on painting in the old Romantic nostalgic mode, or rather, that one can, but it looks like nostalgic fakery, or what Sloterdijk has called "enlightened false consciousness."[36] The point is that Schoenberg, Kandinsky, Picasso, and all the modernist "greats" did not arrive as "truly New" but grew out of the truly old. There is no Schoenberg without the late Beethoven string quartets. In that sense, Beethoven was pregnant with Schoenberg and vice versa. The very emphasis on the *lateness* of Beethoven's string quartets shows that Beethoven himself, however, was *im werden* and also pregnant with himself. Contra Žižek, the desire to return to a pre-Schoenbergian Romanticism could also be seen in a dual way, therefore (and Bloch analyzed fascism in precisely this way), first as a misjudged desire to return to a pre-lapsarian idyll but also as an equally badly misjudged desire to push forward to a post-lapsarian *An-und-für-sich-sein* that carries within it a sublated desire for the Real. Thus what appears to be a harking back can actually be seen as a harking forward to a time when the conscious anti-flow of Schoenberg's disruptive dis-harmonies will be no longer representative or, indeed, necessary.

So Žižek's events and individuals are merely the remarkable points that make the existence of the process clear, unmask it to reveal the void at the heart of existence, or show the darkness of the lived moment, in Bloch's phrase. The need to emerge from both the known-ness and the unknown-ness of that darkness is the true motor of process. It is the very unity of the void with the One which creates Hegel's *für-sich-sein* [being-for-itself]. However, as we know, Hegel's state of *für-sich-sein* was also merely a stage in a process, a *für-sich-werden* [becoming-for-itself] and represented the rope across the abyss between the ape of *an-sich-sein* [being-as-such] and the *Übermensch* of *an-und-für-sich-sein* [*being-of-and-for-itself*]. Thus our desire for a utopia is mistaken for the reality rather than the possibility of utopia. The utopian pregnancy is, in Žižek's terms, "the 'empty' signifier which means meaning as such."[37] It is also, I would contend, a Blochian Not-Yetness. As Bloch points out in his *Subjekt-Objekt: Erläuterung zu Hegel*: "From the very beginning *werden* was the password Hegel used. It opened a path through the apparently static structure of things, just as this structure itself was a path which was itself in motion: a river. . . . The secret of each phenomenon was to be found in its history, particularly in history made by man. It became clear that this was his *Fürsichwerden* (becoming-for-itself), through which the spirit could tear itself free from the bonds of mere natural existence."[38]

As the means by which the subject can become its predicate (S → P) the *werden* is the "Almost Nothing" between S and P. By using the transitive *werden*, though, the Almost Nothing becomes the Potential Everything, the void becomes the new Real, the Event becomes the Process, and as Bloch says at the end of *Principle of Hope*, the true genesis arrives not at the beginning but at the end of the process of prehistory.

To return to Plato, we can see that in Hegelian historical terms it is not just that human beings and therefore human history carry within them "truly new" human beings but that the human being becomes the pregnancy, and in doing so, like Bloch's Hegelian transmutation of a bridge into a river, stops being a being and becomes a becoming. This is the difference between a programmatic, teleological, and technical utopia that we simply carry around with us fully formed until the time is right for its birth, and a processual utopia born out of praxis in which we ourselves become what we are and, with Bloch and Hegel, transform ourselves from bridge to river.

In Lacan and Žižek, the void is not something that can be undone. There is no whole to be gained by filling in the void, even if that were possible, as the void is part of the whole. Žižek posits a difference between desire and drive in that desire is represented by the fetishized *objet petit a*, the thing onto which we project our feelings and needs. We usually repress these desires by repressing the fetishization of them, but the desires are not the end of the matter, for behind them lies the drive that gives rise to the desire, and this drive is provided by the void, the whole, the Big Other. This is the only true thing that cannot reveal itself, but it cannot reveal itself because it is always-already in everything.

In Bloch, I think, the same process exists in that desire is represented by the simultaneously present and absent concrete utopia, whereas hope is the drive which urges us to look for it. Hope in Bloch can thus be seen as an inverted and positivized version of the Žižekian/Lacanian void. Substance and subject, both incomplete and complete at the same time, are therefore constantly moving forward in order to close a gap that can never be closed and search for something that cannot be found. Thus, as Brecht puts it in his play *Mahagonny*, "Those who truly seek will always be disappointed."[39] The emphasis here must, however, be put on the "truly" rather than the "disappointed," since, as with Badiou above, truth is a process, not an illumination. Substance is reality, but reality is not the same as the Real. Subject is consciousness, and it seeks to know not only reality but the Real. Of course, it can never do so, but the process of attempting to do so is what drives humanity on. In Hegel it is the weaving of the spirit concretized in the cunning of reason; in Bloch it is hope concretized in the utopian impulse, and in Žižek/Lacan it is the unknowable Big Other concretized in the *objet petit a*.

Utopia is thus the *objet petit a*, the fetishization of hope. In that sense it is dangerous because it can be programmatized and turned from liberation into commandment. The way to step outside the danger of the fetishized *objet petit a*, however, is to go beyond it into a realm not mapped out by the fetish. It is the difference between the programmatic and the processual utopia. It is concrete because it already exists in our everyday life but also precisely because it doesn't exist other than as a projected and unknown Not-Yetness driven on by the presence through absence of hope. Hope, however, can *only* be present through the absence of its fulfillment.

What constitutes the privatization of hope in today's world is the way in which late capitalist modernity has papered over the lack of an authentic hope and left us only with the fetishized *objet petit a* of a privatized utopia. The end of the religious master-narrative is also the end of the history, not only because of the end of some supposed ontological reality but precisely because of an epistemological lack of the lack and the absence of a new narrative that can take over from the old. We cannot become who we are (which is more than the individual subject), so we only become who we are permitted to be (which is less than the whole we need to be).

Although Bloch was certainly open to Christianity and to what Christianity promises in terms of a utopian and messianic return, he remained an atheist who opposed the Neokantian and Neoplatonic concept of the transcendental sublime. But he did so without rejecting a materialist transcendentalism. For him the idea that a Christian (i.e., truly communist) society could come about by some miracle or apocalypse from outside the material world and without active human revolutionary change was, to paraphrase a German saying, to wish to have one's sins washed away without getting wet. For him the fulfillment of human liberation would also be the fulfillment of misapprehended forms that the dreams of a better life have taken in the past. In this way, what were apparently lost historical opportunities become merely incomplete and latent possibilities for the future, so that we move away from anamnetic circularity to concrete construction of the future out of the wreckage of the old. Religion is a part of the old. It is not jettisoned as a delusion but refunctionalized as the basis for the future. As Bloch himself said, "What is remarkable is that the withering away of the state is an extraordinarily nonviolent, peaceful, indeed Christian expression of something that did not appear within the bourgeois revolution, where roles were simply exchanged ."[40]

The future as a return was one which had to be struggled and worked for. The final two lines of his *Prinzip Hoffnung* are quoted approvingly by many disparate voices: "there arises in the world something that shines in everyone's childhood, but where no one has yet been: home (*Heimat*)." However, just as Marx's famous dictum "religion is the opium of the people" is well known, the essential remainder remains hidden: "it is the sigh of the oppressed creature, the heart of a heartless world," so with Bloch the process by which we return home to a place we have never been often remains hidden:

> Humanity lives everywhere still in prehistory, indeed each and everything is waiting for the creation of a just world. *The true genesis is not at the beginning but at the end*, and it will only start to come about when society and existence [*Dasein*] become radical, i.e., take themselves by their own roots. The root of history, however, is the laboring, creative human, engaged in reshaping and overcoming given conditions. Once he has grasped himself and that which is his, without alienation and based in

real democracy, so there will arise in the world something that shines into everyone's childhood, but where no one has yet been: home (*Heimat*). (*PH*, 1628)[41]

Home, the end of the dialectic, the Third, the return, redemption, salvation, whatever one calls it, is nothing miraculous or spontaneous but the end point of a real, desperate, long, and committed process of change. Just as hurricanes are not caused by the flapping of a butterfly's wings but by trillions of watts of solar energy beating down on the surface of the world's oceans every day, so communism, Bloch maintains, will be the result not of some quasi-miraculous and spontaneous act of violence but of a conscious and determined process, one which we are nowhere near achieving but which we still have to build.

Notes

1 It was this approach which underpinned, for example, the deep chasm between Bloch and Lukács in their famous "Expressionism debate" of the 1930s. See *Aesthetics and Politics* (London: Verso, 1980), 9–59.

2 Bloch, *Subjekt-Objekt: Erläuterung zu Hegel* (Frankfurt: Suhrkamp, 1962), 517.

3 Ernst Bloch, *Experimentum Mundi: Frage, Kategorien des Herausbringens, Praxis* (Frankfurt: Suhrkamp, 1975), 11.

4 Heiko Feldner, "Žižek versus Foucault," in *Did Somebody Say Ideology? On Slavoj Žižek and Consequences*, ed. Fabio Vighi and Heiko Feldner (Cambridge: Cambridge Scholars' Press, 2007), 152.

5 As Žižek points out, of course, Hegel also maintained that there is nothing behind the veil other than "what the subject who is searching has put there." Slavoj Žižek, *In Defence of Lost Causes* (London: Verso, 2008), 392.

6 Apart from the obvious link with Rev. 21:2, this is also an allusion to Richard Wagner and Freiherr von Bodman's *Gesang der Apollopriesterin*, op. 33 (*Vier Gesänge*), no. 2 (1896). Available at http://www.recmusic.org/lieder/get_text.html?TextId=21324. This is particularly likely when one considers the similarity of this idea to that of the radically contingent observation made by Nietzsche in *Über Wahrheit und Lüge im außermoralischen Sinne*, 1873 (which Bloch quotes in *Prinzip Hoffnung*, 1573 ff.) that "in some corner of a galaxy far, far away (irresistible translation) there was a planet on which some clever animals invented knowledge. It was one of the most arrogant and dishonest moments of 'world history': but only for a minute. After nature had taken a few breaths the brain froze and the clever animals had to die" (*PoH*, 1331, translation adapted).

7 "Utopie als Tagtraum und Wachtraum: Ist Zukunft Jugend oder Tod? Ein Gespräch

mit Ernst Bloch," *Die Zeit*, 29 July 1977, no. 32. Available at http://www.zeit.de/19 77/32/Ist-Zukunft-Jugend-oder-Tod? (my translation).

8   Alain Badiou, *St Paul: The Foundation of Universalism* (Palo Alto, CA: Stanford University Press, 2003), 15.

9   Badiou, *St Paul*, 15.

10   Bernard N. Schumacher and D. C. Schindler, *A Philosophy of Hope: Josef Pieper and the Contemporary Debate on Hope*, trans. D. C. Schindler (New York: Fordham University Press, 2003), 110.

11   This was Bloch's self-definition. See Ernst Bloch, *Das Materialismusproblem, seine Geschichte und Substanz* (Frankfurt: Suhrkamp, 1972), 152–64, and his *Avicenna und die Aristotelische Linke* (Frankfurt: Suhrkamp, 1952).

12   Bloch, *Subjekt-Objekt: Erläuterung zu Hegel*, 473–88.

13   Bloch, *Subjekt-Objekt: Erläuterung zu Hegel*, 476.

14   Bloch, *Subjekt-Objekt: Erläuterung zu Hegel*, 476.

15   Heinrich von Kleist, "Über die allmähliche Vefertigung der Gedanken beim Sprechen": http://www.litencyc.com/php/sworks.php?rec=true&UID=13112.

16   Friedrich Nietzsche, *Die fröhliche Wissenschaft*, aphorism 270.

17   Ernst Bloch, *Freiheit und Ordnung* (Frankfurt: Suhrkamp, 1972), 464.

18   Arno Münster, ed., *Tagträume vom aufrechtem Gang: Sechs Interviews mit Ernst Bloch* (Frankfurt: Suhrkamp, 1978), 118.

19   Ernst Bloch, *Leipziger Vorlesungen* (Frankfurt: Suhrkamp, 1985), 4:199–200.

20   Ernst Bloch, *Tübinger Einleitung in die Philosophie* (Frankfurt: Suhrkamp, 1985), 219–20.

21   Ernst Bloch, *Über die Kraft und ihr Wesen* (1902) quoted on opening leaf in Ernst Bloch, *Philosophische Aufsätze zur objektiven Phantasie* (Frankfurt: Suhrkamp, 1977).

22   Slavoj Žižek, *The Puppet and the Dwarf: The Perverse Core of Christianity* (Cambridge, MA: MIT Press, 2003), 86–87.

23   This is also quoted by Lukács in his *History and Class Consciousness* of 1923.

24   Ernst Bloch, *Tendenz-Latenz-Utopie* (Frankfurt: Suhrkamp, 1978), 99.

25   See http://www.ethicalpolitics.org/seminars/davie1.htm.

26   Quentin Meillassoux, "The Divine Inexistence" in *Quentin Meillassoux: Philosophy in the Making*, ed. Graham Harman (Edinburgh: Edinburgh University Press, 2011), 111–12.

27   Slavoj Žižek, *For They Know Not What They Do* (London: Verso, 2008), lxxxii.

28   *Jakob Böhme's Sämtliche Werke*, ed. K. W. Schiebler, 7 vols. (Leipzig: Johann Ambrosius Barth, 1831–46), vol. 4, *De signatura Rerum*, 286.

29   *Jakob Böhme's Sämtliche Werke*, 4:428.

30   Habermas described Bloch as "the Marxist Schelling." Compare Jürgen Habermas, "Ernst Bloch, ein marxistischer Schelling," in Jürgen Habermas, *Philosophisch-politische Profile* (Frankfurt: Suhrkamp, 1971), 141–67. Habermas also describes Bloch's system as one of "speculative materialism" in this text, preempting Meillassoux by some decades: see Harman, *Quentin Meillassoux*, 4.

31   Žižek, *For They Know Not What They Do*, xx–xxi.

32 See Quentin Meillassoux's recent exposition of radical contingency in *After Finitude: An Essay on the Necessity of Contingency* (London: Continuum, 2008).

33 See http://continentcontinent.cc/index.php/continent/article/viewArticle/65.

34 Žižek, *For They Know Not What They Do*, lxxxvi.

35 G. W. F. Hegel, *The Difference between Fichte's and Schelling's System of Philosophy*, trans. H. S. Harris and Walter Cerf (Albany: SUNY Press, 1977), 91.

36 Peter Sloterdijk, *Critique of Cynical Reason* (Minnesota: Minnesota University Press, 1987), 5.

37 Žižek, *For They Know Not What They Do*, xx.

38 Bloch, *Subjekt-Objekt: Erläuterung zu Hegel*, 226.

39 See Bertolt Brecht, *The Rise and Fall of the City of Mahagonny*, in *Brecht: Collected Plays*, vol. 2, ed. John Willett and Ralph Manheim, trans. W. H. Auden and Chester Kallman (London: Eyre Methuen, 1979).

40 Rainer Traub and Harald Wieser, eds., *Gespräche mit Ernst Bloch* (Frankfurt: Suhrkamp, 1977), 166.

41 Cf. POH, 1375–76. Here I use my own translation.

5

The Privatization of Eschatology and Myth: Ernst Bloch vs. Rudolph Bultmann

Roland Boer

The mention of either myth or eschatology today conjures up ideas such as "myths to live by" (anyone can make a billion dollars or become president or prime minister) or sets us pondering on what happens to us when we die. In short, it is a privatized sense of myth and eschatology that dominates our perceptions. But how did it come to this? Why are the deeply collective practices of myth and eschatology now so privatized? In order to explore those questions, I turn to an old debate from the 1930s between Ernst Bloch and the theologian Rudolph Bultmann. Unlike the situation in philosophy and theology today, where both camps can proceed to talk and write about the Bible with only the barest recognition of one another,[1] what we find is a biblical scholar adept at philosophy and a philosopher with a propensity for reading biblical scholarship.[2] Their debate concerned the matters of myth and eschatology in the New Testament. Yet, despite Bloch's collective and political emphasis, it seems today as though Bultmann's existentialist reinterpretation has won the day. In this essay, then, I trace their debate in order to show how Bultmann's existential reinterpretation of myth and privatized eschatology seems to have triumphed over Bloch. In response to a neglected Bloch and a victorious Bultmann, I seek to recover one and recuperate the other by bringing them back into contact with one another.

Before I proceed, there is a preliminary question: how are myth and eschatology connected? The answer is disarmingly simple (and obvious): eschatology is a form of myth. Indeed, stories about the end of the world and the inauguration of a new and better age cannot avoid dealing in the language, metaphors, and narrative structures of myth. Eschatology may be regarded as a subset of mythology, along with what are conventionally called theogonic, cosmogonic, and anthropogonic myths (the creation of the gods, the universe, and human beings). To these I would add "poligonic" myths, not merely because these various types of myths are inescapably political but also because we can speak of a distinct category of political myth.[3] What eschatology does is round out the picture, for all these types of myth actually deal with origins; by contrast, the concern of eschatology is the process of the end of history and whatever might follow.

Myth: Demythologization vs. Discernment

I begin my tracking of their debate with Bultmann's call for "demythologization" [Entmythologisierung] of the mythology of the New Testament. Precisely what Bultmann meant by "demythologizing" is a tricky question, since the common understanding of the term is that he sought to remove the mythological framework of the New Testament. The argument appears most clearly in his manifesto, "Mythology and the New Testament," which produced a howl of controversy when it first appeared in 1941.[4] This essay is worth a patient rereading, not least because of the widespread caricatures of his position. Myth takes on a number of senses in this text: it is a worldview that must be periodized, a pervasive ideology, and dressing for the kerygma. (The Greek New Testament term for proclamation and thereby preaching, in which the Word of God—as both the spoken word and Christ as the Logos—addresses human beings.)

For Bultmann, mythology is the name of a worldview [Weltbild], one that precedes, temporally and logically, a scientific worldview. Mythology in this sense is a thing of the past.[5] Mythology turns out to be periodized: it is the dominant worldview of the time before science, before "modern man," and thus by implication before industrialization and capitalism. It is not the best of arguments, being all too easy to demolish. Bloch gives it scant attention, but we can easily call up Adorno and Horkheimer's argument, namely, that science (enlightenment) and myth are a dialectical pair that have been carrying on their tense dance since the ancient Greeks.[6]

Yet before we rush on to dismiss Bultmann's celebration of the modern, scientific worldview, let us look a little more closely at what he says. Not even an alternative science, as Lévi-Strauss would have it,[7] mythology is rather a nonscientific view of the world that has given way to a very different one. In the New Testament—Bultmann's prime instance— we find a worldview in which heaven is physically above, a place where the gods dwell, the underworld and its demons live below, and earth, our abode, lies in between. In this worldview Jesus comes from heaven, defeats the powers of hell in his death and resurrection, and then rises up on the clouds to return to heaven. From there he will return at some point. At this level, Bultmann is thoroughly convincing or, rather, his argument seems like common sense, at least now. But let me turn the situation on its head: it is not so much that Bultmann's position accords with common sense but that what we now take as common sense is actually the result of Bultmann's residual influence. On this level, he is absolutely correct: the story is inescapably mythological; it trades on a worldview that few if any can seriously hold. The scandal when his argument first appeared is not only in the challenge to the fundamental creeds of Christianity but also in his assertion that one could not believe such a story and maintain one's faith.

The central element, then, of Bultmann's definition of myth is that it is tied to a particular worldview or, rather, to put it more strongly, it is the very expression of a distinct worldview, namely, the prescientific and premodern. A key to this definition of myth is that it removes the element of choice from whether one believes in it or not. Here he comes close to an Althusserian notion of the inescapable pervasiveness of ideology: "no one can appropriate a worldview by sheer decision, since it is already given with one's own historical situation."[8] This is a clever move, for it means that no one can in fact hold to mythology, for it is no longer our worldview.

So what are we to do? We have no choice but to dispense with this mythological framework for the New Testament. We cannot pick and choose the parts we like and discard those we don't. Bultmann seems to take mythology as so much elaborate clothing that needs to be removed carefully to reveal the stark naked kerygma. Statements such as the following fall into this line of thought: "We simply have to ask whether it is really nothing but mythology or whether the very effort to understand it in terms of its real intention leads to the elimination of myth [*Eliminierung des Mythos*]."[9] Here a trap opens up, for too many readers have taken such an "elimination of myth" as the key to Bultmann's well-known program of "demythologization." Mythology is merely the imagery attached to the *kerygma* like so much decoration, and we should not confuse the two.

Bloch pounces, pointing out that Bultmann cannot escape myth entirely and that his theory of myth lacks discernment. Bloch stresses that Bultmann's whole approach presupposes a myth—the "heteronomous arch-myth of the Fall"[10] whereby man must be delivered from himself. Mythical themes remain, such as pride, sin, and error, as does the theme of Jesus' resignation until the moment of his death. Indeed, the great themes of judgment and grace are at the center of Bultmann's reworked theology, as is the transcendent otherness of God, and all of these are inescapably mythical. Bultmann, it seems, is caught in a trap of his own making, despite his protestations otherwise: his argument that beliefs such as God acting decisively in an eschatological manner is not mythological in the "traditional sense" does not hold water, at least for Bloch.

However, the most sustained criticism from Bloch is that Bultmann lacks any discernment of myth. Thus Bultmann "sees all myths, irrespective of their tenor, as nothing but stale worldly talk about the 'unworldly.'"[11] This is a telling point: if mythology is the outmoded worldview of the New Testament, and if such a worldview is no longer viable, then all myths, irrespective of their variations, must go. At first sight, it looks as though Bloch has indeed identified the nerve center of Bultmann's argument. But how does discernment work? Elsewhere I have analyzed the way Bloch doesn't quite live up to his program of discernment, but here I would rather focus on the "best practice" of the discernment of myth. For Bloch, myth is neither uniformly repressive nor liberating. One cannot say that all myth is merely false consciousness and therefore needs to be discarded. Nor is it the most wonderful invention of human beings, one that expresses our deepest truths and highest wishes. What is needed is a dialectical approach to myth. So we find that myths of liberation have a dangerous undercurrent of repression within them. For example, the myth of the Exodus from Egypt bears with it the unwelcome justification for dispossession and conquest in the Promised Land. The victim all too easily becomes the victimizer. Conversely, even the most repressive myth has an emancipatory and utopian dimension about it. There is a moment of rebellion even if it is mercilessly crushed. For instance, the rebellion of Korah in Numbers 16 (a favorite of Bloch's) may be characterized by the story as an unforgivable sin against God and his appointed rulers, Moses and Aaron. But in the very telling of this story, the rebellion itself is preserved. In other words, it is difficult to separate liberation from repression, insurrection from deception and illusion. Bloch's great interest was to draw out the utopian element from the midst of myths of manipulation and domination. Indeed, if one looks carefully, nearly every myth has this utopian residue, an element that opens up other possibilities just when one has given up hope. For this reason, Bloch is particularly interested in biblical myth, for the subversive elements in the myths that interest him are enabled by the repressive ideologies that show through again and again.[12]

In other words, Bloch is in the business of "ein dialektisches Zugleich von Zerstörung, Rettung des Mythos durch Licht," a simultaneous dialectic of destroying and saving myth by shedding light on it.[13] How do we do this? Bloch has two strategies, one that involves distinguishing between myths and another that entails making the distinction within myths. So he sets about distinguishing between myths that are the result of fear, ignorance, and superstition and those—and here Bloch reveals his Romantic roots—that give expression to the quality and wonder of nature. Better known is his identification of different genres—fairy tale, fold tale legend, saga, and myth—and his opting for fairy and folk tales as the most subversive of the lot.[14]

My preference is for the other side to Bloch's approach, namely, discerning the utopian and repressive elements within each myth. The easier part is to search for myths that have some moment of transformation and liberation or perhaps a cunning hero who wins a momentary victory through a ruse? Bloch's attention is drawn to the story of Prometheus in Greek mythology, or of the serpent in Paradise in the Bible, where we find a successful rebellion against the powers that be. The last example brings out a crucial element in this approach, for we need to read against the grain of the dominant narrative. Our hero or heroine may end up being vilified and condemned in the story for an act of willful rebellion, so we need to ask, Why is this characterized as sin or rebellion?

Is this character challenging the powers that be, so often personified as God or the gods? Once we have this principle, it is surprising how many stories do in fact speak of crushed insurrection: the serpent, Eve and Adam in the Garden, Cain challenging God, the Israelites murmuring and rebelling against Moses in the wilderness, Miriam's insurrection against Moses and Aaron, the initial rejection of the Promised Land by the Israelites, the challenges of Job, the fiery bloodcurdling language of the Apocalypse (Revelation), and so on. Like Bloch, I would rather keep both the conformist and nonconformist elements of myth rather than no myth at all, since the banishment of myth discards these utopian moments along with all that is oppressive.

What Bloch has done in response to Bultmann is introduce the issue of politics. The question is not whether the Word addresses us and calls us to follow (Bultmann's deeply Lutheran emphasis), but what side we choose. Is it to be that of the white terror of divine power and sanctioned despots, or is to be those who dare to challenge that power? These myths are deeply political.[15] And the reason for this depoliticization of myth is that Bultmann fails to discern myth. What Bultmann effectively does is take myth "out of the danger area of cosmic history" and reserves it exclusively for the "lonely soul and its middle-class God."[16] In other words, the politically explosive myths, especially those of rebellion and of the last things, are dumped on the side of the road. It is a little like the process of European philosophy crossing the Atlantic to North America: somewhere, somehow, all of its politics is washed off in the ocean. And what takes the place of these explosive myths? It is the private individual in the present liberal world of capitalism. For Bultmann's position, argues Bloch, is none other than a classic reformulation of the deepest doctrines of liberalism. At this point we slip into the critique of existentialism, to which I will return later.

At his best, Bloch's discernment of myth is an extraordinary approach, for it enables us to interpret the myths of any religion as neither completely reprehensible nor utterly beneficial. It is precisely through and because of the myths of dominance and despotism that those of cunning and nonconformism can be there, too. It is not merely that we cannot understand the latter without the former, but that the enabling conditions for subversive myths are precisely those myths that are not so.

Eschatology: Existentialism vs. Marxism

So we have reached the point where Bloch finds that Bultmann's program of demythologization actually ends up depoliticizing myth. Bultmann's mistake is to lump all myths together in a mythological worldview that is no longer our own. What we really need, argues Bloch, is both an awareness of the political charge of myths and a strategy of discernment to identify those shards that offer rebellious hope.

There is more: Bultmann's depoliticized Bible actually removes the world-changing power of eschatology. Now Bultmann does have an eschatology, argues Bloch, but it is very much a realized and present version. Immanent, immediate, the Moment, *hic et nunc*—all these terms describe for Bloch the shift to a present eschatology.[17] All that once judged the present from the perspective of the future has been dragged into the present. If there is a future-oriented eschatology, then it is a highly personalized one: what will happen to me in the future and when I die?

Suddenly we stumble across a problem: if Bultmann has a realized version of eschatology focused on the private individual, then he does in fact have a position. It is not all slash and burn, for there is something he wants either to preserve or grow in its place. In fact, the tendency to associate Bultmann with demythologization is a misreading or perhaps half-reading; he was after an *interpretation* and not an elimination of the myths of the New Testament. Bultmann is not entirely consistent in this respect, for he does speak often of the need to "eliminate myth," as we saw earlier. Yet if we look closely enough, demythologization turns out not to be a process of stripping the New Testament of myth. It is in fact a somewhat different task, namely, the interpretation of myth. Or as Bultmann puts it: "during the era of critical research the mythology of the New Testament was simply *eliminated*, the task today . . . is to *interpret* the mythology of the New Testament."[18] Interpretation, not elimination, is the task of demythologization. In this light, Bultmann's other slogans begin to make sense, especially ones like, "If the New Testament proclamation is to preserve its validity, then the only way is to demythologize it."[19]

But how do we reinterpret myth? Bultmann goes on to interpret the mythology of the New Testament in existentialist terms, especially that of Karl Jaspers and Martin Heidegger. In the midst of all the detail

Bultmann makes two moves. First, he asserts that existentialism says roughly the same things as the New Testament, albeit in secular terms: "Above all, Martin Heidegger's existentialist analysis of *Dasein* seems to be only a secularized philosophical presentation of the New Testament view of *Dasein*."[20] Such a statement would have a ringing endorsement from Theodor Adorno, although it would certainly have made Heidegger's lower lip quiver in anger. Adorno, of course, would find the secular theological nature of existentialism its most pernicious feature, for it smuggles in the authority structures of Christian theology without the figures to which this authority was traditionally attached.[21] It is, in other words, the worst form of idolatry and the personality cult, of which Heidegger is a prime instance.

However, Bultmann is not always consistent. One moment he asserts that existentialism presents a secularized view of existence, a replacement for the language of mythology, but at the next moment he points out that the gospel of Christianity goes beyond existentialism. Or, as he puts it, existentialism describes the world as it is—that is, a fallen world—very well, but it has no story of redemption. For that we need the scandalous gospel of Christianity. Existentialism can get us only so far, for no human philosophy can ultimately provide salvation. Only God through Christ can do that: "This, then, is the crucial point that distinguishes between the New Testament and philosophy, between Christian faith and 'natural' self-understanding: the New Testament speaks and Christian faith knows of an *act of God that first enables our submission, faith, love, and authentic life*."[22]

Now he brings in the language of eschatology, since it provides what is unique about the Christian message. In contrast to existentialism, which has no narrative of redemption, Bultmann suggests that the *kerygma*, with the cross and resurrection of Christ at its center, is "the eschatological fact."[23] Bultmann peppers the last pages of his manifesto with the words "eschatology" and "eschatological" so as to leave us in no doubt. Now the questions begin piling up: What sort of eschatology is it? What does he mean by the cross and resurrection of Christ? After all, that story has to be stripped of its mythological cloak and reinterpreted. And eschatology in its traditional form cannot escape the language of mythology. How is that to be reinterpreted?

Reinterpreted, it really means a direct, personal encounter with the

Word in the here and now. It is God's challenge to the individual to turn his or her life around and give it some meaning. Bultmann is after all a good Lutheran. The life-changing effect of the Word (traditionally God in Christ) is a direct and unmediated encounter. Yet who is that who addresses us? It is "a transcendent power to which both we and the world are subject."[24] We are to waken to the fact that there is something beyond our own existence, that there are powers "beyond all that is known."[25] As for myth—which includes Christ's preexistence, incarnation, resurrection, and ascension—that may be reinterpreted as "the conviction that the known and contingent world in which we live does not have its basis and purpose within itself."[26]

Bultmann was reputedly a great preacher, one who could deliver a rousing and inspiring sermon, but these terms seem to me to lack color and narrative. The vivid imagery of the biblical stories has given way to philosophical terms. Above all, it is a highly privatized reinterpretation. Its focus is the individual encounter with the transcendent, its call to be aware of a greater reality beyond this one, a transcendence that should reorient our lives in light of the big picture.

I will return to this point in a moment, but first let us see how Bloch responds. Bloch condemns such existentialist moves, which had a deep and lasting effect in Christian theology; Paul Tillich (Adorno's supervisor for his *Habilitationsschrift*) and John Macquarie being only the most noted among them. However, Bloch's criticism is again quite astute: he does not criticize Bultmann's existentialism as such; rather, it is what existentialism embodies and expresses that bothers him. Existentialism is a means, a language that gives voice to the deep logic of middle-class capitalist ideology. With its focus on the private and sacrosanct individual, it effaces the social world: "The bodily, the social, the cosmic: it can all, for them, be discarded from religion as worldly, as the world: the soul need not bother about it."[27] What we get instead is a purely individualistic focus on existence. What counts for the individual is the encounter with the Word, an encounter in which we find contact from one existence to another. And the essence of that encounter, the address from God to the individual person, has no content, it is not about anything. In the end, for Bloch, such a position is barely Christian, or rather, by abandoning any eschatological and political change, it preserves "highly unchristian conditions in the world."[28]

Recuperating Bultmann and Recovering Bloch

Where does all this leave us? We have a Bultmann stripped of worldly concerns and yet hanging onto the central message of the gospel and a Bloch who scores a few points. Above all, despite Bloch's criticisms, it seems as though Bultmann has won the day. It is not merely because he is still regarded as one of the great theologians of the early part of the twentieth century. This existential reinterpretation (with a distinctly Lutheran twist) has triumphed. Mythology is more and more a myth to live by for each one of us. We may not buy into existentialism, but we can certainly choose from the supermarket of spiritual or secular options. A little bit of reincarnation perhaps, a general belief in a benevolent power, a sense that our good deeds will count for something, the importance of "choice," and so on. Eschatology boils down to searching for answers to our own individual end. Will it be a material death in which my ashes or decaying body becomes one with the earth? Or will it be a reincarnated life in some other form? Or will I go to heaven, which really just means being with God? The urgency of matters such as global warming or peak oil are really only urgent if they happen in my lifetime. Or if I do look beyond my lifetime, then the only way to imagine it is in terms of how my children will fare — that may inspire me to some action.

By contrast, Bloch's effort to offer a distinctly political interpretation of the Bible has not fared so well. When I mention the discernment of myth, or his politicized focus in biblical interpretation, or the search for utopian shards throughout the Bible, people react as though they are brand-new ideas. But then they dismiss him when they hear he was a communist who lived for many years in East Germany. That "ideology" has failed, after all.

In light of all this, is it possible to recover Bloch and recuperate Bultmann? As far as Bloch is concerned, the liberation theologians have been doing a rather good job. Indeed, Tom Moylan argues that political and liberation theologies served as a conduit for Bloch's work, arguing with it and transforming it, so that it entered into newer areas of politically inspired research such as postcolonialism.[29] Indeed, in the 1960s and 1970s, Bloch's work was deeply influential among a range of theologians, including liberal theologies such as the death-of-God, developmental and secular theologies, along with political and liberation theologies in Germany and Latin America.[30] I would also argue that the figure of a distinctly political Jesus of Nazareth, found in more than one "historical Jesus" today, is a legacy of Bloch's own reading. However, the full recovery of Bloch remains a work in progress.

Bultmann is another story. One way to recuperate his very individualist emphasis is through Bloch himself, restoring the implicit collective, bodily, and political elements of his reinterpretation. The starting point for that must be Bloch's point that Bultmann does in fact have a myth or two. One is of course the arch-myth of the Fall, in which human beings find themselves needing an encounter for the purpose of redemption. Yet I would rather focus on other elements of that mythological structure, especially Bultmann's emphasis on the scandal of the Bible.

Bultmann insists that there is a scandal—*skandalon*—at the heart of the Christian message, or *kerygma* as he calls it. For Bultmann the scandal of the *kerygma* is that this particular person, Jesus Christ, lived an ordinary human life, was killed as a common criminal on the cross, and was raised again—not physically, but metaphorically. This person is the moment when God acts eschatologically in history, so much so that such an event changes the history, the world, and individual lives. Bultmann cannot emphasize enough that this is the scandal at the heart of Christianity: it is folly and a stumbling block. That is it; there is nothing else. Even in this form, the story is inescapably mythological, and Bultmann feels that it is not the least bit persuasive. To write that God acts eschatologically in history through a particular human being is nothing if not mythological. It is also loaded with political implications.

Bloch was not shy about seeking out a very political Jesus, who was on no account a gentle bringer of wisdom, supporter of the powers that be, and teacher of bourgeois morals (family, work, church, etc.). Bloch finds a revolutionary firebrand who opposed the Roman colonial authorities and the Jewish religious leaders in the name of an immanent and imminent Kingdom of God. Bloch is extremely keen on a flesh-and-blood Jesus who emerges from his mythical and political context (*POH*, 1256–65; *PH*, 1482–93). Unfortunately for Bloch, the historical Jesus remains as slippery as ever, and all too many searchers end up finding their own reflection in him. Yet what is valuable about this reading is the way it is resolutely political, both in terms of the apocalyptic urgency of the New Testament and the scandal of that story (*POH*, 1265; *PH*, 1493).

It is a scandal with enormous political punch. For Bultmann it is the scandal of God acting through the ordinary person of Jesus Christ; for Bloch it is the scandal of a revolutionary Jesus.[31] The scandal may take different forms, but a scandal it is. Yet there is one other element of that scandal that is a surprise even for me. It is nothing less than the resurrection. Bultmann argues at length that the resurrection is an inescapable piece of the kerygma. Cross and resurrection are two sides of the same coin, and without the resurrection Christianity has no message. The big surprise here is that Bloch too sees the resurrection as central: for him the resurrection signals *"a thirst for justice"* (*PoH*, 1126; *PH*, 1324). He does not find the resurrection a believable concept (nor does Bultmann in any physical sense); rather, it is a crucial feature of apocalyptic thought, practice, and speculation. On Judgment Day a collective resurrection overruns the merely individual notion, and justice is dispensed by a returned Christ. And this advent of Christ was always more immediate, expected soonest by revolutionary groups at revolutionary moments, such as the Albigensian wars or the German Peasants' War: "retribution for all the living after death, for all the dead after the last trumpet, retained a wishful revolutionary meaning for those that labor and are heavy laden, who could not help themselves in reality or were defeated in the struggle" (*PH*, 1132; *PH*, 1331). As a metaphor for revolution, perhaps it is not such a bad eschatological myth after all.

Notes

1   What we have in fact are two distinct genealogies. For example, the current "neo-Paulinist" philosophical debate rarely mentions the work of biblical scholars; see Alain Badiou, *Saint Paul: The Foundation of Universalism*, trans. Ray Brassier (Palo Alto, CA: Stanford University Press, 2003); Slavoj Žižek, *The Fragile Absolute; or, Why Is the Christian Legacy Worth Fighting For?* (London: Verso, 2000); Slavoj Žižek, *On Belief* (London: Routledge, 2001); Slavoj Žižek, *The Puppet and the Dwarf: The Perverse Core of Christianity* (Cambridge, MA: MIT Press, 2003); Georgio Agamben, *The Time That Remains: A Commentary on the Epistle to the Romans*, trans. Patricia Dailey (Palo Alto, CA: Stanford University Press, 2005); Jacob Taubes, *The Political Theology of Paul*, trans. D. Hollander (Palo Alto, CA: Stanford University Press, 2004); Terry Eagleton, *Sweet Violence: The Idea of the Tragic* (Oxford: Blackwell, 2003); Terry Eagleton, *The Gatekeeper: A Memoir* (London: Penguin, 2001); Terry Eagleton, *Figures of Dissent: Critical Essays on Fish, Spivak, Žižek, and Others* (London: Verso, 2003); Terry Eagleton, *After Theory* (New York: Basic Books, 2003); Gabriele Fadini,

"San Paolo e la Filosofia Contemporanea: Prospettive e Sviluppi," PhD diss., University of Padua, 2005. When it does, it is completely unaware of the "megatext" of Pauline scholarship, namely, its major themes and shifts. By contrast, Pauline scholars are locked into their own concerns, and those concerns do not include what the philosophers are saying about Paul. For examples, see Daniel Boyarin, *A Radical Jew: Paul and the Politics of Identity* (Berkeley: University of California Press, 1994); Troels Engberg-Pedersen, *Paul and the Stoics* (Louisville, KY: Westminster John Knox Press, 2000); Bruce J. Malina and Jerome H. Neyrey, *Portraits of Paul: An Archaeology of Ancient Personality* (Louisville, KY: Westminster John Knox Press, 1996); Dale B. Martin, *The Corinthian Body* (New Haven, CT: Yale University Press, 1999); James A. Smith, *Marks of an Apostle: Deconstruction, Philippians, and Problematizing Pauline Theology* (Atlanta: Society of Biblical Literature, 2005); Richard A. Horsley, ed., *Paul and Empire: Religion and Power in Roman Imperial Society* (Harrisburg, PA: Trinity Press International, 1997); Neil Elliott, *Liberating Paul: The Justice of God and the Politics of the Apostle* (Maryknoll, NY: Orbis, 1994); Neil Elliott, "Paul and the Politics of Empire: Problems and Prospects," in *Paul and Politics: Ekklesia, Israel, Imperium, Interpretation: Essays in Honor of Krister Stendahl*, ed. Richard A. Horsley (Harrisburg, PA: Trinity Press International, 2000), 17–39. Also see Daniel Boyarin, "Paul and the Genealogy of Gender," Diana Swancutt, "Sexy Stoics and the Reading of Romans 1.18–2.16," and Kathleen E. Corley, "Women's Inheritance Rights in Antiquity and Paul's Metaphor of Adoption," all in *A Feminist Companion to Paul*, ed. Amy-Jill Levine and Marianne Blickenstaff (London: T and T Clark International, 2004).

2   Thus, in Bultmann's works we find references to Heidegger, who influenced him deeply, but also to Wilhelm Dilthey, Ludwig Feuerbach, G. W. F. Hegel, J. G. von Herder, Karl Jaspers, Søren Kierkegaard, Karl Löwith, Karl Marx, Oswald Spengler and Jaroslav Pelikan to name but a few. For Bloch, the Bible was one of his great inspirations along with Goethe's *Faust*. So apart from a mix of allusions and citations, he has long stretches of exegesis of biblical texts, including his book-length study of the Bible, *Atheism in Christianity*. And he read biblical scholars, especially Karl Barth, Albert Schweitzer, Julius Wellhausen, K. Budde, Joachim Jeremias, Hermann Gunkel, and, of course, Rudolph Bultmann.

3   See my detailed discussion in Roland Boer, *Political Myth: On the Use and Abuse of Biblical Themes* (Durham, NC: Duke University Press, 2009); Roland Boer, "Phases of the Gonic: Re-Reading Genesis to Joshua as Myth," *Literary Newspaper* (Bulgaria) 13, 21 December 2005–10 January 2006 (2005–2006), 18. As far as definitions are concerned (of which there are many), I prefer the simplest: myth is an important story. Beyond that we need to see what shape that story takes. If we want such a definition, then we can't do much better than Northrop Frye: "myth is a form of imaginative and creative thinking." Northrop Frye, *The Great Code: The Bible and Literature* (New York: Harcourt Brace Jovanovich, 1982), 35. Or, in fuller form, myth tells a society "the important things for that society to know about their gods, their traditional history, the origins of their custom and class structure." Northrop Frye, *Words*

with Power, Being a Second Study of the Bible and Literature (New York: Harcourt Brace Jovanovich, 1990), 30. As Flood points out, most definitions seek a combination of narrative, subject matter, cultural status (myths as true for a distinct community), and social functions (ideology). See Christopher G. Flood, *Political Myth: A Theoretical Introduction* (New York: Routledge, 2002), 6–7. Lincoln's concise definition—"ideology in narrative form"—captures most of these. Bruce Lincoln, *Theorizing Myth: Narrative, Ideology, and Scholarship* (Chicago: University of Chicago Press, 2000). To be avoided is the baleful affect of Mircea Eliade in *The Myth of the Eternal Return*, trans. Willard R. Trask (New York: Pantheon, 1954) and *Myth and Reality* (London: Allen and Unwin, 1964) and the University of Chicago's journal *History of Religions.*

4   Rudolph Bultmann, "Neues Testament und Mythologie: Das Problem der Entmythologisiering der Neutestamentlichen Verkündigung," in *Kerygma und Mythos*, ed. H. W. Bartsch, 2nd ed., vol. 1 (Hamburg: Herbert Reich-Evangelischer, 1951). This exists in two translations: "New Testament and Mythology: The Mythological Element in the Message of the New Testament and the Problem of Its Re-Interpretation," trans. Reginald H. Fuller, in *Kerygma and Myth: A Theological Debate*, ed. Hans Werner Bartsch (London: SPCK, 1960) and "New Testament and Mythology: The Problem of Demythologizing the New Testament Proclamation," in *New Testament and Mythology and Other Basic Writings*, trans. and ed. Schubert M. Ogden (Philadelphia: Fortress, 1984). Whereas Fuller pushes the boundaries of free translation to the point of altering the sense of Bultmann's text, Ogden's translation is, partly in response, so slavishly literal that Bultmann's lucid and direct style becomes stilted and wooden. I have consulted both, but unless otherwise indicated, all translations are my own.

5   Bultmann, "Neues Testament und Mythologie," 16.

6   Theodor W. Adorno and Max Horkheimer, *Dialectic of Enlightenment*, trans. John Cumming (London: Continuum, 1999).

7   Claude Lévi-Strauss, *The Savage Mind* (London: Weidenfeld and Nicolson, 1966).

8   Bultmann, "Neues Testament und Mythologie," 17.

9   Bultmann, "Neues Testament und Mythologie," 22.

10   Ernst Bloch, *Atheism in Christianity: The Religion of the Exodus and the Kingdom*, trans. J. T. Swann (New York: Herder and Herder, 1972), 41; Ernst Bloch, *Atheismus im Christentum: Zur Religion des Exodus und des Reichs* (Hamburg: Rowohlt Taschenbuch, 1970), 47. Swann's translation is generally good, but every now and then he inexplicably leaves out a few sentences and rearranges Bloch's text. Needless to say, I tread warily when using his translation, always double-checking with Bloch's German.

11   Bloch, *Atheism in Christianity*, 39–40; Bloch, *Atheismus im Christentum*, 46.

12   I have used this approach quite fruitfully in a number of places. See Roland Boer, *Rescuing the Bible* (Oxford: Blackwell, 2007); Roland Boer, "An Un-Original Tale: Utopia Denied in *Enuma Elish*," *Arena Journal*, n.s., 25/26 (2006): 136–52.

13   Bloch, *Atheism in Christianity*, 37; Bloch, *Atheismus im Christentum*, 44.

14 Jack Zipes has pursued this angle on the discernment of myth with some gusto. See Jack Zipes, *Breaking the Magic Spell: Radical Theories of Folk and Fairy Tales* (New York: Routledge, 1979); Jack Zipes, *Fairy Tale and the Art of Subversion: The Classical Genre for Children and the Process of Civilization* (New York: Routledge, 1988).

15 See Boer, *Political Myth*.

16 Bloch, *Atheism in Christianity*, 40; Bloch, *Atheismus im Christentum*, 46.

17 Bloch, *Atheism in Christianity*, 40; Bloch, *Atheismus im Christentum*, 46.

18 Bultmann, "Neues Testament und Mythologie," 24.

19 Bultmann, "Neues Testament und Mythologie," 22.

20 Bultmann, "Neues Testament und Mythologie," 33.

21 Theodor W. Adorno, *The Jargon of Authenticity*, trans. Knut Tarnowski and Frederic Will (Evanston, IL: Northwestern University Press, 1973). See also Roland Boer, *Criticism of Heaven: On Marxism and Theology* (Leiden: Brill, 2007), 422–30.

22 Bultmann, "Neues Testament und Mythologie," 40.

23 Bultmann, "Neues Testament und Mythologie," 45.

24 Bultmann, "Neues Testament und Mythologie," 23.

25 Bultmann, "Neues Testament und Mythologie," 22–23.

26 Bultmann, "Neues Testament und Mythologie," 22.

27 Bloch, *Atheism in Christianity*, 39; Bloch, *Atheismus im Christentum*, 45.

28 Bloch, *Atheism in Christianity*, 42; Bloch, *Atheismus im Christentum*, 47.

29 Tom Moylan, "Bloch against Bloch: The Theological Reception of *Das Prinzip Hoffnung* and the Liberation of the Utopian Function," in *Not Yet: Reconsidering Ernst Bloch*, ed. Jamie Owen Daniel and Tom Moylan (London: Verso, 1997); Harvey Cox, "Ernst Bloch and the Pull of the Future," *New Theology* 5 (1968): 191–203; Kenneth Heinitz, "The Theology of Hope According to Ernst Bloch," *Dialog* 7 (1968): 34–41; Johannes B. Metz, "The Responsibility of Hope," *Philosophy Today* 10 (1976): 280–88; Jürgen Moltmann, "Hope and Confidence: A Conversation with Ernst Bloch," *Dialog* 7 (1968): 42–55; Paul Tillich, "The Right to Hope," *Neue Zeitschrift für systematische Theologie und Religionsphilosophie* 7 (1965): 371–77. See also the articles by Walter Capps, Johannes B. Metz, Wolfhart Pannenberg, and Bloch himself in *Cross Currents* 18 (1968), as well as those by Frances P. Fiorenza in *Heythrop Journal* 9 and 10 (1968 and 1969).

30 It is worth pointing out that the first translations of Bloch's work into English were enabled by the theologians Jürgen Moltmann and Harvey Cox, specifically the compilation of various excerpts and essays in *Man on His Own: Essays in the Philosophy of Religion*. There followed soon afterward the translation of *Atheism in Christianity: The Religion of the Exodus and the Kingdom*.

31 I am less enamored with Bloch's suggestion in *Principle of Hope* that there is also a scandal in the practice of Christian love, which is "a love which is almost micrological, one which gathers up its own in their out-of-the-wayness, their incognito to the world, their discordance with the world: *into the kingdom where they accord*" (POH 1262; PH, 1490).

6

The Education of Hope:

On the Dialectical

Potential of Speculative

Catherine Moir | **Materialism**

The Injunction

Philosophical materialism has undergone what has been called a "speculative turn."[1] Although materialist philosophy has had its last rites read more than once, continental thinkers have boldly begun once again to seek realist, materialist answers to the most vital questions. However, the contemporary movement owes a largely unacknowledged debt to Ernst Bloch, who already spoke *ante rem* of the need for a "new materialism" when he was developing his own philosophy, during the 1930s, which he indeed called "speculative materialism" and which prefigures in many respects contemporary materialist debates.[2] Bloch conceives of matter "not only as the measure and bearer of the conditions according to which something can be possible, but more than ever as the substrate of the objectively-real possible."[3] One of the aspects of Bloch's speculative materialism to be explored here is its relation to Hegel: in a sense, it can be said that Bloch makes Hegelian speculation fruitful for materialism analogously with Marx's materialization of Hegel's dialectic. Yet, as Hans Heinz Holz points out, Bloch returns to the speculative in the sense of *speculari* [to look out] while Hegel traces it to *speculum*.[4] While, for Hegel, "speculative thinking is mirror thinking," for Bloch it is a matter of looking out, but crucially not only in the sense of the human looking out on the world in an idealist or dualist sense, but of the world itself looking out: to quote Holz, "the other metaphor leads to a different thought-model."[5] Bloch's speculative materialism is *dialectical* and, as such, approaches the thought-being question in dialectical materialist terms, whereby being determines thought.

Slavoj Žižek takes up the question "How is it possible, for a living being, to . . . *install a non-act, a withdrawal into reflexive distance from being, as the most radical intervention?*"[6] For Žižek, attention to the parallax gap, "the irreducible gap between the phenomenal experience of reality and its scientific account/explanation," constitutes true materialism, with which Bloch would arguably agree.[7] For Bloch this "gap" or "rupture" [*Riß*] is at once an aporia in the form of the being-consciousness relation and an antinomy in the quantity-quality relation: antinomy used here not in the Kantian sense of the scientifically inaccessible parallelism of mutually exclusive claims but rather as the mutual opposition of real categories.[8] Yet while for Žižek, as a Lacanian, the point of the parallax view is "not to overcome the gap that separates thought from being, but to conceive it in its 'becoming,'" Bloch leaves open the possibility of overcoming the gap, a speculative possibility which he describes as immanent in the material world. For Bloch, the hope for knowledge of the absolute is thus not a privatized matter, relegated to an esoteric or purely subjective sphere, but rather a principle of matter itself. Bloch draws on historical materialism in his location of the possibility of realization of the principle of hope in the human mesocosm.

The possibility of knowing the absolute is what connects Bloch's thought with contemporary speculative materialism. According to Quentin Meillassoux, one of the foremost representatives of the contemporary turn, the task of speculative philosophy today is to "take up once more the injunction to know the absolute and break with the transcendental tradition that rules out its possibility."[9] For Meillassoux, access to the absolute is what constitutes speculative thought, and it is the task of speculative philosophy to break not only with what he calls "correlationism"—in his words, "the idea according to which we can only ever have access to the correlation between thinking and being and never to either term considered apart from the other"—but also with transcendentalism in the Kantian tradition as thought that is concerned with the conditions of possibility of knowledge.[10] In *After Finitude*, Meillassoux develops a strand of speculative thought in response to a particular question: "what is the condition that legitimates science's ancestral statements?" Meillassoux is concerned here with the problem of how scientific evidence of a reality anterior to conscious life is intelligible. He acknowledges that his construal of the injunction to think the absolute may at first appear to be a transcendental question, but reassures us that "its primary condition is the relinquishing of the transcendental."[11] However, despite his explicit rejection of the logic of the transcendental *subject*, Meillassoux's speculative reasoning arguably does not entirely escape the transcendentalist trap: in other words, his question—"How is science able to tell us anything meaningful about reality anterior to the emergence of the transcendental subject?"—is essentially the same as Kant's question, "What are the conditions of possibility of scientific knowledge of objective reality?"

While Meillassoux's inquiry into the conditions of scientific knowledge largely focuses on knowledge of the ancestral—that which is anterior to consciousness—contemporary speculative thinkers, including Meillassoux himself, are also concerned with the future dimension, often couched in terms of the posthuman. One of the characteristic features of contemporary speculative thought is its rejection of what I will call the *ideology of the human*. Following Meillassoux's succinct explanation of an ideology as "any form of pseudo-rationality whose aim is to establish that what exists as a matter of fact exists necessarily," the ideology of the human here means that form of "pseudo-rationality" which aims to establish that the human is necessary. Such a mode of thought deserves to be challenged on two grounds: first, since it has been largely responsible for a plethora of immensurable atrocities throughout history and, second, because when faced with scientific facts about the nature and future of the universe, it seems to be unreasonable to put the human on a metaphysical pedestal. Contemporary speculative thought certainly does challenge such an ideological preoccupation, but arguably it also at times conflates the ideology of the human with the human itself. For instance, chiming with a particular scientistic view of the human as a relatively insignificant accident, Ray Brassier has explicitly condemned that brand of thought which empirically overdetermines the human's set of cognitive faculties and imposes it on the speculative imagination.[12] Such a view seems to react to the ideological position that the human is necessary with the assertion that human thought and finitude are beyond the scope of speculative inquiry. Yet faced with the perfectly plausible speculative possibility that there has never been, is not, and never will be—indeed, according to Meillassoux, need never have been—conscious life anywhere in the universe other than on Earth, one might at the very least question Brassier's understanding of overdetermination.

Just as a critique of transcendentalism risks reproducing transcendental arguments, a critique of the ideology of the human risks degenerating into an ideology of the posthuman in which the complete contingency of the human itself becomes ideological dogma. Such an *Ersatz* would be problematic on several fronts. Philosophically because, while contemporary thought must accept that there can be reality without us, the reduction of the human to the purely physical risks becoming a mechanistic rather than a speculative materialism, thus effacing the subject: creative subjectivity is still part of material reality, after all. Meanwhile, the ontoligization of mathematical logic—in its form, no less a product of human consciousness than epistemology—threatens to spill over into idealism, thus effacing the object. Each of these philosophical problems has its sociopolitical and environmental counterpart: an emphasis on material agency at the expense of human agency reduces the human to a passive instrument of the physical process of realization; the reverential deferral to calculating rationality perpetuates the willful destruction of the natural environment without consideration for life, including human life. In short, in its reduction of the human to little more than a thing among things, posthumanism demonstrates a reactionary tendency which itself can be seen, analogously with postmodernism, as an ideological reflex of late capitalism.

Despite the immense potential of speculative materialism, then, it is not entirely bulletproof. A tendency toward transcendentalism, quite in spite of its intentions, and a more or less latent, potentially nefarious anti-humanism has thus far been identified. If human thought and finitude are accepted as within the scope of speculative inquiry, then the un- or anti-dialectical character of much contemporary speculative materialism poses a third potential problem. A recently published volume edited by Diana Coole and Samantha Frost heralds the emergence of speculative materialism among the "new materialisms," which are characterized by a conception of matter as something that "becomes" rather than "is." A general introduction explains that new materialists conceive of matter "as possessing its own modes of self-transformation, self-organization and directedness, and thus no longer simply passive and inert." However, they avoid "dualism or dialectical reconciliation by espousing a monological account of emergent, generative material being."[13] While the editors acknowledge a growing tendency to think of matter in processual rather than static terms, dialectic is apparently also dismissed as inadequate to contemporary philosophical materialism. If dialectic is automatically taken to imply idealism, as seems to be the case here, then this is at the very least a serious inconsistency if new materialisms seek to understand material reality as a self-generative absolute. Yet there is arguably no reason why speculative materialism must abandon dialectic; indeed, a case will be made here for the essential dialectical potential of speculative materialism.

In response to the three problems thus raised with some aspects of contemporary speculative materialism, I will defend a threefold argument. In doing so, I will draw on Ernst Bloch's speculative materialism, which, while it preceded the contemporary turn by at least forty years, offers interesting parallels and discontinuities with current speculative materialist thought. First, it is argued that if the speculative materialist wants to avoid transcendentalism, she must understand materialism as *immanently* speculative, which is to say that she must also understand philosophy as a product of material reality. Second, if she wants to avoid anti-humanism, the speculative materialist must understand the absolute as *immanently not-yet*. And third, if she wants to be able to explain material reality as an immanently speculative process of becoming, and if she intends to overcome correlationism without resorting to dualism, the speculative materialist must be able to make use of the dialectic. The principal question throughout must therefore be: what does "speculative materialism" mean?

Speculation and Dialectic

Drawing on Whitehead, Johan Siebers summarizes speculative thinking as that which "deals with ultimate notions, notions incapable of analysis in terms of other notions, more far-reaching than they."[14] Such notions include being, the absolute, reality, matter, and so on. Meillassoux describes the task of speculative philosophy as to think about what is "capable of existing whether we exist or not," which he calls the absolute or simply "being."[15] Meillassoux argues—quite correctly, I think—that most philosophy since Kant has precluded this, positing the exclusive possibility of thinking that the correlation between thought and being, since I, the speculative philosopher, am always-already in the world. An important exception to the problem of correlationism is Hegel, who obviated it by positing the ultimate identity of thought and being, which, however, can be seen to constitute an extreme form of idealism that views matter as an "embarrassment," as Bloch puts it.[16] While the speculative philosopher would not deny that there is a *relation* between being and thought, then, it is imperative that speculative thought be able to access being without collapsing into a *correlation*. For the fundamental implication of correlationism—that thought determines being—is none other than idealism, the logical conclusion of which, as we see with Hegel, is that thought and being are identical, which they cannot be if we accept that material reality is fundamental to (in the sense of prior to) conscious thought. We can therefore say that speculative philosophy responds to an injunction to think being in a non-correlative, non-identical way, without denying any relation between thought and being, since that would be to defend an extreme form of dualism. How, then, are we to construe the relation between being and thought that makes speculative materialism possible? In order to explore this relationship, which Bloch describes as an aporia, in materialist terms, we must first disentangle certain concepts that often appear to be run together.[17] So Meillassoux opposes "being" to "thought," but never mentions consciousness: the question must be posed, however, whether "consciousness" is synonymous with "thought" and, if not, in what way they can be distinguished and what this tells us about the thought-being relation.[18] Furthermore, Meillassoux appears to conflate "thought" with "subject" and "being" with "object," which immediately raises a contradiction: does the subject have no being? Is thought not part of material reality? As a materialist and a realist, I would certainly want to answer both questions in the positive.

Bloch quotes Engels in this context, who declared that materialism is philosophy that explains the world "out of itself."[19] If there can be an axiom of materialist philosophy, surely it is that material reality is all there is and therefore everything in the world, including the speculative philosopher and her thought, is material and real. Since it is a simple axiom, this says nothing about what material reality consists in. It must nonetheless be the starting point of the inquiry if we want to avoid dualism, which posits that thought is something immaterial; correlationism, which posits that the real in itself is inaccessible to thought; and idealism, which, *in extremis*, posits that there is no such thing as material reality at all. For now, let us equate the process of material reality with being. Departing from the materialist axiom, to paraphrase Marx, the materialist wants to say that being determines consciousness; that is, there is no consciousness without being, but there can be being without consciousness.[20] This relation is expressed clearly in German: there can be *Sein* without *Bewusstsein*, but there can be no *Bewusstsein* without *Sein*. However, thought—*Denken*—is not synonymous with consciousness in ways that are apparent in everyday life. Few would deny that a dog is conscious, but equally few would assert that a dog thinks in the same way that a speculative materialist thinks. It is beyond the scope of this discussion to investigate the truth of this proposition in detail, but taken as a simple example, it can illustrate the difference between thought and consciousness as understood here. Thus we can say that it is evident from a dog's behavior that it is conscious of its *being* in some way, if only through the relation between its own body and things that are not its own body. It is a different question, however, whether or not a dog is conscious of its own *consciousness*. A dog may be aware that it is, in so far as it relates to its environment precisely as a living creature. But this is not the same as saying that it is aware "that it is," which would entail an awareness of its *being conscious*. Such awareness would enable the dog to *reflect* upon itself, not only as a being but as a conscious being. In other words, it is maintained here that one can properly speak of thought where conscious being is able to reflect on itself precisely as a conscious being. In other words, thought is *reflexive consciousness*.

Thought must therefore be determined by both consciousness and, more fundamentally, by being. Meanwhile, being is initially determined by neither consciousness nor thought. Does this mean that the materialist, for whom material reality is all there is, is forced to concede that thought *is* being? Not in the Hegelian sense that thought is identical with being: an impossibility if being determines thought. However, from the materialist axiom, it follows that thought is necessarily just as much a part and product of material reality as anything else. Nevertheless, in its capacity to reflect on being—hence, on itself—thought also retains a measure of freedom vis-à-vis other (i.e., inanimate, unconscious) forms of being. We can therefore characterize thought as that form of material being which cannot be said to be *fully* determined but transgresses this determination in the act of speculative reflection. This is the meaning of Bloch's formula, "to think is to transgress."[21] For the materialist, the problem of speculation—thinking being—is not that we are always-already in the world so much as that the world is always-already in us or, rather, that we and our thought *are material*. If being determines consciousness, and thus also—at least partially—thought, *thinking being* constitutes the internalization of the undetermined in the (partially) determined, which is none other than dialectic. Furthermore, the act of speculation for the materialist also necessarily implies being's reflection on itself. How is this conceivable in materialist terms?

A response necessitates a return to the materialist axiom. If there is nothing outside of or beyond the material that can be said to generate matter, then matter must be self-generative. Diana Coole ascribes such "immanent generativity" to matter, asking, rhetorically, "Is it not possible to imagine matter . . . as perhaps a lively materiality that is self-transformative and already saturated with the agentic capacities and existential significance that are typically located in a separate, ideal, and subjectivist realm?"[22] What does it mean to speak of the "self" of matter, its immanent agency, which Bloch calls the *Agens-Immanenz*?[23] Logically it can only mean that the subject–object relation is fundamental to the thought–being relation, or, to put it another way, that the subject–object relation is immanent in being *qua* material reality. From a radical materialist perspective, that the human subject is not only possible but real cannot help but substantiate the immanence of subjectivity in matter.

It is thus logically correct to speak of "the self of the material" as Bloch does, since to do otherwise would be to admit to something other than the material or beyond it.[24] The materialist axiom is incompatible with the equation of being with object and thought with subject. The latter is dualistic in that it treats speculation as thought's reflection on something from which it is entirely free or from which it has not issued. For the materialist, then, speculation, as the act of *thinking being*, implies a dialectical relation if it does not deny the materiality of thought.

It is the process of the material reflecting on its materiality in the form of the human subject, which can be seen as an expressive incarnation of matter's immanent agency. Thus if, in purely quantitative terms, the speculative materialist admits the Adornian "preponderance of the object," in qualitative terms it is a subject that preponderates, in being as well as in thought, since the one thing necessarily intrinsic to the spontaneous process of materialization is dynamic agency.[25] The idea that the object also has an "inside" is also at the heart of the Hegelian dialectical method: the *Aufhebung* of reflective understanding through speculative reason in the *Phenomenology* takes place on the basis of the claim that substance becomes subject. Bloch formulates this idea thus: "the leap from being to consciousness [takes place] on the basis of material being's will towards self-reflection, while the will of material being towards self-manifestation is to thank for the transition from quantity to quality."[26]

The argument, thus far, is as follows: the radical speculative materialist departs from the axiom that the material world is all there is in order to explain that material world out of itself. Moreover, her fidelity to this axiom forces her to acknowledge herself and her speculative reflection as a form of the spontaneous process of materialization, albeit one with relative autonomy vis-à-vis the substrate as compared with inanimate, unconscious forms. Faced with the reality of contingency and change, however, as well as the apparent aporia of her own existence precisely as a speculative materialist, she is compelled to conceive of creative dynamic agency as immanent to matter. Her speculation thus becomes dialectical, since it is the reflection of the material on the material within the spontaneous process of materialization. What is posited is thus neither the correlation of thought and being, nor their identity, nor their radical difference. The relation between them is a dialectical one. Correlationism, Hegelian idealism, and dualism are thus avoided. But what about transcendentalism? Although he does not always distinguish correlationism clearly from transcendentalism, not least in that he opposes himself to them both equally, there is a distinction between transcendentalism and what Meillassoux calls correlationism. Since I agree with Meillassoux that the speculative materialist must avoid both, I will briefly describe the difference as I see it before explaining how speculative materialism can avoid transcendentalism.

Returning first to Meillassoux's definition, he calls "*correlationism* any current of thought which maintains the unsurpassable character of the correlation . . . between thinking and being" and which "consists in disqualifying the claim that it is possible to consider the realms of subjectivity and objectivity independently of one another."[27] Contrary to Kant, Meillassoux claims that it is possible to "grasp the in-itself," which he runs together with both being and the object.[28] The Meillassouxian "in-itself" is therefore not identical with the Kantian, since for Kant the thing-in-itself is not the object: the object, which can be known, is that which is in relation to the subject, meaning that it is phenomenal, while the noumenal thing-in-itself can never be known. Thus far, in allowing no possibility for subjective thought to get at a reality that exists apart from it, Kant's thought is correlationist as defined by Meillassoux, although Graham Harman, following Meillassoux's distinction between strong and weak correlationism, emphasizes Kant's as a weak one in that it does not prohibit all relation between thought and the absolute, but maintains the thinkability of the in-itself.[29] In that sense, then, all idealism can be said to be correlationist, yet not all idealism can be said to be transcendentalist.

The transcendental after Kant is that which is concerned with the conditions of possibility of something: in transcendental idealism, the conditions of the possibility of *a priori* knowledge, which Kant attributes to the mind's formation of the world in terms of space and time. While it is therefore clear to see why the materialist would endeavor to steer clear of transcendental idealism and the metaphysical necessity of the transcendental subject, it is not immediately obvious why she would seek to avoid transcendentalism per se. With what, for example, would radical transcendental materialism be concerned? None other than the conditions for the possibility of material reality, with or without us.[30] Here thought would find itself at an impasse which science calls the Big Bang. The materialist who begins from the radical axiom that the real, material world is all there is would struggle to call herself a materialist at all if her philosophy took on these sorts of transcendentalist ambitions, since to do so would be to inquire not into material reality as such, but into its ground. Yet although at the beginning of this discussion I suggested that Meillassoux does not entirely avoid transcendentalism, the intention is not to point to a latent concern in his thought for the conditions of possibility of being. For Meillassoux, being is the object and he is concerned to show what is the condition that legitimates science's ancestral statements precisely as statements about an objective reality anterior to conscious thought and hence anterior to a Kantian transcendental subject. His response is that there must be a real world apart from us about which we can know those things that are expressible in terms of mathematics.[31] The object for Meillassoux is therefore expressible in terms of those properties of it that extend in time and space, the latter presented as "ancestrally" real and not only forms of intuition. Thus the object becomes little more than one half of an equation intelligible by us in the form of a synthetic judgment *a priori*, whereby Meillassoux perhaps edges closer to Kant's transcendentalism than he might acknowledge. Nevertheless, the speculative materialist will go beyond transcendentalism, but how? The key to this problem, I think, is immanence.

Only by becoming immanently speculative can materialism avoid slipping into something like a transcendental realism in which thought can access things-in-themselves in so far as the thinking subject is capable of complete cognizance of the limitations of thought; in other words, in so far as we are prepared to limit thought's access to the thing-in-itself to the mathematizable properties of objects. In elucidating what an immanently speculative materialism might look like, I will draw on Bloch's thought, but first the question must be posed: what does it mean to speak of an immanently speculative materialism at all? Here immanence is opposed not only to the transcendent as that which goes beyond the material in a supernatural sense, but also to the transcendental as that which concerns the conditions of possibility of something. Thus we might say that Bloch's materialism can be called immanently speculative in that it locates the condition for the possibility of speculation *in the material itself*. It is because matter is immanently speculative that it is possible to know the absolute, of which we are, not incidentally, part. In order to develop this idea further and discuss its implications, it is necessary to turn in more detail to Bloch.

Immanently Speculative Material

Speculation has here been called thinking about ultimate notions. It is a reflective activity, certainly, but for the materialist also a *reflexive* one. In his discussion of speculative method, Siebers explains that the notions used in speculative philosophy are "incapable of analysis in terms of other notions, more far-reaching than they."[32] Speculative notions presuppose one another such that they cannot be clearly defined in terms of other notions; the movement of the speculative method is therefore a processual one, since no single concept in a speculative scheme can exhaust or be exhausted by any or all of the others. One might say that the *depth* of the speculative notion is immanent in it: the concept is in itself incomplete; its essence is not located in itself alone, but what is essential about it is expressed in its relation to other notions in the process of speculative thought. The speculative materialist as here defined is, however, bound to say this not only about the notion, but about the object as well. In other words, matter is itself speculative in the way that the speculative notion is, namely in that it is inherently incomplete and inessential in itself, but the process of materialization consists in the expression of matter's essentiality in the relations between the forms it becomes.

Bloch calls matter immanently speculative in precisely this way, saying, "One cannot think highly enough of matter as open, as itself speculatively structured in the specific sense of the objectively-real being-in-possibility, which is both the womb and the unfinished horizon of its forms."[33] There are three aspects to Bloch's immanently speculative conception of matter, which I will call here dynamic agency, incomplete entelechy, and the material attributes of potential and *logikon*. In identifying dynamic agency in matter, Bloch takes over Aristotle's material categories of *dynámei on* and *kata to dynaton*. The first, *dynámei on*, is Bloch's being-in-possibility or that which might become possible.[34] This category encompasses the radical possibility immanent in matter and thus represents the fundamental maxim that anything is possible. "It is precisely speculative materialism," says Bloch, "which discovers in the [dynámei on] of matter and its certainly highly dangerous openness forwards every true essential feature of matter the *logikon* of which must be called finality."[35] Yet, as Bloch himself asserts in *Das Prinzip Hoffnung*, possibility presupposes partial conditionality; otherwise it would not be possibility at all: complete unconditionality equates to necessity, complete conditionality to impossibility, a point also made by Meillassoux.[36] What is materially *possible* must therefore be partially conditioned and Bloch follows Aristotle in suggesting that the second main category of matter, *kata to dynaton* or being-according-to-possibility or that which is possible, supplies this very conditionality.[37] *Kata to dynaton* is matter's category of contingency for Bloch, who thus characterizes the material as the "substrate of objectively-real possibility" on the basis of its immanent dynamic agency.[38]

In Bloch's scheme, dynamic agency and possibility thus presuppose one another: dynamic agency requires the possibility that things can be otherwise, even if only in situation, while possibility requires that what is at any moment can change. Bloch thus describes matter as open "forwards" and as such necessarily incomplete.[39] By asserting the openness and dynamic agency of matter, we can therefore say something like: in the process of its own self-substantiation, matter simultaneously creates the conditions for its own self-realization. Or, as Bloch puts it, matter is the "self bearing womb of entelechical formations."[40] By describing matter itself—not only the movement of matter, as with Aristotle—as "incomplete entelechy," Bloch captures the material immanence of the speculative.

Bloch also ascribes two attributes to matter, potentiality and *logikon*, which are inextricably connected in the concept of "forwards matter" as open to the future. If matter is not mere stuff, passive and inert, but rather something which changes form and creates itself spontaneously out of itself, energy is clearly required for the materialization process to take place. In scientific terms, energy is called a force and matter a substance, as though force and substance are straightforwardly divisible. On the contrary, Bloch argues against the divisibility of force and substance by analogy with a critique of idealism in which he asserts that matter does not disappear with the latter. He says: "Matter is dissolved energetically by the indivisibility of force and stuff just as little as it disappears when reason emerges from its idealist reservation and comes forth as that which is guiding and practicable in matter; thus potential and *logikon* are the attributes of matter."[41] Far from being a simple juxtaposition of ideas, I think this analogy implies something more fundamental in Bloch's thought, which has to do simultaneously with the relation between potential and *logikon* as material attributes and with the relation between the material and the ideal as apparently irreconcilable. Bloch's assertion that force and substance are indivisible is not a physicalist one—Bloch explicitly rejects physicalism, which he identifies with mechanistic materialism.[42] The mistake of physicalism, according to Bloch, is to reduce matter to simple *Klotzmaterie*, inert, passive, and static: simply there. Indeed, in Bloch's speculative materialism there is no meaningful sense in which matter is "there" at all, except as "incomplete precisely in its there-ness."[43] The point is rather that if we conceive of the fundamental unit of reality as radical potentiality, as Bloch does, the philosophical distinction between the material and the ideal all but dissolves. Far from degenerating into an illogical muddle, Bloch maintains that speculative materialism must actively acknowledge the debt it owes to Hegelian idealism for the idea of dialectical logic as immanent in the world. "Precisely on this point," Bloch says, "materialism must not . . . take over that dualism . . . which has distinguished sharply between matter and spirit and isolated them against one another."[44] Hence is the significance of Bloch's propensity to cite Lenin in this context, who said: "Clever idealism is closer to clever materialism than stupid materialism is."[45]

The *potential* of matter in Bloch's speculative materialism can thus be identified with the indissolubility of force and substance in the material itself, while the *logikon* of matter is a dialectical logic of immanent teleology. As Siebers explains, in Bloch's speculative materialism, "The teleological dynamic of matter is dialectical: that means that contradiction is proper to it and that the Aristotelian principles of Identity and the *Tertium non datur* only apply in relation to the end goal of material process, thus must be seen as its motor, not as its medium."[46] However, completion and identity are not assured, but subsist within the immanently speculative of the material as radical possibility. The material is a tendency toward that which is latent within; materialization for Bloch is thus a process of expression. He says:

> *Tendency is the energetic of matter in action, driving forth in all its already attained forms towards exodus forms, towards the tendentially implied of the entelechially intended end as is not yet become, but which is utopistically latent. Latency is the entelechial of matter in potentiality, utopian, yet already concretely-utopian by means of the exodus forms in each entelechially intended end which shines back from horizons with such defiance in human history, in significant nature.* [Italics in original][47]

Bloch's debt to historical materialism is thus clearly that, for him as for Marx, the human is not only a contingent incarnation of material possibility, although it is that; rather, precisely *as* a contingent incarnation of material possibility, the human represents a principle of the process of materialization itself, namely immanent speculation as that which is oriented toward the ultimate. In other words, the human never had to materialize and it is possible that matter will one day no longer take human form; but of all the possible realities that could formally be, in the event the human *has* materialized, which is, in view of the conditioning action of *kata to dynaton* in matter, it is not purely accidental. Thus by positing the immanently speculative character of matter, speculative materialism need not be anti-humanist. However, this is not to assert the necessity of the human and thus to collapse into metaphysics after Meillassoux's definition, or the ideology of the human after my own. No: instead it is to deny the charge that the human is materially meaningless and to do what Siebers has called freeing the truth of idealism—that there is mind—from dualism, in the name of developing a consistent and radical speculative materialism.[48]

Hope, Finitude, and the Not-Yet Absolute

In *After Finitude*, Meillassoux declares that contemporary speculative materialism must take up the injunction to know the absolute. I agree that it must, with a fundamental caveat concerning his definition of the absolute. Meillassoux defines the absolute as the "great outdoors"—that which is, the way it is, whether I would ever have been or not. The absolute, for Meillassoux, is that which does not depend on thought in order to be. It is therefore definitely not the subject, which is distinguished sharply from the object, as has been shown: for Meillassoux, being = object = absolute; thought = subject = speculation. However, under the conditions described in this discussion—the materialist axiom, the material as immanently speculative—the speculative materialist cannot distinguish between thought and an absolute that is severed from it. In so far as it is possible to speak of an absolute at all under these conditions, thought must be included in it. The mistake, in my opinion, of materialisms that are anti-humanist on the grounds that, in quantitative terms, the human and its thought are macrocosmically dwarfed by forms of matter that do not think is that it opposes itself to an ideology of the human which would have the human and its thought as metaphysically necessary. The conclusion that the human and its thought somehow constitute a merely insignificant accident, the result of an instance of *ex nihilo* creation in time, as Meillassoux puts it, is knee-jerk and not germane to the kind of radical materialism that seeks to explain the world and everything in it, including thought, out of itself. To borrow from Bloch, "The flowering moment of our mesocosm is missing" from antihumanist materialism.[49]

What kind of absolute, then, are we dealing with of which thought is a form? Žižek provides a clue when he says that the "very difference between the for-itself and the in-itself is encompassed within the Absolute. Only by attending to this gap can we become truly materialist."[50] Žižek thus maintains that the absolute is inherently incomplete, that its incompletion is inevitable and identity of the for-itself and the in-itself—the "what" and the "that"—is eternally impossible. Absolute being in Lacanian terms is thus exactly the opposite of absolute being in metaphysical terms, which conceives of the absolute as that being the being of which is simply to be. For Meillassoux, metaphysics is "every type of thinking that claims to be able to access some form of absolute being," while speculation is "every type of thinking that claims to be able to access some form of absolute" as that which is undetermined by thought.[51] However, for the speculative materialist as described here, this distinction is paradoxical: what is not determined by thought is being *qua* material reality; hence to speak of an absolute that is not absolute being is nonsensical. To the speculative materialist for whom the subject–object relation is fundamental to being as an inherently incomplete process, the absolute, no matter how we define it, must be inherently incomplete. To the extent that he might agree with that, Žižek too can be called a speculative materialist.

Where Bloch's materialism departs from Žižek's is in its refusal to assert the impossibility of identity. If the process is open and being creates itself spontaneously as its own telos, then the possibility of the absolute—that is, absolute being—is immanent in the material, even if its realization is neither certain nor necessary. Meillassoux, too, comes close to saying something like this when he asserts that, although God cannot be said to exist now, we must admit the possibility of his existence in the future.[52] An absolute that would denote identity, however, implies the completion of process, thus the end of time and material reality as it is. If thought is part of the material world, then the absolute cannot be that which does not depend on thought to be, but rather, as Hegel said, that which depends on nothing else at all to be. Such a being would be infinite, infinity thus necessarily inhering in a materialist definition of the absolute. Certainly there is no such being in reality at present: the finitude, not only of the human but of all material forms, attests to that. The absolute by definition cannot be bounded by the finite, which must therefore be included in it, but not in such a way as to make the finite infinite; rather finitude must be an immanent part of the process of realization of the possible absolute.

The absolute is, therefore, what Bloch calls *not-yet*. Absolution is materially possible, but not certain. The injunction of speculative materialism to know the absolute thus consists not only in thinking what is whether we are or not, but also what is possible now that we are. My objection to the anti-humanist tendency of speculative materialism is that its anti-humanism renders its central claim somewhat redundant: what is the point of positing the material reality of radical possibility if we, as real material beings capable of reflecting on this possibility, are powerless to do anything with it? Indeed, such a position would appear to compromise the consistency of one's materialism, if one asserts the dynamic agency of the material. Speculative materialism that is concerned with the ultimate possibility of absolution is thus committed to the potential for the human to change the world for the better. It is, I argue, a concern with the absolute as that which is beyond what is immediately given that marks out speculative philosophy as a mode of thought. As Hans Heinz Holz acknowledges, "The object of the speculative process must be that which goes beyond the description and analysis of the empirical, but on the basis of which the latter has its methodological foundation."[53] As that mode of thought which goes beyond "what is the case"—indeed, which conceives of the material itself as going beyond what is the case—speculative philosophy thus cannot rely on complete knowledge, however, nor can it rely on faith that there is anything beyond the material world. It can, however, hope for a better world the possibility of which is immanent in matter itself. Hope that grasps the latent tendency of the objectively real possible is what Bloch calls *docta spes*, educated hope. To specify on what I suggest the education of hope depends, in the sense of "leading out" (*ex- ducere*) hope from the material substrate of objectively real possibility, I will paraphrase Michael O'Neill Burns writing on "The

Hope of Speculative Materialism": unless it holds onto its potential to offer a radical ideological critique grounded in the potential to think the material possibility of another world, speculative thought will have little to offer twenty-first century philosophy.[54]

Coda: The Salt of the Earth

The reader may think that, for a materialist, I have spent an inordinate amount of time in this chapter talking about thought. In response, I return to my initial axiom that material reality is all there is, from which it follows that thought is a form of material reality; one which is, however, able to reflect on material reality which thus reflects on itself. The critical reader will, at this point, naturally say, "But how is that not simply Hegelian idealism?" And of course Bloch, on whose speculative materialist thought I have drawn, does not deny a debt to Hegel. It nevertheless remains to show how such a philosophy does differ from Hegelian idealism, if the claim to speculative materialism is to be substantiated. In particular, it is necessary to refute the straightforwardly hylozoistic idea that matter "thinks."

As Donald Phillip Verene explains in his introduction to *Hegel's Absolute*, for Hegel, "Reflection placed at the service of reason is the basis of speculation," or dialectical reason, as we would now call it.[55] Hegelian speculation, according to Verene, is essentially dialectic:

> [It] requires us to approach the object as not substance but subject, as having an inner life. . . . Reflection at the service of reason [i.e., speculation] becomes an activity of mediation . . . a process of consciousness wherein the knower meets itself in the known. . . . Reflection is taken up into dialectic. . . . Dialectic is reflection turning back on itself, which can capture in thought the self-movement that is substance becomes subject.[56]

Bloch recuperates the speculative after Hegel, taking over a materialist dialectic from Marx. The question of whether Hegel is a materialist, as Slavoj Žižek obliquely argues in his recent book on *Hegel and the Shadow of Dialectical Materialism*, is something of a moot point: the import of his thought for contemporary speculative materialism, I would argue, with Žižek, is in the inheritance of his speculative-dialectical method.[57] Bloch, like many others, treats Hegel as an idealist, not least because, as he clarifies in his Leipzig lecture on Hegelian phenomenology, with Hegel as with other methodological idealists, "The active side of production is exaggerated, whereby the whole world is produced and of the object nothing contrary or super ordinate to or independent from the human remains."[58] Since for Hegel, the real is rational and the rational real, nothing is intrinsically unknowable. This is where Hegel can undoubtedly be called an idealist.

Yet even some of Hegel's remarks about matter, such as that matter "as such" is the same abstraction as the thing-in-itself, or that "spirit is the existing truth of matter, that matter itself has no truth," come close to Bloch's own materialist position that matter is not "there" in any meaningful sense, but rather manifests itself in its forms.[59] As this chapter aims to demonstrate, Bloch and Hegel seem to be aligned on the point that "freedom is the truth of necessity." A central difference between their two positions is arguably their view of contingency. While the idealist Hegel does not view contingent events as an active part of history or reality, the materialist Bloch would accord contingency a far greater significance. In Hegel's scheme, that "necessity appears to itself in the shape of freedom" is a certainty; for Bloch, a possibility.

It has been suggested that in Blochian speculative materialism, matter spontaneously creates both itself and the conditions for its own realization. As such, the material can be seen as creating its own future, including the possibility of its own completion. It is in this sense that Bloch describes matter as immanently speculative, if we understand by speculation a mode of thought that "deals with ultimate notions."[60] In the process of materialization, matter is the ultimate notion, both genetically and teleologically. In response to the objection that, since speculation can only be a function of consciousness, a description of matter as immanently speculative collapses matter into Hegelian *Geist* in precisely the way it has been proposed that Bloch does not do, I suggest that a radical reappraisal of the relationship between being and consciousness follows from Bloch's philosophy.

Bloch acknowledges the necessity of materialism to be able to deal with consciousness in order to become truly speculative, and I propose that the question of the relation between thought and being must be at the heart of contemporary speculative materialist inquiry. In particular, the idea that matter anticipates its own realization implies proto-consciousness in matter itself. Bloch himself explicitly puts forward the idea that consciousness is not only anamnetic but also anticipatory. He calls this category of consciousness the *Not-Yet-Conscious*. From the materialist axiom together with the notion of its spontaneous self-creation, it follows that the possibility of the emergence of reflective consciousness as we see in human beings and other intelligent life must be immanent in matter itself. Bloch says:

> Consciousness [*Bewußtsein*] emerges from being [*Sein*] as conscious being [*bewußtes Sein*] in that being, indeed first as organic, reflects itself. This self-reflexion is possible because matter is precisely not the external, indeed in the vulgar view the preeminently external, but rather the Agens has all later externality in itself and is as a whole the bearing womb on which the self of matter itself can finally meet its self-reflexion consciousness. However, being reflects itself here with such a strong transition from brain to so-called soul that there appears to be a rupture in what is usually in material terms called being.[61]

Unlike with Hegel, then, for whom being and thought are ultimately identical, in Bloch's speculative materialism, *thought is a form of material being*. It is not identical with matter: for Bloch, the rupture between being and thought is a form of Hegelian negation that inheres in matter itself. It is not problematic for the dialectical materialist to say that brain is radically different from soul without becoming a dualist, since both are forms of the material. Bloch quotes Engels in this context, who said, "There is no more a general matter than there is fruit, but there are apples, pears, grapes, and so on."[62] This brings us back to the beginning of the argument, where it was shown that dialectic is needed to make speculative materialism work. If we can say that pre-conscious matter is what is in-itself, without thought, then idealist philosophy is that form of thought that reflects on being as though it is only real for us, which for the speculative materialist is the same as saying for-itself. Thus for speculative materialism as the inquiry into the possibility of what Bloch calls the in-and-for-itself, idealism is an eventually (not absolutely) necessary moment of the dialectical process of materialization. Hegel's thought is thus for radical speculative materialism a "salt of the earth," but crucially, not the earth itself.[63]

Notes

1 Levi Bryant, Nick Srnicek, and Graham Harman, *The Speculative Turn: Continental Materialism and Realism* (Melbourne: re.press, 2011).

2 Ernst Bloch, *Das Materialismusproblem: Seine Geschichte und Substanz* (Frankfurt: Suhrkamp, 1972).

3 Bloch, *Das Materialismusproblem*, 469.

4 Hans Heinz Holz, "Zum Problem des spekulativen Materialismus," in *VorSchein 30: Polyphone der Dialektik*, ed. Doris Zeilinger, Jahrbuch 2008 der Ernst-Bloch-Assoziation, 17.

5 Holz, "Zum Problem," 17. All translations are my own.

6 Slavoj Žižek, *The Parallax View* (Cambridge, MA: MIT Press, 2006), 6.

7 Žižek, *The Parallax View*, 10.

8 Bloch, *Das Materialismusproblem*, 463–64.

9 Quentin Meillassoux, *After Finitude: An Essay on the Necessity of Contingency* (London: Continuum, 2008), 28.

10 Meillassoux, *After Finitude*, 5.

11 Meillassoux, *After Finitude*, 27.

12 Ray Brassier, "Alien Theory: The Decline of Materialism in the Name of Matter," PhD diss., Warwick University, 2001. Available at http://www.cinestatic.com/trans-mat/Brassier/alientheory.pdf, 163.

13 Diana Coole and Samantha Frost, eds., *New Materialisms: Ontology, Agency, and Politics* (Durham, NC: Duke University Press, 2011), 10–12.

14 Johan Siebers, *The Speculative Method: An Essay on the Foundations of Whitehead's Metaphysics* (Kassel: Kassel University Press, 2002; originally Leiden, 1998), 10.

15 Meillassoux, *After Finitude*, 28.

16 Bloch, *Das Materialismusproblem*, 30.

17 Bloch, *Das Materialismusproblem*, 461.

18 Meillassoux, *After Finitude*, 5.

19 Bloch, *Das Materialismusproblem*, 361.

20 From the "Preface to *A Contribution to the Critique of Political Economy*," available at http://www.marxists.org/archive/marx/works/1859/critique-pol-economy/preface-abs.htm. The original sentence in English reads: "It is not the consciousness of men that determines their being, but their social being that determines their consciousness."

21 Ernst Bloch, *Das Prinzip Hoffnung* (Frankfurt: Suhrkamp, 1998), 2.

22 Diana Coole, "The Inertia of Matter and the Generativity of Flesh," in Coole and Frost, *New Materialisms*, 92.

23 Bloch, *Das Prinzip Hoffnung*, 777.

24   Bloch, *Das Materialismusproblem*, 465.

25   Theodor Adorno, *Negative Dialectics* (London: Routledge, 1990), 183.

26   Bloch, *Das Materialismusproblem*, 464.

27   Meillassoux, *After Finitude*, 5.

28   Meillassoux, *After Finitude*, 26.

29   Graham Harman, *Quentin Meillassoux: Philosophy in the Making* (Edinburgh: Edinburgh University Press, 2011), 16; Meillassoux, *After Finitude*, 35.

30   Rainer E. Zimmermann, "Beyond the Physics of Logic: Aspects of Transcendental Materialism or URAM in a Modern View," in *Journal of Ultimate Reality and Meaning*, November 2001, available at arXiv:physics/0105094v1.

31   Meillassoux, *After Finitude*, 3.

32   Siebers, *The Speculative Method*, 10.

33   Bloch, *Das Materialismusproblem*, 469.

34   Bloch, *Das Materialismusproblem*, 142–43.

35   Bloch, *Das Materialismusproblem*, 473.

36   Bloch, *Das Prinzip Hoffnung*, 260; Meillassoux, *After Finitude*, 67.

37   Bloch, *Das Materialismusproblem*, 142–43.

38   Bloch, *Das Materialismusproblem*, 469.

39   Bloch, *Das Materialismusproblem*, 472–73.

40   Bloch, *Das Materialismusproblem*, 475.

41   Bloch, *Das Materialismusproblem*, 475 (italics mine).

42   Bloch, *Das Materialismusproblem*, 356.

43   Bloch, *Das Materialismusproblem*, 473.

44   Bloch, *Das Materialismusproblem*, 472.

45   Bloch, *Das Materialismusproblem*, 132.

46   Johan Siebers, "Logos/Logikon," in *Ernst-Bloch-Wörterbuch*, ed. Beat Dietschy, Doris Zeilinger, and Rainer Zimmermann (Berlin: Walter de Gruyter, 2012).

47   Bloch, *Das Materialismusproblem*, 469.

48   Siebers, "Logos/Logikon."

49   Bloch, *Das Materialismusproblem*, 358.

50   Bryant, Srnicek and Harman, "Towards a Speculative Philosophy," in *The Speculative Turn*, 5.

51   Meillassoux, *After Finitude*, 34.

52   Michael O'Neill Burns, "The Hope of Speculative Materialism," in *The Speculative Turn*, ed. Bryant, Srnicek, and Harman, 321.

53   Hans Heinz Holz, "Zum Problem des spekulativen Materialismus," 16.

54   Burns, "The Hope of Speculative Materialism," 317.

55   Donald Phillip Verene, *Hegel's Absolute: An Introduction to Reading* The Phenomenology of Spirit (Albany: SUNY Press, 2007), 6.

56   Verene, *Hegel's Absolute*, 7.

57   Slavoj Žižek, *Less than Nothing: Hegel and the Shadow of Dialectical Materialism* (London: Verso, 2012), 638, 80.

58   Ernst Bloch, *Neuzeitliche Philosophie II: Deutscher Idealismus; Die Philosophie des 19.*

Jahrhunderts. Leipziger Vorlesungen zur Geschichte der Philosophie, band 1950-1956 (Frankfurt: Suhrkamp, 1985), 307.

59 From the *Enzyklopädie*, chapter 389, cited in Bloch, *Das Materialismusproblem*, 245.

60 Siebers, *The Speculative Method*, 10.

61 Bloch, *Das Materialismusproblem*, 461.

62 Bloch, *Das Materialismusproblem*, 127.

63 Bloch, *Das Materialismusproblem*, 449.

7

Engendering the Future: Bloch's Utopian Philosophy in Dialogue with Gender Theory

Caitríona Ní Dhúill

On the whole, the difference between the sexes lies in a different field to the artificial differences which the class society has produced; thus it does not disappear with the latter.
—Ernst Bloch, *PoH*, 56

Central to Ernst Bloch's philosophy is the thought that the unredeemed content of the past provides the desiring subject of the present with signposts to a future that has yet to be claimed. *Das Prinzip Hoffnung* accounts for the function and significance of hope in the dialogue between history and possibility. Complex relationships between past, present, and future are expressed by Bloch in terms of anticipation, militant optimism, and the forward glance: all modes in which the omnipresent phenomenon of hope can activate the world's latent utopian content and wrest a *Heimat*, a truly habitable world, from the wreckage of history.

This chapter looks into the ways in which these modes of "not-yetness" relate to the structures of human reproduction, to their social articulation in the practice of gender, and to the experience of desiring gendered subjects. Contemporary feminist and gender theorists tend to conceptualize gender as a complex of changing and interactive social and cultural practices. What concerns us here is the relationship between current theoretical approaches to gender and the encyclopedic Marxist cultural critique carried out by Bloch, with its insistence on open horizons of possibility. By scrutinizing the processes through which the sexed and gendered subject comes to be, gender theorists bring a specific focus to the critique of social conditions. As we shall see, much gender theory has a utopian core in the Blochian sense, in that it, too, involves a dialogue between history and possibility and an insistence on horizons that open out beyond the "badly existing" [*das schlecht Vorhandene*]. However, while feminist thought has developed in a lively awareness of Marxism,[1] the reverse cannot be as easily claimed; both Bloch's writings and the critical responses to them have tended to underplay the importance of feminist perspectives and questions of gender. For precisely this reason, it is worth bringing these two theoretical orientations into conversation with each other.

I have examined elsewhere the presence and function of gender discourse in *Das Prinzip Hoffnung*.[2] Here I seek to go beyond the analysis of the discursive residues of patriarchy in Bloch's thinking and writing, in order to suggest more fundamental affinities between reproduction and the Blochian production of the future and between gender and the generative force of hope. It is worth emphasizing from the outset the perhaps obvious point that while gender is related to and in part enacted through human reproduction—sex, family, child-bearing, and child-rearing—it is not reducible to these domains, but is played out in an array of identities, behaviors, and practices that vary according to their social, cultural, and historical location. The concept of reproduction thus exceeds the confines of procreation; it encompasses the reproduction of the social, the transmission into the future of established or prevailing structures, values, and norms. This kind of social reproduction, in the sense used, for example, by Nancy Chodorow in her classic feminist psychoanalytic study *The Reproduction of Mothering*,[3] has been a key target for gender-aware critique. Many feminist critics have scrutinized the processes through which gender norms are reproduced—in language, child-rearing, systems of education, the media, and other social and cultural institutions. On the other hand, it is precisely the reproductive moment in social practices which, while it seeks to guarantee their continuation into the future, constitutes the chink in the armor of their normative force. As exact reproduction—whether of bodies, values, or behaviors—is impossible, always only ever approximate, it is in the fault lines between one generation and the next, one historical moment and the next, that possibilities for transformation, for the formulation of alternatives, can be realized. This seemingly paradoxical relationship between reproduction and transformation has long engaged the attention of gender theorists. Judith Butler, for example, has argued that the very *citationality* of gender—the fact that it is a social practice consisting of the iteration and performative imitation of an "original" that can never be traced—opens up spaces for critical agency and subversive or oppositional possibilities.[4]

Butler has written of gender as "a practice of improvisation within a scene of constraint,"[5] and this is a useful starting point for a closer consideration of how gender theory and Bloch's analysis of the relationship between history and possibility might speak to each other. Already in Butler's pairing, we can align *improvisation* with possibility and *constraint* with the limitations imposed by the social order, in this case a sex/gender system (a term to which I return below), prevailing at a given moment in history. The two elements of the above pairing stand in a dialectical relationship to each other: constraint sets the conditions of improvisation, yet improvisation acts in turn upon constraint and has the potential to undo or reconfigure it to some extent. A closer look at some of the most significant developments in recent gender theory will enable us to identify more precisely some illuminating parallels with Bloch's dialectical thinking.

Gender theory is a diverse body of thought, a set of concerns and perspectives that arose in the first instance from feminism but has continued to evolve beyond it. A central tenet of recent theory is the idea that one's gender is something one "does" rather than "has" or "is."[6] Another significant feature is the cultivation of what has been called a "hermeneutic of suspicion"[7] with regard to such concepts and categories as masculine and feminine, homosexual and heterosexual, nature and culture, norm and deviation, self and other. Gender theory not only inquires into the relationship between these categories but it questions the operation of categorization itself. Many contemporary theorists emphasize that gender is not, or at least not necessarily, a binaristic scheme according to which individuals are allocated predetermined roles (although this traditional model does continue to determine gender practices), but is more usefully thought of as a field of tension between structure and agency. The linguistic and behavioral norms, cultural expectations, available roles, and prohibitions to which we are variously subject as gendered beings come up against the negotiation, resistance, subversion, and improvisation of individuals and groups in an infinitely varied array of practices and experiences of gender. Crucial to a critical understanding of this process has been the analysis of the ways in which masculinities, femininities, and the spectrum of positions and possibilities in between are constructed and enacted (although the metaphor of a spectrum with opposite ends is itself problematic, indebted as it is to the binaristic model which gender theory has done so much to destabilize). In fact, gender "identities" and gender relations cannot be considered apart from each other; it is more apt to speak, as many recent theorists do, of "sex/gender systems" (a term coined by Gayle Rubin), in which subject positions are constituted through relation, including relations of difference. This is clearest where "masculine" and "feminine" continue to be understood as a mutually constituting binary, but also in contexts where this traditional opposition becomes self-questioning, parodic, opaque, diversified, or unstable, as for instance in times of social transformation or crisis, in situations of intercultural encounter, through the cross-cutting effects of other differences (such as those of class, age, or ethnicity), or in queer identities. The term *sex/gender system* has the further advantage of highlighting the embeddedness of gender within other systems of social and economic relationships, with which it interacts.

In seeking to establish gender theory's supposed utopian core, we presuppose that any theoretical perspective critical of existing practices must be motivated by and committed to an alternative, even if this alternative is nowhere explicitly formulated. Beginning with the early feminists of the "first wave," gender theorists in all their variety have combined the analysis of existing sex/gender systems with the hope that these systems can be changed.[8] Yet it is far from being the case that their efforts are underpinned by a shared vision. In fact, the alternatives to the sex/gender status quo that have been envisioned by different theorists and activists at different times are strikingly at odds with each other, as the following broad summary of key themes suggests: the reclaiming of a "true" gender in the face of inauthentic social roles; the overthrowing of constraining or oppressive gender norms; the utopia of gender equality; the utopia of authentically lived, or consciously cultivated, sexual difference;[9] and, provocatively, the negation of the future through a cultivated awareness of the void of death that undergirds all desire.[10] Even this schematic, incomplete summary of what we might call "utopias of gender" (the last of which is decidedly anti-utopian) reveals serious tensions, even contradictions, a problem to which I return below.

Where might the Blochian dimension of transformative hope be located in all of this? The changes that have been effected in women's rights and gender relations, from the weakening of social taboos such as those surrounding female virginity, unmarried motherhood, and homosexuality, to concrete political gains such as improved labor rights and enfranchisement, cannot be solely attributed to the transformative power of hope. Nevertheless, we can usefully speak of a dynamic interaction between vision, critique, and changing social norms and cultural practices, one only partially, even grudgingly, acknowledged by Bloch in his own remarks on the sex/gender system and the condition of women.

From "Truth" to "Construction": Currents in Gender Theory

We have already seen the difficulty of attempting to harmonize the differences between various theories of, and approaches to, questions of gender through any reference to a supposedly shared vision or utopian horizon. Nevertheless, it can be claimed with some confidence that for all their differences, gender theorists are united by a concern with the tension between possibility and historical conditions: with what gender *has* been or *is*, and with what it *can* or *could* be. Critical analysis of the relationships, identities, and practices that go to make up sex/gender systems makes it possible to envision changes to these systems. Evidence of the close relationship between critique and transformation is provided by the concrete advances in women's rights, gay rights, and reproductive freedoms that have been achieved in the last half-century, even when other, contingent factors are taken into account. Each of these social transformations effects systemic change, creating new, hitherto unforeseen conditions and challenges for individuals, for societies, and for gender theory. Changes achieved *within* a given order actually effect transformation *of* the order—the changes cannot be thought away, and no comparison with their absence is possible. Once women have entered large areas of the paid labor market, for example, the debate on women's labor rights is complicated by the necessity to negotiate changes in childcare systems, to identify the social and cultural factors that contribute to the glass ceiling effect, and to pay heed to new relations of exploitation and vulnerability that arise through the increasing feminization of low-wage global migration.[11]

The formulation of possibilities for change, then, is utopian, not in the sense of an unreal or unrealistic fantasy, but rather in the Blochian sense: imaginable alternative futures provide the horizon for the critique of the now.[12] Classic texts of feminism, from de Beauvoir to Chodorow and from Kate Millett to Christa Wolf, irrespective of the marked differences in their immediate context and in their approach to questions of political economy, share a utopian dimension insofar as they project possibilities, reaching beyond the rejected givens to imagine these givens overthrown or, to use Bloch's words: "Every barrier, when it is felt as such, is at the same time crossed. For just coming up against it presupposes a movement which goes beyond it and contains this in embryo" (*PoH*, 444; *PH*, 515).[13]

Bloch is not primarily concerned with questions of gender and gender relations, yet he nevertheless acknowledges that the overcoming of barriers described here can also be observed in this area, as for example when he speaks of "the prospect of venturing beyond an undetermined sexual barrier" (*PoH*, 598; *PH*, 698).

While the subject of history in Bloch's work may be gendered male—and there is ample evidence that this is the case[14]—this maleness, like all gender categories, depends on difference, on its position relative to the term it excludes and against which it is defined. Where can this difference, this excluded term, be located in Bloch's philosophy, and what is its function? How does Bloch deal with the two mythic poles of feminine and masculine and the multitude of gendered and engendering subjectivities from which these are abstracted?

Bloch's thoughts on gender tend toward the utopia of authentically realized sexual difference, toward the emancipation of what he calls the "contents of gender" or more specifically with respect to femininity "the utopian possibilities" of "female content" (*PoH*, 596; *PH*, 695). The sense that the prevailing social order somehow distorts or fails to recognize the "truth" of gender implies a correlated utopian vision of people being able, and free, to live their genders and sexualities more authentically. Yet the utopia of "true" gender is not inherently emancipatory, as it can lead to prescriptive models of "natural" or "essential" gender difference. This accounts for the theoretical shift that has occurred in recent decades, away from an emphasis on authenticity to an interest in performativity, the implications of which I revisit below. While the authenticity or "truth of gender" trope may have been more or less superseded by the performativity trope in current theoretical discourse, it is most relevant to *Das Prinzip Hoffnung*. Where Bloch writes of the feminine — "das Weibhafte" — and of the complementary binary of male and female idealized in the figure of the "High Pair" (*PoH*, 327), his debt to traditional stereotype, and also to archetype, is clear: "It [*das Weibhafte* — female nature] is something gentle and wild, destructive and compassionate, it is the flower, the witch, the haughty bronze and the efficient life and soul of business. It is the maenad and the ruling Demeter, it is the mature Juno, the cool Artemis, the artistic Minerva and all sorts of other things. It is the musical capriccioso (the violin solo in Strauss's "Heldenleben") and the prototype of the lento, of calm. It is finally, with an arc which no man knows, the tension between Venus and Mary" (*PoH*, 596; *PH*, 695–96).

To a feminist sensibility, this gesture of defining the feminine, even in such a way as to recognize its internal diversity, has a prescriptive aspect that makes it questionable. Nevertheless, this "truth of gender" trope has appealed powerfully to some feminists and other critics of the sexual status quo at various times. The argument that if social norms are preventing me from living my gender "truly" or authentically, then these norms must change to accommodate my "natural" or "innate" capacities and desires, can carry a certain strategic advantage when it is a question of achieving concrete changes, such as the adoption of more progressive legislation. An example of the strategic use of the "truth of gender" trope is offered by Charlotte Perkins Gilman's utopia *Herland* (1915), which deploys the essentialist rhetoric of maternalist feminism. While Gilman's text relies on a problematically idealized "true" femininity that is thoroughly aligned with fully realized motherhood, the utopia it constructs nevertheless serves to expose what the author regards as the "false" or degraded femininity of Victorian patriarchy. As the male narrator surveys the radically different practices of the matriarchal society portrayed in the novel, his eyes are opened to the distinction between "true" and "false" gender: "These women, whose essential distinction of motherhood was the dominant note of their whole culture, were strikingly deficient in what we call 'femininity.' This led me very promptly to the conviction that those 'feminine charms' we are so fond of are not feminine at all, but mere reflected masculinity—developed to please us because they had to please us, and in no way essential to the real fulfillment of their great process."[15] Here, the premise of a "true" femininity, realized in the utopian society, facilitates the critique of the gender norms actually in place in Gilman's time.

The idea that certain gender categories can be strategically invoked for the purposes of critique and transformation returns in recent thinking on gender. The invocation or mobilization of what Gayatri Spivak has called "the necessary error of identity" proceeds in the knowledge that any signifier of identity can be destabilized or contested.[16] Put more simply, any claims we make about our genders can be called into question, but that does not mean there is nothing to be gained by making such claims. Nancy Chodorow's study of gender roles in *The Reproduction of Mothering* shows this dynamic at work. Chodorow posits that relationality is a feature of feminine identity—a risky hypothesis, as it can be used to shore up the patriarchal practice of defining women in terms of their relationships with men. However, this claim about femininity, while it may be contested, rejected, distorted, or even abused, does have heuristic value for an inquiry into gender relations and social structures. The strength of Chodorow's by now classic analysis is that it does not hypostatize relationality as some inherent quality, or strength, of an ahistoric, universalizable "femininity," but rather relates it to a specific, socially constituted, and historically located organization of the labor of reproduction and parenting.

The concern with difference in gender theory, then, has yielded fresh perspectives and challenged a facile universalist equality discourse that would negate the irreducibly different experiences of differently positioned subjects; but the move to place difference at the center of concern carries its own risks, and the perception and interpretation of gender difference have their own troubled history. The feminine types evoked by Bloch's "tension between Venus and Mary," problematic even in the context of his broadly sympathetic argument, take on quite another cast when viewed from the perspective of a *fin de siècle* misogynist such as Otto Weininger, whose widely read polemic *Geschlecht und Charakter* of 1903 located the "essence of woman" precisely in the "always and absolutely sexual" types of mother and whore.[17] Moving forward to late twentieth-century *Differenzfeminismus*, we find quite a different deployment of essentialism, for example in the writing of Verena Stefan;[18] here we could not be further, in gender-political terms, from Weininger, but the risk of overemphasizing bodily and sexual experience as constitutive of femininity arguably remains.[19] The utopian "truth of gender" trope thus combines strategic advantage with risk; yet, if we look at the history of utopian thought in the modern era, we can conclude that this ambivalence is a common feature of all utopian projections. That ideals formulated in the service of a critique of an oppressive reality (let us not forget that even Weininger struck an anticipatory note with his theory of universal bisexuality) themselves have the potential to become static, hegemonic, or oppressive is perhaps the key insight of dystopian thinking.[20]

The converse of the "truth of gender" trope—the idea that there is no "true" or "authentic" gender, but rather that gender is constructed by social practices and cultural discourses—also contains a utopian core: if gender identities and gender relations are socially constructed, surely we can remake them to our liking? Taking the constructivist position to its logical extreme, I may reject the prescribed gender role and gender identification of my social context and fashion an alternative, or several alternatives, from the array of cultural practices available to me, changing and subverting these as I appropriate them. One thinks of Monique Wittig's radicalization of de Beauvoir's "one is not born a woman"; if woman is something one becomes rather than is, one can become something else instead. For Wittig, because "woman" only exists as a term that "stabilizes and consolidates a binary and oppositional relation to a man,"[21] a lesbian is not a woman. Such radical constructivism is balanced in poststructuralist gender theory by an emphasis on the conditions that define, determine, and delimit the "I" itself. Lacan's re-inflection of the term *subject*, away from notions of autonomy and self-identity and toward the notion of *subjection*—the condition of being subjected to language, discourse, and other systems and regimes—highlights the fact that the conditions under which the subject might fashion her own "identity" are not themselves of the subject's choosing. Foucault similarly emphasizes processes of *subjectivation* through which the subject is positioned within a social apparatus.[22] The notion of the subjectless subject of poststructuralism, produced and traversed by discourse, may itself be a simplistic caricature, but at least it provides a provocative counterpart to the myth of the self-engendering subject, freely constructing her gender identity within a marketplace of options. Butler formulates the poststructuralist challenge to gender theory and practice as follows: "If there is no subject who decides on its gender, and if, on the contrary, gender is part of what decides the subject, how might one formulate a project that preserves gender practices as sites of critical agency?"[23]

The opposition of constructivism versus essentialism—itself a variation on the theme of nature/nurture—has lately given way to a more nuanced inquiry into the production of identity through the sedimentation of social and cultural practices and into operations of difference, dissidence, and desire.[24] Of lasting significance for the ways in which these questions are approached has been an increased emphasis on performativity, along with a heightened awareness of the constraints to which the "performance" of gender is subject: "The 'performativity' of gender is far from the exercise of an unconstrained voluntarism. . . . rather, constraint calls to be rethought as the very condition of performativity."[25]

This dialectical model, which identifies the limitations placed *on* possibility while conversely acknowledging how these limitations are only thinkable in their tension *with* possibility, shows clear affinities to the dialogue between history and hope that is the larger theme of *Das Prinzip Hoffnung*.

Gender and the "Humanization of Nature"

The constructivist position alluded to here may seem far from Bloch's commitment to the unfolding of a "utopian content of gender," yet there are some aspects of his thought to which this central theme of recent gender theory is highly relevant. What I would like to suggest is that Bloch's conceptualization of the relationship between humanity and nature is sufficiently complex to accommodate aspects of gender constructivism. The concept of nature is highly problematic for gender theorists. This is an understandable consequence of its frequent mobilization in antiprogressive discourse, but it continues to haunt gender theory nonetheless, not least at the edges of the debate about what constitutes sex and what gender.[26]

Bloch's Marxist account of the human/nature relationship as a dialectical process which involves the "humanization of nature" and the concomitant "naturalization of (the hu)man" offers a way out of the problem that the concept of nature poses to gender theory. Bloch writes: "The means by which man first became human was work, the basis of the second stage [of becoming human] is the classless society, its framework is a culture whose horizon is surrounded purely by the contents of founded hope, the most important, the positive being-in-possibility" (*POH*, 210; *PH*, 242).

Bloch's view of the complex process whereby human labor both *initiates* and, as currently organized, *hinders* the unfolding of human potential is admittedly gender-blind. But his blind spot should not prevent us from seeing both the relevance of his account to questions of gender and, conversely, the need for gender theory to complete his account. The division of labor entails the construction of differences of gender, class, and race, thus marking an incomplete *Menschwerdung*, a falling short of the task of becoming fully human. But this first Menschwerdung paves the way to a second Menschwerdung (Bloch, unlike his translators, does not speak in terms of "phases," rather expressing these as two distinct processes). The second Menschwerdung, which completes the work of the first, is heralded in cultural expressions of hope and anticipation. The articulation of possibilities for change and self-fashioning and the rejection and refashioning of the "badly existing" (*POH*, 147; *PH*, 167) are, for Bloch, among the most important tasks of culture.

Negotiations in the field of gender and gender relations can be understood on this model as a kind of "humanization of nature": in gender, biological/anatomical difference is restated as a cultural/social question. While this restatement has traditionally taken the form of a hierarchical social code, involving prescription, normativity, and constraint, it does not necessarily take this form; it can also open the possibilities for resistance, improvisation, and subversion discussed above. In other words, the very insight that gender is more or other than biology offers a way out of the trap of biology as destiny that so preoccupied earlier feminists such as Simone de Beauvoir.[27] The "nature" of sexual dimorphism is "humanized" in the practice of gender, but in the first instance this achieves only a partial, incomplete Menschwerdung that remains subject to the social divisions of patriarchy, just as the "humanization" achieved through labor remains incomplete as long as it is subject to the social divisions of class. The second Menschwerdung would reconcile *Mensch* (both woman and man) with *Welt* [world] and vice versa (*PoH*, 210; *PH*, 241–42). Bloch's "humanization of nature" confronts the question of how labor might serve freedom through the establishment of radical democracy and the achievement of full humanity; therefore, it cannot be thought apart from the question of gender, as the divisions which it presupposes and seeks to overcome include the gendered division of labor, the estrangement of women from nature and themselves in patriarchy, and their exploitation by men. Bloch, caught in his gender-blind spot, may be quick to dismiss feminist activism as the privilege-grabbing antics of a bourgeois sisterhood whose case dissolves once the revolution has happened (*PoH*, 589–98; *PH*, 687–98). But the history of feminism might more appropriately be read as compelling evidence of the tenacious hope that the "badly existing" is not the only possible world.

It is this very hope that relates feminist and gender theory to the central category of Bloch's thought. *Das Prinzip Hoffnung* demonstrates that expressions of hope, while they are unthinkable apart from the prevailing social reality and bound by the constraints of this reality, testify to a continued resistance to, and transgression of, these constraints. Blochian hope encompasses subjective and objective, or "warm" and "cold" strands. These correspond to the imaginative anticipation and desire of the subject (warm), and the concrete response to the objective reality of socioeconomic structures (cold). As with all conceptual pairs in Bloch's thinking, the relationship between the "warm" and "cold" strands is dialectical:[28] "Both factors, the subjective and the objective, must rather be understood in their constant dialectical interaction, one which cannot be divided or isolated" (*PoH*, 148; *PH*, 168). The mutually transformative interaction between the "warm" and "cold" strands of hope constitutes historical progression, the two strands together driving history forward. We can conceptualize this process as follows: The subjective desire for change comes up against the wall of social reality. This reality is what engenders desire to begin with. "From early on we are searching. All we do is cry out. Do not have what we want" (*PoH*, 21; *PH*, 21) we read at the opening of *Das Prinzip Hoffnung*, in the section headed "We start out empty." Through the encounter between the desiring subject and external conditions, reality itself is altered, the subject's desire acts upon it. An example is the relationship, discussed above, between vision, critique, and transformation, as concretely manifested in specific gains such as women's enfranchisement. Bloch's insistence on the importance of hope in history allows us to write subjective desire, both individual and collective, back into our understanding of how such transformations are achieved. The "cold stream" of practical circumstances and material factors cannot be separated out from the "warm stream" of anticipatory consciousness, daydreams, and desires.

Desire in History

The hope of Bloch's philosophy, then, is a socially oriented form of desire. Bloch's insistence on historicizing desire and the human drives and passions is fundamental to his critique of psychoanalysis. The fact that the opening sections of *Das Prinzip Hoffnung* are devoted to a critical summary of Freud's and Jung's theories suggests how significant Bloch considered the then emerging discipline to be and also how much he saw his own work on hope as a response, and corrective, to the psychoanalytic account of desire. While he is critical of Freud, he is nothing short of damning of Jung. (This is a primarily political aversion; in fact, archetypes play quite a significant role in Bloch's thought, as his discussion of the "High Pair" trope and the "utopian content of femininity," quoted above, reveals. This is not to suggest that his reference to archetypes makes him a Jungian, but it does relativize somewhat the stark opposition between the two thinkers suggested by the hostility toward Jung expressed in *Das Prinzip Hoffnung*.) Bloch's quarrel with psychoanalysis is that Freud and his colleagues seem to accept all too readily the reality in which they find themselves. Their focus, he argues, is on what is and has been, rather than what is not or not yet: "The unconscious of psychoanalysis is . . . never a Not-Yet-Conscious" (*POH*, 56; *PH*, 61). In Bloch's opinion, Freud, Adler, and especially Jung have a tendency to hypostatize the unconscious and the drives, isolating them from social and economic conditions: "an idolized libido arises . . . which] is never discussed as a variable of socio-economic conditions" (*POH*, 64; *PH*, 71). Bloch also finds the psychoanalytic model of the unconscious to be thoroughly de-historicized, and maintains that its proponents exhibit a willful blindness to history.[29]

The psychoanalytic significance allocated to (night-)dreams also leads, in Bloch's view, to the underestimation of the importance of day-dreams, which play a hugely important role in his own anatomy of hope. In Bloch's view, the daydream, unlike the night-dream, has a collective dimension, an expansive quality, and a commitment to "Welt-verbesserung" [world-improvement]; furthermore, it is fundamentally communicative and communicable. This makes it congenial to his utopian philosophy in a way the night-dream cannot be. "Above all revolutionary interest, with knowledge of how bad the world is, with acknowledgement of how good it could be if it were otherwise, needs the waking dream of world-improvement" (PoH, 92; PH, 107).

For Bloch, the daydream provides evidence of the integral relationship, discussed above, between critical analysis of existing conditions and visionary formulation of alternative possibilities. Yet however compelling Bloch's objections to psychoanalysis may be, one comes away from his discussion of Freud and Jung with the uneasy sense that he—Bloch—has excessive faith in desire. He is insistent that desire is a positive force, in and of itself, and that any problems generated for and by desire are a result of prevailing socioeconomic conditions and will vanish when these are overcome. The psychoanalytic project to understand the workings of desire is, for Bloch, a questionable digression from the more urgent task of enabling the fulfillment of desire through the creation of appropriate social conditions.

Desire, hope, anticipation, orientation toward the future: the central Blochian concepts all involve a potentially precarious relationship to the now. Where the future is given the heavy burden of having to redeem an unsatisfactory present, this redemption risks being perpetually deferred and the present lived in the shadow of a promised future. Bloch acknowledges this risk, for example in his discussion of the melancholy of fulfillment or of the Trojan Helen. These figures of disappointment, in which the realization of desire falls short of its promise, underline the necessity of constant dialectical mediation between present and future, *Weg* and *Ziel*. The future-oriented attitude of militant optimism can avoid the risk of disappointment if sufficient attention is paid to the *latency* of the now, to that which it holds within itself to unfold. The analysis of possibility thus not only contributes to the envisioning of the future; it also heightens awareness of the anticipatory or latent aspects of the present moment. It is to be noted that Bloch's discussion of latency and disappointment draws on a long tradition of feminizing utopia: in his figuring of fulfillment as sexual consummation, of disappointment as sexual disaffection, and of hope as sexual desire, the desiring subject is male, the desired object female (*POH*, 178–94, and 997; *PH*, 204–12, and 1172).[30] Yet while gender theory can sharpen our awareness of Bloch's reliance on this kind of discourse, the traffic goes in both directions: key concerns of gender theory also can be illuminated by Blochian concepts. Perhaps the most important shared ground here is the commitment to radical democracy, to which we now turn.

The Utopia of Radical Democracy

A critical insight into the world we have ("the badly existing"), a collective desire for a different and better one (a Marxian "realm of freedom"), given endlessly varied expression in anticipatory cultural practices. This formula of Blochian utopianism begs some fundamental questions, not least: who is covered by "we"? How might the *Heimat* of such freedom be attained? How might it even be recognized? These questions must also be asked of the utopian visions that—often tacitly—underpin theories of gender. Recent theoretical work on gender frequently takes these questions as its point of departure, reflecting on the difficulties of articulating a valid collective position and on the impossibility of formulating a definitive "task" or "goal."[31] Nevertheless, gender theorists do at times come close to formulating such a task, at least in broad outline. For example, Butler names "defiance" and "legitimacy" as two central concerns of gender theory, as follows: "defiance of the established meanings and values attached to sexual practices and gender identities, along with a quest to legitimise that which has been deemed illegitimate or beyond the pale. . . . The task is to refigure this necessary 'outside' as a future horizon, one in which the violence of exclusion is perpetually in the process of being overcome."[32]

In order to overcome the violence of exclusion, categories and practices "which had seemed fixed" need to be opened up.[33] The reevaluation of seemingly fixed practices and norms, their "re-description" as Richard Rorty would term it,[34] is a crucial step toward the achievement of a more radically democratic sex/gender system. In the passage just quoted, where Butler does set forth a task of sorts for gender theory, her formulation makes striking use of the horizon metaphor so familiar to readers of Bloch. The utopian attitude is described in *Das Prinzip Hoffnung* as a pioneering position at the boundaries of an advancing world, one which continually exceeds each available horizon (*PoH*, 126; *PH*, 142). This horizon is both internal and external to the subject of history: man [*der Mensch*], Bloch writes, is "not an established being, but one which, together with his environment, constitutes a task" (*PoH*, 119; *PH*, 135); elsewhere, Bloch writes "der Mensch ist nicht dicht" (*PH*, 225) evoking—in the porous, unfinished quality of "nicht dicht" far more so than in the translators' "man is not solid" (*PoH*, 195)—an open-ended process that sits well with the accounts of subject formation and self-construction offered by gender theorists. Gender, according to Butler, is "an assignment which is never quite carried out according to expectation."[35] In a similar vein, Brigitte Weisshaupt has argued that the category of femininity, while a bearer of anthropological tradition, can also be inherently open ["'Weiblichkeit' ist tradierte Anthropologie und zugleich offener anthropologischer Entwurf"].[36] This insistence on openness in contemporary theories of gender identity bears comparison with Bloch's account of human history, in which the limit of the given and the horizon of the possible are constantly in the process of being overcome.

Despite their clear differences in scope and emphasis, where Bloch's philosophy and contemporary gender theory appear to coincide is in their shared commitment to a radical or real democracy, a democratic future which constitutes the horizon of their thought. Butler situates her own thinking within a "radical democratic theory" and writes of the "democratic notion of futurity" that informs the work of gender critique.[37] By exposing the aporia of gender "identity" and rethinking gender in terms of its instability, Butler aims toward "a more democratizing affirmation of internal difference"—the difference internal both to the subject and to the sex/gender system.[38] Other feminist thinkers also invoke democracy in like manner: for instance, the reflections on a feminist theory of authority offered by Rebecca Hanrahan and Louise Antony are grounded in a commitment to "the development and maintenance of truly democratic institutions."[39] The use and understanding of the term *democratic* in such contexts provides a further key to the utopian dimension of recent gender theory. This is not to suggest that democracy be equated wholesale with utopia—an equation that, leaving aside its problematic political implications, would weaken the semantic specificity of both terms. Rather, the point is to identify the role played by democracy in Bloch's utopian philosophy and to acknowledge its similarity to the function of the democratic horizon of gender theory. It is worth quoting once more the familiar finale of *Das Prinzip Hoffnung* in order to take a closer look at Bloch's invocation of democracy there: "But the root of history is the working, creating human being who reshapes and overhauls the given facts. Once he has grasped himself and established what is his, without expropriation and alienation, *in real democracy*, there arises in the world something which shines into the childhood of all and in which no one has yet been: homeland" (*PoH*, 1376, emphasis added; *PH*, 1628).

The humanly habitable world toward which Bloch's thought never tires of pointing is a real democracy, beyond alienation. While many of Bloch's assumptions concerning the concrete appearance of this world, as derived from the "real existing socialism" of the Soviet Union, have not stood the test of history, nevertheless his overall project of identifying those tendencies in human history and culture which anticipate real democracy, those areas in which this democracy shows itself in latent, unrealized yet realizable form, remains compelling. *Das Prinzip Hoffnung* underscores the importance of retaining a radical conception of democracy as the horizon of social critique. And, as we have seen, where social critique focuses on sex/gender systems, the democratic horizon is indispensable.

In their analysis of the interaction between the social and the subjective, gender theorists seek to locate sites of resistance to normativity. The utopian dimension of gender theory is dynamic rather than static. The aim is not to cancel history and instate a new perpetual order, but rather to identify both emancipatory and oppressive tendencies within the history of gender relations, and to offer critical perspectives on oppression and constraint with a view to expanding the scope and effectiveness of emancipation. From this viewpoint, history is not only a narrative of suffering and struggle; it is also a resource. Through active engagement with the past, including the past of gender and the genders of the past, its seeming fixity is ruptured, its utopian potential activated, its relation to the now rendered urgent.[40] Which returns us to where we began: the task of the present, as articulated by Bloch, is to identify and activate the unredeemed content of the past in such a way as to shape a more habitable future. This creative, praxis-oriented conception of the relationship between hope and history is everywhere at work in gender theory. The critical analysis of what gender is and has been contributes to a fuller vision of possibility, a permanent expansion of the horizons within which sexed subjects can live (and live against) their genders.

Notes

Ernst Bloch, *POH*, 56; Ernst Bloch, *PH*, 695.

1 Significant early voices in the dialogue between feminism and Marxism are, of course, Friedrich Engels, August Bebel, and Simone de Beauvoir. More recent feminist perspectives to engage with Marxism would include Gayle Rubin, "The Traffic in Women: Notes on the 'Political Economy' of Sex," in *Toward an Anthropology of Women*, ed. Rayna R. Reiter (New York: Monthly Review Press, 1975), 157–210; see also Donna Landry and Gerald M. MacLean, *Materialist Feminisms* (Cambridge, MA: Blackwell, 1993), and the work of Silvia Federici.

2 Caitríona Ní Dhúill, "'One loves the girl for what she is, the boy for what he promises to be': Gender Discourse in Ernst Bloch's *Das Prinzip Hoffnung*," in *Exploring the Utopian Impulse: Essays on the Terrain of Utopian Thought and Practice*, ed. Michael Griffin and Tom Moylan (Oxford: Lang, 2007), 272–92.

3 Nancy Chodorow, *The Reproduction of Mothering: Psychoanalysis and the Sociology of Gender* (Berkeley: University of California Press, 1978).

4 Judith Butler, *Bodies That Matter: On the Discursive Limits of "Sex"* (London: Routledge, 1993), 21, 108, 191.

5 Judith Butler, *Undoing Gender* (London: Routledge, 2004), 1.

6 Candace West and Don H. Zimmerman, "Doing Gender," *Gender and Society* 1, no. 2 (1987): 140. See also Butler, *Bodies That Matter*, 2.

7 The expression "hermeneutic of suspicion" derives primarily from Paul Ricoeur's reading of Freud, Marx, and Nietzsche. See Ricoeur, *Freud and Philosophy: An Essay on Interpretation* (New Haven: Yale University Press, 1970). See also Jonathan Dollimore, *Sex, Literature, and Censorship* (Cambridge: Polity, 2001), 11–15, for a discussion of this concept in the context of gender theory and queer theory.

8 On the utopian content of early feminism, see Harriet Anderson, *Utopian Feminism: Women's Movements in fin-de-siècle Vienna* (New Haven, CT: Yale University Press, 1992); Angelique Richardson, *Love and Eugenics in the Late Nineteenth Century: Rational Reproduction and the New Woman* (Oxford: Oxford University Press, 2003).

9 For a vision of consciously cultivated sexual difference—predicated on a "culture in the feminine"—see Luce Irigaray, *I Love to You: Sketch for a Felicity within History*, trans. Alison Martin (New York: Routledge, 1996).

10 Lee Edelman, *No Future: Queer Theory and the Death Drive* (Durham, NC: Duke University Press, 2004).

11   See Barbara Ehrenreich and Arlie Russell Hochschild, eds., *Global Woman: Nannies, Maids, and Sex Workers in the New Economy* (New York: Metropolitan Books, 2003); also Evangelia Tastsoglou and Alexandra Dobrowolsky, eds., *Women, Migration, and Citizenship: Making Local, National, and Transnational Connections* (Aldershot, UK: Ashgate, 2006).

12   On the wide semantic range of the term utopian, see Caitríona Ní Dhúill, *Sex in Imagined Spaces: Gender and Utopia from More to Bloch* (Oxford: Legenda, 2010), chapter 1.

13   See Angelika Bammer, *Partial Visions: Feminism and Utopianism in the 1970s* (New York: Routledge, 1991).

14   See, for instance, Bloch, *Das Prinzip Hoffnung*, 1:132. For a more detailed discussion of the ways in which Bloch's subject of history is gendered, see Ní Dhúill, "'One loves.'"

15   Charlotte Perkins Gilman, *Herland* [1915] (New York: Signet Classics, 1992), 60.

16   Gayatri Spivak, quoted in Butler, *Bodies That Matter*, 229.

17   Otto Weininger, *Geschlecht und Charakter: Eine prinzipielle Untersuchung* (Munich: Mathes & Seitz, [1903] 1980).

18   Verena Stefan, *Häutungen* (Munich: Frauenoffensive, 1976).

19   For a critical discussion of Stefan's essentialist feminism, see Bammer, *Partial Visions*, 67–79.

20   See Horst Glaser, *Utopische Inseln: Beiträge zu ihrer Geschichte und Theorie* (Frankfurt: Lang, 1996); Krishan Kumar, *Utopia and Anti-Utopia in Modern Times* (Oxford: Blackwell, 1987); Jost Hermand, *Orte. Irgendwo: Formen utopischen Denkens* (Königstein, Ts: Athenäum, 1981); Ní Dhúill, *Sex in Imagined Spaces*, chapter 2.

21   Judith Butler, *Gender Trouble: Feminism and the Subversion of Identity* (New York: Routledge, 1990), 112.

22   See Butler, *Bodies That Matter*, 189.

23   Butler, *Bodies That Matter*, x.

24   See Butler, *Gender Trouble*; Jonathan Dollimore, *Sexual Dissidence: Augustine to Wilde, Freud to Foucault* (Oxford: Clarendon, 1991); Dollimore, *Sex, Literature, and Censorship*.

25   Butler, *Bodies That Matter*, 94–95.

26   West and Zimmermann, "Doing Gender." See also Sherry B. Ortner's classic essay "Is Female to Male as Nature Is to Culture?" (1972) and her own later response to criticism of her earlier thesis, "So, *Is* Female to Male as Nature Is to Culture?" in her book *Making Gender: The Politics and Erotics of Culture* (Boston: Beacon, 1996), 21–42 and 173–80, respectively.

27   Simone de Beauvoir, *The Second Sex* (1949), trans. H. M. Parshley (London: Everyman, 1993).

28   For a personal account of Bloch as a dialectical thinker, see Jean Améry, "Nachruf auf Ernst Bloch," in Améry, *Der integrale Humanismus: Zwischen Philosophie und Literatur. Aufsätze und Kritiken eines Lesers, 1966–1978* (Stuttgart: Klett Cotta, 1985), 64–68.

29 "The bourgeois individual, seen by Freud in a bourgeois way, wears down his Dionysian horns on 'reality,' as Freud calls his bourgeois environment (the commodity world and its ideology)." *POH*, 52; *PH*, 57.

30 See Ní Dhúill, "'One loves.'"

31 A major focus of the debate among feminisms, particularly in the light of postcolonial theory, has been precisely this question of how to articulate a valid collective position in a way that does justice to the differences between subject positions. See Kum-Kum Bhavnani, ed., *Feminism and "Race"* (Oxford: Oxford University Press, 2001).

32 Butler, *Bodies That Matter*, 52–53.

33 Butler, *Bodies That Matter*, 29, 89.

34 Richard Rorty, *Contingency, Irony, and Solidarity* (Cambridge: Cambridge University Press, 1989).

35 Butler, *Bodies That Matter*, 231.

36 Brigitte Weisshaupt, "Begriff und Metapher des Weiblichen," in *Wissen Macht Geschlecht: Philosophie und die Zukunft der "condition féminine,"* ed. Birgit Christensen et al. (Zurich: Chronos, 2002), 137.

37 Butler, *Bodies That Matter*, 191.

38 Butler, *Bodies That Matter*, 219.

39 Rebecca Hanrahan and Louise Antony, "Because I Said So: Toward a Feminist Theory of Authority," *Hypatia*, 20, no. 4 (2005): 63.

40 Anna Wolkowicz, "Bloch als (postmoderner?) Hermeneutiker der Utopie: zu einem Motiv in der Rezeption seines Denkens in den letzten zwanzig Jahren," in *Zeitgenössische Utopieentwürfe in Literatur und Gesellschaft: Zur Kontroverse seit den achtziger Jahren*, ed. Rolf Jucker (Amsterdam: Rodopi, 1997), 184. The inaccurately quoted phrase is from Ernst Bloch, *Thomas Münzer als Theologe der Revolution* (Munich: Wolff, 1921), 19. The passage in fact reads, "begriffene Geschichte, gestellt unter die fortwirkenden revolutionären Begriffe, zur Legende getrieben und durcherleuchtet, . . . ist keineswegs . . . ein *festes* Epos des Fortschritts und der heilsökonomischen Vorsehung, sondern harte, gefährdetste Fahrt, ein Leiden, Wandern, Irren, Suchen nach der verborgenen Heimat" (emphasis added).

8

The Zero-Point:

Encountering the Dark

Frances Daly | **Emptiness of Nothingness**

Introduction: "Deciphering the Palimpsest of Hope"

"The path to ourselves is never narrow":
The Problematic Openness of Being

"What to seek, what to flee," reflects Ernst Bloch, commending Cicero's words, seeing in this postulate the central problem involved in what it is to become human (*POH*, 933). And the difficulty is not simply the presence of indecision, capriciousness, or a lack of precision in the face of wishful questions. It is because desired images of what humanity might become are themselves ambivalent. *That* humanity might become is itself a potential question, and so it is most immediately to the contradictions and equivocations in the juxtaposition of images that "beckon and hover before us" that Bloch wants to draw our attention (*POH*, 933). "Hope knows," he tells us, that "defeat pervades the world as a function of nothingness."[1] A lack of reconciliation troubles and yet animates a sense of what could be, and this is played out in Bloch's layering of image upon image, sometimes as insight into a state of dissatisfied agitation, sometimes as conceptual point of departure for his own aesthetic pursuit of what else a discontentment could and might be.

At one level, a sense of untethered hesitancy and uncertainty suits the contemporary period well. We question what it is that could amount to something better and have long doubted any glib attribution of authenticity or its lack. Creativity, substantiveness, and wakefulness fall prey to the mundane and the mendacious; doubt, desperation, and destructive tendencies expose the hollowing out of ways to better being. A citadel culture subjects most to a permanent state of emergency, turning paranoia, fear, and a diminution of rights into a self-sustaining ideology of security.[2] At the same time, a festering, unfinished refusal repeatedly insinuates itself, and capitalist accumulation is fraying not at the edges but at its very core. And yet, at another level, vacillations between acceptance and doubt have been ever thus and a sense of what might be genuine or undefeated within hope, never unequivocal. For a wide array of writers from the early decades of the twentieth century, something different is detected in this pattern of uncertain disquiet—that of a disconcerting wavering within a rapidly shifting, fragile landscape of near catastrophe, duplicity, and fragmentation. Everything changes, Bloch reminds us, "from one day to the next."[3] Bloch sees in much human expectancy an ambivalence that has, at its basis, the driving force of a state of ferment that takes on especially agitated, restless forms within the context of modernity.

It is the significance of a specific element of this state of uncertainty that will be investigated here—the relevance for us today of what Bloch sees as a complex, undecided darkness permeating conditions of ambiguity. For as much as Bloch is known as the preeminent philosopher of utopian impulses within troubling conditions—the illumination within "the darkness of the lived moment,"[4] as he frequently refers to it—what is not appreciated is how fundamental an emphasis on the anti-utopian elements of this moment is for his work. An analysis of the darkest of obscure darkness can bring to light the very reason why Bloch is a philosopher of hope, and this is, I would argue, a necessary and entirely appropriate way to understand the most provocatively mystical of twentieth-century radical critics. Bloch pursues a sense of an uncertainty sufficient to open paths for the realization of possibility and a "still nameless future" via what he refers to as "sigillary" signs—symbols that remain unfulfilled and yet encapsulate a desired image of what might be, and this involves, I will set out, a problematic starting point (*Literary Essays*, 105; *Spirit*, 24). For signs that occupy a not-yet exhausted past and an uncertain becoming will be inherently unstable, veering between creative possibility and conformity. Every illuminated moment is in danger of being captured by the dull, the fraudulent, the constricting, or diverting, if not the cunning, embittered, or spiteful. And the lived moment, as Bloch repeatedly underlines, is difficult to observe, lurching as it does between closeness and distance. It is often mired in necessity and boredom but also a restlessness, a strangely seductive obscurity that can equally deceive and enlighten in its "dark-brightness," partly because its actuality has not yet been realized but also because humanity, divided, incomplete, not yet known to itself, and "full of ambiguities," could always be something else (POH, 939, 948).

The current times present profound challenges to any understanding of tendencies toward or away from a better world. Knowing that something better would be preferable does not prevent an overwhelming distrust of its possibility. Moments of both the rapid and slow destruction of social democracy, violent state suppression, mass murder, war, and the rise and perpetuation of forms of fascism, as well as the unending bankruptcy of economic inequality and instability — moments that were, for Bloch, unfinished interruptions marking "dialectical moments of the dialectical context" — seem not only all the more discontinuous and haphazard a process but often more depleted than any Hegelian "pulse of liveliness" would entail (POH, 291). And whilst we might no longer face the same type of hegemony, in which a dismal disbelief in another world than this gained easy traction, what a present dissatisfaction might mean is not in any sense straightforward. It is difficult to say quite when a justifiably widespread anguish over a sense that society was "slipping towards atrocity" without noticing the slide, as Siegfried Kracauer referred to it,[5] became more associated with forms of Pyrrhonistic disillusionment. Certainly by the post–Second World War period, perhaps most tellingly in Theodor Adorno's overcompensating and yet obviously concerned, sweeping skepticism of culture and reason, a way of attributing responsibility for the darkness had been advanced that would set the terms of much subsequent debate. A totalizing cultural hegemony was placed in relation to an assumption that reason and science held complete sway over the guileless masses, the "self-loathers" who desire their own deception.[6] In the decades shortly after, which would see postmodernism have its brief moment in the theoretical sun, only the subject of the drama underwent a reconsideration. Clearly, an absolutist ascendency of a dominant culture, unabraded, splinterless, and without challenge, and its attendant end of history, subjectivity, and refusal, are not the problems that we currently confront. The social order is presently under intense scrutiny and irruption. But we do face unnervingly opaque and fragmented tendencies in which liberatory impulses are distorted or ignored. And in this sense it is much more difficult for us to see expansive horizons against which one might detect presentiments of betterment.

Bloch's first forays into surveying these Goethean horizons of life as an "exceeding of limits" saw him delicately prise open the intention of music, for him, the realm of the most utopian of experiments in human intensity. This then allowed him to turn to the vast openness of forms of creativity and the particular cultural surplus and potential for breakthrough they can generate to write his magnum opus, *The Principle of Hope*. In the expansive array of creative wishes, Bloch maintains that we strive and dream, thereby recasting whatever we experience within the imagination to make attentiveness open to both what is concealed and what is anticipated. Dreams, he tells us, are the "outriders of our escape" (*PoH*, 24). Images and symbols have meanings that require deciphering, he argues in accordance with Novalis (*PoH*, 100). There is a continual play of "what is opened and what is cloaked" (*PoH*, 177), a transitoriness through which longing, anticipation, and distance can be felt. However difficult or deceptively easy a time humanity's dreams might actually have in the world, their ability to reveal tendencies within the present has not yet been exhausted, and it is this movement or rotation beyond immediacy that interests Bloch. Indeed, it is the inclusion of an unsettled dynamic into his presentation of images that is, I suggest, a distinctive aspect of Bloch's work and of his influential contribution to a "thought-image" approach more generally.[7] As I will argue in this essay, the aggressively antithetical and yet interrelated and precarious nature of this relationship between anticipation and its inimical other has much to tell us about the fate of hope today.

For Bloch, even the most hopeful of expectations manifest in conditions of darkness and hollowness. This too is the case with apparent non-utopias, but the non-utopian is distinctive in that its tendency would seem more bleakly final and hopeless. Bloch considers various examples of hopelessly constrained hope and tendencies destructive of the imagination, but I wish to draw out those which provoke the greatest force of emptiness, from which little renunciation seems possible—death and the attempted realization of necessary, tragic, desperate striving.[8] The images I have selected of death and Promethean striving reveal the seemingly contradictory aspects of the passage within what remains of the past and a wished-for future. In the face of death there can well arise a respect for the mystery of life as much as can wishful images that never detach themselves from a sense of the abyss from which they wish to escape. In the tragedy of realizing being, just as a necessary audacity motivates Prometheus's attempt to sequester from the gods the secret of fire, so too can this remain an impulse without satisfaction. Bloch writes tellingly of the difficulty in remaining caught in an Apollonian/ Dionysian dualism that supposes fixed polarities of what it means to be a divided self—an either/or of driven sensuality and domesticated acceptance. Both facets of this supposed divide are challenging aspects of being and play a vital part in the ambiguity of the convoluted path to the self; but both require a radical break with a sense that they must always constitute static alternatives. The formation of transit points for a mediation between darkness and a future dimension, between what is foreseen, dreamed, or wished for and the cracks, or even the abyss, in realization, needs to be felt and "set free" (*PoH*, 3, 4). Bloch attempts to find in the "roaring nothingness" a reshaping and overhauling of the present that allows for resonating, open narratives that differ radically from those which remain suspended in the given.[9]

The possibility for the sort of self-encounter Bloch theorizes in conditions of otherwise difficult darkness, what he sometimes refers to as an "expanded darkness" (*Spirit*, 201), would seem to seep away beyond the grasp of tragic being and death. For here, the montage through which the self moves and interacts is often one of a difficult estrangement, as continuously evolving forms of alienation and externalization make for an ever more haunted circle of emptiness and unreality. It is in order to analyze this difficulty that it seems to me it is necessary to bring to attention one of Bloch's overlooked and yet most provocative terms. Bloch variously refers to "zero-points" or "zero-limits" and does so, I would maintain, to indicate a place of extremity in which a confrontation between what exists and has been realized strikes against the undetected or eclipsed.[10] Attempting to locate subversive processes and transformation within a zero-point of seeming emptiness and nothingness places the latency and immediacy of contradiction under enormous strain and yet it is this very contradiction of a zero-limit that exposes a condition for hope. I wish to argue that in using the idea of a zero-point to intimate the difficulty of the process involved in realizing hope we might better appreciate the significance of the anti-utopian within hope. Death and defeated striving would seem to be self-evidently without hope, and yet both must be deciphered anew in order to understand their troublesome place for hope today. Bloch provokes us to think that only in the intensity of exceeding seeming limits, in engaging with a distorting, disorienting darkness of being and the alienated conditions of existence, is a venturing forth possible.

As emblematic of the unstable process of transgression, a transgression we can take to be evinced in dissatisfied existence, I will select three particular instances. The three unfulfilled states of being—being that is "enfolded," being "unfamiliar" to ourselves, and being that is "missing" (*Spirit*, 201, 200)—are each mentioned in different contexts in Bloch's work, and each is centered in a complex imagery appropriated from mysticism. Each explains an aspect of the problem of uncertainty at the heart of instances of anti-utopianism. The unfamiliarity of existence I will consider in the most acute of its instances—in the face of death. A sense of being that is missing I will pursue by way of the image of Promethean striving. It is a form of longing, of hunger and desire where a sense exists that the self is not enough, that existence is somewhat askew, that there is "something missing," as Bloch, using a Brechtian term, repeatedly expresses it.[11] And this question of longing remains unredeemed (*Spirit*, 236). Hence longing is the "not" of a process of "not-yet," the anti-nothingness and anti-emptiness; it is what becomes expressed in dissatisfaction as "unappeased denial" by way of positively positing itself—the constant contradiction between hunger and intended, although rarely achieved or artificially inhibited, fulfilment. What is missing, what is played out as an extreme force of "negativity" is thus, for Bloch, subversively utopian, as even the most hollowed out of hollow spaces contains sparks.[12] The significance of enfolded being will be highlighted in an image Bloch uses repeatedly to indicate the problem of a reading of reality—that of the attempted unveiling of the goddess Isis, the goddess representing the secrets of nature or the mystery of being.

This image is, for him, bound up in the "inconstruable" question of what being might be and is suggestive for an understanding of the problematic terrain of possibility today.

A dissonance within an uncertain darkness, the "primeval chance" of being which Friedrich Schelling had also highlighted, is what we repeatedly encounter today.[13] But perhaps this dialectic of darkness and illumination, or even darkness with sparks, seems too unencumbered an interpretation of the problems we currently face. When we pose the question of our being today, we are immediately struck by how much darker the lived moment appears to be, how much more hollow the hollow spaces and how much more at ease we are in Auerbach's cellar.[14] So much of the determination toward a self-encounter in the contemporary world seems debilitated. We search hard to find countervailing tendencies to greed, coldness, and forgetting. The folly of immediate, limited wishes seems almost touching in these current times of the will to control and annihilate—a will now rupturing but whose strongest desires barely attempt to cloak the corruption and disrespect out of which they emerge. The tensions we encounter take us only a little further along a somewhat familiar playing out of chance, adventure, anxiety, and bad conscience. In its present incarnation the unraveling of hoarded avarice gives way to *ressentiment*; the destruction of curiosity turns the gray, empty reality of so much of life into an unstable alloy of sentimentality and nostalgia. Can we, in such circumstances, still discern, let alone welcome, the deep "joyousness" of the darkness that is closing in, as Bloch saw it, believing our longing for the darkness and the darkness itself, to be the preconditions of any becoming?[15]

For Bloch, a possible "something," a restless urging, an "open dimension" to things is there in the process of the experience of the moment, in its "forward-surging" (*PoH*, 288, 292). It is perfectly possible for this "tiny spark," as Meister Eckhart referred to it,[16] to become extinguished. But to infer from this that desolation would then be all that could ever be would mean assuming an endlessly static experience of the self and world. The Promethean would be without any element of movement, a Zeus without Prometheus, an existence without opposition or, at the very least, a questioning. A life without restlessness, fluctuations, or change is inconceivable to Bloch. The site of hope, he consistently maintains, is in an ethics of community, in the relation of self to other, the I and We of existence. This is not put forward on the assumption of the existence of a dualistic model in which an original condition of unity and mutuality can be contrasted with the instrumentality of society, as Ferdinand Tönnies had argued in the late nineteenth century.[17] For Bloch, the *humanum* is radically open equally to "everything and nothing," to "fulfillment and to ruin." It is an *experimentum mundi*, pulsating and uncertain. It is a darkness, Bloch says, "still veiled to itself and seeking itself," but it is also a ferment.[18] In this space what is most open to the future, Bloch contends, what most anticipates the future, is the ethic of human dignity and the values of freedom, equality, and community. This is a possible content for an experimental, experiential world, not the basis of a preordained authenticity. Humanity's dream, its "oldest daydream," Bloch recounts from Marx's dream, is to overcome all those conditions in which humanity has been degraded, subjugated, forsaken, and treated with contempt (*Literary Essays*, 344).[19] It is this dream that provides archetypes of the "human landscape" of the future. But it is this same future and its connection to the present that seems to us so severely compromised. Having sold our birthright for very much less than a mess of potage, what remains of the self, let alone the relation between the self and other?[20]

At the very least what remains is a tension. What then intervenes in or breaks through this process matters decisively—the tendency for humanity's dream to be postponed or quarantined again and again, in numerous forms of distraction, cynicism, resentment, and reactionary "idealism," has marked the passage of modernity. The tragedy is not merely that the self remains "enfolded" but that barren or uncertain soil would often seem to await a spirit of rebellion. Bloch frequently talks of the need for a "social mandate" (Moses against the Pharoah, Jesus against Caesar, the revolt of the people against the "old enemy" of alienation and dehumanization) for the defiance of the age to blossom—and, even more tellingly, considers entire eras where this spirit disappears and becomes forgotten (*PoH*, 1213).[21] But he also sees in this the basis for the dynamic of a zero-point, a type of negation from which humanity turns and rebounds. The "shudder of sublimity" never really leaves us, he wants to suggest, the "heliotropism of the wondrous" persists, even in the darkness (*PoH*, 312; *Spirit*, 207).[22] This is the provocative, problematic terrain of Bloch's theorization of hope. For it is certainly here that real limits and the actual difficulties involved in hopeful living with and through these limits are met. Our times force us to take seriously the fate of hope when it is at its most tested, to sense whether hope persists not merely against delays and concealment of a nonetheless long pre-served memory but against the decidedly more difficult and seemingly unyielding circumstance of an undreaming void.

Discerning the unpredictable and contradictory attenuation of hope and the tension of impeded, contained, and at times besieged possibili-ties is what, I argue, offers us some critically important elements for the retrieval and reimagining of an uncompleted venturing beyond the given. Images we find in Bloch's work repeatedly provoke a radical re-consideration of possibility. This is not to claim that his analysis pro-vides the basis for an unproblematic critique of contemporary incursions upon hope. What we encounter in his work is a very different theoretical approach from those we tend to take as illustrative of the bifurcations of modernity and find scattered across nihilism, vitalism, idealism, and historical materialism—polarized arguments of the clash between sub-ject and object, emptiness and otherness, society and community. Bloch presents a radically different way of looking at humanity, one which places the not-yet of becoming at its center. Humanity is conceived as a possibility, as a challenge to become, not as a given, and this means that no actual assumption concerning the content of being can be made. In-deed, Bloch's starting point is astonishingly elemental: something stirs, there is the living moment, a bare, naked urging that reaches forth, a stimulus, a movement to all life, and only when this striving is felt, does it become a desire for something, a restlessness, a hunger, an imagining, and a searching. Many philosophies of being, I would argue, are dazzled or disappointed by the passage of the self into the modern world. Bloch focuses instead on the profound implications of what it means to be *homo absconditus*, ones who are yet to see themselves face-to-face and who exist in a momentariness (*Atheism*, 163, 211). Humanity, he indicates, in words that evoke Schelling, does not have possession of itself simply as it is. Rather, it "is something that has yet to be discovered" (*Traces*, 18).[23] This then is Bloch's opening gambit: confronted with desires and fear, humanity strives for something and often something better. Modernity intensifies the dangers involved in making oneself the rope across the abyss, and yet, just as one is hurtling headlong into the void, the void

itself might generate the very possibilities that fear of the abyss has prevented one from seeing. The path to ourselves, crisscrossing any number
of unpredictable voids, is never narrow.

The First Instance of "the Darkness of the Lived Moment": Being Enfolded

"The forest wanders into the desert":
The Problem of Nearness and Distance

Cicero's apothegm on seeking and fleeing permits us to see the importance of the image of ambiguity that reverberates throughout Bloch's
philosophy, in the ideas of uncertainty, discontinuity, and what he calls
the "transitive character of all moments" (*PoH*, 292). In ambiguity there
is both nearness and distance, the creation of sharp perspectives, distortions, and shadows. Cast into darkness, humanity might not "even see
the claws of the lion" (*Literary Essays*, 197). And if, more often than not,
history passes humanity by, unnoticed or unprepared for, the basis for a
self-realizing humanity to achieve hope is radically uncertain. Humanity
can sometimes be too close to reality, Bloch suggests, or too distracted
from its significance. But neither is distance any guarantee of perspective. Even at a remove, "moments still beat unheard, unseen" because
their present "is still not conscious" (*PoH*, 295).

We might be led to think that Bloch's sole emphasis is on the ambiguity of the darkness as, according to this conceptualization, uncertainty is at the core of humanity itself—humanity is an abyss, he notes,
concurring with Georg Büchner, "one shudders, looking down there"
(*Literary Essays*, 69). This shuddering, a constant motif used by Goethe,
Schelling, and Kant to depict humanity's response to the mysterious-
ness of life, is in Bloch (and in Nietzsche's *Zarathustra*) not always or
necessarily the result of fear or an awkward self-recognition. Perhaps
humanity beholds a "happy abyss" Bloch conjectures, "one with all
kinds of overlooked gains" (*Literary Essays*, 69). For those who would
"long for the other shore," there are a number of different interpretations
for a "happy" or "lovable" trembling at the edge of the abyss.[24] Indeed,
sounding ever more Zarathustrian, Bloch finds a fullness in a reality that
contains both destruction and illumination. We are "wanderers," "it is

our coming and going that occurs within things" (*Spirit*, 129). Humanity becomes what it might be by "venturing beyond" (*PoH*, 4), by subjecting itself to the uncertain expectations and dangers of hope and, in so doing, whether motivated by fear or desire, activating tendencies within, what he terms, a "high road," a "structured openness" (*Literary Essays*, 73). But this might not necessarily require a developed sense of anticipation. It might be that history gives rise to displacements and interruptions in orientation or experience, and this can perhaps allow for feelings of the uncanny and a reactivated past to develop.

Bloch wants to draw our attention through ambiguity back to the nearness of the darkness. Indeed, he states that "the knot of the riddle of existence" (*PoH*, 292) is to be found in the darkest nearness. According to the images of which he is particularly fond, there are sparks within the darkness and clearings in the forest and, within these, the presence of the unforeseen and the unappreciated hovers. An entire history of driving forces and transformations exists, even if a consciousness of this must struggle to emerge. But in any case, we can be reassured that possibility would not exist unless there were a sense that something should be other than it is. But are we assured? Why is Bloch so certain that by detecting the presence of contradiction at the basis of experience he can find traces of joyful or, more often, fearful anticipation?

Difficult experiences might leave one disoriented but might instead enable one to see beyond the immediacy. Bloch mentions Ovid's account of the dryad Syrinx, in book 1 of the *Metamorphoses*, in order to explain the presence of seemingly vanished entities. Syrinx is the one who has "vanished and yet not vanished," Bloch states.[25] Having asked the Arcadian water nymphs of the Ladon to transform her so that she might escape from Pan's unwanted entreaties, what remains of Syrinx is a haunting lament through the reeds. Her eventual permutation as the flute of Pan's construction resounds—the music played on the reeds of her once former self, the presence of a limit that has been exceeded.[26] A contradictory dynamic means that the possibility to trace lines within the invisible exists. There are, of course, "a thousand paths never taken," as Nietzsche, in a decidedly utopian manner, says—and the most as-yet undiscovered are certainly those that Bloch wants us to acknowledge as our cultural inheritance and anticipated future.[27] But if, as Bloch argues, no one "is really here yet," what sort of encounter with the darkness could enable those who act within the "sharp turning-points of existence" to bring a questioning astonishment to what is present and what is hoped for within the darkness (*PoH*, 293)?

The Image at Saïs

There is one image that is so replete with meaning and suggestion across ages and cultures that its particular significance for philosophies of transformation has tended to become blurred in a hazy, generalized depiction of nature and its hidden identity. The image is that of a veiled goddess. Partly veiled, partly encased, sometimes wrapped with strange animal protomes, sometimes with a zoomorphical headdress, often oddly multi-breasted, perhaps multi-testicled, certainly more often appearing with rows of pendulous, elliptical shapes adorning the chest, symbolic of fertility and originally possibly suggesting an association with a tree deity, abundantly gravid with fruit—the image is ripe for interpretation. The earliest depictions of the image, at times in the form of Neith, the Egyptian goddess of hunting, wisdom, water, and weaving of Saïs, nursing crocodiles, and weaving the world anew each day, have elements that, under the influence of a Hellenistic vogue for Egyptian cults, are found on the statue of the goddess of the temple of Ephesus and are then assimilated, from the nineteenth century overwhelmingly so, as Isis, the veiled goddess representing light, nature, truth, and mystery. As a syncretistic deity she has been variously depicted in art, literature, and philosophy across the centuries.[28] In dispute is the meaning of what is hidden by her veiling and what is then revealed by her unveiling or by her reluctance to be unveiled.

Bloch's attraction to a goddess of such potential ambiguity is hardly surprising—indeed, she provides for him the very image of conflictual openness that he transfers to humanity's uneasy relationship with hope. Bloch's goddess is gleaned from Plutarch, Proclus, Goethe, Schiller, Novalis, and perhaps even Nietzsche, although it is the unfinished essay, *The Novices at Saïs* by Novalis and Friedrich Schiller's poem "The Veiled Image at Saïs" that most prompt Bloch to construct his own version of the occurrence at Saïs.[29]

A young man is intrigued by what lies beneath the veil of the statue of Isis at Saïs. Perhaps as a result of being warned against entering the temple by the hierophant, perhaps by reading the statue's inscription, "I am all that has been, that is, and that shall be; no mortal has yet raised my veil," the youth's appetite for a knowledge of the secret of Isis is irrevocably whetted and, returning to the temple at night, he lifts her veil. In Schiller's depiction, the youth is so horrified by what he beholds that a deep melancholy overwhelms and destroys him. For Novalis, this dislocation reflects a necessary preparedness to immortalize oneself, even if, on raising the veil, the youth sees "wonder of wonders! himself." Bloch too suggests that the crucial issue is that the youth sees his own reflection but remarks additionally that it is the image of the self he encounters that is problematic (*Spirit*, 226). Frightened by the guardians at the entrance to the temple, the youth's "unpurified eye" can discern only his own "twofold form"—that of the experience of sorrow before a transcendental entrance. This image and not any discovery of truth is what provokes the youth's demise. Bloch maintains that what the youth perceives is both his self within the existing darkness and an image of self as "it might radiate in full, redeemed, future glory," away from active disbelief and fear. The guardians play dual roles of the divided self—one a railing, furious god of a *mysterium tremendum*, the other a god of love and fervor, of a *mysterium fascinosum*.

This moment of conflict is the stated but unconstrued question of existence that awaits us all. In this sense, following Bloch's reasoning, mere guilty curiosity cannot lift the veil from Isis. But the youth recoils in horror not only because he glimpses his double self but because he sees beyond himself, past the guardians, a "far more terrible abyss"—an absolute, demonic guardian before the threshold of the "great in vain," the eternal death "without peace" of "absolute frustration." In this void the youth can discern his own image, petrified, immobilized, and yet still aware, "burning with an aimless longing in perfect nothingness." His histrionic, blustering cry, "What do I have, if I do not have everything?" belies his false bravado. If he possessed sufficient knowledge, he would realize that he has no need to grasp at complete truth, for this world is never going to furnish him with it. The best this world can offer, a warmth and a remembering, is only a preparation for an entirely different existence than this. We must be poised to "go through," but only by understanding what it is we leave behind and what it is we intend to embrace (*Spirit*, 227). Only via this can an engagement with the suffering that enfolds a being so tightly take place.

The image at Saïs allows Bloch to put forward a key argument concerning self-overcoming. The choice would seem stark: To the abyss we can bring either a searching without knowing or an ability to break through fear. In the former case, this is a searching that, however reflective of a need to create and remember, remains captive to an inability to reclaim who we are. It is exemplified in much restless, empty, hidden motivation, vulnerable as it is to glimpsing the void, the nothingness that is the image of humanity shackled to a perpetual sameness of living out an unchanged, unemancipated existence, the "eternal death without peace." In the latter case, we can foist ourselves into fear and, with awareness, drive ourselves outward without any need to behold the "truth" of Isis unveiled.

In this sense it is apparent that Bloch is arguing for the possibility to move beyond the alternatives of uninformed seeking or endless trepidation but so too is he rejecting the possibility of an accommodation with the given. For Nietzsche, joyful wisdom is having the good taste to know when to leave the pursuit of knowledge alone. "We no longer believe," Nietzsche declares, "that truth remains truth when the veils are withdrawn." And in any case, perhaps reason has good reason for not revealing her reasons.[30] Nietzsche's sense of courage to terminate one's journey at the surface is that which Bloch finds in going through. This is the path to ourselves, to death as well, into the emptiness of nothingness and against it—it is an emergence. Encircling the strange, intoxicated feeling of sadness and longing, Bloch imagines "a smile," "a winking": the smile is the veiled image of Saïs.[31] Both Bloch and Nietzsche give us an inkling of the playful revenge of the mystery held intact, deflecting all attempts at unveiling but, for Bloch, the life which we might want to affirm is still dark in both amazing and shattering ways. Thus the same problem of the "Dionysian wishful image" involves, in addition, a knowledge of "the lust of the future" (*PoH*, 950). Bloch's choice beyond choice is made difficult to construe as a question of our being because what it means to *be* becomes enfolded within conditions of an often quite forlorn, vacant darkness. What is both feared and hoped for opens up within any orientation toward the future, but certain conditions, particularly those Bloch associates with declining, fragmenting societies, riddled by crisis phenomena, seem to contract and deactivate the experience of hope. The "Saïs-like aspect of the world" comes to the fore in these conditions, but it also underlines and extends the void. But who is this self who struggles to remember and imagine?

The Divided Self

According to Schiller, Bloch notes, being that chooses between a joy of the senses and the peacefulness of the soul will be condemned to an "anxious choice" (PoH, 948).[32] But perhaps this is also a crossroads upon which the self can loiter endlessly without ever arriving at a decision. For Bloch, it is only by sensing the future that humanity will be able to recognize why it acts and what it posits of the world and moment. With enigmatic suggestiveness he says that "the beginning will only have happened completely at the end" (Spirit, 227), which might well be so and, yet, knowing quite where we are within this process surely then becomes fraught.

Like Nietzsche, Bloch is drawn to the concept of the Dionysian to understand why it is that conscious life veers between apocalyptic horror and a self-realizing amazement. Recognition or anagnorisis is the ability to wonder into the future by way of the past and present. It is not Dionysian rapture in the sense of an abstract romantic reaction to falsity and inauthenticity, but it is Dionysian in its encounter with the "glowing core" of humanity (Spirit, 206), the shock, the utopian "flash of lightning" (Heritage, 331). Dionysus, Bloch argues, is not the "approximate subject," the predator between monster and superman. He is, perhaps, somewhat overplayed as the problem of unfinished humanity (the lone hero repeatedly striking out against and with eternal recurrence) because the drive that Dionysus represents is a renunciation of emptiness, a turn from the zero-point of repression and distraction. The true Dionysian Anti-Christ, Bloch argues, is the heretical Jesus—the one who "does not remain in the grave his whole imposed death long" (Heritage, 331). We are capable of preventing ourselves from slipping into the tragedy around us, of interrupting its duration, but not by the force of our character being made to coincide with destiny, as Bloch attributes to Novalis; not by the realization of the "occurrence that always recurs," via

Nietzsche; and not, Bloch argues, in contradistinction to Hegel (and as Georg Lukács would in his early writings contend) by limiting a sense of the tragic outcome to a fatal divergence between soul and deed (*Spirit*, 220).[33]

For Bloch, the real drama of life is one that is riven through by the historical and, as Novalis stated, the mysterious.[34] Humanity exists within world processes that are a discontinuous playing out of the lived experience of darkness and of dark being as well. And what is experienced is also "the most inexperienced thing that there is" (*PoH*, 293), for we are *homo ignotus*, we do not know who we will become but, in being, we resist and embody. Our encounter with ourselves and the world is an "encounter with the obstacle" (*Spirit*, 221). If, as we have argued, it is the openness of profound possibilities, recondite horizons, and the undiscovered that gives substance to a sense of the mysterious, it is also the reason why Bloch refuses to pit the Dionysian against the Apollonian. The drive, the will, the life force and fluidity placed against the spirit, the clarity, and contained awareness, is too rigid a choice and one which fails to recognize that neither tendency is finished. Apollo remains the "abyss on high" and Dionysus the "dark fire in the abyss" whilst being remains incomplete; only when humanity sees itself face-to-face will these alternatives disappear (*PoH*, 952). This is Bloch's sense of the divided self, a reinterpretation of Goethe's Faustian conflict of two souls within one breast and of the Apollonian/Dionysian divide. But the problem is, as Bloch is well aware, that what is unexplored of us and the dark, deep forest through which we might venture or simply become lost, is as often alien to us as it is tempting as we try to find in it a passage of the self. It is an uneasy mix of familiar and unexplored terrain, one of searching and frequently not finding.

The Second Instance of "The Darkness of the Lived Moment": Being Unfamiliar to Ourselves

"Going out in search of the great perhaps": Death as Unfamiliarity

It is not surprising that to open his examination of hopeful images against death, Bloch quotes both Rabelais, the supreme celebrator of a life freed from servitude with his testament to the openness, the "great

perhaps" beyond life, and Kierkegaard, the champion of the self's knowledge through difficulty and the necessity of awakening with his Pauline
description of the hopelessness of death into which the spirit brings a
"hope which is hoping against hope."[35] For Bloch's understanding of
death is first and foremost an analysis of the seemingly contradictory difficulty that death poses for hope in the lasting noncoincidence death has
to being, as well as the profoundly open consequences this "extreme annihilation" has for the living (POH, 1109). "Our space," Bloch argues, is
"always life, or something more," and it is this "something more" that
is poked and prodded at by a consciousness of the inevitability of death
(Traces, 30). We cannot know death in the same way that we know that
it will extinguish life, nor can we know anything of an "afterdeath," and
so something of the future, an unknown something, imposes itself on
death. It is a leap not merely into but through the abyss. "We live without
knowing what for. We die without knowing where to," Bloch notes (POH,
1105, Spirit, 275). If life is not quite right, death is decidedly strange, and
this strangeness throws into confusion a sense of hope and newness. It
is a disorienting frontier of near and far, a dislocation involving separation and unfamiliarity. Bloch describes this oscillating realm with the
surrealistic words: "the clouds are corals from the ocean floor; death has
the brightness of green turquoise."[36] And yet it is precisely in this disconcerting terrain that death becomes "audible" (Traces, 97). Although
death is the journey from which there is no return, the destroyer of the
witness to change, the canceller of existence and the capacity to experience, what exposes it to an ambivalence is that it is also a provocation for
setting wishful evidence against its "so little illuminating certainty" (POH,
1107). Longing and desires, including a sense of wonder for and beyond
the chaos of existence, subject death to conjecture. On this basis, death
first involves a basic antagonism between ending and possibility that is
centered in the irresolution of lived experience. But there are a number
of ways to read this confusion, this restless, sublime shudder, whose
promise is both freedom from, and yet somehow also a renewal of, life.

At one level we must know that we are moving toward death, and how
we proceed toward this seeming nothingness, whether via repressed fear
or by a sense of the wondrous and marvelous or by any number of states
in between, will shape an understanding of what it is of life that is re-
ceptive to awakening before death, a state that Bloch sometimes refers

to as the "undeath" in death or a "*Novum* against death."[37] At his most
undaunted, Bloch would like us to consider that a type of consciousness
exists which has already bypassed the need for consolation into death
via an empowered, transcending humanity capable of understanding and
engaging with freedom as much as the sacred and that this would then
allow for a reconsideration of a radical incompleteness in the face of
death (*PoH*, 1172, 1173, 1175). It must be remembered, however, that the
sheer weight and perpetuation of consoling myth and avoidance would
make us question just how far any such engagement has moved beyond
fear and how thoroughly it has been able to reject conquest. Attempts at
liberation from a given way of life undoubtedly create a powerful symbolism, and yet it is unclear how this might lead to a readiness to be open
to a death-ending life. It is important to bear in mind that we are both
the inheritors of Feuerbach's anthropologization of religion and critics
of its mechanistic limitations.[38] We are the occupiers, too, of Nietzsche's
accusation that we are God's murderers.[39] Where humanity once approached death with a "sacred horror," it has been perfectly possible to
sever much of the connection to the marvelous that has distinguished a
human contemplation of death.[40] Far from meaning that we have thus
dispensed with guiding images of death, what would instead appear to
be the case is a repeated replacement of those images not conducive to
any contemporaneous relation to life with images deemed more easily
amenable.

Humanity has always created images of death. That modernity has
both destroyed religious mystery and made a virtue of prosperity cults,
theistic and anti-theistic, is undoubtedly problematic for a guidance
into death today, but it is entirely in keeping with societies in which the
idolatry of money and its signifiers reign supreme. Whilst necessity has
any purchase on freedom, there will exist what Bloch refers to as a "snare
over the void," a "trap door into bottomless illusion" (*Traces*, 145). But
how we deal with forms of entanglement in death—whether it encloses
and eventually entombs or whether we manage to break through what
it is that enchains us—is our difficult test. How the transcendent negativity of death, its "emptiness of nothingness,"[41] its turning point, might
be viewed is thus fundamental, for it should follow that this bare "nothingness" is also the possibility of a type of renewal.

"Utopias of the night with no morning":
Dark Guiding Images against Death

Bloch's study of hopeful images against death scans across a vast array of symbols and images of an afterlife, but we are particularly interested in anti-utopian images—images revealing a zero-point that are most able to shed light upon the contemporary philosophical problem of death. Two images, I contend, would seem to express this tendency: both involve death by suicide, the first provoked by alienated despair, the second by a sense of irredeemable failure. The first image we can derive from Bloch appears in an utterance that he mentions by a character in Frank Wedekind's play *Spring Awakening*. Bloch's interpretation of a youth's statement is that it is a taunt: "Been in Egypt and never saw the pyramids." It is a "scornful" statement from someone who is to die "without experiencing the joys of love," Bloch states (*PoH*, 1106). The young man, Moritz Stiefel, is in fact about to take his own life; he is desperate and disappointed. Life has given him "the cold shoulder," and something warm and friendlier beckons "from the other side." This act carries with it an intense anguish—Moritz fears the darkness and knows he will never again return home once he has drained "the bitter cup" and allowed himself to taste the "mysterious terrors of departure." He wants to set himself free and yet knows that in so doing he is surrendering any chance to experience love and desire and considers it "shameful" to be human and yet never to have known the "most human thing of all." It is this painful thought that provokes his dark rumination about being in Egypt yet never seeing the pyramids. To be able to exit life, he needs to see existence as empty and illusory and pretend to himself that suicide is as "innocuous" as "whipped cream."[42] The second image we find in Bloch is from Émile Zola's *The Masterpiece*.[43] Zola's acutely disturbing story involves the artist Claude Lantier, who, in repeated attempts to paint his life's ultimate work, increasingly realizes his inability to achieve his intention. The novel culminates in Lantier's suicide, his cold, limp body discovered against his unfinished painting.

If what we have in both these examples is a bleak withdrawal from life, suggesting an unwillingness to deal with life and death as well, do these images constitute a zero limit for a contemporary understanding of death? Neither Wedekind's Moritz nor Zola's Lantier are able to attenuate the fear of a nonlived life in the face of death. Certainly, in substituting fear and wonder in many of their ritualized and religious forms with a "meager" nothingness, the substance of dying has become hollowed out (*PoH*, 1157). And in the absence of any urge to reach a place beyond death via life itself or of the mystery surrounding the meaning of death, a type of hope can barely persist, let alone achieve any type of transformation. When an engagement with death becomes more a need to find a type of security beyond life, this is increasingly spurred by an uncertainty and a lack of confidence in existence itself. Would a successful execution of his imagined work have saved Lantier from ending his life, or would he have never deemed his work adequate to his dream? Despite knowing that alienated despair remains, whether or not it can be cut short by death as a last desperate form of control over the chaos of life, we are confronted with a radical interruption to the expected trajectory of being. There is a decisive halt to the future by these attempts to retreat from a continuing present but also a blunt assessment on its unfinished suffering. It is both a seeking and a fleeing from extremes of familiarity and the unknown. If a type of freedom exists in these examples of letting go of the rope across the abyss, it is a troubling zero-point for a release from alienation.

A problem for images of death today is that we live within the strange reality of the obscuring of significant aspects of individual death and yet, at the same time, are bombarded by a knowledge and direct images of multiple or mass death, whose meaning is presented according to an entirely arbitrary schema of relative significance or gravity, which is oddly detached from a sense of the death of the self. We are the recipients of an extended, discontinuous period in which the assumption of human dignity has been met with numerous instances of violation and indifference. And yet we still want death to be meaningful, even at its most malign and contemptuous of life. Is this the zero-limit that death elicits for hope today? There is an element of "extra-territoriality" to the demise of the self, and this would mean, for Bloch, that in the death and disappearance of what has not yet become, something appears (*Atheism*, 263). The power of death, he stresses, is such that it can provoke a sense of a "recurrent beginning," and this can be the "witch's potion" against the "horrible" force of death, the "dream of a final, undefeated self-presence at the end of the world" (*Spirit*, 264). Certainly, the self is marked by a meaning bound up in a duration that is finite and yet one which cannot ultimately be experienced as such. There is something anticipated but not experienced. It is an enigma before death that throws into relief the problem of hope. But Bloch's "extra-territoriality" emanates from the not-yet of life, against which death seems the much weaker force. Because he understands being as bound to a not-yet being, an incompleteness of being that is not finished in life, it is, he would argue, not terminated by death. This can manifest itself in an enlightened *un*awakedness, a type of brittleness and skepticism in the face of death. No matter how emptied of meaning death becomes, there are still, he avers, the flowers that "have to be put somewhere" (*Atheism*, 263, 262), the reminder to and acknowledgment by the living of one's somewhat less than calmly awaited fate. But today many an unacknowledged, unmourned passing of the self occurs, without liberation, dream, or even flowers. If we accept that human orientation is to the future, is it still possible to contend that death can alter hope, thereby transforming hope for the living? Bloch attempts to create philosophical space for a sphere of hope both within the process of life and as a realm for the preparation for death. This depends upon a necessity to comprehend the world on something other than its own terms, for to do otherwise, the "dreams of illumination," of which Bloch writes (*PoH*, 1107, 1109), the paradoxical dreams of both annihilation and non-renunciation would become overwhelmed by the nightmare of living without the possibility of hope. The search for escape of Wedekind's Moritz and Zola's Lantier gives meaning to their deaths but little to their cancelled and yet unfinished lives.

The Possibility within Death: "metamorphosis into nothingness"

Death unsettles life. It is certainly the disquietude that death elicits which permits a questioning of the relation between existence and non-existence. And this question probes the possibility that the self, having deracinated so many of the values making each of us human, is no longer able to relate to the sort of promise of transformation of being that death holds out to life, instead, bringing to death only an empty, unredeemed past. Fear cannot be elided, but there is the possibility that it can give to life its substance rather than only an endless affirmation of the abyss. Fear can also be infused with a genuine, unfulfilled desire in which, without the possibility of any certain knowledge, we nonetheless connect with the question that death poses and situate this question in an interrogation of our own relation to being. Where Emmanuel Levinas might refer here to the "paradox of the infinite" as ultimately underscored by an interrogative mode that cannot really constitute a question because there can be no response, and George Bataille would maintain that in any such question resides only a seriously derisive reflection (indeed he says, "the most profound practical joke"), Bloch sees a "paradox of non-renunciation" (PoH, 1109).[44] The seeming contradiction is that thoughts of annihilation exist alongside those of awakening. Both are, however, subject to the nature of the passage toward or away from humanization. Thus what is implicated in the persistence of a woeful adjustment, or complete lack of adjustment, to "human finality" (Atheism, 121) is as much a world of rampant greed and selfishness as it is an unrealistic wish to cling to or exit life.

At one level, this has always been the dilemma death poses: If death is the ultimate non-utopia—it is, after all, only in breathing that we "seethe," Bloch says—then how might it also be the sign, the direction for an entry into a "workable fate"?[45] We considered previously the image at Saïs. What the idea of a veiled Isis provoked for many was the importance of a respect for the mystery of being—Isis holds behind her coverings the secret of life and thus of death as well. What is born will tend to disappear but not without leaving a trace. Like Syrinx, there are traces, even in the invisible. If death lays bare the enigma of being, the search for its elucidation is in understanding what the mystery is rather than in any demystifying of it, and this is the primordial problem of humanity's relation to the darkness. And yet this underlines the persistently difficult contradiction that death presents to unfamiliar life. We considered earlier that Bloch situates being in relation to a type of openness, a destructive and creative experience of the possibility of one's existence. On this basis, death could be the possibility to be open to expectation and curiosity; it could even be the basis for imaginatively accessing a sense of the mystery of existence and, in so doing, allowing the knowledge of departure to be transformed into a sense of the future. And yet much about the contemporary experience of death militates against this.

Indeed, our present engagement with death is less troubled by consolations of ultimate avoidance and fear than it is by a much starker substitution of the meaning of death with banal distraction. If longing in the face of imminent extinguishment here compels us in any direction, it is back to the blandishments of a plasticized, empty, false self that suffices in place of either meaning or discovery. Where this leaves the possibility of a journey past fear and instead into "the great expedition" is wholly uncertain (PoH, 1177). Without distance and familiarity, the strangeness of life toward death tends to overwhelm. Bloch senses that this living on an "expired belief" whose apparent direction is the complete evaporation of the enlivening fear humanity once felt in the face of death can lead toward only an ever more helpless "horror" (PoH, 1104, 1157). It is, paradoxically, a place where even the fear of death becomes flat and unrecognizable as fear. And yet the strangeness of certain death somehow remains. It is just that we seem ill-prepared for an understanding of its significance or potential meaning. What this anxious, uncertain state is most able to tell us is that the significance of the uncompleted nature of being is first felt in a profound unfamiliarity in being. Death hovers as the great unremembered, its sense of departure, which should induce the clarity of distance, instead taking on the strangeness and confusion of nearness. In the face of death this unfamiliarity is amplified whether or not euthanizing conceits are resorted to in order to lessen the impact of what will unfold and however tragic and difficult their realization. Whilst Bloch maintains that there is both inavertible and avertible fate, the problem is surely that death is an unavoidable certainty (PoH, 1280).

To know how to live—to philosophize, in Montaigne's sense—is to learn how to die.[46] And this is what should be left for those "who suffer and are dark," those who "hope far ahead" (PoH, 276)—a consideration of the meaning of life. What Bloch in effect contends is that this is the most basic and profound trace that death leaves. It marks not only a past but issues to both the present and the future a constant obligation to consider the purpose and enactment of life. This realm is qualified by a not-yet conscious that is open to becoming conscious to a knowledge of its content only in the act of anticipatory imagination. If death does not exhaust its meaning in death, then we must look to what it is that concerns being beyond its own finiteness, to the fragile, uncertain, unstable encounter with life that suggests the something more of the ruin of dark being. What is heading irrevocably into death is the not-yet become and, in its sublime emptiness of nothingness, in its zero-point, some-thing—the humane, ethical meaning of life—can be posed. Death, as Bloch writes so evocatively, is a "metamorphosis into nothingness" (*POH*, 1108). It is a strange homeland where we have never been (*Traces*, 58). We cannot know if the life process allows the posing of the question of transformation, but we cannot dismiss the question itself (*POH*, 1109). A "transitional state," not an "inflexibly formative" end point, "lies far be-yond death" (*Spirit*, 269, 265). Something, Bloch tells us, is extractable from our passage toward death; it is and remains unburied (*Spirit*, 265). Even the *idea* of death is able to rescue the self from a type of immobility because it can imagine possibility, even the expectant illumination of an end (*Spirit*, 264). It might well be that it is just as likely that a "bad con-science" of the end will arise as might any type of awakening in the face of death, but this bad faith is already present in a placid, unreflective contentment with the way the world currently is. *This* is the "veiling of the self" and the "distortion of the beyond," the Saïs-like problem of the world. And yet it is also, at its most basic, a space that can open into the question of being, which also contains a response, the indispensability of ethical responsibility.

The Third Instance of "the Darkness of the Lived Moment": Being Missing

Attempted Overcoming: The "revolt of the people to the sacred mountain"

If the "key to us all is death," as Bloch says in Tolstoyan fashion, it is so because it holds the potential for one's own self-concealment to dissolve to a sublime nothingness (*Traces*, 97). But not only death is capable of disturbing us in this manner; there is something else that can act as a "knock on the door." Bloch observes that there is a recurring likeness between "exit" and "exodus" (*Traces*, 99). And if the problem with exiting is that its potential self-encounter can be overwhelmed by fear, then exodus is liable to an equally intense vulnerability in the act of de-parting, for departure is marked by an expectation that can be subjected to a cruel reversal. The potential joy available to the departing and the finally arriving is not any guarantee for the journey outward. As Bloch says, the ones staying back are susceptible to a form of melancholy (*Traces*, 99). Staying, turning, or being turned back—each carries the risk of allowing the inability of escaping or breaking through one's time to distort both the age and the self, condemning humanity to a type of eternal return. As we considered at the outset, at its most powerful, Dionysus as a symbol of anti-nothingness represents both the problem of an unfinished world and the drive forward—Dionysian unrest "thinks" the darkness of the lived moment. But without content or history, as a mere "placeless subject," Dionysus can only remain in the realm of an abstract wish against indeterminate life, where "confused noise" can overwhelm (*Heritage*, 327, 299). At its least worst, this becomes occultish myth, reaction "mitigated by weeds," as Bloch calls it (*Heritage*, 171). Worse are those who remain within history but who wish to smash its "false forms," fueled by the resentments of the "little man," the Babbitt, the "employee who dreams of the whip," who is full of embittered, peevish, accumulated rage, exploiting any power against the most defenseless.[47] Worse still is the intoxicated blood-myth of the "malicious, fossilized" fascist; this culture, Bloch tells us, quoting Kracauer, is "an escape from revolution and from death."[48]

If death presents a difficult path to overcoming, there is, in life, a fate worse than death and that is the darkness of tragic being. In the "creatural will" that screams, there can be a type of rebelliousness that stakes its claim against the very sort of intoxication that we might recognize as it has staggered through our modern times.[49] Against this, the most expressively "fermenting" subject, whose instinct is to leave given reality, is that subject who most reveals and breaks open the tension between humanity and its own estrangement (*Heritage*, 327). The subject of tragic being, of the most "numinous shudder," is that subject who, through suffering and revolt, searches for a way out (*POH*, 1194).[50] In seeking a place beyond the "oppressed expanse," in setting sail on the "Genoese ship" into the "wide blue yonder," humanity embarks on a precarious journey into the illuminated light of the not-yet lived life (*Heritage*, 327). This exodus is prompted by a recognition that we lack something—and we sense this via a mixture of expectation and disappointment—but also by a dream-filled wishful world of releasing enslavement into freedom. The cry of life, the battle cry for the "detour-maker," humanity, is the invocation to freedom. It is indeed the very existence of freedom that allows for extremes of attempted overcoming. The "revolt of the people to the sacred mountain" is the explosive hope against an aimless nothingness. It is not the idle or secret-shattering curiosity of the youth at Saïs, propelled forward in the certainty that all knowledge is within one's grasp. It is, rather, the intervention of the enslaved in the historical situatedness of enslavement, a yearning for freedom via the power of exuberance and ferment but by way of seeing the darkness that this surely entails.

Prometheus against the Cliffs: The Attempt to Overcome

If Dionysus is the symbol of the unarrived, the god of fermentation, it is Prometheus who, for Bloch, represents a fore-thinking or acting into change, a bringer of a "sparking, flaming" light to suffering and passivity.[51] Bloch's Prometheus is the Aeschylean realizer of freedom, the knowledge bringer with his "own flower," his "flashing fire," the Luciferian light-bringer, the Titan, the champion of mortals and the enslaved against rulers and tyrannical power, the demiurge, the Faustian figure of tragic knowledge and the sorrows of Job, as well as the Jesus figure who bears his intense suffering for the salvation of others.[52] He contains not only what is pent up within us—the impulse without satisfaction—but also the protest against injustice, the "blazing element" against the "age-old heraldic emblem of oppression." He is an "immortal hope," a "considerer of the future" (PoH, 979, 978). This is Schelling's Prometheus as well. Prometheus, Schelling argues, suffers because of his "inner feeling" of injustice and oppression. But his suffering is not a subjection or necessary fate; rather, it is caused by the tyranny exacted against him and thus is also a defiance, a rebellion.[53] The example of Prometheus signifies how necessary the content of hope is to utopian longing. An exuberant spirit is not enough to dare us to reach for freedom. What is imprisoned within humanity is not simply an urge for change waiting to be set free but the self herself, unbecome and not fully known to herself and, through this, the numinous—in the daring to overturn the suffering of all. The dreaming, the willing outward needs courage and hope but also a consciousness of the new. It needs, Bloch writes, an "intention of sublimity," a metamorphosis (PoH, 980).

Longing for the "blue flower," the drive to transcend, need not, of course, always place us in contention with our times. But to break through the present time, to overcome the obstacles of its controlling, selfish motive, its "shoddy product," and "flimsy, barbaric content" requires a will of defiance and hope (*Atheism*, 31; *Spirit*, 267). But what is it that shifts this rage and wishful thinking, this daring joined to zeal, the "lurking mischief" Oceanus would accuse Prometheus of indulging in, into a productive hope?[54] Rage and daring might possess a sharpness, even a "dash of confusion" that is necessary in the face of tyranny, but they might not in themselves open the content of hope (*PoH*, 983). Zeus himself is attacked by many, most notably by Typhon, the spirit of darkness and grotesque uncle of Prometheus, covered in coiled serpents and full of "boiling rage" who himself gives birth to the eagle who will be the unbidden banqueter on Prometheus's liver.[55] But only Prometheus possesses an unconquerable will against despotic power.

Bloch argues cogently that the self-encounter is a moment of conflict. Nothing, he says, would break through from before if it remained calm and alone. Defiance is the "metaphysics of tragedy" (*PoH*, 1213). Defiance and hope are the "two tragic emotions" that refuse to capitulate before fate (*PoH*, 430). Prometheus, for Bloch, is the figure of torment, of an excruciating "incubation," of a "forward-dawning"; he holds a "demanding gaze" (*PoH*, 981). His ambition supersedes everything else, and it must do so to open the expanse of the "fulfilled moment" to any present view, to "hear the unheard" (*PoH*, 982). What we know is that Prometheus would recast in understanding that which is "wrought in confusion," that which is "witless." This is not pride or willfulness, although it requires both and more to achieve; it is understanding the needs of others. And this lesson is one that Prometheus savors for Zeus to learn — he will be forced to see how very different it is to be "a sovereign and a slave."[56] Only then can the external world be shaped or reshaped to follow the contours of a hope against incursions upon hope. This sublimity, a greatness, a hope beyond us, is the mystery, the metamorphosis that resisting oppression and even momentarily grasping at a perfection before us can ignite. It requires a "magnificent hubris," a "blind hope," the promise of which can spill out from Pandora's box as much as has evil. Only when "I have been bent by pangs and tortures infinite," says Prometheus, "am I to escape my bondage."[57] The sort of effort needed to break through a contemporary fate, short of having one's liver, the organ of prophecy, gnawed at and torn to pieces every third day, is difficult for us to contemplate today, but it is only by denying a present suffering that we imagine a fate worse than death could not be the promise of exodus.[58]

When we consider what it is that propels humanity into this departure, it is important to know whether opposition to the given is carried by dissatisfaction alone or if it requires something more. What negativities, what incongruities transform dissatisfaction and, indeed, need it to be transformed if it is to project a type of ferment rather than hesitation or resignation? If, in any case, there is a constant rotation of "contaminated" space, at which point on Ixion's wheel is humanity at the present moment?[59] A guilty embodiment of an age of craven distraction can, only with enormous difficulty, place its hopes in a realm of unfamiliarity, as Bloch's argument would need us to contend. Bloch tells us repeatedly that it is our nearness that is strange and our exile, familiar; we sense and yet misconstrue what it is that is missing. But perhaps we have learned to ignore the decay and enslavement of life, thereby pacifying, transmogrifying its strangeness beyond any real recognition. We are capable, it would seem, of bending even the most contradictory realities into an easy compromise. Prometheus might have had more "leisure" than he craved and thus time to contemplate the necessity of his grand impetuosity, bringing fire to all mortals in the first place—but do we? Despite the "strange preexistence" of an "orientation and anticipation"[60] within us, the god, the Promethean will within us, we would seem to find much harder to locate.

The issue of tragic being is both necessary and challenging for hope. Like death, tragic being demonstrates the instability of hope—and this is of benefit to hope but also constitutes a potential reversion. What is unstable within hope reinforces the idea that hope can go forward as much as it can regress. Ultimately, Zeus might never relent, he might never be moved by Artemis's tears, he might never feel the need to send Hercules as his emissary, Hercules might never arrive, he might find the apples of the Hesperides without needing Prometheus's directions, his arrow might miss the eagle, and Prometheus might, in any case, be bluffing as to his possession of secret knowledge that would ensure Zeus's downfall.[61] And, as Franz Kafka would say, there remains the "inexplicable mass of rock."[62] What we want to know is what we cannot yet know: whether attempts to defy authority and to seek freedom for all are destined to fail.

Will hope be realized and just as quickly evaporate? With the benefit of the greatest, most powerful hope, we might sense the divine, the marvelous that can, at its best, enable us "to see around the corner, where different, unfamiliar life may be going on," as Bloch wishes (*PoH*, 1193). But what if hope is repeatedly disappointed—do we start to doubt if it is ever realizable? In the battle for hope, the constant wonder is whether those who would deny freedom will always be on the winning side, and this might be a source of enervation as much as potential provocation.

Freedom, Bloch argues, implies a "release from something," and this makes for emptiness. We need to be emptied out; we need a "purifying emptiness" (*Atheism*, 18). And the attempt to achieve this changes something about constraint itself rather than simply momentarily displacing its intention. This underscores the tragedy of tragic being. Only when the courageous have become essential do they die or endure punishment. But this immediately returns us to the question of what this release into emptiness is for and what direction humanity might take in the realm of hope. Bloch's most suggestive riposte to this would be to emphasize that whether we choose to use it or not, humanity has a freedom of transition. We can be Luciferian makers of consciousness, creators of light, and changers of the world; we can find a Paracletan will, a morally engaged capacity for the concern of others. And there is a relationship between the contradictions of freedom and hope, freedom and courage, rage and hope. Hope reshapes freedom as much as freedom must shape the hope it generates. This link is important because, without the urge and rage for freedom, humanity will not have freedom, and if this is the case, then freedom is likewise unable to rebound back on any Promethean courage we might be able to muster. Wherever salvation exists, Bloch says, inverting this argument, "danger increases" (*Literary Essays*, 345). The zero-point here must then shift between the "adamantine wedge's stubborn edge," the shaft being driven straight through Prometheus's chest, and what this implies (the preparedness of any pitiless Hephaestus to do the bidding of the powerful) *and* Prometheus's rage and "blind hope" crying out on the desolate, dreary, "joyless rock" at the end of the world.[63] In other words, the risk of defeat and the likelihood of a continued triumph for the forces of repression are always part of the attempt to overcome. These are, of course, high stakes in the revolt of the people to the sacred mountain.

The Problem of a Wolf-like Nature: "Homo homini lupus"

Typhon gives birth to the ravening liver-eater because he seethes with revenge. He teaches his children that all humans are the creation of their uncle, Prometheus, and are incarnations of evil. His motivation is not complex; it is, indeed, shockingly simple. His elongated hands and legs writhing in snakes, his eyes throbbing with fire, his enormous body covered in hysterically flapping wings—he is repulsive, even to his own brothers. And for this he is prepared to hurl mountains, destroy cities, and assist in condemning those close to him to eternal punishment. He is the ruthless seeker of vengeance, the original "man being wolf to man."[64] Giving expression to a wolfish nature is not the key to some supposed human essence, but it does bring into question a sense of any straightforward path to the *humanum*. More fundamentally still, it makes us question where we are in relation to the openness that the *humanum* entails and whether it is not the cracked surface and its dull darkness that gives us meaning. For while the *humanum* must be equally open to "everything and nothing," its subjective element must also imply a searching "for the where to and what for" of not only being but better being.[65]

For this to be something other than endless searching and never finding, an orientation through suffering and away from dehumanization must be its antagonistic basis. Hegel, Feuerbach, and Marx took as their starting point human self-alienation—the clear sense that being and its active energy condition everything. For Bloch, there is being whose attempts to change the world, whose relations with others, occur in an actual and yet "not-yet" existing sense (*POH*, 1323). Unguaranteed and at the same time unprevented, there is available to us what is genuine in us (*Spirit*, 166). But at the same time he repeatedly reminds us that, given the opportunity, disregard and nastiness will prevail. And so what we have is a difficult and problematic conceptualization of an anticipatory consciousness. To transcend is not to realize the true, there is no lifting of the veil; it is to begin. That this can coincide with something "genuine" in us—perhaps "substantial" would be a better way to phrase it—is something to be arrived at, something to be tested. Bloch undoubtedly understands that what we are or could be is not fate or endless recurrence and yet, because it is the *humanum* that awaits a realization and because interventions in any passage toward this involve a telic content, there are values he assumes must exist rather than a bare emptiness. It is this that we approach with a world-weary wariness today, not because we actually believe in our own emptiness, indeed, far from it—we stuff all kinds of delusions into a sense of who we are—but perhaps because the assumption that we "enter as good and depart as better," as the inscription at the temple of Aesculapius reads, strikes us as ambitiously hopeful. Are we still able to say in the decay of today not only that there is something not yet finished and fully shaped but that this something is still open and confused, that there are ciphers in hollow space? (*Heritage*, 223, 221). And if we do, how, then, do we contend with the wolf within our midst?

Bloch asks us to consider the image of the serpent. Its meaning is complex, both "seductive but also rousing." It contains both poison and healing. It is the "dragon of the abyss" but also the "lightning high-above." It is the bringer of sorrow and promise (*Atheism*, 85). And its promise also is not straightforward. The serpent tells Adam he can be like God, wanting forbidden, concealed wisdom, the wisdom of renewal and divine intoxication, the fruit of the Tree of Knowledge of good and evil. But with an experience only of the coarsely drawn garden of animal baseness and no knowledge to bring to Paradise, Adam is expelled into the fear, rage, and vengeance of the "lower world." In clearly gnostic fashion, the serpent, Bloch argues, represents the shard of light to tempt humanity out of a "hollow submissive slave-guilt" (*Atheism*, 86). And this light persists, confusing and informing those kindred "nocturnal chthonian" spirits. *This* serpent is not the collection of hissing emanations from Typhon's thighs, the vipered body deliberately fathering Prometheus's tormenting eagle; it is not Zarathustra's serpent wound comfortably around its eagle's neck, its appearance at noon heralding Zarathustra's desire to return to his Dionysian spirit by sloughing off his demiurge skin.[66] Bloch's image of the serpent, I would argue, connects with the tragically heroic attempt to break through times in which wrongfulness and injustice are perpetuated. It represents a zero-point from which renewal is possible. Despite the punishment, the timidity, and reluctance and despite its problematic promise, humanity has sought the fruit of the Tree of Knowledge for a reason. And not even Heracles can subdue the serpent and steal the apples in the garden of the Hesperides without the assistance of Atlas. It requires a certain overcoming, a breakthrough, a departure from the self. And it is this issue that under-lies the difficulty of any metamorphosis today.

To seek emancipation conveys us directly into the contradictions of deep sorrow and scant promise. We face death in ever more unnatural ways and are entombed by its shadow; the most plaintive cries for jus-tice are hindered and shackled in ways that might give even Prometheus pause. And still the strange fear that the apple at which we grasp, which we are balefully fortuitous to have discovered, will remain for us unripe. But in the "sublimity of the tragic world," defiance and hope emerge in and against a feeling that "something is not quite right" about the tragic being's downfall.[67] This remains a powerful challenge to any resignation to the given world.

Conclusion: "A Rethinking of the World Is at the Door"

Beyond the Zero-Point: "We are or could be what the forest dreams"

It is difficult today to contend that much about hope has not been di-verted into wishful thinking, often in gimmicky, greedy, self-interested ways with a narrowing down of a sense of the mystery of being or, worse still, that it has not been channeled into cold, calculating acts of disre-gard for all except one's own monstrous self. If the "thousand folds" of being still buttress the self, their distinctiveness dissolves and dissipates into an uninteresting, unbroken sameness. It is not that everything is a lie but the space for exodus is narrow, and we find it difficult to sense much of a navigable entanglement of humanity and world. Kafka's insistence that there is an abundance of hope but none for us seems only all the more pertinent to current conditions.[68] Do we then assume that there is simply a presumptuous belief that the truth of Isis has already been re-vealed and that we can blithely, inconsequentially outstare her, or would an overwhelming skepticism or insufficient curiosity to even want to lift the veil greet any such attempt in any case?

Bloch's most interesting and challenging claim in relation to hope is that it involves danger and fundamental insecurity and that this is its dark ambivalence. At its most difficult, it approaches and resides in a zero-point of emptiness and darkness. But this is a place where fear creates yearning and longing against that which the darkness most obscures and depreciates. The tenebrous realities of death and tragic being can provide a motivating uncertainty in which a renewal might occur. As we have considered, the true image at Saïs is the figure of the self-encounter, the encounter that sees the darkness and its light of what is not yet known but sees beyond this as well. This is the horizon toward which Bloch's whole compelling story of hope is directed. It is a discontinuous, troubling state that brings with it different angles of destructiveness, new serpents lying in wait, and a remembered or anticipated "dangerous abyss."[69] We could be "Dionysiacally opening and turning" with collected impulse, we could be overhauling with Promethean adventure, but instead of attaining a "coactive" status with the self-encounter, uncertainty seems to be the very reason why the tragic battle seems both close to and yet far removed from us.[70] A relationship still exists, of course, between the encounter and hope but perhaps not all glowering rage and every daydream is the suppressed battle between Lucifer and the demiurge. Indeed, is what we experience in gnashing resentment and, equally, in banal, self-aggrandizing not the end result of an extended time of frustrated hope?

When a Promethean will unites intensely, perhaps excessively, with the contents of hope and occasionally breaks through, and when the zero-point of death carries with it the significance of life, then perhaps these infrequent and yet timely examples of exceeding the limits is sufficient. The exodus in life and the promise offered by a hope against hope are a metamorphosis as well, but only by shifting the rage and exuberance against living death and, in all expectation, of unjust suffering into a consciousness of a freedom beyond enslaved life. Each extreme difficulty of life—death and tragic being—offers something that disturbs the given in a departure, an exit, an exodus, but only via a zero-point are limits exceeded. Seneca writes that "fear follows hope," and perhaps we can add that hope can follow fear or, more tentatively, like Job, that after darkness "we hope for light."[71] The conditions for hoping are as much refracted through empowering capacities as they are the limitations to and distractions from the ability to hope and wonder. The emptiness of diversion can, however, become misdirected intoxication, the endless pull of sickly sweet dreams and deceptively enlivening rage (*Heritage*, 54). It is perfectly possible for the self to become brutalized and still dream. Likewise, feelings of discontentment, even those in which there might be recognition of one's sense of imprisonment, can merely persist. The wolf forages on rage and the dreamer undoubtedly possesses hope, but one is too much and the other is not enough. Both lack a metamorphosis into hope. As we have seen, the zero-point of fear into death requires the dream of the new, just as the zero-point of Promethean suffering and Paracletan intercession requires rage and courage. Of course, distraction or rupture, intoxication or provocation, it is not merely the wishfulness of the dream that matters: "One can also just dream," Bloch reminds us, of "having one more sausage" (*Traces*, 26). The dream's fulfillment, which might falter on its own success, can also keep us indefinitely suspended in the darkness out of which desire first arises.

It is as much the undecidedness of the world and how we have learned or unlearned to engage with this that shapes a waking dream from a lived nightmare. And this is Bloch's real strength, in both detecting instances of the impulse toward hope—the sparks in everything we shape—and in understanding the problems that emerge within hope itself, transformed as it is by the dark and uncertain ground of the world. Indeed, Bloch's central theoretical question concerns not merely what it is to hope but what it is to hope in a world of alienated disenchantment where we dream alone and in the dark of an "enormous night" (*Traces*, 148). The actual significance of the dream is in what festers and gathers within it as a persistent eruption of types of uneasiness with the existing world and dissatisfaction with who we are. It is an engagement with an inheritance as much as a "trying out," of leaving behind an imprisoned, unfree existence (*Atheism*, 198).

"What to seek, what to flee" remains humanity's conundrum. For us, the ones who do not yet possess ourselves in hope, to recognize what it is that we are, to understand the sign of our incompleteness and indeterminacy, we need to find a way back through to what Bloch takes to be the fundamental problem of life—our relation to each other. It is here that the dark, deep dream that tends toward enclosing the self can instead suggest a "horizon of humanization," one which "transgresses all limits" (*Experimentum*, 102). Each step poses a further question; freedom is always the possibility of another occurrence (*PoH*, 934).

The forest, Bloch tells us, "draws us in," it "looks at us unfathomably," it contains what is "secret and unrevealed."[72] But we dream of the forest, and "we walk in the forest and we feel we are or could be what the forest dreams" (*Spirit*, 34). As we have seen, the path through this dark-ness proceeds sometimes enchantedly, sometimes with dread, some-times with an understanding that is not renunciatory but still fulfilling. This is not a paradise, seducing us, waiting for us to fall. In the forest there is death, and there are valiant struggles for life that fail to achieve their aim. But there is also the search for light, longing, and hope. It is here that the full adventure of the shaping subject, being as she wishes to be, can take place. Here, precisely where the wrench of anti-utopian extremes is most turbulently felt, a space that remains open for what is missing can be found and perhaps propagate the "enigmatic shimmer" through which an "overhauling" of the world could take place."[73] The very difficulties we encounter in occupying a space between the self and other, between ourselves and our world is precisely that which needs the perspective of hope, the "long, sunlit corridor with a door at the far end" (*Spirit*, 9). The corridor can, of course, only be illuminated when a capacity to create images of a better life is activitated, where images are driven at their most fundamental by a searching, a hunger, and a wish to overcome dissatisfaction. Without this element of hope, the door re-mains firmly shut. It is perhaps in the persistence of this question, as damaged and as threatened as it presently is, that we can locate a basis for hope. But more importantly still, Bloch writes persuasively of a need to *learn* hope as much as we have learned fear. It is only really in doing so that we might find something available to us in order to venture beyond (*POH*, 3). Barriers, he tells us, are there to be crossed, and if they are felt as such, they have already been.[74]

Notes

1   Ernst Bloch, *Literary Essays*, trans. Andrew Joron et al. (Palo Alto, CA: Stanford University Press, 1998), 345. Henceforth *Literary Essays* in parentheses in the text.

2   The idea of consciousness influenced by the role of the citadel has long interested phi-losophers from the Stoics to Berlin and Werckmeister. See Isaiah Berlin, "Two Concepts of Liberty," in *Four Essays on Liberty* (Oxford: Oxford University Press, 1969) and Otto Karl Werckmeister, *Citadel Culture* (Chicago: University of Chicago Press, 1991).

3   Ernst Bloch, *Heritage of Our Times*, trans. Neville and Stephen Plaice (Berkeley: University of California Press, 1990), 145. Henceforth *Heritage* in parentheses in the text.

4   Ernst Bloch, *The Spirit of Utopia*, trans. Anthony A. Nasser (Palo Alto, CA: Stanford University Press, 2000), 161. Henceforth *Spirit* in parentheses in the text.

5   Siegfried Kracauer, "Murder Trials and Society," *The Weimar Republic Sourcebook*, ed. Anton Kaes, Martin Jay, and Edward Dimendberg (Berkeley: University of California Press, 1994), 740.

6   Theodor W. Adorno, "Culture Industry Reconsidered," *New German Critique* 6 (fall 1975): 16.

7   For a discussion of the *Denkbild* tradition in the work of some twentieth-century German writers, such as Benjamin, Bloch, Kracauer, and Adorno, see Gerhard Richter, *Thought-Images: Frankfurt School Writers' Reflections from Damaged Life* (Palo Alto, CA: Stanford University Press, 2007).

8   Bloch's work mentions these themes repeatedly as fundamental examples of the non-utopian. See *POH*, 16, 112, and *Spirit*, 222.

9   The expression "roaring nothingness" is one Bloch borrows from the dramatist Georg Büchner's play *Woyzeck* (*POH*, 301). Bloch, *Spirit*, 129; Ernst Bloch, *Traces*, trans. Anthony A. Nassar (Stanford: Stanford University Press, 2006), 99. Henceforth *Traces* in parentheses in the text.

10   In various essays included in the collection *Heritage of Our Times* and elsewhere, Bloch refers to the "zero-point." See, for example, Bloch, *Heritage*, 305.

11   Bloch refers to this idea in a discussion with Adorno. Ernst Bloch, *The Utopian Function of Art and Literature: Selected Essays*, trans. Jack Zipes and Frank Mecklenburg (Cambridge, MA: MIT Press, 1988) 15.

12   Bloch, *Heritage of Our Times*, 111, 112, 209, 8.

13   See F. W. J. Schelling, *First Outline of a System of the Philosophy of Nature*, trans. Keith R. Peterson (New York: SUNY Press, 2004).

14   See Johann Wolfgang von Goethe, *Faust: A Tragedy*, trans. Walter Arndt, ed. Cyrus Hamlin (New York: W. W. Norton, 2001), part 1, scene v.

15   Bloch, *Spirit*, 144, 202. Ernst Bloch, "Recollections of Walter Benjamin," in *On Walter Benjamin: Critical Essays and Recollections*, ed. Gary Smith (Cambridge, MA: MIT Press, 1991), 343.

16   Meister Eckhart, *The Book of Divine Consolation, from the Book of "Benedictus,"* in *Meister Eckhart: Selections from His Essential Writings*, ed. Emilie Griffin, trans. Edmund Colledge (New York: HarperCollins, 2005), 134.

17   Ferdinand Tönnies, *Community and Society (Gemeinschaft und Gesellschaft)*, trans. and ed. Charles P. Loomis (East Lansing: Michigan State University Press, 1957), 33–102.

18   Ernst Bloch, *Atheism in Christianity: The Religion of the Exodus and the Kingdom*, trans. J. T. Swann (New York: Herder and Herder, 1972), 221. Henceforth *Atheism* in parentheses in the text.

19   See Karl Marx, "A Contribution to the Critique of Hegel's *Philosophy of Right*," in *Early Writings*, intro. Lucio Colletti, trans. Rodney Livingstone and Gregor Benton (Harmondsworth, UK: Penguin, 1984), 251.

20   See Karl Marx, *Grundrisse: Foundations of the Critique of Political Economy*, trans. Martin Nicolaus (Harmondsworth, UK: Penguin, 1973), 307.

21   The "old enemy" is also death.

22   The idea of the "sublime," as it appears in Kant, Schopenhauer, Hegel and Schelling, informs Bloch's use of the concept.

23   See F. W. J. Schelling, *The Ages of the World*, trans. Jason M. Wirth (Albany: SUNY Press, 2000).

24   Friedrich Nietzsche, *Thus Spoke Zarathustra: A Book for All and None*, ed. Adrian del Caro and Robert B. Pippen, trans. Adrian del Caro (Cambridge: Cambridge University Press, 2006), 1: §4, "Zarathustra's Prologue," 7.

25   Ernst Bloch, *Essays on the Philosophy of Music*, trans. Peter Palmer (Cambridge: Cambridge University Press, 1985), 196, 197.

26   Ovid, "The Transformation of Syrinx into Reeds," *Metamorphoses*, book 1, ed. Sir Samuel Garth, trans. John Dryden et al. (Hertfordshire, UK: Wordsworth, 1998), lines 689–721.

27   Nietzsche, *Thus Spoke Zarathustra*, 1: §2, "Of the Bestowing Virtue," 58.

28   Lynn Li Donnici considers the association between Artemis Ephesia and Isis in her article, "The Images of Artemis Ephesia and Greco-Roman Worship: A Reconsideration," *Harvard Theological Review* 85, no. 4 (October 1992): 389–415.

29   Novalis, *The Novices at Sais*, trans. Ralph Manheim (Brooklyn: Archipelago Books, 2005); Friedrich Schiller, "The Veiled Image at Sais," in *The Poems and Ballads of Schiller*, trans. Sir Edward Bulwer-Lytton (Edinburgh: William Blackwood, 1852).

30   Friedrich Nietzsche, *The Gay Science: With a Prelude in Rhymes and an Appendix of Songs*, trans. Walter Kaufman (New York: Random House, 1974), preface for the 2nd ed., 38.

31   Ernst Bloch, in Walter Benjamin, *On Hashish*, trans. Howard Eiland et al. (Cambridge, MA: Belknap Press, 2006), 30.

32   See Friedrich Schiller, *On the Aesthetic Education of Man*, trans. Reginald Snell (New York: Dover, 2004), 74, 79, 67.

33   According to Bloch, Hegel's tragic individual reaps only the fruits of his own deeds and "these fruits are those of the most sublime destruction and death." Ernst Bloch, *Natural Law and Human Dignity*, trans. Dennis J. Schmidt (Cambridge, MA: MIT Press, 1986), 252.

34   The "mysterious way leads inwards," Novalis writes in his "Miscellaneous Observations." Novalis, *Philosophical Writings*, trans. and ed. Margaret Mahony Stoljar (Albany: SUNY Press, 1997), aphorism 17, 25.

35   In his letter to the Romans, Paul writes "in hope he believed against hope." Rom. 4:18.

36   Bloch, *Atheism in Christianity*, 258; Bloch, *Traces*, 130.

37   *POH*, 1171; Bloch, *Traces*, 103; *POH*, 1173.

38   Ludwig Feuerbach, *The Essence of Christianity*, trans. George Eliot (New York: Prometheus Books, 1989).

39   Nietzsche, *The Gay Science*, book 2: §125, "The Madman," 181.

40 "Sacred horror" is Bataille's term for the sense of the miraculous that emerges with prehistoric humanity. See Georges Bataille, *The Cradle of Humanity: Prehistoric Art and Culture*, ed. Stuart Kendall, trans. Michelle Kendall and Stuart Kendall (New York: Zone Books, 2009), 102.

41 In an appreciation of the work of the nineteenth-century writer Gottfried Keller, Bloch uses this expression, the "emptiness of nothingness," to describe Keller's use of the image of the journey into death (*PoH*, 1149, 1174).

42 Frank Wedekind, *Spring Awakening: A Play*, trans. Jonathan Franzen (New York: Faber and Faber, 2007), act 2, scene 6: 47, 45, 46.

43 Émile Zola, *The Masterpiece*, trans. Thomas Walton and Roger Pearson (Oxford: Oxford University Press, 1999). Bloch mentions Zola's work in *Literary Essays*, 71.

44 Levinas sees limitations to Heidegger's view of being as ultimate event, as against Bloch's "ontological modulations" of the incompleteness of self and world in relation to the sense of threat that death presents. Emmanuel Levinas, *God, Death, and Time*, trans. Bettina Bergo (Palo Alto, CA: Stanford University Press, 2000) 105, 104; Georges Bataille, *The Unfinished System of Nonknowledge*, ed. Stuart Kendall, trans. Michelle Kendall and Stuart Kendall (Minneapolis: University of Minnesota Press, 2001), 119. Death, for Bataille, is unable to teach us anything, for it is most fundamentally the end of thought. Thinking on death or perhaps thinking on the death of thought comprising this "practical joke" is a type of rebellion, a nonacceptance. Bataille, *The Unfinished System of Nonknowledge*, 128.

45 Bloch refers to death as the "hardest counterblow to utopia" (*PoH*, 16; *Traces*, 42).

46 Michel de Montaigne, *The Essays of Michel de Montaigne*, trans. M. A. Screech (Harmondsworth, UK: Penguin, 1991), 1:20, 89.

47 *Heritage*, 328; *PoH*, 32, 1279. Bloch derives the idea of the Babbitt from Sinclair Lewis's 1922 novel *Babbitt* (New York: Bantam Books, 2007). Bloch acknowledges Siegfried Kracauer's perceptive analysis of the employees. See Bloch's essay "Artificial Centre" (1929): On Kracauer's 'The Employees,'" in *Heritage*, 24–26. See Siegfried Kracauer, *The Salaried Masses: Duty and Distraction in Weimar Germany*, trans. Quintin Hoare (London: Verso, 1998).

48 *Heritage*, 148, 25, 26. Kracauer writes: "The flight of the images is the flight from revolution and from death." Kracauer, *The Salaried Masses*, 94.

49 Bloch refers to the creatural in various senses. See, for example, *PoH*, 221. The expression "creatural will" Bloch derives from Jakob Böhme, who uses the idea of the "creatural" throughout many of his works. See, for example, Jacob Boehme, *Mysterium Magnum Part One or an Exposition of the First Book of Moses Called Genesis*, 2 vols., trans. John Sparrow, ed. C. J. Barker (London: John M. Watkins, 1965).

50 Bloch takes the term *numinous shudder* from Rudolf Otto, the German theologian and author of the 1917 work *The Idea of the Holy*. Rudolf Otto, *The Idea of the Holy*, trans. John W. Harvey (Oxford: Oxford University Press, 1958).

51 *Heritage*, 327; *PoH*, 1212, 975.

52 Aeschylus, *Prometheus Bound*, trans. Herbert Weir Smyth (Cambridge, MA: Harvard University Press, 1926).

53   For Schelling, Prometheus is the "greatest human inner character, and thereby also the true archetype of tragedy." F. W. J. Schelling, *The Philosophy of Art*, ed. and trans. Douglas W. Stott (Minneapolis: University of Minnesota Press, 1989), 261.

54   Aeschylus, *Prometheus Bound*, line 384.

55   Aeschylus, *Prometheus Bound*, line 371. In other versions of the myth of Osiris and Isis, Typhon murders Isis's husband, Osiris, an act for which Isis seeks revenge.

56   Aeschylus, *Prometheus Bound*, line 927.

57   Aeschylus, *Prometheus Bound*, lines 513–14.

58   Hesiod's *Prometheus* talks of Prometheus's liver growing by night as much as the eagle could devour by day. Hesiod, *Theogony, Works and Days, Testimonia*, ed. and trans. Glenn W. Most (Cambridge, MA: Harvard University Press, 2006), 507.

59   Bloch talks of the contamination of drives and the will by egocentrism (*Spirit*, 189).

60   This is the basis of what can become a "concrete anticipation" in latency and tendency. Ernst Bloch, *Experimentum Mundi: Frage, Kategorien des Herausbringens, Praxis* (Frankfurt: Suhrkamp, 1975), 147.

61   This range of possibilities I have derived from a variety of sources dealing with the Promethean myth, including Aeschylus, Callimachus in his *Hymns, Epigrams, Select Fragments*, trans. Stanley Lombardo and Diane Rayor (Baltimore: Johns Hopkins University Press, 1988) and Pseudo-Hyginus in the *Astronomica*, in *The Myths of Hyginus*, ed. and trans. Mary Grant (Lawrence: University of Kansas Publications, 1960).

62   Franz Kafka, "Prometheus," in *Franz Kafka: The Complete Stories*, trans. Willa and Edwin Muir, ed. Nahum N. Glatzer (New York: Schocken Books, 1971), 432.

63   Aeschylus, *Prometheus Bound*, lines, 64, 269, 30.

64   The expression "man as a wolf unto man" is attributed to Plautus in his *Asinaria*. Titus Maccius Plautus, *Amphitryon, The Comedy of Asses, The Pot of Gold, The Two Bacchises. The Captives*, in vol. 1 of *Plautus*, trans. Paul Nixon (Cambridge, MA: Harvard University Press, 1916).

65   *Atheism*, 221; Ernst Bloch, *A Philosophy of the Future*, trans. John Cumming (New York: Herder and Herder, 1970), 140.

66   Nietzsche, *Thus Spoke Zarathustra*, 1: §10, "Zarathustra's Prologue," 15.

67   *POH*, 431; *Spirit*, 224.

68   This was Kafka's response to the following question put to him by Max Brod: "So could there be hope beyond this particular manifestation of the world?" Franz Kafka in discussion with Max Brod, cited by Walter Benjamin, "Franz Kafka—Zur zehnten Wiederkehr seines Todestages," in *Über Literatur* (Frankfurt: Fischer, 1959), 159.

69   *Atheism*, 87, 85; *Spirit*, 119.

70   *Traces*, 104; *Spirit*, 223.

71   Lucius Anneaus Seneca, *Moral Epistles*, vol. 1, trans. Richard M. Gummere (Cambridge, MA: Harvard University Press, 1917–25), Epistle V, 7. Job 17: 11–13.

72   *Traces*, 141; *POH*, 882.

73   *Spirit*, 58; *POH*, 1056.

74   Bloch, *The Utopian Function of Art and Literature*, 11.

9

A Marxist Poetics:

Allegory and Reading in

David Miller | ***The Principle of Hope***

So we must turn to allegory, the method dear to men with their eyes opened.
—Philo Judeus

Allegory has by its very nature extended application for it is a kind of
representation founded deep in the nature of speech and thought.
—Philip August Boeckh

In short, it's good to think in stories, too.
—Ernst Bloch

Reading *The Principle of Hope* can be a demanding and even forbidding task. Even readers who come to the book already well versed in German philosophy and literary history often confess to being bewildered by the range of its intellectual reference points and the depth of its philosophical and theological expertise. Should the reader engage in a literary, philosophical, sociological, or theological reading?

These aesthetic and interpretative challenges are often presented as a problem of Bloch's style. Vincent Geoghegan adopts this line of reasoning in his critical biography of Bloch, in which he claims that Bloch's style is "forbidding," "opaque," and full of "overblown" rhetoric.[1] Faced with the apparently meandering conceptual paths and the intricate interlocking literary, philosophical, and theological connections, many critics and translators are apt to blame the form of the book for obscuring its philosophical and political message. J. K. Dickinson, for example, characterizes Bloch's method of composition as "baroque," and for Ronald Aronson, Bloch is quite simply "a torture to read."[2] The traditional and altogether rational impulse when faced with such apparent resistance to any process of stable reading is to clarify rather than engage in immediate interpretation as such. In the case of *The Principle of Hope*, more often than not, this configuration involves the glossing of the philosophical and conceptual density of the book, followed by a series of evasive gestures aimed at alleviating or bypassing the "style," so as to assuage the effort the book demands from the reader. In "Reading *The Principle of Hope*," Douglas Kellner adopts this approach in order to smooth the path for the uninitiated reader: "If Bloch is to have any real impact on political and cultural analysis in the English-speaking world, efforts must be made to explain and interpret what he is up to, and convincing arguments must be provided by us to persuade people that *reading* Bloch is worth the time and effort."[3] Bloch's "style" gets in the way of his arguments, and the formal strangeness of the book acts as a barrier to wider popular consumption. Even as an astute a commentator on critical theory as Stephen Bronner argues that there is an esoteric and Neoplatonic strand to Bloch's thinking. Although Bronner is an enthusiastic supporter of Bloch's "romantic anti-capitalism," he nonetheless finds Bloch's "free flowing . . . expressionistic literary style" problematic and implies that this is one of the primary reasons that his "categories" and "formulations" lack the criteria of analytical and "logical validity."[4]

Yet as Theodor Adorno recognized, the impulse to "correct" Bloch's "philosophical flaws" is often the result of a misreading. In "The Handle, the Pot, and Early Experience," Adorno argues that it is misguided to "criticize" Bloch's offenses against "the ceremonials of intellectual discipline." Moreover, Adorno goes on to argue that Bloch's rejection of any "abominable resignation to methodology" is actually the result of an intricate and deliberate formal choice that emerges from Bloch's perspective on critical thinking in general. For Adorno, the initial "bewilderment" experienced on first reading Bloch is the necessary first moment of a complex and demanding encounter that leads to the possibility of increasing levels of *unexpected* insight. To take the initial resistances of Bloch's work as simply the result of intellectual eccentricity or modish literary over-embellishment is to misconstrue the deep literary and hermeneutic roots of Bloch's critical enterprise. By this account, the apparent stylistic resistances are not a regrettable flaw but rather a necessary primary stage of estrangement or discomfort that will lead the reader into a journey of increasingly intensified levels of awareness. As Adorno phrases it, reading Bloch is a risk in which the habitual expectations and subjective false security of the reader are "not self-enclosed and self-positing like an idyllic inwardness but rather a space through which the thinking hand leads one to an abundance of content not offered by outward life."[5] The initial moment of stuttering readability then, mirrors Bloch's philosophical position that we embark upon the journey of discovery precisely because we *are* bewildered. This alternative and perhaps less repressed version of what Adorno terms "amazement" connects Bloch's work to, rather than severs it from, the older philosophical and hermeneutic traditions, albeit in a radically altered way. (In this context Adorno references Plato's dictum that the philosophical quest for an alternative world "originates in amazement.")[6] This implies that the difficulties of reading Bloch are more an intentionally arranged ordeal in which we put our preconceived orders of understanding to the test rather than some compositional fault. Certainly, in a critical engagement such as this, one can no longer rely upon established logical or epistemological categories or accumulated empirical evidence, for these systems of knowledge also fall within the categories that are being put into question.

Adorno aside, in the passages that follow I want to show that hostile and defensive reactions to Bloch's "style," while in many respects accurate in terms of describing the initial difficulties of reading the *Principle of Hope*, inevitably lead to a serious misunderstanding of the essential dynamics of the *form* of the book. By extending the notion of "style" to encompass a dialectical concept of "form," one takes a step closer to grasping the fact that the form of the book is not the result of "baroque" idiosyncrasy but rather an utterly consistent compositional strategy. A clearer understanding of the form of *The Principle of Hope* will show that far from being a stylistic anomaly or "problem," the difficulties of its form are *intrinsic* to its "message" and are in fact entirely commensurate with its hermeneutic agenda and political categories. However, this by no means implies any lessening of the resistances the book presents, for as I will argue later, the possibility of a *finished* and complete reading is incompatible with the book's own claim that "understanding must repeatedly prove itself anew" (*POH*, 25).

When the literary difficulties of *The Principle of Hope* are approached in this way, the complex interlocking form and discontinuous but connected levels of conceptualization become a necessary ordeal that the reader must journey through in order to arrive at some crucial moment of illumination. By taking in philosophy, theology, politics, and art, the book projects the possibility of a complete but alternative universe of meaning. What the form of the book offers, then, is a different system of reality that exists as the shadowy and veiled counterpart to the everyday world of habitual experience. This alternative world is attached to the recognizable objects and experiences of social existence, but also acts as the critical counterweight by which the new landscape of existence can be conceived. Under this pattern of thought, the "real," including all the intellectual and theological disciplines that purport to define and explain it, is the index and degraded pattern of the better world that exists beyond its surface textures. In other words, the form of the book encompasses both social critique and utopian projection. These are considerations that go well beyond the simple question of the incorporation of literary devices into philosophical prose, for they indicate that the true "critic," as the young Georg Lukács wrote in *Soul and Form*, is one who "glimpses destiny in forms."[7]

The notion of a complete and serene reading is also inimical to the book's particular version of time. Any claim to absolute understanding in the *present* would imply a perfect reader of a perfected book in a perfected world; this is a situation the book projects as a desirable possibility but rejects as an impossible falsehood in the present. The impossibility of a full incorporation of the book into our preexisting expectations is one of the results of Bloch's concept of *What-Is-in-Possibility*. To believe that what Bloch calls the "subject-matter" of the book could be realized in the "Here and Now" is actually to entertain an insufficient concept of "realization." For Bloch, this false assumption of complete realization produces only the "melancholy of fulfillment" (*POH*, 299). This is the case because for Bloch there is always a "crack" and a "remainder" that opens out onto some "future society" in all assumptions of completion. It is in this aperture, exposed by the assumption of fulfillment, that the "not yet fulfilled aspect in the fixed material announces itself" (*POH*, 229). As Bloch emphasizes, "there is a great deal that is not fulfilled and made banal through the fulfillment—regardless of the deeper viewpoint that each realization brings a melancholy fulfillment with it" (*POH*, 2). By virtue of its own formulations then, a "fulfilled" reading of *The Principle of Hope* is literally impossible. Thus the object that the language of the book seeks to represent is, in an oddly spectral way, here and not here, waiting silently just beyond its own semantic capabilities. The "other" utopian world can be figured but not fully represented, and so the book functions as an allegory of what could and *should* be. The contours of the redeemed world that hovers on the other side of bourgeois social existence can be glimpsed but not wholly conceived. Unlike previous critical utopian works, such as Thomas More's *Utopia*, for example, Bloch understands that the better life has to be striven for rather than simply discovered. As Bloch makes clear, at the moment technological modernity fails to deliver on its promises of a liberated life, utopian hope shifts from space to time. It is no longer a preexisting island or city waiting to be found but a moment of "new contents" on the edge of the "not-yet" (*POH*, 215–30, passim). *The Principle of Hope* mirrors this hope-filled longing for "new contents" (that politically redeemed existence will be qualitatively different than the one we already have) by virtue of its complex pattern of surplus *uninterpretability*.[8] It is to the literary language just as much as to the hermeneutic system of the book that this surplus belongs.[9] Further, it is clear that the textual and conceptual superfluity of the book is worked up as both the result of, and possible solution to, the inadequacy or emptiness we sense in contemporary life. This is a condition that is typical of allegory, for allegory is one of the primary modes by which something that is lacking or degraded in the world can be prefigured and outlined against a critical ideal. The most appropriate and obvious analogy is with Dante's *Divine Comedy* and with allegory in general, for as Adorno rightly observed, Bloch's "attitude" is always "that of the allegorist."[10]

It was Fredric Jameson who first grasped the full significance of Adorno's observation that Bloch should be understood as an "allegorist."[11] In *Marxism and Form: Twentieth-Century Theories of Literature*, Jameson suggested that the work of Bloch should be "grasped" as an attempt to furnish Marxism with a full-blown "allegorical hermeneutics." Taking his cue from the Dante analogy, Jameson writes that Bloch should be understood "as an attempt to do for Marxism what the four levels of meaning did for Medieval Christianity, to furnish a hermeneutic of great flexibility and depth." Having made the assertion, however, he simultaneously acknowledges that there is a "suspicion . . . floating over the whole enterprise." Given the specifically "medieval" and "Christian" version of allegory that Jameson outlines, this "suspicion" relates to an implied "affinity between Marxism and religion." This "affinity," Jameson claims, is based on a shared "historical situation" in which both movements attempted to project a "universal culture" and versions of radical social change out of a period of decline and repression. It is therefore no real surprise, according to Jameson, that the "intellectual instruments" and "techniques" of Marxism bear a "structural similarity" to the figural and allegorical configurations of medieval hermeneutics.[12] As impressive and suggestive as this formulation is, it is clear that there are a number of very important extensions and clarifications that must be made in order to deepen our understanding of the complex formal configurations and literary and theoretical implications of allegory for Bloch's writing.

The first point that can be made is that an emphasis upon medieval Christian allegory tends to obscure the substantial philosophical, literary, and hermeneutic heritage that lies behind the mode. This broader inheritance is important not only because it sheds some light on the various strands of Bloch's intellectual and philosophical influences, but also because it represents an additional and *alternative* mode of conducting philosophical and theoretical inquiry that is woven into the very texture of Bloch's work. A concentration solely on medieval allegory tends to bypass the continued elaboration and importance of allegory in the work of thinkers such as Philip August Boeckh, for example, who are significant within the history of German philology and hermeneutics and with whom Bloch was utterly familiar. A conception of allegory that relies too heavily upon medieval Christian versions will also tend to suppress the importance of those Romantic writers such as Ludwig Tieck and Novalis, who sought to reconfigure allegory and fairy tale within German literary culture.[13] Such writers, along with Hegel, Marx, and Kierkegaard, figured prominently in the eager discussions between Bloch and the young Lukács in their student days at Heidelberg.[14]

Taking Bloch principally as a version of the Christian and medieval allegorist also overlooks the substantial inheritance of Judaic writings on allegory. For example, patterns derived from Hebrew hermeneutics and the Kabbalah can be traced in Bloch's work, and as Jürgen Habermas has recognized, this plays a role in the kind of expectations and patterns of interpretations imposed upon the reader.[15] Finally, there is the intellectual inheritance of Stoic allegorical commentary on Homeric and poetic texts that had a significant impact on the debates that took place within German hermeneutics in the nineteenth century. Such debates, principally but not exclusively concerned with allegory and the status of a reliable hermeneutic theory, are not merely of historical interest and can still be traced in the work of important modern Marxist theorists such Peter Szondi.[16] With its troubling of theological, poetic, and philosophical boundaries, Stoic allegory has more than coincidental affinities with Bloch's mode of composition and with his refusal to conform to institutionally delineated subject areas. To approach the work of Bloch principally as a version of medieval Christian hermeneutics certainly brings one closer to recognizing the singular importance of allegory, particularly when it comes to grasping the full extent of his particular contribution to Marxist theory. Yet, on the other hand, the initial insight raises the broader question of the role and significance of allegory *in general* when it comes to engaging with the formal and intellectual difficulties of Bloch's work.

There is a further point that is unavoidable if one takes the idea of Bloch as an allegorist seriously. This is the fact that allegory is not only an interpretative method but also a literary mode. Although Jameson develops his formulation toward a fully conceived Marxist hermeneutics, examining both the ramifications and shape such an interpretative model might take, he says very little about what the figural demands of allegory do to Bloch's whole compositional and theoretical enterprise. Despite his clear recognition of allegory as essential to Bloch's writing, he veers away from a full confrontation with the question of the poetics of allegory. Prefiguring some of the unease shown by subsequent critics when confronted with Bloch's style, Jameson lets the issue rest under terms such as *hieroglyphic*, *enigmatic*, and *mysterious*.[17]

Allegory unavoidably involves a *poetics* as well as a hermeneutics, and it is therefore possible and necessary to consider the poetics of allegory in *The Principle of Hope* in conjunction with the hermeneutics that underpin its claims. By extension, it can be shown that a poetics of allegory is fundamentally attached to the concept of utopia that the book projects, and this in turn has far-reaching ramifications for the version of political hope that the book proposes.[18] The poetics of allegory, therefore, cannot be isolated from the complex demands that *The Principle of Hope* makes upon the reader. A better understanding of the nature and configurations of what can be broadly termed the "allegorical poetics" of the *Principle of Hope* will not only highlight the full explanatory and utopian potential of the book but also go some way to explaining why those commentators who are more familiar with the logical and argumentative procedures of the social sciences find the form of the book so disturbing. It is also clear that the question of allegory in relation to *The Principle of Hope* goes well beyond the straightforward issue of influence and sources and implies not just an "affinity" between Marxism and Christianity as Jameson indicates but also a more general affinity between Marxist theory and allegory.[19]

Terry Eagleton makes a persuasive argument for the affinities between dialectical materialism and allegory, and his assessment has the additional benefit of outlining the basic elements of the allegorical mode: "What might undo the "totalitarian" implications of Kantian aesthetics is the idea of affinity or mimesis—the nonsensuous correspondences between disparate features of the artefact, or more generally the filiations of both kinship and otherness between subject and object, humanity and nature, which might provide an alternative rationality to the instrumental. One might even name this mimesis *allegory*, that figurative mode which relates through difference, preserving the relative autonomy of a set of signifying units while suggesting an affinity with some other range of signifiers."[20]

This mode, as Eagleton argues, "carries significant political implications." Although not explicitly mentioned by Eagleton, at least one major advantage of the allegorical mode is that it maintains a narrative vision of the future without reducing such a gesture to simple determinate and predictable teleology. Allegory therefore does not reduce the literary to the political or vice versa. This idea of a *telos* without determinate teleology is surely part of what Adorno had in mind when he characterized Bloch as an "allegorist."[21]

The projection of a future utopian landscape patterned out of the degraded emblems of the everyday world indicates a complex relationship in the book to the literary heritage of allegorical dream vision.[22] Writing principally of the role of dreams in Freud and Jung, Bloch quickly subverts the idea that Freud can be used to fully explain literary and dream versions of the "wish-landscape." Bloch indicates that literary manifestations of "dream vision" better encapsulate the longing for utopia embedded in dreams. Stories that "contain the utopianizing character" of the "dream landscape" are "non-sublimated" and therefore operate in the "common property" of language (*PoH*, 94). This "common property" of the narratives of dream vision acts as a corrective to the assumed private inwardness of the dreamer supposedly available only to the psychoanalyst. In other words, literary versions of the dream landscape return the "dream wish" to collective ongoing expression, whereas the Freudian model seeks to isolate the utopian wish-landscape in the sublimated realm of the inner mind. Bloch makes the literary power of dream allegory explicit by citing *Faust* and the "circles of Dante's *Paradiso*" as primary examples of his argument. Bloch uses the literary authority of Dante and Goethe in order to claim that literary dream visions "radiate" rather than sublimate "utopian consciousness" (*PoH*, 92–98).

It is not only that *The Principle of Hope* makes a case for the value of dream allegory. The book also enacts the conventions of the genre in the common property of its form. One result of the reader's entanglement in this allegorical dimension of the book is that he or she enacts the role of the dream wanderer or allegorical proxy. In much the same manner as the Christian Everyman of Bunyan's *The Pilgrim's Progress from This World to That Which Is to Come*, the reader is subject to a difficult journey of constant self-questioning as he or she progresses through the book toward some final point of illumination. In this way, the book functions as an allegorical map of the historical journey that hope itself must take.[23] In this sense, the book itself plays Virgil to the reader's Dante. Again, this allegorical pattern is entirely commensurate with the idea that we are "not yet" full and "start out empty" and with Bloch's notion of the "topos of possibility."[24]

As far as the reader goes then, Bloch's commitment to the necessity of bewilderment and its cognates and to what Bloch later elaborates as "positive astonishment" (*PoH*, 312) becomes combined with the ultimately unfulfilled nature of the material of hope and tends toward a certain uninterpretable superfluity. The idea of an uninterpretable surplus also hints at the book as a self-cancelling artifact. The "principle" of hope, both as a force in human history and the book itself, will always fail (knowingly in Bloch's case) to correspond with its stated objective. This is entirely coherent with Bloch's dialectical Marxist outlook, of course, because the "yearning and overhauling image of a world without alienation" (POH, 15) that drives the principle of hope has to be concretely achieved rather than simply stated or imagined. Moreover, the achievement of the unalienated life would render the book itself redundant, and so the book also functions, again knowingly, as an emblem of the moment when it will no longer be needed. In other words, much like the disappearance of the proletariat into the classless communism it ultimately brings about, the book is an allegorical emblem of both the pathos and nobility of its own vanishing. Again, this is not some literary inflected deviation but entirely commensurate with Marxist dialectics, for as Bloch rightly explains, "In Marxism, the act of analyzing the situation is entwined with the enthusiastically prospective act. Both acts are united in the dialectical method, in the pathos of the goal" (POH, 208). Using the emblems of the existing world as the figural index of the better life, allegory remains intrinsically attached to the existing order of things. But it also acts as the critical envisioning of the correction of that order. This intrinsically doubled configuration allows allegory and dialectics to avoid what Bloch calls "utopian fanaticism." What dialectical materialism and allegory have in common, then, is that they maintain a "liberating intention" alongside the "materialistically humane" (POH, 208–9). This is one of the main reasons that Bloch can quote the great utopian allegories of early humanism by the likes of Tommaso Campanella and Francis Bacon, for example, and yet remain confident that he is not impugning his own critical position.[25] Similarly, it is allegory that allows the book to retain the rigor of a method and the dynamism of narrative movement (the story of the journey of hope through the fallen landscape of the commodity-filled world) and at the same time avoid the risk of predetermining its objective.

This doubled allegorical pattern, in which poetic and referential language is intertwined, is also essential to Bloch's notion of the "two truths of the world." In a late interview, Bloch made his determination to exact the maximum possibility from the relationship between literary form and philosophical critique explicit. His insistence on the simultaneous existence of the two truths of the world is emblematic in this case. The two truths are, on the one hand, a "positivist," experiential "fact" based— and a justificatory one—"truth-as-justification-of the world" [*die Welt rechtfertigend*]—and on the other hand, a subversive truth that establishes itself as "truth-as hostile-to-the-world" [*zur Welt feindlich*].[26] For Bloch, Juvenal's *tempestus poeticus* is just one example of this subversive truth. The incorporation of this critical and hostile truth is clearly visible in the form of *The Principle of Hope* and in the seemingly unconventional demands the book makes upon the reader. The doubled allegorical form permits the close and detailed cultural and social analysis, but also inscribes a poetic excess that insists upon its own truth. It would be an odd kind of error to complain that this latter truth does not conform to the analytical categories of the former, for that is precisely its purpose. Although *The Principle of Hope* undoubtedly contains stylistic elements drawn from modern movements such as Expressionism, those formal configurations that at first appear so strange and "bewildering" to the reader can actually be traced to a much older but no less "subversive" lineage of critical and literary writing. I do not suggest that *The Principle of Hope* is simply a philosophical version of *tempestus poeticus*, but rather that this intellectual and formal inheritance necessitates a configuration in which the analytical and empirical claim of "truth-as-justification" is combined with the "value" and ethically based "truth-as-hostile-to-the-world."[27]

One can see from Bloch's own formulations that a certain "ludicrous" gesture toward the "unconstruable" (*PoH*, 299) adheres to the activities and objects of hope, and one must surely accept that reading *The Principle of Hope* is an example of such a hope-filled encounter. This resistance to full hermeneutic assimilation is intrinsic to Bloch's idea of the "melancholy of fulfillment" (*PoH*, 299). Writing of the work of E. T. A. Hoffman and Stendhal, he stresses the worth of the "non-satisfaction and what lies within fulfillment" (*PoH*, 179). Using relations of sexual love as a metaphor, Bloch outlines his idea that a certain sense of "fiasco" always attaches itself to assumptions of absolute consummation and completion. This pattern can be extended to include the relationship of reader and work, so that any claim to simplify and clarify Bloch's works in order to make them more intellectually consumable results in a rather banal "fiasco" (*POH*, 180). In other words, to try and correct *The Principle of Hope* for the sake of some putative average reader is ridiculous (*POH*, 179). A certain sense of unsettling dissatisfaction and delayed climax is an utterly necessary part of both the book's allegorical configuration and its political project. *The Principle of Hope*, then, is configured to resist complete consumption, and it is in the form of the book that this resistance really lies. As Adorno's remarks make clear, it is by means of its complex use of allegory that the book can maintain its "advanced literary" status and at the same moment resist absorption into the facile domain of the standardized "private" reader demanded by the culture industry.

Due to its traditional links with medieval and early Renaissance religious, and even doctrinal, conventions of thought and representation, allegory has often been seen as an overly didactic and restrictive mode.[28] However, as we have seen for the work of Jameson, Benjamin, and Bloch, allegory is an indispensable mode for understanding modernity. By plaiting the patterns of allegorical interpretation and narrative to the modern situation, new and unsettling configurations of thought and critique emerge. In short, understood as a complex allegory, *The Principle of Hope* critiques modernity from within and also from without, not only by means of its internal capabilities and patterns of thought but also by way of its status as a sort of useful anachronism.[29] The continued existence of allegory acts as a sort of literary and philosophical rebuke to the claims of modernity. According to standard literary and intellectual history, allegory really should have passed fully into cultural memory, but its shady existence between older and modern forms of representation implies a stalled history—a sort of purgatory of the "Not-Yet." It was surely timely and felicitous for Jameson to highlight the allegorical basis of Bloch's Marxist hermeneutics, but I hope to have shown here that by that same allegorical token, Bloch's great book is also the closest we have yet come to a Marxist poetics. The pathos and "bewilderment" engendered by the fact that we lack an ideal reader for the task the book presents is the fault of a failed history, not of the book. As an allegorical adventure of all that still awaits us, the book acts as a constant reminder that the private individual is a poor substitute for the unalienated subject that still remains to be achieved. It is not so much that *The Principle of Hope* patterns itself on an allegory of perfect reading, but rather that it enforces itself upon the reader as a rebuke to all notions of subjective complacent knowing that would underpin any such concept of a perfect or secure reading. What is at stake is the allegorical vision of an altered and redeemed humanity. What the book achieves by means of its formal complexities is the opening up of an allegorical understanding of what a secure subject *might* be able to achieve in a liberated and nonexploitative world. In this, the book resists any basis for private knowledge and maps an allegorical route toward a different subjectivity and an alternative version of history.

Notes

1   Vincent Geoghagen, *Ernst Bloch* (London: Routledge, 1996), 3.

2   J. K. Dickinson, "Ernst Bloch's *The Principle of Hope*: A Review and Comment on the English Translation," *Babel* 36, no. 1 (1990): 7–31 (8); Ronald Aronson, "Review of *The Principle of Hope*," *History and Theory* 30, no. 2 (1991): 220–32.

3   See Douglas Kellner, "Ernst Bloch, Utopia and Ideology Critique," *Illuminations*. Available at http://www.uta.edu/huma/illuminations/ke111.htm. The italics are mine.

4   Stephen Eric Bronner, *Of Critical Theory and Its Theorist* (Oxford: Blackwell, 1994), 62–72.

5   Theodor W. Adorno, *Notes to Literature*, vol. 2, trans. Shierry Weber Nicholsen (New York: Columbia University Press, 1992), 211–14.

6   "Wonder," and associated and cognate terms such as *amazement* and *bewilderment* have an interesting philosophical lineage. See principally Plato's *Theaetetus*, translated by Seth Benardete (Chicago: University of Chicago Press, 1986), 155. Adorno may have allowed the idea a degree of intellectual credibility as it is reiterated, by way of Aristotle, in Hegel's *The Philosophy of History*. Hegel writes of "Aristotle's dictum that philosophy proceeds from wonder." See G. W. F. Hegel, *The Philosophy of History*, trans. J. Sibree (New York: Dover, 1956), 234. The significance of "wonderment" or simply "wonder" in the history of German literature and criticism can also be traced to the aesthetics of Baumgarten and the literary theories of Johann Jakob Bodmer and Jakob Breitinger, especially Breitinger's *Critische Dichtkunst* (1740), which had a major influence on subsequent notions of imaginative "genius" and stylistic effectiveness. It is worth considering this aspect of Bloch's writing, because it tends to show that far from simply rejecting or overthrowing the older philosophical and hermeneutic texts, his work seeks to cast them in a new and estranging light by which some latent and long obscured utopian content might be released. In turn it

shows how Bloch can attach himself to the great works of the past and yet still adopt a radically transforming approach to them.

7   Georg Lukács, *Soul and Form*, trans. Anna Bostock (London: Merlin Press, 1974), 8–9.

8   "Something's Missing: A Discussion between Ernst Bloch and Theodor W. Adorno on the Contradictions of Utopian Longing," in Ernst Bloch, *The Utopian Function of Art and Literature: Selected Essays*, trans. Jack Zipes and Frank Mecklenburg (Cambridge, MA: MIT Press, 1996), 2–5.

9   The English translators of *The Principle of Hope* are convinced that the book is "certainly a literary work in its own right" and hazard that Bloch is "perhaps a poet of light," xxi. This is only partly accurate, and I hope to show that in a similar form to the great allegorical works of the past, *The Principle of Hope* is both a poetic and a critical philosophical work. At a secondary level, I insist that an understanding of the book's allegorical form is a crucial issue rather than supplementary stylistic matter.

10   Adorno, *Notes to Literature*, 2: 217.

11   In the pages that follow I will not offer a definitive concept of allegory. Part of my argument concerning the affinity between Marxism and allegory is that in a manner akin to Marxist theory, the power of allegory resides in the perpetual dialectic energy produced by its simultaneous existence as both imaginative projection (literary and figural) and as a method of critical commentary (hermeneutic and substantive). Broadly speaking, this double configuration corresponds to the twin poles of figural and literal meaning, although this binary is subject to considerable complications. Nevertheless, I am aware that some basic definitions of both the history and the formal components of allegory are needed. The best introduction I am aware of in English is Angus Fletcher's *Allegory: The Theory of a Symbolic Mode* (Ithaca, NY: Cornell University Press, 1982). For a more detailed account, see Brenda Machosky, ed., *Thinking Allegory Otherwise* (Palo Alto, CA: Stanford University Press, 2009).

12   See Fredric Jameson, *Marxism and Form: Twentieth-Century Dialectical Theories of Literature* (Princeton, NJ: Princeton University Press, 1971), 116–59.

13   Liliane Weissberg explores this connection with fable and fairy tale more fully in "Philosophy and the Fairy Tale: Bloch as Narrator," *New German Critique* 55 (winter 1992): 21–44.

14   Michael Lowy, "Interview with Ernst Bloch," *New German Critique* 9 (autumn 1976): 39–45.

15   For a convincing account, see Jürgen Habermas, "The German Idealism of the Jewish Philosophers," in which Habermas suggests a connection between Bloch's engagement with Kabbalah and Protestant philosophy, in Habermas, *Religion and Rationality: Essays on God, Reason, and Modernity* (Cambridge, MA: MIT Press, 2002), 54–57. Habermas also hints at a role for Lurianic ideas such as *sheviret ha-kelim* [shattering of the vessels] in Bloch's writings.

16   Dilthey, for example, claimed that the traditions of Stoic allegorical interpretation had a "lasting influence" and were, moreover, based on "sound principles." Wilhelm Dilthey, *Hermeneutics and the Study of History: Selected Works*, vol. 4, ed. R. A. Mak-

kreel and F. Rodi (Princeton, NJ: Princeton University Press, 1996), 5. For an informative discussion of Stoic and classical versions of allegory, see *Metaphor, Allegory, and the Classical Tradition: Ancient Thought and Modern Revisions*, ed. G. R. Boys-Stones (Oxford: Oxford University Press, 2003). For a fine example of Peter Szondi's work in relation to the issues raised here, see *An Introduction to Literary Hermeneutics*, trans. Martha Woodmansee (Cambridge: Cambridge University Press, 1995).

17 Jameson, *Marxism and Form*, 1, 59.

18 It goes without saying, of course, that I imply that this poetic/hermeneutic dialectic follows a "master and bondsman" relation, that it is impossible to claim outright at any given moment, and that the "hermeneutic" always functions as the theoretical "master." Part of my claim here is that Jameson unconsciously relegates the "poetics" of allegory in favor of the assumed "master" of "allegorical" hermeneutics and that this underestimates Bloch's affinity with the resources of "hope" embedded in the poetics of allegory.

19 Jameson, *Marxism and Form*, 118–20.

20 Terry Eagleton, *The Significance of Theory* (Oxford: Blackwell, 1990), 58.

21 There are clear connections here with allegory and Bloch's version of "polyrythmic" time. For a further discussion of this strand of Bloch's thinking, see Frederic J. Schwartz, "Ernst Bloch and Wilhelm Pinder: Out of Sync," *Gray Room* 3 (2001): 54–89.

22 Allegorical dream visions were popular in the Middle Ages, and as a literary form they cover a wide array of narratives from fairy stories to elaborate political commentary. The most prominent allegorical dream visions include Macrobius's *Commentary on Cicero's Dream of Scipio* (400 ACE), the thirteenth-century *Roman de la rose* and *Piers Plowman* (1362–87), and Bunyan's *Pilgrim's Progress* (1678). William Morris's *Dream of John Ball* (1866) is an example of the political use of the genre as a form of socialist utopian critique.

23 Obviously, following Jameson's and Adorno's formulations, the allegorical form remains, but dialectical materialism has replaced the Old and New Testaments as the theoretical guide that underpins the logic and direction of travel.

24 See Bloch's "The Wish-Landscape Perspective in Aesthetics: The Order of Art Materials According to Their Profundity and Hope" (1959), in *The Utopian Function of Art and Literature*, 4–6. Here we may productively contrast Bloch's allegorical poetics of hope with Walter Benjamin's bleak version of allegory as the pathos-laden mode that best exemplifies a frozen and catastrophic history. Here we have two approaches of dialectical critical theory that, far from invalidating the role of allegory I am outlining here, actually designates the fecundity and applicability of the mode. As argued by Warren S. Goldstein, for example, in "Messianism and Marxism: Walter Benjamin's and Ernst Bloch's Dialectical Theories of Secularisation," *Critical Sociology* 27, no. 2 (2001): 246–81, both approaches share a version of allegory in which the guiding and prefiguring presence of God and thus the theology has been expunged. What is often missing from such sociological accounts, however, is any analysis of the means by which this process of the secularization of messianic redemption is enacted. I believe

that what may be termed the "objectification" of the process of the "secularization" of messianic hope takes place for Bloch not only at the level of political practice but most importantly in the work of art. That is to say, the forms, modes, and aesthetic of the artistic work takes over from what was the religious role of Messianic hope. This process of the transference of the principles of hope from religion to art is obviously linked to the argument concerning allegory and dialectical materialism I am developing here.

25   Principally, Tommaso Campanella's *City of the Sun* (1637) and Bacon's *New Atlantis* (1627).

26   Michael Lowy, "Interview with Ernst Bloch."

27   The necessity of incorporating and enforcing a version of "hostile" and "poetic" truth goes some way toward explaining how Bloch could come to appreciate and incorporate useful images, devices, and ideas from writers such as Kierkegaard, Schopenhauer, and Dostoevsky in his work, who would otherwise appear, on the basis of their political pronouncements, to be far too anti-Hegelian and reactionary to be significant influences.

28   See Erich Auerbach's famous claim that the vitality of "serious realism" was nearly "choked to death by the vines of allegory." Erich Auerbach, *Mimesis: The Representation of Reality in Western Literature*, trans. Willard R. Trask, with an introduction by Edward W. Said (Princeton, NJ: Princeton University Press, 1953), 261.

29   Adorno writes that "in a social order, which liquidates the modern as retrograde, then what may befall what is retrograde, if it is overtaken by the judgment, is the truth over which the historical process rolls. Because no truth can be expressed, than the one which is capable of filling the subject, the anachronism becomes the refuge of what is modern." See *Minima Moralia: Reflections from a Damaged Life*, trans. E. F. N. Jephcott (London: Verso, 1974), 219.

10

Singing Summons the

Existence of the Fountain:

Ruth Levitas | **Bloch, Music, and Utopia**

The dearth in Anglophone sources of serious discussion of the utopian force of music is striking. Most commentators on Bloch's utopianism note the particular power and role that Bloch ascribes to music. Fredric Jameson's 1971 *Marxism and Form* tells us that for Bloch, "There exist . . . existential experiences which may be understood as foreshadowings of what the plenitude of such an ultimate Utopian instant might be like: this . . . is the most genuine function of music as a limited and yet pure feeling of that unity of outside and inside which Utopia will establish in all the dimensions of existence . . . [M]usic is profoundly Utopian, both in its form and in its content."[1] Wayne Hudson, in the first full-length study of Bloch in English in 1982, notes, "For Bloch, music is the most utopian of the arts. It is speech which men can understand" and "Music expresses something 'not yet.' It copies what is objectively undetermined in the world. . . . In this sense there is a pre-appearance . . . of the realisation of the realising factor in music: a proleptic promise of a new heaven and a new earth."[2] Curiously, however, few go much further than a passing acknowledgment of this.[3] Until 2010, despite occasional specialist articles,[4] the two principal exceptions in the core Bloch literature in English were Vincent Geoghegan's 1996 *Ernst Bloch* and David Drew's introductory essay in the 1985 Cambridge edition of *Essays on the Philosophy of Music*, on which Geoghegan draws. Geoghegan devotes about four pages to the question of music, providing a succinct summary of Bloch's position as set out in *The Principle of Hope*. Drew's thirty-page essay sets out the social, intellectual, and institutional context of Bloch's writings on music, as well as stressing its uniquely utopian content. Both Geoghegan and Drew emphasize the biographical importance of music for Bloch: he studied music at university, along with philosophy and physics, and played the piano, and in 1974 said that he "would probably have been a mediocre Kappelmeister but for . . . a certain talent for philosophy."[5] Benjamin Korstvedt's *Listening for Utopia in Ernst Bloch's Musical Philosophy* thus provides a serious addition to the corpus of work on Bloch.[6] Korstvedt both explores and develops Bloch's discussions of music, elaborating them through his own musicological analyses of Wagner, Mozart, Brahms, and Bruckner.[7] Korstvedt offers explorations of the figures of the *teppich* or carpet, melisma, the darkness of the lived moment, and the relationship between subject and object in Bloch's musical philosophy. This is an invaluable account of *how* music, for Bloch, carries utopian intensity. The mysterious question of *why* music is accorded so privileged a position as a vehicle of utopia remains unclear. Bloch argues not only that music is the most utopian of cultural forms but that it is uniquely capable of conveying *and effecting* a better world. Music's alleged abstraction, its nonconceptual and nonverbal character, and its direct route to human emotion underlie its capacity to express what is not (yet) utterable.

The Principle of Hope

As is well known, the early drafts of *The Principle of Hope* were written in exile when Bloch like so many of his compatriots, fled Germany in the 1930s and revised and completed after his return to the German Democratic Republic in 1949. Bloch was in his seventies when the final volumes of *The Principle of Hope* were published in 1959. The third volume contains a fifty-page section, "Venturing Beyond and Most Intense World of Man in Music." Geoghegan's account concentrates on this as Bloch's mature position, although noting some changes from *The Philosophy of Music*. In *The Principle of Hope* Bloch locates the origin of music—as distinct from noise—in the invention of the panpipe or shepherd's pipe, whose purpose is to reach the distant beloved. He recounts the myth of Pan and Syrinx as told by Ovid, in which Pan pursues Syrinx, but is left with only reeds in his hands, which he makes into pipes. Syrinx has both vanished and not vanished, remaining in—or as—the sound of the flute. "Thus music begins longingly and already definitely as a *call to that which is missing.* . . . The panpipe . . . is the birthplace of music as a human expression, a sounding wishful dream" (*POH*, 1059). The mysterious character of music is also here at the start, originating in a hollow space. The motif of the vanished Syrinx is identified in Berlioz's *Symphonie Fantastique* as the vehicle of "the unenjoyed . . . the Not-Yet, indeed even the Never" (1061). Here, the evocation of absence rests not only on the notes but in the silences and pauses around the notes—an aspect of music also stressed by Daniel Barenboim and enacted in the compositions of John Cage. Thus Bloch says: "Here that which is absent, indeed unconditional, dwells not in the finale, which is the most dubious part of every symphony anyway. It is in the faint thunder of the scene in the fields, in the answer which is no answer but which contains the unfound answer in the context which the significant pause before the thunder produces in this coda. And with this fine adagio and its evening-like, long-drawn-out, distantly familiarized heath of sound, with a rest which is not silent" (*POH*, 1062).

Bloch makes three distinct claims about music. First, he argues that it is the most socially conditioned of all arts. Much of the ensuing discussion is an attempt to trace the history of musical form and expression in a manner more musicological than sociological, but the sociological claims are sweeping:

> No Haydn and Mozart, no Handel and Bach, no Beethoven and Brahms without their respective precisely varied social mandate; it extends from the form of the performance right to the characteristic style of the tonal material and its composition, to the expression, the meaning of the content. Handel's oratorios in their festive pride reflect rising imperialist England, its aptness to be the chosen people. No Brahms without the bourgeois concert society and even no music of "new objectivity," of supposed expressionlessness, without the gigantic rise of alienation, objectification and reification in late capitalism. It is the consumer class and its mandate, it is the emotional and goal-world of the respective ruling class, which in each case becomes expressive in music. (*POH*, 1063)

Overwrought romanticism and sentimentality, "effect from affects or affect from effects," in Wagner and especially in Tchaikovsky, similarly have social causes: "the broad bourgeoisie of the large towns with its need for amorphous nerve-stimulation, and on top of this above all the petit bourgeoisie with its cut-price consumption of feeling" (POH, 1068). Sonata form itself "presupposes capitalist dynamics" while the fugue "presupposes class, static society." And "atonal music would not have been possible in any other periods than those of late-bourgeois decline," to which it responded "as bold helplessness" (1071).

Were this Bloch's core argument about music, it would be easily dismissed, especially for its failure to address processes of mediation. But the second claim is that "music, by virtue of its so immediately human capacity of expression, has more than the other arts the quality of incorporating the numerous sufferings, the wishes and spots of light of the oppressed class" (POH, 1063). In other words, despite the socially conditioned form and content of music, it has a direct route to human emotion. And the potential contradiction between the first two claims is squared by the third. Bloch uses the concept of cultural surplus to acknowledge the capacity of art in general to be more than a reflection of its historical location and conditions of production, to overspill that frame and point toward that which is not yet. Where music is concerned, "no art has so much surplus over the respective time and ideology in which it exists" (1063). Bloch asserts a utopian surplus that transcends the relations of production, reproduction, and consumption of musical works at any given time, *and* argues that music is unique in its utopian function. Even where texts are set to music, it is the music that is quintessentially utopian:

> The textual expressive stimulus serves only the most characteristic aspiration of music: to be, to find, to become language sui generis. Indeed because the expressive power of music lies beyond all known names, in the end expression in music is no longer under discussion at all but *music itself as expression*. This means the *entirety of its intending, signifying, depicting and of that which it depicts in such a clouded but, in both senses of the word, moving way*. And music . . . goes towards this alone, towards the hour of its own language, of its poesis a se which is pre-formed in powerful expression and nonetheless still unknown. . . . Musical expression as a whole is thus ultimately a *vice-regent for an articulation which goes much further than anything so far known*. (POH, 1069)

There is something here, too, about what it means to be human. Bloch refers back to the 1918 edition of *Geist der Utopie* [*Spirit of Utopia*] in which he claims that "music is one great subjective theurgy" and adds that this theurgy "proposes to sing, to invoke, that which is essential and most like proper human beings," that which expresses "adequateness to our own core" (*PoH*, 1070).[8] It is partly that "experience of music provides the best access to the hermeneutics of the emotions, especially the expectant emotions," but also that it touches on the subject as agent, or as the agent that is still forming, is not yet: "Thus music is that art of pre-appearance which relates most intensively to the welling core of existence (moment) of That-Which-Is and relates most expansively to its horizon;—*cantus essentiam fontis vocat* [singing summons the existence of the fountain]" (1070).[9] The relation to the latent subject is a key element of music's importance and a contributory reason why the "language sought and intended in music . . . lies much further beyond existing designations . . . than any other art" (1080). It conveys "intensive root, signalled social tendency," and moves "towards the wellspring sound of as yet unachieved self-shaping in the world" (1080). This reaching to a latent subject does not presume an essential human nature so much as a route to possibility, a "cracked, cracked-open nature, a nature illuminable into regnum hominis." Music drives toward the "core of human intensity" (1096). Or again: "This world is not that which has already become but that which circulates within it, which, as the regnum hominis, is imminent only in future, anxiety, hope. The relation to this world makes music, particularly in social terms, seismographic, it reflects cracks under the social surface, expresses wishes for change, bids us to hope" (*PoH*, 1088).

The same image can be found elsewhere: "The New comes in a particularly complex form. . . . But above all in the involuntary crack and some of its shimmering signs."[10] Or as Leonard Cohen put it, "There is a crack, a crack in everything: that's how the light gets in."[11] In Bloch, Beethoven appears in terms of musical content and musical forms as category rather than composer. His music is described as "pervaded by moral passion, by that will which is a will to Becoming Bright, not to mindless life" (*PoH* 1087). Thus Bloch can hear in Wagner "a reverberation, something Beethovenian, true to man, for which a sounding wellspring space . . . cracks open . . . and *morality of music* appears" (1086).

And "the category of Beethoven as the venturing beyond" describes the sonata form with its capacity to develop its thematic possibilities and its "hugely charged, hugely forward-pressing essence" (1094). Here again, music outstrips the other arts in its pre-illuminating and shaping of human intensity, especially in the slow movements of sonatas and chamber and symphonic works: "Music excavates its treasure on that gold ground of a most distantly immediate mindfulness which strikes into the most closely Intensive and to which literature and painting are only applied: the treasure of *intensive essence*" (1097).

The culmination of "Venturing Beyond in Music" is the discussion of music's relation to death: "If death . . . is the harshest non-utopia, then music measures itself against it as the most utopian of all arts" (*POH*, 1097). The light of music is bound to and intensified by the darkness of death. The Requiem Mass is the traditional form of this, with music working to "bring forth . . . the symbols of expectation which are at work in the requiem" and which are "inscribed in the music" (1099). Yet the most powerful examples are those free from conventional liturgy. Here we have Bloch's celebration of *Fidelio*, bypassing the *Missa Solemnis* (which he discusses in *The Philosophy of Music*) in his claim that Beethoven did not write a requiem other than in this secular form: "*If one seeks musical initiation into the truth of utopia*, the first, all-containing light is *Fidelio*" (1100). Bloch acknowledges that *Fidelio* itself makes use of a culturally available form, the opera of salvation, but argues that this "merely provided the external material for the morality of this music" (1103). He claims that the trumpet call, which overtly announces the arrival of a key character (which Bloch regards as a superficial interpretation) "announces the arrival of the Messiah" (1102). He then quotes the words of Verdi's Requiem, *Tuba mirum spargens sonum* [The trumpet scattering its amazing sound] (1100). Bloch's own messianism is reflected in the claim for the utopianism of the work, and music, as a whole:

> Every future storming of the Bastille is intended in *Fidelio*, an incipient matter of human identity fills the space in the sostenuto assai. . . . Bee- thoven's music is chiliastic. . . . More than anywhere else music here be- comes morning red, militant-religious, whose day becomes as audible as if it were already more than mere hope. It shines as pure work of man . . . thus music as a whole stands at the frontiers of mankind, but at those

where mankind, with new language and the *call-aura around captured intensity, attained We-World,* is still only forming. And precisely the order in musical expression intends a house, indeed a crystal, but from future freedom, a star, but as a new earth. (*PoH*, 1103)[12]

The discussion of Brahms's *German Requiem,* with its biblical rather than liturgical texts, concludes with the claim that: "All music of annihilation points towards a robust core which, because it has not yet blossomed, cannot pass away either; it points to a *non omnis confundar.* In the darkness of this music gleam the treasures which will not be corrupted by moth and rust, the lasting treasures in which will and goal, hope and its content, virtue and happiness could be united as in a world without frustration, as in the highest good;—*the requiem circles the landscape of the highest good"* (*PoH*, 1101).

Bloch's discussions are not confined to the classical tradition, although this does dominate in *The Principle of Hope.* Even here, Schoenberg's music "reflects the hollow space of this age and the atmosphere brewing in it, noiseless dynamite, long anticipations, suspended arrivals" (1090), just as Mahler's *Song of the Earth* "moves with an unresolved suspension into an immense Eternal, eternal" (1092). The new music is "a hollow space with sparks" (1091). In *The Philosophy of Music* the highest accolades are reserved for Bruckner, whereas during the Kroll period it is Kurt Weill who is elevated to utopian primacy.[13]

The Philosophy of Music

The Philosophy of Music is strikingly different from *The Principle of Hope* and from the intervening essays. The ground for the later work is laid in relations to music's role in both inward and outward, or forward, illumination. This involves *"placing at the end of music the interior realm of all that is hearing itself, moulded sound, as simply the aura of the listener re-encountering himself"* (*Essays,* 130). The text is suffused by religiosity, and the not yet that is carried in music is more than once declared not to be realized on Earth.[14] There are a number of tendentious claims about the naturalness of, for example, musical scales, as well as the elemental and natural character of music in general. Correspondingly, in this earlier work Bloch denies the level of social conditioning of music that he later

acknowledges. One might perhaps say that he was first trying to identify the character of cultural surplus carried by music, or that in his own
terms *The Principle of Hope* carries more of the cold stream of analysis
and *The Philosophy of Music* more of the warm stream of human passion and desire. The crude leaps from economic base to musical super-
structure in the later work may be seen either as a welcome corrective to
the idealism of *The Philosophy of Music* and a manifestation of maturity,
or alternatively as an irritating ideological accretion. And indeed, if the
latter work is more conventionally materialist, the earlier work is more
rooted in material human experience. The central trope of "Venturing
Beyond in Music" is the note or the tone: pure, explicitly disembodied,
sound, even though the discussion opens with the prior claim that "it
is not possible to avoid hearing a call in singing" (*POH*, 1058).[15] Thus "a
freedom from pressure, death and fate is expressed in the Still-Nowhere
medium of the tone, and cannot yet express itself in definite visibility"
(*POH*, 1101). In contrast, the argument in *The Philosophy of Music* begins
with and is structured around the embodied practice of singing—and indeed the embodied practice of listening.

It opens with "We hear only ourselves."[16] The quality of consciousness and self-consciousness is from the beginning embodied and heard.
It cannot be directly grasped. Here as elsewhere Bloch alludes to the
darkness of the lived moment, the inability to grasp our immediate situation because we are too close to it. "But the note flares out of us, the
heard note, not the note itself or its forms . . . [and] shows us our historically inner path as a flame in which not the vibrating air but we ourselves
begin to tremble" (*Spirit*, 34). Beethoven is already central in terms of
the preappearance of a particular human subject whose "voice becomes
cries for help and of outrage." This cry rises "loudly and recklessly,"
"whom nothing in this illusory life satisfies, who stands above even the
highest level of what the real world can encompass, who like the genius
of music itself is exemplified or welcomed nowhere in the world" (*Spirit*,
64–65). Beethoven is "Lucifer's benign offspring, the daemon that leads
to the ultimate things" (*Essays*, 61).[17] The *Missa Solemnis* is here used
to draw attention to the shift from collective, communal singing to the
human voice as the supremely expressive element in orchestral setting,
such that "the word, hitherto so important, loses ground in the process"
(*Essays*, 26). The history of music, primarily as a sung form, is set out,

drawing on the concept of "carpet," or a constraining and structuring ground, which Bloch ascribes to Georg Lukács.

Despite Bloch's insistence on the superiority of music over words, he suggests that people would find music easier to hear if they knew how to talk about it. Indeed, Korstvedt suggests that part of the difficulty of interpreting Bloch's musical philosophy lies in Bloch's own struggles to verbalize an essentially nonverbal experience. But hearing is, for Bloch, based on a human and physical response to a human expression. We understand inflection in song because "our own throat, gently innervated in sympathy, permits us to see and understand from within, as it were, what is being directed at us, what is speaking here" (*Essays*, 67). It is not the disembodied note but the humanly created sound that conveys crucial meaning: "What it contains of the actual person singing, and thus what quality the singer or player 'puts into' the note, is more important than what his song contains purely in terms of note-values" (67–68).[18] Music may be abstract in being beyond categories, but it is precisely "unabstract" in its dependence on "the act of utterance" or performance (72, 73). We find our way about the musical beat "by virtue of breathing" (99); our "pulses throb audibly" (100). Beethoven's compositions work by drawing on "the changing states of our energy" (102). The tone and the note are already central to Bloch's thinking, but "[t]o become music it [the note] is absolutely dependent on the flesh and blood of the person who takes it up and performs it" (117). Already, though, for Bloch music carries the utopian and indeed messianic essence in a way unparalleled in other arts: "The time is imminent when the overflowing inner life, the breakthrough and the divining of a most immediate, ultimate latency, can no longer express itself other than in the musical, ethical, and metaphysical domain" (65).

The Kroll Years

Many of Bloch's examples in both *The Principle of Hope* and *The Philosophy of Music* are taken from oratorio or opera. They include extended discussion of Wagner (where Bloch, like Otto Klemperer, had a settled preference for *Tristan und Isolde* over the Ring cycle), and particular criticism of conventional performances of Wagner's work. The essays for the intervening period are frequently related to specific productions, especially those taking place at the Kroll. Bloch's concerns at this time reflect both his embeddedness in this milieu and the embodied actuality of performance. Hans Mayer argued that "true thought always begins from some concrete experience," but locates that experience in the reception or consumption of the musical work: "without Beethoven's *Fidelio*, the concept of *The Principle of Hope* would not have occurred to . . . Bloch."[19] The concrete experiences surrounding Bloch's different writings about music need to be understood as something more than this. For although there are references to *Fidelio* in *The Philosophy of Music*, the iconic significance ascribed to this work appears to have emerged later. The trumpet call is not mentioned at all in *The Philosophy of Music*. The contrasting prosaic and redemptive interpretations appear in a passing reference in the short essay *Magic Rattle, Human Harp* (*Essays*, 142). Yet Bloch's son, Jan Robert Bloch, was to recall, "Whoever knows Bloch knows the meaning of the trumpet signal for him. Everything was in it. Nothing moved him more." Again, despite Ernst Bloch's own claims about music *rather than* words carrying the utopian content, Jan Robert Bloch's elaboration of the importance of *Fidelio* refers back to the libretto and the plot: "Florestan, Bloch's matador of the upright gait, sings, 'Words of truth I bravely uttered, and these chains are my reward.' Florestan's 'To freedom, to freedom in heaven above,' Leonora's answer to 'O my Leonora, what have you endured for me?': 'Nothing, nothing, my Florestan!' brought tears to his eyes."[20]

Beyond the discursive meaning may lie a biographical significance. The publication of *Geist der Utopie* brought Bloch into contact with both philosophers and musicians. It was the impetus for Adorno to seek him out in 1928. It led eventually to his close involvement with avant-garde opera and musical theater in Berlin in the 1920s at the Kroll Opera.[21] The Kroll was constituted in 1927 with the twin, though perhaps contradictory, aims of encouraging innovation and reaching a broad public. The conductor and musical director was Otto Klemperer, committed both to treating opera as a unified work of art and to making it relevant and accessible in the present. Klemperer, Bloch's exact contemporary, had been introduced to *Geist der Utopie* in 1916 by Georg Simmel, and he regarded it as the work of a genius. Later, Bloch and Klemperer became close friends, and Bloch was brought into the ambit of the Kroll. He wrote articles for the Kroll programs and contributed to the music journal *Anbruch*—and allegedly danced a minuet with Igor Stravinsky at the Kroll's opening performance of *Oedipus Rex*.[22]

The Kroll's programs included both new music and opera and new interpretations and stagings of classical and recent works. Besides radical reinterpreted versions of Beethoven, Wagner, and Mozart's *The Magic Flute* and *Don Giovanni*, there were Stravinsky's *Oedipus Rex* and *A Soldier's Tale*, the commissioned suite by Kurt Weill, *Kleine Dreigroschen-musik*, works by Hindemith, and a controversial production of Offenbach's *Tales of Hoffmann* with sets by László Moholy-Nagy. Curiously, in the first two seasons there were no works by Schoenberg or Alban Berg, although this was to change, and vacillation by Klemperer meant that Brecht and Weill's *Mahagonny* was not premiered at the Kroll as originally intended.

The first Kroll production, for which Bloch wrote the program notes, was *Fidelio*. It was an adaptation of Klemperer's earlier production at Wiesbaden in 1924 with Ewald Dülberg, who regarded his task as designer to be "to provide a visual accompaniment to the score by means of form, color, and space."[23] Klemperer himself was influenced by developments in Soviet theater, including the work of both Stanislavsky and Meyerhold. The Wiesbaden production is described by Patrick Carnegy: "Dülberg's sets were built of cube-like blocks and rectilinear platforms corresponding to the elemental structure of Beethoven's score and subject. Rocco's quarters were bare of domestic furniture, while there were fierce blood-red walls for the prison yard, pierced by holes, rather than doors leading to the cells. In the finale the blocks rolled away to reveal a wide and limitless open space."[24] Then, quoting Hans Curjel, Carnegy continues: "The prisoners formed an undifferentiated mass with shorn hair and whitened faces and in the finale the chorus was again deployed in static blocks, this time against a brilliant, blue background."[25]

The production was controversial, but critical acclaim included the assertion that "All historical accretions, all implausibilities of plot and text are swept away. Myth emerges from anecdotal story, archetypes out of operatic characters. Most splendid of all, Beethoven is reborn out of the experience of our own time, fashioned out of our feeling for space and sound."[26] The Berlin production was less successful than its earlier counterpart and provoked the claim that "*Fidelio* under Klemperer [represents] the complete triumph of the conductor and producer over Beethoven."[27] Nevertheless, *Fidelio* inaugurated the brief period of Bloch's embeddedness in the Weimar avant-garde before its destruction and loss, and it is during this period that *Fidelio* becomes an evident reference point.

Bloch's writing at this time discusses not only "the music itself" but the productive context. He is explicit about the importance of this to the utopian effect of music. Bloch clearly saw music, and especially music by Kurt Weill, as a revolutionary force. In his review of *The Threepenny Opera*, he wrote: "Whereas music cannot change a society, it can as Wiesengrund [Adorno] rightly says, signalize an impending change by 'absorbing' and proclaiming whatever is decomposing and re-forming beneath the surface. Most of all it sheds light on the impulses of those who would be marching towards the future in any case, but can do so more easily with its help. Weill's music is the only one today with any socio-polemic impact; the wind whistles through it, the wind that can blow freely only where there are as yet no structures to curb it, where time has not yet turned into reality."[28]

This approbation is certainly about Weill's music: "In Weill, the music is thoroughly simplified, possessed of bare, sharp, and angular means, and plays upon the contemporary surface. Yet his music is also uncanny, evocative of a surrealistic jungle; for all its transparency it is replete with dense atmosphere, revolutionary and religious; it is full of wishes, dreams, prophecies" (*Literary Essays*, 137). But it is also about something beyond that. He refers to Weill having "a sphere of being that he sets to music," and then, again, to the "collaborative space" created by Weill and Brecht in *Mahagonny* whose "entire utopian ensemble is as evocative of its time as the theme of redemption and the story of Fidelio." The issue is openness to the future: "A wind blows through it, an honest wind where no building can stop it, every place where time has not yet actualized itself" (138).

Of course, Weill stands out precisely because Bloch did not think all music was equally utopian or revolutionary, any more than he thought all wishes for the world to be otherwise were radical and transformative; many simply reflect "how the ruling class wishes the wishes of the weak to be" (*POH*, 13). Music plays its part here, too, as Bloch observed in 1933: "For every 'La Marseillaise' there are a hundred thousand folk songs of the nineteenth century, designed to leave no room for any thought." Such music "sustains an unconsolable life by administering consolation." Moreover, "music is very much the softest means of molding the people's body according to the masters' will" (*Literary Essays*, 58). Just as Bloch is anxious to distinguish abstract from concrete utopia, wishful thinking from anticipatory illumination and willful action, so he is concerned throughout his discussions on music to distinguish the most utopian—or that with the most utopian surplus—from music which is, in this sense, less laden with hope and futurity.

That utopian surplus resided not in the music itself but in its specific realization in a given historical context. The issue of cultural reproduction recurs in the essays from this period—the need for a Brechtian estrangement, so that the work can be experienced anew, rather than simply as historical repetition. Bloch opens a discussion of *The Tales of Hoffmann* with "It is deeply affecting to hear music like this again today. How much has changed since the 1880s, but also since 1905, the previous occasion on which this piece was revived." In this production, "the 'new slickness' was overturned for the first time, and the sense of interiority that had previously been abandoned was present once more" (*Literary Essays*, 247)—a claim immediately followed by a description of the set and staging. His discussion of *The Magic Flute* refers directly to Brecht and to the contemporary relevance of Mozart's themes. "How bitterly new, how convincingly new the following lines sound, if they are no longer spoken by Sarastro and no longer pacifistic: 'The rays of the sun drive back the night, destroying the hypocrites' illegitimate power'" (254). In the same essay, Bloch discusses the utopian force of both *The Magic Flute* and *Fidelio*. There is indeed something "of the perennial, real and as yet unrealized Tendency" in both, he claims (255), but this does not reside in timelessness or completeness, but rather their push toward the future. They are "immortal because of their continuing relevance, their ongoing call to action" (255), "their purposeful striving to open a realm of premonitory dreams" (251), and because "in order to travel with such works something is demanded of us" (252). But for this very reason, they require re-presentation: "Thus these works must be staged in new and different ways if they are to maintain their presence" (251), as when Klemperer conducts *The Magic Flute* and "the listeners feel themselves to be not on historical ground but on living earth" (251). Much later, in a birthday tribute to Klemperer in 1965, Bloch refers to the Kroll years and to Klemperer's distinctive capacity to conjure "reproduction without regression" (495).

The Kroll Opera was closed in 1931 for both political and financial reasons. Some of the antipathy was directly racial: "The Klemperer ensemble, which consists mainly of aliens, is bit by bit devouring the entire repertory. It presents the best loved operas "according to the spirit of the times," that is, according to the Jewish spirit. . . . Klemperer and Legal would do well . . . to declare their cultural bolshevist undertaking a "Jewish Opera." What goes on in it has nothing to do with German artistic spirit."[29]

And, indeed, Bloch's writings added to the political animus against the Kroll. The 1929 production of Wagner's *Der fliegende Holländer* [*The Flying Dutchman*], based on the original score, with sets by Dülberg and very different from the prevalent Bayreuth style, opened "with police at the doors anticipating riots." Public controversy included demands that the production be withdrawn, and Hans Curjel was hauled before the Prussian Parliament to account for this mockery of Wagner. "It had not helped that the philosopher Ernst Bloch had written an introductory piece arguing that to treat the opera as a nautical adventure story by Captain Marryat, but with surrealistic overtones, was as good a way as any of liberating it from the kitsch fantasy [*Traumkitsch*] in which first Wagner and then his heirs had cocooned it."[30] Indeed, the production was flagged in a 1938 Nazi exhibition of degenerate music as "one of the greatest cultural outrages of the Weimar Republic."[31]

Two years after the Kroll's closure, most of the key players had fled Germany—Bloch to Zurich, Vienna, Paris, and Prague before his move to the United States in 1938. After the Reichstag fire in 1933, the Kroll Opera House was used by the Nazi Parliament for its sessions. The Kroll's significance is debated. Klemperer asserted, "Whenever this approach to opera is revived, it will have to start where we have been obliged to leave off. They may shut our theatre, but the idea underlying it cannot be killed."[32] John Rockwell describes it as "the high point of Weimar operatic progressivism." Patrick Carnegy asserts that "it is hard to overestimate the importance of the Kroll Opera's four years of existence for opera production in the twentieth century."[33] In contrast, Klemperer's biographer, Peter Heyworth, says that the repertoire of the Kroll and its "reputation as a hotbed of radicalism has been exaggerated."[34] But whatever its overall significance, its importance as the principal period during which Bloch was embedded in cultural, and especially musical, life has been overlooked.

In a general sense, it is understood that the conception and drafting of *The Principle of Hope* took place in the context of loss. In relation to the musical writings in particular, it is worth being a little more specific. The apparently more materialist, but also more disembodied and disembedded, character of the discussion of music in *The Principle of Hope* can plausibly be related to the process of deracination and loss. Despite serious illness following a brain tumor in 1939, Klemperer was able to establish a career as an acclaimed conductor in the West. Eisler and Weill continued composing, and although Adorno was not happy in exile and returned to Frankfurt immediately after the war, he did assimilate successfully into western academic life—perhaps in part because he was significantly younger and more competent in English than Bloch. Although Bloch maintained connections with the émigré German intellectual community, relations were dramatically altered. The specific social milieu of the Kroll and Weimar culture was disbanded. More than that, the whole central European cultural inheritance that made Kroll possible was erased by Nazi supremacy, war, and the subsequent division of Europe. This was a culture in which music held a particular significance. It was not just that concert-going was part of the pattern of bourgeois life. A real musical literacy, including the ability to play an instrument, was part of the expected cultural capital of the educated classes, in a manner inconceivable in the United States or Britain. The place of music and musicianship in this prewar period and the contrast with North America are underlined by Eva Hoffman's account of moving from Poland to Canada in 1959 at the age of thirteen: "'Being a pianist' . . . means something entirely different in my new cultural matrix. It is no longer the height of glamour or the heart of beauty. 'What a nice tunc,' my friends say when I play a Beethoven sonata for them, but I see that they don't care. . . . 'You're too intelligent to become a musician,' others tell me. But there is nothing in the world that takes a more incandescent intelligence, the intelligence of your whole being! I want to reply."[35]

Both Bloch's and Adorno's responses to music in the United States have to be understood against this background. Adorno's cultural elitism and his attitude toward jazz are well known. Bloch, despite drawing extensively on a canonical tradition across philosophy, literature, and music, was far less elitist in his judgments than Adorno. It was that propensity to draw on popular culture, to recognize its utopian valencies, that caused so much difficulty in the essay on *The Flying Dutchman*. But having extolled Weill's work during the Kroll period, Bloch was profoundly critical of his later, less "political" music.

The political shift that runs through *The Principle of Hope* is usually discussed in terms of Bloch's communism, his return to the GDR, and his pinning of hope upon the building of a postwar socialist state. The existential significance of Bloch's Jewish identity in Weimar Germany, in exile, and in the postwar years is less often explored. Like so many German intellectuals and musicians, Bloch was an assimilated Jew, and the religious language and tradition most accessible to him and visible in his work is Christian. Nevertheless, the fact of his Jewishness was inescapable. Anti-Semitism was rife in Germany in the late nineteenth and twentieth centuries, including among university students. After his formal studies, Bloch participated in the private circles first of Georg Simmel in Berlin and then of Max Weber in Heidelberg. Weber's Sunday meetings included a number of young Jewish intellectuals and discussions of Judaism and Zionism. Marianne Weber described Bloch as "a new Jewish philosopher . . . a young man with an enormous crown of black hair and an equally enormous self-assurance" who "evidently regarded himself as the precursor of a new Messiah and wanted to be recognized as such."[36] Both Max and Marianne Weber could be exasperated by Bloch, who is further described as "a most peculiar fellow, very clever . . . but with extremely uncivil manners, importunate and arrogant and definitely . . . a little mad."[37] Marianne called Bloch and Lukács the "messiah kids, because they hope for a future Messiah and want to create the philosophical atmosphere for his coming." Weber himself was inclined to dissuade young Jewish scholars from pursuing university careers, partly for the less than commendable reason that he felt under pressure to support them, but partly because of the general anti-Semitism of the German university establishment.[38]

If Bloch's formative years as well as his adult life were in the context of overt anti-Semitism, all work after 1938 (by which time Bloch was fifty-three), and especially after 1945, necessarily took place against a background of the profound grief, existential threat, and terror consequent on the extermination of European Jewry in the Shoah. There are specific, nameable losses such as the death of Bloch's friend Walter Benjamin, but more significantly there was the huge, unnamable, inexpressible loss of a people and culture. This absence is architecturally figured in the voids in Daniel Libeskind's Jewish Museum in Berlin. The period when *The Principle of Hope* was revised was characterized by relative silence in the wake of the Shoah. Parents in the West did not talk much to their children born into the postwar world about this period of horror, but attempted to protect them from it, a silence discussed in different ways by writers including Victor Seidler in *Shadows of the Shoah* (2000), David Grossman in *See Under—Love* (1990), and Eva Hoffman in *After Such Knowledge* (2004). In the GDR, the failure to acknowledge inadequate denazification would have exacerbated this. But the overwhelming sense of loss carried by all survivors of the Shoah must have contributed to Bloch's intensified response to *Fidelio*, and Bloch's own arguments about cultural reproduction and the simultaneously shifting and enduring character of musical works should make us doubly aware of this. How could the overthrowing of arbitrary power signaled even in the most prosaic interpretation of the trumpet call *not* represent that liberation which was not, as well as that which is not yet? Moreover, the trumpet sound might be construed as analogous to the sound of the Shofar blown on Rosh Hashanah, the Jewish New Year, with a liturgy translated as "You shall cause the Shofar to be sounded . . . and proclaim liberty throughout the earth to all its inhabitants." Some modern commentators interpret the sound of the Shofar as "a call to hear the sound of weeping humanity, to feel . . . the unspeakable pain of the world."[39]

Coda

How should we read Bloch's claims about music in the twenty-first century? For Bloch, the nonlinguistic character of music is fundamental to his claims for music's superior utopian force. He was not alone in this belief. As Gustav Landauer put it, "Doesn't everyone who has tried to put dreams into words know that the best is dissolved and destroyed when they are cast into language?"[40] Music's "abstraction" in the sense of being nonverbal is critical for Bloch, as is its consequent direct access to human emotion: "the ear perceives more than can be explained conceptually" and "we sense everything and know exactly where we are, but when it is transferred to the intellect, the light burning in our hearts will go out" (*Essays*, 113). He is scathing about program music that is intended to conjure particular images and argues repeatedly against the attempt to "explain" music in program notes. Romantic music in particular, he writes, "has sometimes given its expression literary signposts which are superfluous" such as the title of Beethoven's *Pastoral Symphony*, or as in the case of "elaborate program symphonies from Berlioz to Strauss" leading to inferior music (*PoH*, 1068). Words are always music's poor relation: "the note actually draws . . . whereas the word is just used" (*Essays*, 78); "The one settled factor . . . is that the note overtakes the word" (*Essays*, 80). Even in opera and music dramas, which constitute a large proportion of Bloch's musical examples, "the whole of the action that can be spoken is latently overtaken . . . by the sounds originating in us, by the subjective streak in the note" (*Essays*, 79). Bloch is adamant that music has a "latent expressive power which goes beyond all known words" and should not be treated as "a mere illustration of literary aids to the imagination" (*PoH*, 1068): "The dark primordial sound of music dissolves every word, even every drama within itself, and the deepest transformations, a multitude of mysterious shapes concealing future revelations, are crowding past us in the singing flames of great music. Hence there is no *great* music at all . . . whose prerequisites do not exceed the limits of even the most masterly and polished poetry" (*Essays*, 83).

Moreover, Bloch's own practice in identifying the locus of utopian substance is contradictory. He quotes Albert Schweitzer in a passage suggesting a more complex relationship between libretto and score: "Rather than resigning himself simply to writing beautiful music for the text, [Bach] attempts the impossible in order to discover a feeling in the words which, multiplied by a certain heightening emotion, becomes portrayable in music" (*PH*, 1066). In other places, Bloch himself clearly finds the verbal content more accessible or at least explicable. Thus his reference to the "sublimely rich expression" of the duet of the cranes in Bertolt Brecht and Kurt Weill's *Mahagonny* is to the words: "poetry of extraordinary value and not unworthy of late Goethe" (*Heritage*, 230). The musical figure is not mentioned.[41] In the specific discussions of *Fidelio* and Brahms's *German Requiem*, there is as much reference to text as to music. In particular, Bloch emphasizes the freedom of the Brahms *Requiem* from the liturgy of the Requiem Mass—although, of course, the text remains biblical, unlike Benjamin Britten's later *War Requiem*. He quotes: "For here we have no continuing city, but we seek one to come"; "Behold I shew you a mystery: We shall not all sleep, but we shall all be changed"; "Therefore the redeemed of the Lord shall return, and come with singing unto Zion; and everlasting joy shall be upon their head" (*PoH*, 1100).

Bloch's claims here do, therefore, need to be treated with skepticism, partly because his own writing about music itself conjures, as it is intended to, that which is not yet. Strong claims can be made about the power of language. For example, Christopher Caudwell's *Illusion and Reality* is, like *Geist der Utopie*, a pre-Marxist work by a Marxist writer. For Caudwell poetry has a similar expressive *and instrumental* function in its transformation of agency and thence the world.[42] Moreover, abstraction is a feature of the visual arts as well as music; color, in particular, is argued to have a direct route to the emotions.

Second, we need to consider the impact of new technologies that have transformed listening practices (and that were doing so for much of Bloch's own lifetime). If disembedding was a feature of the life experience against which Bloch's "mature" writings were composed, it is also very much a feature of present conditions of musical reception. The development of technology has progressively detached music from its live performance. Radio broadcasting became widespread in the 1920s and 1930s, competing with the gramophone, which had made recorded music available from the late nineteenth century. However, the records themselves were heavy, played at 78 rpm, and they fragmented longer works: HMV released a Verdi opera on forty single-sided discs in 1903. Even in the 1930s, the quality of recording and reproduction was relatively poor. This may have contributed to some hostility to recorded music on the part of musicians and critics such as Victor Gollancz, and strenuous arguments in favor of live performance. For other reasons—notably the livelihood of musicians—this later resurfaced in the Musicians' Union slogan "Keep Music Live." Later technology such as the LP (long-playing record) reduced but did not eliminate the fragmentation of works, and the CD moved yet further in this direction. With the MP3 player (and even more so with electronic sound sampling), fragmentation increases, as individual tracks can be selected and rearranged at will. What this does is to detach music, or bits of music, from the work as a whole and from live performance, and also from listening as a social, or collective, act. The view that much is lost here remains: as the saxophonist John Harle put it, "the point of grace between audience and performer only happens live."[43]

The MP3 player means that music becomes more than ever a background to other activities such as exercising, traveling, working. It can be a means of insulating the self from the social environment rather than being fully present in it, a compensatory turning away from reality. This turning in to the self rather than out to a transforming, transformable world is exacerbated by a difference in the experience of music heard through headphones and music as ambient sound. The social aspect of musical performance is distanced, and the social experience of shared listening is wholly absent. The MP3 player creates the extraordinary illusion of the music emanating from within the listener's own head, as it does when you dream music. The music itself becomes internal rather than external. We hear only ourselves.

But the use of recorded sound cannot be read off from technology. Daniel Barenboim, with typical evenhandedness, accedes that the question of the merits or otherwise of technologies of recorded music lies only in the uses to which they are put. They may be an aid to genuine listening or understanding, and above all they make music more accessible to more people. One effect of the MP3 player is that music becomes ubiquitous, rather than a sequestered, heterotopic experience. Barenboim's fear is that this increases the risk of not concentrating, not thinking, not listening. "Recorded sound, which artificially preserves the unpreservable, increases the likelihood of hearing without listening, since it can be listened to at home, in cars, in airplanes, thus allowing us to reduce music to background activity and eliminate the possibility of total concentration—i.e., thought."[44] Both fragmentation and distraction work against musical understanding, for "listening to music entails hearing it as well, in order to understand the musical narrative. Listening . . . is hearing with thought" (*Everything* 37). Concert audiences, as Bloch noted, do not necessarily listen in this way, but new technology makes treating music as background easier, encouraging what Adorno called regressive listening.

Research on the uses of music in everyday life is ambiguous. Andersen found that listening to specific pieces of music was used as part of deliberate remembering, in ways he construed as utopian in an explicitly Blochian sense. It can offer "experiences of intensified affect that provide ways of being and living" and that, "within the context of a specific everyday life, take on a utopian function."[45] Practices of using music touch "that which is present but 'not-yet-become' in order to re-order the ordinary sense of domestic everydayness."[46] Tia DeNora insists (like Bloch) that music is constitutive of agency, seeing it as a resource with and through which people construct and configure themselves as agents. She therefore emphasizes the importance of looking at how people actually use music and the potential for appropriation and control given to the listener. Evidently, people choose music to alter mood and specifically to raise or lower energy. On the other hand, classical music was described by one of DeNora's listeners as useful because of its wordlessness and its capacity to override and eliminate random thoughts and thus aid concentration—but not concentration on the music.[47]

Yet contemporary discussion of music, especially by Daniel Barenboim and Edward Said, return us to the idea that there is something in music itself that overspills technological and social change. Barenboim shares with Bloch the belief that music's abstraction enables the expression of that which is verbally unutterable: "Music is . . . an abstract language of harmony . . . which makes it possible to express what is difficult or even forbidden in words" (*Everything*, 68). He also insists on the physicality of music: "Music possesses a power that goes beyond words. It has the power to move us and it has the sheer physical power of sound, which literally resounds within our bodies for the duration of its existence" (115). And music's essential temporality is also important: "The inevitable flow in music means constant movement—development, change, transformation" (134). And he shares with Bloch a belief in music's utopian potential, although this lies not just in the music itself but in the socially embedded character of musical performance.

Barenboim's discussions of music are embedded in decades of professional performance, but above all in the contemporary politics of the Middle East. In 1999, Barenboim and Said set up the West-Eastern Divan Orchestra to organize workshops bringing together young musicians across the political divide.[48] The orchestra was subsequently offered a permanent home in Seville, reflecting Andalusia's historic significance as a place where Muslims, Jews, and Christians have coexisted peacefully for centuries. Barenboim and Said were well aware that such a project could not solve the political conflict. Indeed, music as "sonorous air" does not "solve problems." (*Everything*, 182). Music can, however, foster a different way of thinking and at a deeper level enable the construction of a different subject position on the part of the player. Barenboim argues that there is an inherent dialogic character in music. This resides in the music itself in the different voices within compositions. It arises in a complementary way in the process of their performance or realization, because it is impossible to play in a musical ensemble without simultaneously playing and listening. Orchestral playing, then, is "not simply a common activity . . . but an existential process that encourages reflection and understanding" (79) This becomes utopian in both a visionary and a transformative sense: "Through music it is possible to imagine an alternative social model, where Utopia and practicality join forces, allowing us to express ourselves freely and hear each other's preoccupations" (68). "The idea of music . . . could be a model for society; it teaches us the importance of the interconnection between transparency, power, and force" (133). In the end, "Music teaches us . . . that everything is connected" (134). Barenboim's position here seems close to Adorno's, who, when comparing Franz Kafka and Samuel Beckett with the "engaged" stance of Jean-Paul Sartre and Bertolt Brecht, argued that "the inescapability of their work compels the change of attitude which committed works merely demand."[49]

Both the Celts and indigenous Australian peoples believed that the world was not created but sung into being—and that singing into being was an ongoing necessity. Bloch's "singing summons the existence of the fountain" echoes this. Andersen's discussion of music and memory insists that "a practice of remembering with music does not represent the past but enacts time-space, and thus the past, into becoming," while arguing that this also enacts the not-yet.[50] Barenboim's argument, like Bloch's, goes beyond musical performance as social education or the claim that the relations between players prefigure those of a better world. Rather, there is something *in the nature of music itself and our making of it* that reforms us as subjects and agents, and thus it conjures the possibility of a new world and moves toward it.[51] Just as Bloch's own responses and arguments must be understood in terms of his own embedding/disembedding in musical cultures, so the relationships between performers, music, and listeners are changed by new technologies. Both making and listening to music are material practices. And yet, it seems, the elusive and utopian cultural surplus of music is such that it continues to open, in many different ways, to that which is not yet.

Notes

1   Fredric Jameson, *Marxism and Form: Twentieth-Century Dialectical Theories of Literature* (Princeton, NJ: Princeton University Press, 1974), 143.

2   Wayne Hudson, *The Marxist Philosophy of Ernst Bloch* (London: Macmillan, 1982), 175–76.

3   Jürgen Moltmann's 1971 introduction to Bloch's *Man on His Own* merely notes that "In Pirate Jenny's song from *The Threepenny Opera*, Bloch heard something like the melody of 'the possible resurrection of the dead.'" Ernst Bloch, *Man on His Own*: *Essays in the Philosophy of Religion*, trans. E. B. Ashton (New York: Herder and Herder, 1971), 23. Maynard Solomon, who went on to provide the most wonderful Blochian readings of music in his biographies of Mozart and Beethoven, makes only passing reference to music in his short essay in his 1979 *Marxism and Art*, although he does provide a translation of Bloch's essay on *The Threepenny Opera* in Maynard Solomon, ed., *Marxism and Art: Essays Classic and Contemporary* (Sussex: Harvester, 1979). Hudson devotes less than two pages to music in *The Marxist Philosophy of Ernst Bloch*. The short translators' introduction to Bloch's *The Principle of Hope* (1986) refers mainly to the structure rather than the content of Bloch's magnum opus: "The symphonic structure of the work is also clearly evident. Bloch considered music to be the most important of the arts, in which the Not-Yet and the utopian could be most perfectly realized. Reprises, refrains, codas, the musical gestures are unmistakable. Bloch was not only anxious to include the ontological and utopian gestures of music in his catalogue of hope . . . but also to incorporate these gestures into the *structure* of his major work itself." Ernst Bloch, *The Principle of Hope*, trans. Neville Plaice, Stephen Plaice, and Paul Knight (Oxford: Blackwell, 1986), xxx–xxxi. The 1988 introduction by Jack Zipes to Bloch's *The Utopian Function of Art and Literature*, trans. Jack Zipes and Frank Mecklenburg (Cambridge, MA: MIT Press, 1988), contains virtually nothing about music and, although the collection is claimed to represent Bloch's "most significant views on music, art, architecture, theatre, film, and literature" (ix), it is similarly light in this regard. My own *The Concept of Utopia* (Hemel Hempstead, UK: Philip Allen, 1990) offers half a page on music, most of which is taken up by two substantial quotations from Bloch. The brief translators' introduction to the 1991 English edition of *Heritage of Our Times*, which includes some essays on music, concentrates on debates around expressionism. John Miller Jones goes no

further: "For Bloch, music is the most utopian of the arts": John Miller Jones, *Assembling (Post)modernism: The Utopian Philosophy of Ernst Bloch* (New York: Lang, 1995), 22. He quotes Bloch: "Music is 'the supreme art of venturing beyond . . . whether it drifts or builds'" (*PoH*, 1057), and says, "Music is most utopian because it is completely temporal: it nowhere touches space and thus is ideally suited for expressing that which cannot be found in space, *Heimat*, although it does this only in an abstract way" (Jones, *Assembling (Post)modernism*, 118). Anthony Nassar's translation of the 1923 edition of *Geist der Utopie* [*The Spirit of Utopia*] (Palo Alto, CA: Stanford University Press, 2000), includes no introduction, nor does Andrew Joron's edition of *Literary Essays* (Palo Alto, CA: Stanford University Press, 2008). Even Ben Anderson, who uses Bloch's utopianism to frame discussions of contemporary listening practices, does so without close analysis of Bloch's discussions of music per se, arguing that "further work is needed to tease out the complexities of the approach to music contained in *The Principle of Hope*." Ben Anderson, "A Principle of Hope: Recorded Music, Listening Practices, and the Immanence of Utopia," *Geografiska Annaler* 84B, 3–4 (2002): 211–27 (217).

The relative dearth of writing in Anglophone sources may be partly explained by problems of translation. Many of the essays from the period between the *Philosophy of Music* and *The Principle of Hope* remain untranslated, making it an act of hubris for anyone who does not read German to address this topic. Moreover, the translations of Bloch's work that do exist are of variable quality. For consistency and accessibility I have used the 1986 Plaice et al. translation of *The Principle of Hope*. Some of the sections on music were translated earlier by Peter Palmer, as part of the 1985 edition of Bloch's *Essays on the Philosophy of Music*, and in some cases I have given that alternative translation in a footnote, as Palmer is sometimes more elegant and less opaque. *The Philosophy of Music* forms part of *Geist der Utopie*, the 1923 edition of which was translated in 2000 by Anthony Nassar as *Spirit of Utopia* (henceforth *Spirit* in parentheses in the text). Again, much of this was translated by Peter Palmer for the 1985 collection. My preference is for the Palmer translation, although I have included some references to Nassar's translation, and again I have sometimes included a comparison in the footnotes. The translation of Bloch's *Literary Essays* by Andrew Joron, which contains a substantial amount of material on music including essays from the Kroll period, is admirably clear and readable (henceforth *Literary Essays* in parentheses in the text).

4   Compare Christopher Norris, "Utopian Deconstruction: Ernst Bloch, Paul de Man, and the Politics of Music," in *Music and the Politics of Culture*, ed. Christopher Norris (London: Lawrence and Wishart, 1989), 305–47; Gerhard Richter, "Bloch's Dream, Music's Traces," in *Sound Figures of Modernity: German Music and Philosophy*, ed. Jost Hermand and Gerhard Richter (Madison: University of Wisconsin Press, 2006), 141–80; Gary Zabel, "Ernst Bloch and the Utopian Dimension of Music," *Musical Times* 131 (1990): 82–84.

5   Drew, "Introduction," in Ernst Bloch, *Essays on the Philosophy of Music*, trans. Peter Palmer (Cambridge: Cambridge University Press, 1985), xiii; Vincent Geoghegan, *Ernst Bloch* (London: Routledge, 1996).

6 Benjamin Korstvedt, *Listening for Utopia in Ernst Bloch's Musical Philosophy* (Cambridge: Cambridge University Press, 2010).

7 Korstvedt does not cite Solomon, though, at any point, inviting a comparative reading of their different Blochian readings of *The Magic Flute*.

8 Palmer translates this as "invoke the essentiality most in the likeness of men" (*Essays*, 208).

9 Palmer translates this as "Music names the essence of the fountainhead" (*Essays*, 208).

10 Ernst Bloch, *Heritage of Our Times*, trans. Neville and Stephen Plaice (Cambridge: Polity, 1991), 1 (henceforth *Heritage* in parentheses in the text).

11 Leonard Cohen, "Anthem," *The Little Black Songbook* (London: Wise, 2008), 14.

12 The translation by Peter Palmer here is much clearer: "Every future storming of the Bastille is implicitly expressed in *Fidelio*, and an incipient substance of human identity fills up the space in the Sostenuto assai. . . . Beethoven's music is chiliastic. . . . Here and nowhere else . . . music becomes a rosy dawn, militant-religious, the dawning of a new day so audible that it seems more than simply a hope. It shines forth as the pure work of man. . . . Thus music as a whole stands at the further limits of humanity, but at those limits where humanity, with a new language and haloed by the call to achieved *intensity, to the attained world of 'we'* is first taking shape. And this ordering in our musical expression means a house, indeed a crystal, but one derived from our future freedom; a star, but one that will be a new Earth" (*Essays*, 243).

13 On Weill's work in this period and its utopian resonance, see Robert Hunter, "The Music of Change," *Utopian Studies* 21, no. 2 (2010): 293–312.

14 Zabel suggests that the religious symbolism in Bloch is to be understood metaphorically. This seems to erroneously read Bloch's later position in *The Principle of Hope*, and indeed *Atheism in Christianity*, back into *The Spirit of Utopia*.

15 Palmer translates as "Here we cannot help hearing a summons in the singing" (*Essays*, 196).

16 Bloch, *The Spirit of Utopia*, trans. Nassar, 34.

17 Alternatively, in Nassar's translation, "Beethoven is Lucifer's good son, the psychopomp to the last things" (*Spirit*, 62).

18 Jonathan Letham, writing about rock, soul, and pop singing, also draws attention to this physicality of the voice, singing and bodily hearing, and the importance of what the voice puts into the song. Jonathan Letham, "What Makes a Great Singer?" Available at http://www.rollingstone.com/news/story/24200601, accessed 27 November 2008.

19 Jones, *Assembling (Post)modernism*, 21.

20 Geoghegan, *Ernst Bloch*, 52.

21 On the Kroll Opera, see Patrick Carnegy, *Wagner and the Art of the Theatre* (New Haven, CT: Yale University Press, 2006), chap. 8, and Peter Heyworth, *Otto Klemperer: His Life and Times*, vol. 1, *1885-1933* (Cambridge: Cambridge University Press, 1983). Other sources not consulted for this piece include Hans Curjel, *Experiment Krolloper, 1927-1931* (Munich: Prestel, 1975) and Rachel Nussbaum, "The Kroll

Opera and the Politics of Cultural Reform in the Weimar Republic," PhD diss., Cornell University, 2005. http://ecommons.library.cornell.edu/handle/1813/2130.

22   Heyworth, *Otto Klemperer*, 26.

23   Heyworth, *Otto Klemperer*, 200-201.

24   Carnegy, *Wagner and the Art of the Theatre*, 251.

25   Carnegy, *Wagner and the Art of the Theatre*, 252.

26   Cited in Heyworth, *Otto Klemperer*, 202.

27   Cited in Heyworth, *Otto Klemperer*, 260.

28   Solomon, *Marxism and Art*, 577.

29   Cited in Heyworth, *Otto Klemperer*, 286.

30   Carnegy, *Wagner and the Art of the Theatre*, 256.

31   Heyworth, *Otto Klemperer*, 283. An account of the production and its reception is given in Carnegy, *Wagner and the Art of the Theatre*, 255–60. The production was also a decisive influence on interpretations of Wagner when Bayreuth reopened in the 1950s, under the guidance of Wieland Wagner, with whom Bloch remained friends. For a translation of (a version of) Bloch's piece, see "Rescuing Wagner through Surrealistic Colportage" (Bloch, *Heritage*, 338–45).

32   Heyworth, *Otto Klemperer*, 377.

33   John Rockwell, "Kurt Weill's Operatic Reform and Its Context," in *A New Orpheus: Essays on Kurt Weill*, ed. Kim Kowalke (New Haven, CT: Yale University Press, 1986), 57; Carnegy, *Wagner and the Art of the Theatre*, 248.

34   Heyworth, *Otto Klemperer*, 256.

35   Eva Hoffman, *Lost in Translation: A Life in a New Language* (London: Vintage, 1998), 158.

36   Geoghegan, *Ernst Bloch*, 12.

37   Joachim Radkau, *Max Weber: A Biography* (Cambridge: Polity, 2009), 432.

38   Radkau, *Max Weber*, 432, 433.

39   Andrew Goldstein and Charles H. Middleburgh, eds., *Services for the Days of Awe* (London: Union of Liberal and Progressive Synagogues, 2003), 92, 151.

40   Russell Jacoby, *Picture Imperfect: Utopian Thought for an Anti-Utopian Age* (New York: Columbia University Press, 2005), 107.

41   For a discussion of the utopian impulse of Weill's music and the crane duet in particular, see Hunter, "The Music of Change."

42   Christopher Caudwell, *Illusion and Reality: A Study of the Sources of Poetry* (London: Macmillan, 1937).

43   John Harle in conversation with Robert Winston, University of Bristol Art Lectures, November 10, 2008.

44   Daniel Barenboim, *Music Quickens Time* (New York: Verso, 2008), 37; Daniel Barenboim, *Everything Is Connected: The Power of Music* (London: Weidenfeld and Nicholson, 2008), 37 (henceforth *Everything* in parentheses in the text).

45   Ben Anderson, "Recorded Music and the Practices of Remembering," *Social and Cultural Geography* 5, no. 1 (2004): 3–20.

46   Anderson, "Recorded Music," 16.

47 Tia DeNora, *Music in Everyday Life* (Cambridge: Cambridge University Press, 2000).

48 The name is taken from a set of poems by Goethe published in 1819 and reflecting his deep interest in Islam. Barenboim also notes that the publication of the poems coincided with the composition of Beethoven's Ninth Symphony.

49 Eugene Lunn, *Marxism and Modernism* (London: Verso, 1985), 274.

50 Anderson, "Recorded Music," 16.

51 The Weidenfeld British edition of this book is called *Everything Is Connected: The Power of Music*, the Verso US/UK edition *Music Quickens Time*. It is notable that this essay, "Sixty Years of Israel," does not appear in the Verso edition, presumably because it is far too critical of the Israeli state. It is replaced by a brief piece on dual citizenship that is less controversial.

Rainer E. Zimmermann

For Bloch, the starting point of his concept is the intrinsic existential contingency that lies at the roots of irritation within daily life. This irritation can be visualized as a form of some ontological type of alienation producing what we call *existential anxiety* [*Angst*]. So for Bloch, it is necessary to develop a new reflexive strategy in order to overcome this anxiety, or rather, in order to accept, endure, resist, and withstand it, in a progressively organized social motion of authenticity: "The point is to learn Hope. Its work does not renounce, it is enamored of success rather than failure. Hoping, situated above fearing, is neither passive like the latter nor imprisoned in its nothingness. The affect of hoping comes out of its shell, extends humanity instead of contracting it, cannot at all know enough of what makes it well-aimed inwardly, of what may be allied to it outwardly" (PH, 1).[1]

Human life is thus permeated by daydreams of which one part is referring to the tendency of escaping from what is causing a permanent suffering from failure and despair: "The other part has hope as its nucleus, and it is teachable" (PH, 1). Bloch utilizes here an imperative that reminds us of Marx's Eleventh Thesis on Feuerbach: "No human being ever lived without daydreams, but the point is to know them in more and more detail and, by doing so, to hold them peremptorily and helpfully, pointed towards the right thing" (PH, 1). It is exactly in this sense that thinking means transgressing, but not when performed in an arbitrary manner: "Real transgressing knows and activates the dialectically mediated tendency which is intrinsic in history's design" (*PH*, 2).

The architecture of Bloch's monumental work *The Principle of Hope* reflects in detail the various levels of reflection on which this real transgressing by means of daydreams is actually being organized. Starting from "little daydreams," passing on to the "anticipating consciousness" of primarily mythological qualities, and to the mechanisms of the leisure industry, Bloch spans the arc of his panoramic view up to the constructive techniques of concrete utopian reflections, represented in the end in terms of the arts and sciences and of philosophy proper. By doing so, he tries in fact to replace that concrete actuality which is to be criticized in structural terms by some appropriate utopian actuality as proposed by contemporary Marxist theory. Ernst Bloch has in common with Jean-Paul Sartre, who sets out to stage a similar project,[2] that his Marxism is different from the official Marxism, that he is visualizing a not-yet available yet concrete form of Marxism which is able to explicitly reconcile the antagonistic tendencies of the subjective and objective aspects of social life. In fact, the whole exposition leads invariably to the famous last sentence of Bloch's work, which evokes the concept of *home* [*Heimat*] as that which is ideally the final collective result of all efforts: "*True genesis is not at the beginning, but at the end*, and it starts to begin only when society and existence become radical, i.e., grasp their roots. But the root of history is the working, creating human being who reshapes and overhauls the given facts. Once he has grasped himself and established what is his, without expropriation and alienation, in real democracy, there arises in the world something which shines into the childhood of all and in which no one has yet been: homeland" (*PoH*, 1375–76; *PH*, 1628;).

With this concept of home, Bloch tries to visualize an essentially *virtual* world, a world that is full of possibilities and can be thought of as being *artificial* in the sense that it is being produced by human reflection and (political) action as an improvement of what there already is. (This was the crucial point of conflict in the ancient debate between Montaigne and Shakespeare: whether it would be possible to improve nature by means of human civilized activity, as the latter illustrated in terms of *The Tempest*, or rather that humans should not interfere with the original state of nature, as contended by the former.)[3] Indeed, Bloch's striving for a concrete utopia is not very different from the traditional search for the "pearly gates of cyberspace," as Margaret Wertheim has called her recent book on the human tendency toward parallel realities.[4] Unfortunately, however, the concept of utopia carries the connotation of its own impossibility in the very wording, because the Greek prefix *ou* qualifies an absolute form of negation meaning that utopia is a place [*topos*] which is impossible per definition. On the other hand, the prefix *mè* qualifies a relative form of negation. So we should actually speak of *metopia* rather than utopia when visualizing something that *is not yet* but that *could be* (because it is possible). Concrete utopia in the Blochian terminology means thus what can be approached by reflection and action such that eventually it would become reality, contrary to what is purely utopian and therefore impossible. But the latter is nevertheless not useless altogether, because it serves the orientation of activities undertaken toward something that is defining the "right direction," similar to a direction finder. And on the way to this impossible end (concrete) metopian goals can then be actualized in the sense and under the horizon of that which is aimed for.

It is interesting to note that it is not really literature which is at the center of Bloch's discussion in his main work. Of course, he mentions the standard authors of literary utopian models such as Dante (1265–1321) and Thomas More (1478–1535). And he also refers to Campanella and Milton. But besides an explicit reference to Ovid and frequent references to Goethe and Schiller, literature is not really visualized as the main carrier of utopian thought. Consequently, Bloch fails to differ precisely between the two intrinsic tendencies of literary utopian contents: that is between the older tradition of placing the utopian location into some religious beyond (Dante, Milton), on the one hand, and the more recent tradition of visualizing utopia as a sort of social alternative criticizing present society (More, Campanella), on the other.[5]

Originally, and I would agree with Wertheim's opinion here, the idea is to refer to two distinct types of space: one in which our bodies move, and another in which our soul moves.[6] In this case a soul is equated with mind in a straightforward simplification. It is in fact only the human mind which is able to eventually overcome the strict boundary of space and time. For Dante, as for the last pre-Renaissance painters, the medieval *empyreum* [empyrean heaven] is representing the actual beyond as the *habitaculum Dei* [dwelling place of God]. For the space between the world of daily life and empyrean's boundary, Dante himself describes a complex ascending hierarchy of nested structures covering the *inferno* (with the lowest point situated in the very center of Earth) as well as the nine heavens (which start on the mountain top representing the earthly paradise). This intermediacy is being entered by a gate that serves a transitory function (by this gate one does not actually enter another room or cavern, but another *space*), and one also leaves it, if successfully purified, by a second gate in order to enter the *empyreum*. The point is that even then, it is obvious that existence as inhabitant of the *empyreum* does not imply any form of earthly existence. In other words, one cannot actually say what the concept of existence means. This is an ancient clarification undertaken by St. Paul already, who states that heavenly bodies are ontologically different from earthly bodies (1 Cor 15: 40–47): "It is sown in corruption; it is raised in Incorruption."

This systematic approach to a utopian world is clearly different from a utopian model that criticizes the present society. This is mainly so because, in the first case, it is the *state of existence* itself which is being transformed such that the result cannot be compared anymore with the initial state (of common daily life). In the second case, it is the *state of organization* that is being transformed such that the result displays an alternative *earthly existence* which can actually be compared with the initial (present) state. Even if one enters the latter worlds by some suitable gate of transition, this is merely a signification of distance, a means of explaining the isolated location of that alternative world, which is nevertheless referring metaphorically to the well-known world at hand.

For a *realm of freedom* to exist in the Marxist sense would mean that a given critique in social terms can only be useful if it refers to altered living conditions within the well-known world of daily life rather than to an altered state of existence that cannot be described at all. Neither Marx himself nor Bloch has marked this crucial difference clearly. On the one hand, this opens the proposed model to quasi-religious speculations; on the other, it actually hampers the development of explicit techniques in order to introduce social improvements. It is necessary instead to transform the utopian character of the approach to an explicitly *metopian* character and to concentrate on the question of what can be possible in practical terms within the concrete world in which we are living.

More recently, within the development of cyberspace technologies, the aspect of an alternative state of worldly organization has been mixed with the aspect of changing the state of existence altogether. The idea is that eventually it might be possible to map the contents of consciousness onto suitable software so as to re-store this consciousness, together with all its perceptive and cognitive properties including the properties of a chosen environment, which then becomes the concrete emulation of the original human person. In this case, the crucial point is to live on in a world that is essentially the old world, under the old living conditions, with the difference that now this world is itself an artificial world and its conditions are emulated rather than real. This progressive mixing of alternative states can be visualized as a kind of revision of the ancient idea of Dante's. As Wertheim quotes Woody Allen: "I would not actually like to achieve immortality in terms of my works, but simply by not dying instead."[7]

In this chapter I will try to assemble the most important aspects that refer to the problems mentioned in this introduction. In the first section I will discuss the recent literary tendencies that deal with alternative worlds in more detail. In the second section I will concentrate on aspects of cyberspace as an example for the continuation of these literary tendencies within a new technological context. In the conclusion I will try to reconcile the results with even more recent formal results in the mediation of space and language. As it turns out within the framework of the chosen examples, the search for metopian structures is a common project that transforms itself into a personal (private) project after all. In other words, by visualizing virtual worlds as metopian alternatives and by striving thus for an actual improvement of the world as it is observed, the new variety gained shows up mainly in terms of an innovative and most flexible variability expressed in terms of individual desires. It is perhaps this aspect that opens up the route toward reconciling the *bourgeois* with the *citoyen* as it will be discussed in this chapter.

Literary Artificial Worlds

Cornelia Funke's *Inkheart Trilogy* (2003–8) is both a classical as well as a modern approach to the problem of virtual realities. It is classical with a view to the literary medium and style in which it is being presented, but it also strives to satisfy the needs of a reading public that associates with the concept of virtuality and the electronically generated environments of our time.[8] In fact, Funke follows the traditional strategy of declaring her work as one for children, although it is quite unlikely that most of the children, if reading at all, will be able to actually grasp the deeper aspects of what the plot is implying. Essentially, she starts by appealing to the memory character of reading itself: "If you take a book with you for travelling, . . . then something odd happens: The book will begin to collect your memories. Later, you will simply have to open it, and at once you will be back at the place where you have read it for the first time."[9] Insofar as the printed story is in fact reinterpreted while reading, with a view to personal experiences, or with respect to a personal, individually visualized world, it is in fact a superposition of several stories in the end: "Perhaps behind the printed story there is another, far bigger one which changes in the same way as our world is changing? And the letters tell us about this just so much as a look through a keyhole would."[10] In this sense the question is whether we do actually belong to various stories and not only one.[11] In any case, the story that is read changes the reader who at the same time changes the story. Hence a story is obviously more than the written text.[12] The respective worlds can be said to actually *consist of words*, and their reality will be mediated by means of concrete communication about them.[13]

Although this line of argument is not very different from the usual exposition of the techniques of interpreting literary works and of talking about them in terms of an appropriate hermeneutic, the message is quite clear: by reading books one can create one's own personalized virtual worlds. Indeed, within the process of socialization, literary narration is probably the first sort of institutionalized virtuality beyond the games of very young children. So far, so good. But the *Inkheart Trilogy* offers a further generalization of this perspective. The idea is that any narration, in particular the one which is self-made and subject to a spontaneous outbreak of fantasy, can achieve this sort of virtuality. And more than that, it is proposed that the concept of virtuality be visualized in its original sense, not as something that is not real and/or concrete (like an optically generated picture that can be observed but cannot be projected onto a screen), but rather as something that can be possibly concrete and can form a real alternative to the given world. The virtuality here not only is alternative in formal terms but also is *parallel*. It thus fulfills the conditions of the daydream in a Blochian sense. But note that in general, this virtuality which is parallel to lived actuality is not very different from the world of daily life. It is probably not more than a minimally modified variant of the latter, adjusted according to the wishes of the author. Completely different variants of daily life are extremely rare. We deal mostly with variations in the state of organization rather than with variations of the state of existence.[14] In fact, Funke's work belongs to a traditional line of narration which, in a sufficiently modern language, seems to have started with Lewis Carroll's story of Sylvie and Bruno.[15] This dates back to 1889 and introduces style elements that will become commonly known to readers of literature only after the advent of the innovations introduced by James Joyce. Indeed, as to the compositional techniques employed, Carroll can be visualized as a precursor of Joyce.[16] The three parallel worlds of Carroll's novel (our own world, Outland, Fairyland) are still accessible directly within states of dreaming. They are essentially worlds of daydreams (and because of their explicit intermediation, this means that our own world of daily experience is actually included in these states of dreaming rather than operating on a different "ontological" level). On the other hand, in this very text, Carroll establishes an explicit satirical treatment of the real world by referring especially to the children's literature of his time. In principle, he performs what Steiner has later called a *specific form of literary critique* within a generalized kind of "secondary literature": Carroll criticizes the literature of his time by writing his own.[17]

This aspect of critique leads to the complete unfolding of ideological strategies in the later series of *Narnia* novels by C. S. Lewis. Again, this goes under the name of children's literature and follows a standard scheme of development that will remain an invariant in later epochs. Five key points of this scheme can be readily identified: 1. Young protagonists who have an important life mission (in the beginning unknown to themselves) are being addressed through a crucial, otherworldly adventure. 2. An excursion takes place into an invented world that may have well-defined boundaries or more abstract configurations. 3. Perilous journeys provoke mind- and life-altering events and consequences. 4. There are adults and other guides who offer information and assistance. 5. The protagonists return to the primary world with new information and abilities to address problems that they left behind in the first place.[18]

This key structure clearly follows that of ancient mythological narratives which can be traditionally read as mapping the biographical development of the protagonists involved.[19] However, without mentioning it directly, this mythology is being altered in an explicitly Christian form. And it is no coincidence that the novels with children as their protagonists aim at children. There are essentially two reasons for this: first, the technical reason (or the ideological reason in the strict sense) is that this sort of literature which appears primarily to be an entertaining adventure, similar to fairy tales for even smaller children, can easily be utilized as a subversive medium that is able to instrumentalize the immanent polarization between forces of Good and Evil in order to transport (in the case of Lewis *Catholic*) Christian ideas. On the other hand, the more metaphysical reason is that children as agents of the story imply a fundamental state of innocence that opens up a new beginning of history from where concrete improvements can be induced. The famous lion in *Narnia* carries multifarious connotations of Jesus Christ, while the protagonists become actual kings and queens of virtual reality enthroned by him. And in this sense they are a refined sort of mini Adams and Eves. But once the protagonists are of adult age, they cannot reenter Narnia because they have lost their innocence. And the cycle continues with other children.

Together with Tolkien's *Lord of the Rings*, which is very much on the same line of development as the *Narnia* books,[20] these novels follow the same mythological structure by talking about some suitable *Otherworld* that can be accessed by daydreaming and being entered metaphorically by means of special gates.[21] As we have seen, these windows or portals have been introduced much earlier by Dante. (And also Carroll works with them in his Alice books.) Even in their explicit ideology they are nothing but projected drafts of alternative (virtual) worlds. The interesting point is that over the years their ideological content becomes increasingly concealed such that the common readers take these books at their face value as adventure stories full of action, especially if transformed into suitable Hollywood movies.

This can be particularly recognized in the case of Philip Pullman's *His*

Dark Materials trilogy, which has been called a "triumph of intertextuality."[22] Here, Pullman follows the same setting when presenting his children's mythology, except that he refers to recent terminology taken from physics: he talks about many-world theories, superstrings, smallest agents (called *dust*) constituting nature, and so forth. His portals into other worlds can easily be verified when manipulating windows in the computer software that is readily at hand today. In other words, Pullman joins the circle of the above-mentioned novelists, but at the boundary to cyberspace proper. And he differs from his predecessors in that his ideology is rather an *anti-ideology*. This is so because he also quotes the common literary systems of reference in starting with Milton. The structural scheme of the story is very much the same as that mentioned earlier, and in the end, the children are separated, again being confined to live in their own respective worlds once they have become adults. Here the form follows the traditional function.[23] On the other hand, Pullman introduces explicitly satirical elements hinting at a universal (obviously Catholic) organization that oppresses people in the virtual Oxford 2.0 (not altogether different from the real Oxford, as it appears) or talking about a Chief Angel who tells the other angels that he would (could?) be the Lord, although he is not, merely the first angel created, while the true Lord is being kept in a container where he is conserved but unable to act because of his enormous age. And indeed, in the end, the compassionate children will liberate him from his prison such that he disintegrates into dust.

Obviously, Pullman is challenging the narration of Lewis and Tolkien by means of an atheistic counterproject, introducing aspects of existential ethics instead: "Mary Malone explains that she still believes in good and evil, but not in powers 'outside us . . . good and evil are names for what people do, not for what they are.'"[24] Indeed, this is something Jean-Paul Sartre could have said. And Marina Warner has recovered the (secular)[25] roots of this sort of narration in Ovid's *Metamorphoses*.[26] In the whole line of literary tradition, these roots are often interpreted in a strictly idealistic manner (choosing the spirit as a kind of invariable substance among the worldly multitude). But in Pullman, they are being given an explicitly materialistic context when they show up in terms of what he calls *dust*.[27] Warner states correctly: "Ovid's picture of natural generation, assuming a universe that is unceasingly progenitive, multiple, and fluid, organizes the relationships between creatures according to axioms of metaphorical affinity, poetic resonance, and even a variety of dream punning."[28]

We clearly recognize here the basic elements of what the creation of virtual spaces is all about. The same principles have been applied in Italian Renaissance literature, notably in Colonna-Alberti's "Hypnerotomachia Poliphili,"[29] which can be visualized as a modern version of the *Metamorphoses*. In fact, in the meantime, this work, after a long and complex process of translation, has been reinterpreted again (and criticized in a literary sense) by another novel and a commentary following the novel's publication.[30] In particular, the relevant elements of style survive also in the later works that we have already mentioned: "Science and magic converge in ways of thinking about shadows, ghosts, and out-of-body experiences, in a uniquely Victorian amalgam of spiritual quest and rationality."[31] The actual representation performed in the narrative structures acts as a form of doubling: "[It] exists in magical relation to the apprehensible world, it can exercise the power to make something alive, apparently. . . . *Simply put, figures of speech turn into figures of vitality*."[32]

Aspects of Cyberspace

In a straightforward generalization of the ideas mentioned above, we find that a practical implementation of them into the present versions of cyberspace makes the underlying epistemic principle, namely, to visualize a virtual space explicitly constructed out of propositions, much more clear after all. In fact, what we can observe on the computer screen (or by means of more intricate machinery connected directly to the pathways of cognition) is nothing but the immediate result of a relevant set of propositions written in the program. This program is to what happens on the screen or elsewhere what the traditional substance is to its attributes under which human observation can actually take place.[33] A larger complex structure such as *Secondlife* or similar scenarios is essentially a web constituted of language, and the virtual space representing this very web is ultimately *made* out of language.

The first fully developed story of this kind was published, however, as a literary novel. Tad Williams, originally a writer of fantasy fiction, traveled into the field of science fiction and created a novel that combined all the diverse aspects of virtual (artificial) worlds while the plot took place in cyberspace proper.[34] The considerable merit of this work of literary fiction is primarily that it is able to illuminate the possibilities that a further development of cyberspace will have. At the same time, various alleys to useful and less useful applications are being indicated within a considerably realistic framework of everyday tendencies in media technology. Also, Williams does not refrain from the treatment of somewhat more metaphysical questions related to cyberspace, not quite covering the scope of the famous predecessor novel *Permutation City*,[35] but at the very least comparable in a quite profitable manner.

But the really important point is something else: beyond the literary context of lived adventures,[36] the central aspect of possible applications is in the concrete modeling of everyday environments which are not more than variants of the world we actually live in. In other words, this sort of modeling by means of planned variations of artificial worlds contributes to what we may call "experimental philosophy" in the sense of creating scenarios according to theoretical principles and drawing conclusions about their feasibility in practice.[37] Here the line of Blochian arguments loops back to practical achievements such that we gain a clear indication as to what *concrete utopia* would actually mean. As can be shown, cyberspace produces itself *within the framework of its own everyday handling* of new forms of communication and cooperation that enable the development of concrete political projects that are well able to change social conceptions in the long run. Especially, the recent works of Antonio Negri and Michael Hardt refer to this aspect.[38] Indeed, the confrontation of the early twenty-first century between the "Empire" on the one hand and the "Multitude" on the other can be explicitly defused by resorting to emergent innovative structures of society. This is very much what Bloch once anticipated when thinking of his concept of concrete utopia.

Nevertheless, the ancient difference between *bourgeois* and *citoyen* is still unresolved. While on the theoretical level of discussion, notably in Negri and Hardt, this is clearly shown by means of the difficulties arising when introducing the two-sided implication of two identities which do not necessarily appear to be mutually compatible in the first place:

virtus = potentia ⇔ civitas = multitudo

This is also shown in the concrete tendencies of everyday practical life where indeed a kind of "privatization of hope" can be noticed.

First of all, in the terminology of Spinoza, the implicational formula above links the concepts of "virtue" and "potential," on the one hand, "citizenry" and "multitude," on the other. The respective identities of the two pairs of concepts, however, which are always understood in terms of being a postulated ideal and thus an ethical demand rather than a concrete given, cause various difficulties because their realization in terms of practical daily life seems counterintuitive and not quite a straightforward operation of illustrating an idealized principle. The underlying problem is in fact one of mediation: this is so because the implication's identity of the left-hand side refers to *individual people* while the identity of the right-hand side refers to (social) *groups of people*. Hence any practical realization of the inferred principle should operate on two different levels, which are dialectically mediated, and this turns out to be the most difficult problem of any ethical approach. (In fact, as it appears, this may also pose a serious problem for the approach offered by Negri and Hardt themselves, because making the multitude topical, as they do, is only half of the task, and perhaps it is thus that the latter's ideas occasionally appear somewhat abstract.)[39]

Nevertheless, it is very much along similar lines that a possible reconciliation of both sides of the above implicational formula comes into view. Cyberspace technology opens up a much wider scope for a practical utopian field than literature, because it enhances the concrete cooperation necessary in order to develop and utilize the new technology (this is the mediative aspect between the left-hand side and the right-hand side of the above formula) and because it increases the range of applied fantasies quite considerably (such that the gain for the individual person increases with the gain for others). Of course, the danger of eventual failure is always immanent. This is illustrated in a particularly clear manner in the *Otherland* novel. But the *possible failure of hope* is an invariant within the Blochian context in the first place. Or to be more precise, the failure of humankind on this very planet does not entail the failure of other humankinds on other planets. This should not, however, hold us back from trying our utmost to achieve the metopian states of the world.

Note that from the start, the concept of cyberspace as we have used it here is not at all restricted to some computer-screen scenario as we know it. In fact, it is the research field of *biospherics* (close to the field of space exploration) that opens further perspectives on practical applications of cyberspace technology, especially with a view to urban systems.[40] Within the framework of this ongoing research we enter directly the space of concrete realizations of those possibilities which span the field of virtual reality in the strict sense. And this is nothing but the consequent approach to what Bloch once called "concrete utopia." In other words, although it appears as if within the context of the industrialized parts of the world a strong tendency toward the privatization of hope is unfolding itself, far beyond the traditional structures of social solidarity, there is nevertheless another, not so obvious, but equally strong tendency toward a reestablishment of what in classical terms can be called *polis*, aiming at a resystematization of urban social space which becomes more and more influenced by cyberspace technology and is transferrable, in principle, to settlements on other planets as well. This concept does not refer to a *polis* in the ancient Greek sense, of course, but to one which incorporates the achievements of modern societies. This means that the Blochian approach is still quite adequate after all, though we have to generalize and thus modify its context and consequences accordingly. In fact, the merit of a philosopher is less in the affirmation of what he or she has written but more in the productive generalization of his or her thoughts. So the Blochian principle of hope is still governing our life provided we apply it in a creative manner rather than simply copying it from what has been written long ago, under a horizon of knowledge and insight that Bloch himself could not actually anticipate at the time.

Today, it is the recently emerging (mathematical) *topos theory*[41] which has become relevant for quite a number of research fields that offer a more precise approach to the problem of mediating space and language. The important point is that a topos (as mathematical structure) turns out to be a Lindenbaum-Tarski algebra for a logical theory whose models are the points of a space.[42] In other words, we can identify an appropriate space with a logical theory such that its points are the models of this theory, its open sets the propositional formulae, the sheafs the predicate formulae, and the continuous maps the transformations of models. At this point logic connects with model theory. Essentially, a Lindenbaum-Tarski algebra A of a logical theory T consists of the equivalence classes of propositions p of the theory under the relation $\cong$ defined by $p \cong q$ when p and q are logically equivalent in T. That is, in T proposition q can be deduced from p and vice versa. Operations in A are inherited from those available in T, typically conjunction and disjunction. When negation is also present, then A is Boolean, provided the logic is classical. Conversely, for every Boolean algebra A, there is a theory T of classical propositional logic such that the Lindenbaum-Tarski algebra of T is isomorphic to A. In the case of intuitionist logic, the Lindenbaum-Tarski algebras are Heyting algebras. (Hence we deal here with an algebra of logical propositions in which logically equivalent formulations of the same proposition are not differentiated.) We recognize immediately that it is model theory that relates representation to interpretation: model theory is the mathematical discipline that checks semantic elements of structures by means of syntactic elements in a given language. The latter can have logical as well as non-logical symbols and grammatical rules, but in principle, it is always the explication of a logical theory. If L is such a language, and M some set, then M becomes an L-structure by means of the interpretation of each of the non-logical symbols in L. Each proposition that is formulated according to the rules gains some *meaning* in M. So representation entails interpretation and vice versa.

It is not the proper place here to enter deeply into the discussion of model theory.[43] But what we can already see is the relevance of the spatial approach to topoi. We recall from philosophical epistemology that essentially a *theory* is a set of propositions that satisfy certain rules. If we visualize the theory as an abstract space, then the points of this space are subsets of propositions. Generalized (abstract) spaces (not only within the field of mathematics) are nothing but sets of propositions or subsets of languages. Obviously, the languages serve the purpose of drafting a picture of the world so as to orient oneself within its complex network of social and nonsocial interactions.

This aspect is directly projected onto a plane representing an abstract space of reflexive operations in the case of what we call a *glass bead game*.[44] The projection takes place here on a two-dimensional plane that is represented in terms of vertices and edges of a network, where the vertices are points that represent propositions and the edges are logical connectives of these propositions. In principle, this is a graphical representation that maps nicely what the topos concept means when referring to its spatial aspect. The glass bead game consists of sequences of points being consistently connected by appropriate edges such that the resulting path within the network of propositions is the picture of a research process that mirrors the model building common in the sciences. (The idea is taken from the well-known novel by Hermann Hesse.) The glass bead game essentially maps a section of social space (namely, its scientific section laid down in scientific scripture). And in doing so it illustrates that this space is intrinsically dynamic because it is actually constituted by the processing of the sequences of propositions according to given rules. In other words, we are dealing here with the processing of information (including its organization and interpretation). This concept is compatible with Alfred Lorenzer's theory of "language games," which stress the importance of predicators for the explicit training of social interactions in daily life.[45]

One aspect is still missing: the concrete *multi-perspectivity* of social space. This is dealt with in detail in Guerino Mazzola's work on the theory of music, which explores how various perspectives are taken into account that determine the modes of interpretation of given works of music. But this aspect is equally important for social spaces in general. And as it turns out, it can also be included in the terminology of topos theory. This can be shown in terms of what is called "Yoneda lemma." For Mazzola, the Yoneda lemma serves as a foundation of multi-perspectivity among local interpretations. In music (Mazzola's favorite field), let R and S be appropriate vector spaces, and let K in R and L in S be two local compositions.[46] The relations then between the two compositions can be expressed as a morphism K → L. Essentially, this morphism defines a perspective under which L can be visualized. The Yoneda lemma certifies then that the system of all L-perspectives determines the isomorphy class of L. The morphisms can be visualized as essentially hermeneutic instruments in order to classify and understand local compositions. It is quite straightforward then to generalize this aspect to more "unspecialized" cases as instances of social space. The important point is that most of the time we do not talk here about a space *as it is actually observed*, but instead about a space *as it could be observed*. The number of possible interpretations is larger than the number of actual interpretations. (Remember that in common social space, collections of these interpretations form the practical "worldview.") Not only does space show up as social space in the first place, and not only does social space show up as a space whose points are propositions of logical theories, but social space shows up as well as a *virtual space*. Strictly speaking, the concrete social space is a *special case* of virtual space, and not vice versa, because the latter's "virtuality" refers to the field of possibilities rather than to the field of actualities that can be empirically observed.[47]

What we see now is that traditionally, there have been many connections between the human techniques of spatial representation (what has been called *anthropological graphism* elsewhere)[48] and the mapping of processes in terms of logical formulae. And we have seen elsewhere that this kind of discussion visualizes processes in the general sense as percolation phenomena,[49] and what is being percolated is information then. And we have seen that it is topos theory that provides an appropriate language in order to deal with these aspects of spatial representation. More than that, a topos can be essentially interpreted as the algebraic expression of the fact that spaces utilized in human cognition are basically constituted by propositions of logical theories. On the other hand, the procedures of deduction and induction as well as creative abduction, available to human logic, can be rephrased in terms of algorithmic pro-

Cognition	Communication	Cooperation
Space	Network	System

cedures. Hence they are both accessible by means of programs as they are utilized in computation, and by means of game theory, because on a fundamental level of reflection, games are essentially algorithmic procedures whose strategies are given by their rules.[50] What we realize then is that all of this relates nicely with the approaches of the Kassel and Salzburg schools as described at earlier occasions.[51]

Remember that the conceptual nucleus of these approaches is given by two triadic arrangements of concepts of the form:

The first triadic structure mirrors the close relationship between cognition and communication on the one hand—as a pair of concepts characterizing the process of reflection—and cooperation on the other hand—as characterizing the transition from reflection to action.[52] While the first pair of concepts cannot be separated in practice, the latter concept is structurally separable from the other two. Reflection and action represent thus two different time scales which show up with the systematic updating process involved in the sequential organization which is underlying both reflexion and action, respectively. The producing of models belongs to the pair of concepts in the first place and is primarily based on a generic self-model which defines the framework according to which cognition is normalized. Essentially, this is the onto-epistemic picture of the grasping of the world by humans.[53] Earlier stages of evolution can be visualized as conceptual approximations of this onto-epistemic picture.

In *methodological* terms the second triadic structure is associated with the first such that there are intrinsic pairwise correspondences between cognition and space, communication and network, and cooperation and system, respectively. Space is the conceptual structure from which that world of daily life is being reconstructed, which is derived from the process of cognition. Network is the conceptual structure from which those social interactions of daily life can be reconstructed, which are derived from the process of communication. System is the conceptual structure from which those joint manipulations of the material world can be reconstructed, which are derived from the process of cooperation. Obviously, the first and second pair of concepts from the two triadic structures regulate the actual flow of information and the interpretation of meaning while the third pair regulates the production of matter. This is a result of the fact that the complete system is more than space and network, because it encompasses not only social interactions but also tangible matter.[54] In a sense, space is the region in which the system unfolds its actions, while the network is a skeleton of both space and system. This systematic viewpoint can show clearly how humans construct their various spatial representations by editing the propositions of their theories.

And in fact, this is what we have tried to develop in this chapter by means of referring to recent developments in dealing with virtual worlds as interpreted in terms of the concept of *metopia*: the essential idea is that while the utopian nucleus of evolving virtual worlds (e.g., in the field of cyberspace development) can be visualized as one that strengthens the right-hand side of Spinoza's isomorphism relationship (civitas/multitude) and hence the public part of collective interests, at the same time its practical application strengthens also the left-hand side (virtus/potentia) because of the variability achieved. The public aspect of life can be reconciled with its individual (private) aspect. This kind of equilibrium of desire and interest can be interpreted within a framework of privatizing hope in the Blochian sense.

Notes

1   Note that I quote according to the text of the German edition in my own translation. Note also that "to come out of its shell" the English version of the original meaning of the Latin "existere, existo, exstiti" is indeed such that an explicit existential connotation is being produced here. Also, "to be well-aimed" carries here the connotation of "being objective."

2   In fact, while *The Principle of Hope* is published in 1959, Sartre turns to Marxism explicitly in his *Saint Genet* of 1952 for the first time, and he continues then to lay out his principles for a future Marxism around 1960 in his *Search for a Method* and in the first part of his *Critique of Dialectical Reason*.

3   Rainer E. Zimmermann, "Prosperos Buch oder Echolot der Materie," *VorSchein* 15 (1996): 40–57.

4   Margaret Wertheim, *Pearly Gates of Cyberspace: A History of Space from Dante to the Internet* (New York: W. W. Norton, 1999).

5   Note that in practice, a really precise distinction is not quite possible, though, because the one tendency always ends up overlapping with the other.

6   Wertheim, *Pearly Gates of Cyberspace*, 21.

7   Wertheim, *Pearly Gates of Cyberspace*, 292. Note, however, that this cyberspace version of immortality is not really one for eternity, because it is necessary to look after and attend to the memory system in order to service it and provide energy for it, and so forth.

8   Cornelia Funke, *Tintenherz, Tintenblut, Tintentod* (Hamburg: Dressler, 2003, 2005, 2007): published in English as *Inkheart, Inkblood, Inkdeath*, trans. Anthea Bell (Frome: Chicken House, 2004, 2005, 2009).

9   Funke, *Tintenherz*, 24 (always my translation).

10 Funke, *Tintenherz*, 163.

11 Funke, *Tintentod*, 288.

12 Funke, *Tintentod*, 466, 472.

13   Funke, *Tintentod*, 700.

14   As far as I know, the only case where the narration encompasses completely alien variants of (conscious) existence is the world of the science fiction novel series on the planet Dune by Frank Herbert: *Dune, Dune Messiah, Children of Dune, God Emperor of Dune, Heretics of Dune, Chapterhouse Dune* (New York: Ace—Penguin/Putnam, 1965, 1969, 1976, 1981, 1984, 1985). There are some other candidates, especially within this same genre, but except perhaps Doris Lessing's *Canopus in Argos: Archives* cycle, most of them are far off the mark. A strictly parallel world like that of J. K. Rowling's Harry Potter is not really alien in this sense, because it is essentially mapping a traditional English public school novel plus a transformation of everyday life into one which is being enriched by certain magical properties and facilities of the protagonists.

15   Lewis Carroll (Charles Lutwidge Dodgson), *The Complete Sylvie and Bruno* (San Francisco: Mercury House, 1991).

16   See in particular the editor's note to the above-mentioned edition by Thomas Christensen, "Dodgson's Dodges," in *The Complete Sylvie and Bruno*, ix–xvi.

17   George Steiner, *Real Presences* (London: Faber and Faber, 1989). Here quoted according to the German edition (Munich: Hanser, 1990), 24.

18   Paraphrased according to Karen Patricia Smith, "Tradition, Transformation, and the Bold Emergence: Fantastic Legacy and Pullman's HDM," in Millicent Lenz, Carole Scott, eds., *His Dark Materials Illuminated: Critical Essays on Philip Pullman's Trilogy* (Detroit: Wayne State University Press, 2005), 135–51 (136).

19   Rainer E. Zimmermann, *Die ausserordentlichen Reisen des Jules Verne: Zur Wissenschafts- und Technikrezeption im Frankreich des 19. Jahrhunderts* (Paderborn: mentis, 2006), 291–309.

20   In the *Lord of the Rings* the world is not really parallel, though, but it is essentially an earthly world much older than human beings. From the general plan of Tolkien's cycle (essentially consisting of *The Hobbit, The Lord of the Rings, The Simarillion*) we can see that the late days of the struggle against Sauron (when the master ring is being destroyed) play shortly before the first historical humans take the rule over the world such that we could even give a date to that, namely, about 6,000 BCE. Nevertheless, there are also gates in the story that can be utilized to enter other worlds (the underworld, the world of the dead, the fairy world beyond the Sea, and so forth).

21   Various types of methods to enter other worlds are discussed in Jane Langton, *The Weak Place in the Cloth* (New York: Hiern Books, 1973), 433–41.

22   Carole Scott, "Pullman's Enigmatic Ontology: Revamping Old Traditions in HDM," in *His Dark Materials Illuminated*, ed. Millicent Lenz and Carole Scott, 95–105 (96). Scott refers to Philip Pullman, *His Dark Materials* (*The Golden Compass, The Subtle Knife, The Amber Spyglass*) (New York: Random House, 1995, 1997, 2000). In fact, the motto to volume 1 illustrates clearly the underlying conception when quoting from Milton's *Paradise Lost* and giving the trilogy its name: "But all these in their pregnant causes mixed / Confusedly, and which thus must ever fight, / Unless the almighty maker them ordain / His dark materials to create more worlds."

23 As defined in Alastair J. Minnis, Alexander B. Scott, and David Wallace, eds., *Medieval Literary Theory and Criticism* (Oxford: Clarendon Press, 1998), 267: "Littera gesta docet / Quid credas allegoria /Moralia quid agas / Quo tendas anagogia" [The letter teaches history; / Allegory, what you must believe; / The moral sense, what you must do; / The anagogical, your future destination]. These are the fundamental rules of interpreting narratives, also applicable to children's literature.

24 Scott, *His Dark Materials Illuminated*, 98, quoting *The Amber Spyglass*, 470.

25 With "secular" within the age of (Roman) polytheism we mean here the universal nucleus within the multitude of mythological deities which is interpreted in the sense of an underlying cross-cultural "administration" of what is actually independent of specific cultural forms constituting a ritual framework for the Empire similar to the republican administration practiced until the first century BCE and later for a short period subject to a trial of reconstruction under the emperor Julian.

26 Marina Warner, *Fantastic Metamorphoses, Other Worlds* (Oxford: Oxford University Press, 2002).

27 Essentially, this complies with *Metamorphoses* 15:165: "utque novis facilis signatur vera figures / nec manet ut fuerat nec formam servant eandem, / sed tamen ipsa eadem est, animam sic semper eandem / esse, sed in varias doceo migrare figuras" [As the pliant wax is stamped with new designs, / and is no longer what once it was, but changes form, and still / is pliant wax, so do I teach that spirit / is evermore the same, though passing always to ever-changing bodies] from *Ovids Metamorphosen*, 2nd ed., ed. Gerhard Fink (Munich: Artemis und Winkler, 2007).

28 Warner, *Fantastic Metamorphoses*, 5.

29 Francesco Colonna, *Hypnerotomachia Poliphili*, ed. Joscelyn Godwin (London: Thames and Hudson, 1999).

30 Ian Caldwell and Dustin Thomason, *The Rule of Four* (New York: Dell, 2004). See also Joscelyn Godwin, *The Real Rule of Four* (New York: Disinformation, 2004). A study on the work's impact on modern architecture has been given by Liane Lefaivre, *Leon Battista Alberti's Hypnerotomachia Poliphili. Re-Cognizing the Architectural Body in the Early Italian Renaissance* (Cambridge, MA: MIT Press, 1997). Note that the question as to whether Alberti himself or the more apocryphal Colonna is the author of this work is still disputed somewhat.

31 Warner, *Fantastic Metamorphoses*, 28.

32 Warner, *Fantastic Metamorphoses*, 165, 169.

33 The relevant principles of this viewpoint have been discussed in more detail in Rainer E. Zimmermann, *New Ethics Proved in Geometrical Order: Spinozist Reflexions on Evolutionary Systems* (Litchfield Park, AZ: Emergent Publications, 2010).

34 Tad Williams, *Otherland*, 4 vols. (*City of Golden Shadow, River of Blue Fire, Mountain of Black Glass, Sea of Silver Light*) (Brookfield, CT: DAW Books, 1996, 1998, 1999, 2001).

35 Greg Egan, *Permutation City* (London: Millennium, 1994).

36 Although the Blochian wedding of *fair* and *objective fantasy* (of Karl May and Karl Marx) is always immanent within these conceptions. Compare Ernst Bloch, "Über

Märchen, Kolportage, und Sage" [On Fairy Tales, Trashy Literature, and Legend], in Bloch, *Erbschaft dieser Zeit* (Frankfurt: Suhrkamp, 1985), 168–86.

37   Rainer E. Zimmermann, "'. . . the exact size, shape and color of hope itself'" Virtual Environment and Concrete Utopia," in *Heimat in vernetzten Welten*, Jahrbuch der Ernst-Bloch-Gesellschaft 2006, ed. Francesca Vidal (Mössingen: Talheimer, 2006), 67–82.

38   Compare Christian Fuchs and Rainer E. Zimmermann, *Practical Civil Virtues in Cyberspace: Towards the Utopian Identity of Civitas and Multitudo* (Aachen: Shaker, 2008).

39   Fuchs and Zimmermann, *Practical Civil Virtues in Cyberspace*, 7.

40   Rainer E. Zimmermann, "Impact of Artificial Life on Climate Change," in *Second International Conference* IT *and the Climate Change*, ed. Klaus Fuchs-Kittowski and Volker Wohlgemuth (Berlin: ITCC, 2009), 58–67. See also Zimmermann, "Metopien in Anderland. Ansätze zu einer experimentellen Philosophie," in *Naturallianz — von der Physik zur Politik, Jahrbuch der Ernst-Bloch-Gesellschaft* 2006, ed. Francesca Vidal (Mössingen: Talheimer, 2004), 47–62. And for more practical applications in urban space, see Zimmermann, "From Utopia to Metopia: Brecht's *Mahagonny* as a Counter Project to Progressing Civilis and Actual Bologna as Its Negation," in *"Können uns und euch und niemand helfen": Die Mahagonnysierung der Welt*, ed. Gerd Koch et al. (Frankfurt: Brandes und Apsel, 2006), 113–23; Zimmerman, "Die Raumdeutung: Ein erster Ansatz," *VorSchein* 29 (2007): 13–25; Zimmermann, "Sartre steht im Raum: Überlegungen zur Einholung der Philosophie in die soziale Praxis," in *Carnets Jean-Paul Sartre — Eine Moral in Situation*, ed. Peter Knopp and Vincent von Wroblewsky (Frankfurt: Lang, 2008), 211–32; Zimmermann, "Konzeptuelle Dialektik I: Leid & Elend," *VorSchein* 30 (2008): 225–42; Zimmermann, "Konzeptuelle Dialektik II: Topoi der Systeme," Berliner November 2007 (Leibniz-Sozietät Berlin); Zimmermann, "Topoi der Architektur: Zur approximativen Harmonie der Raumgestaltung oder: Bauhaus Revisited," *Jahrbuch der Ernst-Bloch-Gesellschaft* 2008 (Mössingen: Talheimer, 2008), 17–32.

41   Zimmermann, *New Ethics Proved*, 28, 35.

42   We follow here the terminology of Steven Vickers, "Locales and Toposes as Spaces," in *Handbook of Spatial Logics*, ed. Marco Aiello, Ian Pratt-Hartmann, and Johan van Bentham (Berlin: Springer, 2007), 429–96: preprint version available at: http://www.cs.bham.ac.uk/~sjv/papersfull.php#LocTopSpaces.

43   For a useful survey refer to Wilfrid Hodges, *A Shorter Model Theory* (Cambridge: Cambridge University Press, 1997).

44   Cf. Rainer E. Zimmermann, "The Modeling of Nature as a Glass Bead Game," in *Conference Human Approaches to the Universe: An Interdisciplinary Perspective*, ed. Eeva Martikainen (Helsinki: Agricola Society, 2005), 43–65. More details in Zimmermann, *Was heißt und zu welchem Ende studiert man Design Science? Münchener Schriften zur Design Science*, vol. 1 (Aachen: Shaker, 2007).

45   Cf. Alfred Lorenzer, *Sprachspiel und Interaktionsformen* (Frankfurt: Suhrkamp, 1977); Lorenzer, *Sprachzerstörung und Rekonstruktion* (Frankfurt: Suhrkamp, 1970). Origi-

nally, Lorenzer looked for a theoretical combination of Wittgenstein's and Freud's approaches.

46 We refer here to Mazzola's earlier paper [with Oliver Zahorka] "Topologien gestalteter Motive in Kompositionen"; www.uni-koeln.de/phil-fak/muwi/fricke/145maz zola.pdf. The complete outline of Mazzola's approach is given in the monumental book by Guerino Mazzola, *The Topos of Music: Geometric Logic of Concepts, Theory, and Performance* (Basel: Birkhäuser, 2002).

47 As a referee once correctly stated on another occasion, virtual space is an extremely rich and complex concept. But note that, in principle, it is identical with what we might call *reality*, while social space, in so far as it is observable, is *modality* instead. In fact, as far as it goes, communication in terms of language is concrete rather than abstract, though its interpretations are abstract rather than concrete, but can unfold concrete actions undertaken.

48 Rainer E. Zimmermann, *Graphismus & Repraesentation Zu einer poetischen Logik von Raum und Zeit* (Munich: Magenta, 2004). The idea goes back to a formulation of Henri Lefebvre, *The Production of Space* (Oxford: Blackwell, [1974] 1991), 33: "A conceptual triad has now emerged. . . . : 1) *spatial practice* which embraces production and reproduction, and the particular locations and spatial sets characteristic of each social formation. . . . 2) *representations of space* which are tied to the relations of production . . . , hence to knowledge, signs, codes . . . 3) *representational spaces* embodying complex symbolisms . . . linked to the clandestine side of social life." In this book the problem of space is posed for the first time in a sufficiently modern language. There are even remarks on Hesse's *Glass Bead Game* (24, 136).

49 Cf. Dietrich Stauffer and Amnon Aharony, *Introduction to Percolation Theory*, 2nd ed. (London: Taylor and Francis, 1994).

50 Cf. Robin Houston, "Categories of Games," master's thesis, University of Manchester, 2003.

51 Cf. the volumes of collected essays presenting the results of the INTAS cooperation project "Human Systems in Transition" with the universities of Vienna, Kassel, and Kyiv and the Academy of Sciences, Moscow, led by Wolfgang Hofkirchner (then Vienna, now Salzburg): Vladimir Arshinov and Christian Fuchs, eds., *Causality, Emergence, Self-Organization*, vol. 1, Russian Academy of Science (Moscow: NIA-Priroda, 2003); Iryna Dobronravova and Wolfgang Hofkirchner, eds., *Science of Self-Organization and Self-Organization of Science*, vol. 2 (Kiev: Abris, 2004); Rainer E. Zimmermann and Vladimir G. Budanov, eds., *Towards Otherland: Languages of Science and Languages Beyond*, vol. 3 (Kassel: Kassel University Press, 2005).

52 For more details, see Rainer E. Zimmermann, "Konzeptuelle Dialektik I and II."

53 In other words, it is the human mode of being to produce knowledge. For humans, ontology and epistemology fall into one. Higher and lower animals, in principle also plants, represent the same scheme, but on lower levels of organization. Essentially, even physical systems on a very fundamental level can be thought of as satisfying the general framework of this scheme, though by extremely simple means of organization. In the sense of Stuart Kauffman in *Investigations* (Oxford: Oxford University

Press, 2001) the most fundamental physical (autonomous) agent can be defined by satisfying a minimal condition from thermodynamics, namely, that the system is able to perform at least one thermodynamic work cycle. This is probably true for spin networks on the level of quantized physical space. Hence evolution shows up as a multi-shifted hierarchy of complexity as to the unfolding of various forms of organized collectives of (autonomous) agents. Humans thus represent systems with (up to now) a maximal degree of organization. In between we would expect a manifold of biological structures with different degrees of organization smaller than that degree in humans.

54 Of course, these two make no difference with respect to both the energy balance and the entropy balance. Matter belongs to the additional term which has to be added on the entropy's side in order to make both balances equal, because it can be visualized as a kind of stored information (memory).

12

Unlearning How to Hope: Eleven Theses in Defense of Liberal Democracy and Consumer Culture

Henk de Berg

"It is a question of learning hope."[1] This sentence from *The Principle of Hope* could serve as the motto to most of the philosophical theories developed during the last hundred years. Bloch may have bewailed the lack of proper theoretical reflection on man's *dreams of a better life* in the history of Western philosophy,[2] but the twentieth century has more than made up for this apparent neglect. The majority of thinkers in and after Bloch's lifetime have been preoccupied, even obsessed, with the attempt to transcend what Hegel delineated as the domain of philosophy, the realm of *das, was ist*—reality. If they have not heeded the prescription of the Eleventh Thesis on Feuerbach that the point of philosophy is to change the world, they have at least sought to keep the flame of utopia burning, recasting the act of philosophizing itself as an instance of transcendence and hence as a *promesse de bonheur*.

Behind the multifarious philosophical expressions of hope lies a single central assumption: the conviction that there is something fundamentally wrong with modernity—that modern life does not live.[3] The main target of this critique is the combination of liberal democracy and capitalism characteristic of the West (and increasingly of other parts of the globe as well). The more extreme manifestations of modernity, by contrast, tend to be scrutinized less suspiciously by the type of cultural critique that is at issue here. They are seen either as solutions to, or as expressions of, structural problems that are supposed to have been caused by a modernization process driven by the mode of production that is at the very heart of Western societies. Thus National Socialism and Stalinism were, and various forms of communism still are, hailed as ways out of the supposedly life-negating nature of the modern world; here it suffices to mention the names of Heidegger and Bloch.[4] The other approach is to insist on the similarities and connections between totalitarianism and economic liberalism. Fascist, Stalinist, and real-existing socialist societies are then viewed, for example, as having been generated by capitalism or as varieties of it: that is to say, as instances of state capitalism fraught with the same social antagonisms as market capitalism (rationalization, bureaucratization, alienation, oppression, and so forth), or as alternative paths toward man's *retour à l'animalité* in a full-blown consumerist brave new world.[5] Whichever approach is taken, the prime target remains the same: the form of social organization that Francis Fukuyama famously described as the end point of mankind's ideological evolution.

The arguments put forward by the various strands of this type of cultural critique are also remarkably similar across the ideological spectrum. Man is seen as a slave to a capitalist system that reduces him to a mere cog in the self-perpetuating machine of production and consumption, robbing him of his autonomy. This dehumanization purportedly extends to his social life: capitalism, it is argued, atomizes society and alienates its members by destroying the bonds that hold them together. The result is a lonely crowd of other-directed individuals without any true individuality.[6] What makes this state of affairs especially pernicious—so the argument goes—is that the vast majority of people are not even aware of it. Straitjacketed as they are by the system, they have developed a false consciousness that blinds them to the reality of their situation. In other words, today's capitalism exploits people not by giving them too little but by offering them too much. Consequently, they become dependent on a host of false needs (the desire for fashion items, for gadgets, for cheap entertainment, and the like) while repressing their true needs.[7] Modern man, in this view, has turned into a purely materialistic creature, having been "corrupted," as Bloch puts it, "by economic progress and the so-called cooperation between the employers and the unions" to the extent that he is now "completely aligned with the capitalist mode of production."[8]

The only way of life left open, it is propounded, is that of the consumerist bourgeois, of Nietzsche's *last man*; in his guise of the "all too private person," who builds himself "a little narrow wig-wam" only to "perish in privacy," or in the form of "his contrasting brother," whose "mere sprint of industriousness" counts as equally empty and lacking in progression (*PoH*, 1354). Only occasionally, it is believed, do man's repressed desires and aspirations light up the *darkness of the lived moment*, providing the perspective of an unalienated, autonomous, and truly authentic human existence.[9] It is here that cultural critics of the ilk I have been discussing see their task; to wit, to preserve and clarify this perspective and, on this basis, to resist the system's totalizing tendencies and expose its inhumanity. The more optimistic of these critics, such as Bloch, go even further and claim that philosophy should contribute actively to the founding of a new social order. But whatever the level of utopian confidence, they always envisage a type of society beyond the present one. After all, if, as is assumed, the liberal-democratic and capitalist order is fundamentally flawed, no reformism will do. The philosophical hope is therefore not the wish to improve this imperfect reality. It is the yearning for a different reality, for wholeness, harmony, for what Bloch calls *Heimat*.

Such are the views typical of the dominant current of twentieth- and twenty-first-century social thought, a current of which Bloch's philosophy is an integral part. But are these views correct? In other words, is the gloomy analysis of modern liberal-democratic and capitalist society justified? And is the attempt to transcend this reality a good thing? It is my contention that both the diagnosis and the cure supplied by our critical "doctors of culture" (Nietzsche) are fundamentally mistaken. In order to demonstrate this I shall formulate eleven theses targeted, directly or indirectly, at the views I have just outlined.[10]

I

Let me start with the criticism that today people are more materialistic than ever before. This is a misconception induced by a failure to recognize the peculiar nature of progress. Progress tends to make itself invisible retrospectively. In other words, once people are actually in possession of this or that commodity, it is no longer viewed as something special, but taken for granted.[11] The washing machine, for instance, in the 1950s the epitome of luxury, is now a perfectly ordinary household item. Hence the mistaken view that our grandparents had no extravagant wishes, whereas we appear to be obsessed with consumer goods. This false impression seems to be confirmed by the fact that nowadays these goods are bought by people from all walks of life. However, this too is no sign of increased decadence; it is merely the logical outcome of the ongoing process of economic democratization.

Now I will not contradict the argument that people today have more needs and want more than previous generations. They do. But the simple fact is that today there happen to exist more things they *can* want—in the past, people also desired what was there.

This is not to deny that capitalism creates needs and desires. As Hegel already pointed out in the *Philosophy of Right*, modern markets produce an increasingly abstract (that is, nature-independent) and complex network of socioeconomic relations, which generate different types of consumers with different tastes, leading to a demand for increasingly higher numbers of increasingly variegated commodities (clothes, trousers, jeans, designer jeans, etc.) so that, due to people's desire both to emulate others *and* to distinguish themselves from them, "[i]n the end, it is no longer need but opinion which has to be satisfied."[12] However, this insight should be relativized against what we know of the history of humanity. To put it metonymically, Laban's sons envied Jacob his prosperity (Genesis 31:1) and the soldiers played dice for Jesus' garments (Mark 15:24). In other words, man's desire for consumer goods does not spring from a capitalist deformation of his "essentially un-materialistic" nature. It is hard to imagine a society with a modern economy, be it market-oriented or plan-based, that would somehow do away with what empirically appears to be a rather stable feature of man.[13]

II

A related objection put forward by cultural critics is the charge that modern capitalist life is hectic and restless, that everyone is rushing from one form of entertainment to the next without any regard for or interest in higher values.[14] This, too, is a misconception. Never before did man have so much leisure time and so many different ways to make use of that time. If there is one social order that has achieved Marx's *realm of freedom*, it is today's bourgeois capitalist society. We have more holidays, more part-time jobs, more hobbies, and more time for our partners and children than any society before.

Why then do cultural critics think that modern life is so restless? The answer is because the number of things we can do with our increased leisure time increases more rapidly than the amount of leisure time itself. On one and the same day, we cannot work *and* go to the cinema *and* play football with our children *and* watch a film on TV *and* go to see an exhibition of modern art *and* organise an Open Day for the local branch of Amnesty International. In other words, if we want it to be so, our diary is always full. So cultural critics jump to the conclusion that we are living in a society corrupted by consumerism, a society whose members are almost desperately on the lookout for entertainment, a society in which people have become slaves to the market. In fact, this supposedly hectic and unfree existence is *more* autonomous than that of our ancestors. Besides, most of us appear to be sufficiently adept at handling this increased autonomy, quite apart from the fact that more and more people now have the opportunity to work less or stay indoors. But what about man's higher spiritual values? They do not go by the board at all: more leisure time also means more time for charity work, reading, self-study, visits to museums and concerts, and of course for religious and political activity.

Admittedly, not everybody is successful when it comes to managing this increased autonomy. The growth of individual freedom is accompanied by an increase in failed attempts at self-realization, which then triggers criticisms about a "lack of meaning" in modern society. There can be no doubt about the reality of such existential problems. But they are not, as our cultural critics claim, forced on us by some totally administered society squeezing the meaning out of everything. Rather, they are the flipside of the *increase* in individual freedom.[15]

III

The pessimistic view that modern man has lost his autonomy and has been reduced to a mere cog in the capitalist machine is linked to our experience of increased social interdependence. This experience is not without objective foundation. Hegel already identified "the interlinked dependence of each on all" as one of the central features of modernity,[16] and there can indeed be no doubt that nowadays people are increasingly dependent on the economic, political, technological, and organizational activities of other people. However, these indubitable interdependencies cannot simply be attributed to a loss of human autonomy. First, less autonomy in one area is often accompanied by more autonomy in another. Thus the very same Internet and mobile phones on which we are increasingly dependent allow us to move about more freely and make better-founded decisions. Second, we should not forget that previous generations were also subject to all manner of dependencies. Whereas today we are concerned about the reliability of MRI scans, a hundred years ago a brain tumor was a death sentence. In the past, the West knew famines; now its inhabitants sue McDonald's.

This brings me to the third and last consideration in this context. In the past, dependencies were often brought about by external factors that could not be influenced (the natural environment, for example, or biology); nowadays they increasingly result from social factors. Hence they are, in principle and to a certain extent, increasingly within our control. Sociologists have described this development as the transformation of *dangers* into *risks*: the transformation of situations that are *impervious* to human decision-making (the harvest is good or bad depending on weather conditions that can neither be predicted nor influenced) into situations in which any potential damage is the *result* of human decision-making (depending as it does on our willingness to act upon weather forecasts, for example).[17] However, with this increase in human autonomy and control, our *desire* for security and our *sensitivity* to risk increase as well. Hence the so-called litigation culture. No accident is simply bad luck or fate anymore. Everything is a question of blame and responsibility. In other words, the objective rise in our levels of autonomy and security paradoxically produces a sense of vulnerability, and this in its turn generates the misguided view of modern man's "loss of autonomy."

IV

Cultural critics such as Bloch consistently point to the many problems facing capitalist democracies: crime, discrimination, social inequality, unemployment, and so forth—problems, they argue, that require a radical overhaul of the current social order. What are we to make of this criticism? It is true, of course, that these problems exist and that they are serious. However, no social order has ever produced more freedom, more equality, and more justice than the combination of bourgeois capitalism and liberal democracy. Certainly the utopias of Stalin, Mao, and Pol Pot never did. As Hegel put it in one of his Jena manuscripts when criticizing the liberation theology of his day: seeking to create heaven on earth is like trying to make fire under water.[18] The revolutionary critique of modern society must be seen for what it is: the result, as Edward Shils once wrote, of a blind "attachment to an impossible ideal of human perfection."[19]

What our cultural critics cannot accept is human finitude. In the case of Bloch, this implies an almost willful neglect of man's destructive urges. Thus daydreams are construed as the anthropological basis of utopian thinking *in spite of the fact that they are frequently violent and sexually aggressive*. To brush this dimension aside as somehow inessential is not just theoretically implausible but also morally reckless. For it is precisely this lack of respect for what Immanuel Kant called "the crooked timber of humanity," out of which "no straight thing was ever made,"[20] that leads philosophers such as Bloch into absolutism: "The hope of the goal . . . is necessarily at odds with false satisfaction, necessarily at one with revolutionary thoroughness;—crooked seeks to be straight, half to be full" (POH, 336).

But even if human beings were, or could be, better than they are, this would not mean that *society* could be. Society is more than simply a collection of people; it is made up of processes that transcend individuals and groups and their subjective intentions. Social processes possess their own logic. Good intentions may well lead to nothing or have bad consequences (just as bad intentions may have good consequences). And good consequences may have bad side-effects or in turn lead to bad consequences further down the road. Of course, one can argue (as Bloch does) that there is a latent tendency in history toward the postulated goal—that one is dealing not just with human hope and human intentions but with subjective factors that possess an objective correlate in reality. However, this merely takes us back to where we were before. For how are we to know that this is true? Human finitude excludes not only omnipotence but also omniscience.

To avoid misunderstanding, this does not mean that our society cannot or should not be improved. All I am saying is that there are limits to what we can improve and that we should do well to accept that. The road to hell is paved not so much with good intentions that are not carried out as with intentions that are too good and too radical and are nevertheless acted upon.[21]

V

Much of the criticism directed at bourgeois society has its roots not simply in an unrealistic perception of actual problems but also in what Odo Marquard has termed the princess-and-the-pea syndrome: the fewer social ills there are, the more unbearable the remaining ones become.[22] And what happens when many of the remaining ills, too, are decreasing in number? Then, Marquard argues, bourgeois man, the true successor to the aristocratic *sensibilissima* that was the princess, begins to distrust the mattresses, the duvets, and the fact that the pea is no longer there. The very things that help us to reduce pain and suffering then come to be seen as ills just as bad as the ones they were meant to combat.[23] To take some of Marquard's examples, the more successful modern medicine becomes, the stronger the tendency gets to view its methods as being themselves pathological (hence the rise of alternative medicine); the more benefits modern chemistry brings, the stronger the suspicion that it is poisoning people; and the more repressions liberal democracy eliminates, the stronger the worry that this form of government is itself a form of repression.

The reason for this is to be found in the nature of culture. Culture is aimed at delivering man from things such as danger, disease, and want. It is, one might say, a kind of automatic problem-processor. So when there are fewer and fewer problems left to be solved, our problem-processor will automatically start treating the solutions as problems.[24]

A similar mechanism explains the totalizing tendencies inherent in cultural critique. Many of the remaining problems of capitalist democracies (say, the question of how to deal with under- or overregulated markets) require solutions based on highly specialized knowledge and on finely tuned political compromises—solutions, in other words, to which cultural critics have little or nothing to contribute. In this situation, the only thing left for them to solve is the "real" problem, Western modernity as a whole—and so the whole becomes the false.[25]

VI

A good deal of cultural criticism can be explained by the fear of supporting the wrong side: with many intellectuals, the disastrous effects of identifying with the political systems of fascism and communism have produced an almost reflex-like aversion to identifying with liberal democracy and market capitalism. The paradox here is obvious. First, this refusal is by no means politically innocent; one need only think of the Weimar Republic.[26] Second, there is no guarantee that the situation will not get worse—and the bourgeois capitalist and liberal-democratic system has much that we would do well to preserve.

This is not to say that any criticism of the current social order is misguided or out of place. There are many wrongs that need exposing, from instances of dubious political lobbying to shameful practices such as extraordinary renditions. But one can have too much of a good thing. That point is reached, it seems to me, when the negatives of the current system are highlighted in such a way as to obscure its positives—as if criticizing what is wrong were somehow more honorable than supporting what is right, and lamenting what is missing better than praising what has been achieved.

It is sometimes mistakenly assumed that identifying with market capitalism and liberal democracy leads to political quietism. If anything, the opposite is true. It is only in the context of existing society that questions about, say, the level of unemployment benefits or the size of economic stimulus packages gain the political relevance that the people concerned attach to them. From a "genuinely critical" (that is to say, utopian) perspective, by contrast, such questions are at best side issues and at worst manifestations of reprehensible reformism.

How problematic the refusal to identify with capitalism and liberal democracy can be is demonstrated by Bloch's philosophy. At first sight, the central concept of utopian hope may (to some anyway) appear to be the much needed product of a free spirit trying to think beyond the narrow confines of his own repressive society. On closer inspection, it becomes apparent that this concept can be used to justify *any* kind of revolutionary overhaul of society, including revolutions aimed at installing a theocracy or a fascist dictatorship. For the distinction between hope that is "merely empty or exhausting escapism, an easy prey for swindlers" and hope that "is provocative, is not content just to accept the bad which exists, does not accept renunciation" and that approaches existing reality "not in the way of merely contemplative understanding, which takes things as they are and as they stand, but of engaged understanding, which takes them as they go and hence as they could go better" (PH 3–4, translation modified) is entirely rhetorical and politically empty. It is a distinction that is an easy prey not only for swindlers but also, which is worse, for honest revolutionaries. After all, which revolutionary does not believe that his hope is of the right kind?[27]

VII

What about the criticism that capitalism atomizes society by destroying the bonds that hold people together? It is of course true that nascent capitalism uprooted traditional ways of life. Nor can it be denied that capitalism is a dynamic force that constantly renews and remakes itself, requiring people to adapt, to be mobile and flexible, to abandon cherished patterns of behavior and familiar ways of working together. That this is often a difficult and painful process, of that too there can be no doubt. However, all this does not mean that economic liberalism and social cohesion are antithetical. Capitalism may undermine existing ties between people, but it also allows, indeed encourages, new ones to emerge.

There are at least two reasons for this.[28] First, if, as seems to be the case, people are social beings that need to relate to other social beings through shared values and experiences, then they will forever be seeking to create the manifold types of associations that make this possible—and it is precisely economically and politically liberal social orders that, due to their fundamental disjunction of civil society and political system, provide the best context for such associational life.[29] Second, capitalism itself generates new patterns of interaction and value systems because it could not function properly without such *social capital*. As Hegel put it: through the division of labor "the work of the individual . . . becomes *simpler*, so that his skill at his abstract work becomes greater, as does the volume of his output. At the same time, this abstraction of skill and means makes the *dependence* and *reciprocity* of human beings in the satisfaction of their other needs complete and entirely necessary."[30] In other words, the division of labor and the specialization that are central features of market capitalism require increasing coordination between the various areas of society, and hence increased social cooperation, which in its turn demands the development of a set of shared values and of a common legal and normative framework.[31] This process is underpinned by the modern world's increasing technological interconnectedness, which itself is in many ways the result of globalizing capitalism. "Atomization" is thus but one half of the story of modernity. The other half is the emergence of new, non-traditional, social bonds.

The process through which capitalist societies renew and remake their social foundations is often disruptive in the extreme. For all its problems, however, the continuous undermining of existing relations also has liberating effects: the capitalist melting down of all that is solid—of "natural" hierarchies, inherited privileges, time-honored patterns of behavior, and conventional assumptions[32]—sets the individual free from the tyranny of the past, *decolonizing* him.[33]

VIII

A surprisingly popular criticism is the charge that the modern bourgeois is drowning in a sea of mediocrity—that his cowardly existence leaves no room for the achievement of anything great. The most famous expression of this view can be found in Nietzsche's *Zarathustra*: "No shepherd and one herd! Everyone wants the same, everyone is the same: whoever feels different goes voluntarily into a madhouse. . . . One has one's little pleasure for the day and one's little pleasure for the night: but one has a regard for health."[34] Today, so the criticism goes, there is no place left for what makes us truly human: our desire to be special and accomplish something extraordinary—to "give birth to a dancing star."[35] The *Übermensch*, who always strives to surpass himself and others, is neither needed nor wanted anymore. The charge, then, is essentially a double one: that bourgeois existence is unheroic, boring, banal and that it is conformist, not expressive of our individuality, inauthentic.

Is Nietzsche right? It is certainly true that bourgeois societies are not favorably disposed toward excesses and exceptions. They prefer the middle way to extremism, the ordinary to the extraordinary. But is that so bad? Nietzsche thinks it is, and many writers and thinkers have followed in his footsteps. Yet it seems to me that this type of criticism is fundamentally erroneous.

That people seek recognition is undeniable. That they want to be seen as special seems to me to be correct as well. But the identification of this kind of desire with a striving for "heroism" or "greatness" is a normative assumption that has no basis in reality. It is a form of over-philosophizing, typical of so many intellectuals who, yearning for a life of revolutionary action,[36] expect the same yearning from their fellow citizens. (Having been disappointed in that expectation, they then put their revolutionary efforts into criticizing this "passivity" and educating humanity to their own radical dreams.)

But what about the charge that bourgeois existence is inauthentic? Here, too, we are dealing with a confusion of *is* and *ought*—a confusion, on the part of the cultural critic, of what he thinks is right with what other people think is right (or what they would think is right if they were "truly free"). It is assumed, first of all, that there is no objective meaning to life—that human beings create their own values. This seems reasonable enough. But it is *also* assumed that it is up to each individual how to do that, and here Nietzscheanism runs into trouble. For this is precisely what the *Übermensch* is about (but then it is no longer up to the cultural critic to decide whether someone's existence is authentic or not), whereas only *some* choices count as "truly" individual, "truly" authentic (but then the *Übermensch* has become little more than a stooge expressing the cultural critic's personal preferences). This paradox may be hidden from sight by rhetorical obfuscation (such as Nietzsche's exhortation that what man should *really* do is "give birth to a dancing star") or by variations on the concept of false consciousness (Sartre's *mauvaise foi*, Bloch's *darkness of the lived moment*, Marcuse's *false needs*, and so forth), but that does not make it any less problematic.[37]

IX

The real question is not whether bourgeois society is sufficiently "heroic." The real question is: does it offer people enough opportunities to satisfy their need to be special? Does it allow them to realize their potential, improve themselves, and surpass other people? And *this* question, it seems to me, must be answered in the affirmative. Work, hobbies, even bourgeois family life offer excellent ways of doing precisely that. Working toward getting a promotion, combining our job with charity work, spending more time with our family even when we are busy, becoming good at a particular hobby—all these bourgeois activities allow us to go beyond where we are at any given moment in time. They also enable us to surpass other people. The lawyer who wins a court case, the associate professor who is appointed full professor, the secretary who explains the new computer system to her boss—all of them have the satisfaction of being able to do things that others are incapable of. Even the stamp collector possesses a sense of superiority. And when a technologically or athletically ungifted father manages to repair the CD player or plays football with his kids, he too feels special. It would be naive to overlook the selfish component in such actions. As Freud has taught us, altruistic social behavior is always also motivated by selfish drives.

Fashion, or rather consumerism in general, too, offers people ever new opportunities to distinguish themselves from other people (however unappealing some of us may find the more extreme manifestations of this phenomenon). The fact that fashions are always group-specific makes no difference: all consumerism is a way of combining our desire to stand out with our need for conformism.[38]

People assert their freedom and achieve self-realization by negating the given with a view to creating something new. They do so through their cultural activity in the broadest sense of the term, from the production of their means of subsistence to the choice of their holiday destinations. Their work is thus not simply the creation of products that are needed or desired but a way to create themselves. By acquiring a house of their choice and deciding what clothes to wear, they objectify their individuality.[39] And it is capitalist democracies, more than any previous societies, that allow people to gain and sustain their subjecthood in this way. They have generated and continue to generate a plurality of lifestyles that gives the lie to all predictions, and all pseudo-descriptive claims, of man's de-individualization in a homogeneous mass culture.

X

All this does not mean that we are no longer able to give vent to our more excessive desires within a bourgeois framework. On the contrary, it is one of the great achievements of modern consumer culture that it allows us to simulate the most exceptional actions, the most heroic deeds. It offers us a plethora of opportunities for sublimation and surrogate satisfaction through novels, comic strips, TV programs, films, and computer games. Here, too, Freud's assessment is still valid: cultural progress consists first and foremost of an increase in the number and type of mechanisms that allow us to satisfy our more excessive drives in a manner commensurate with the well-being of society. Moreover, this process must be understood as including low as well as high culture—sex on the Internet as well as Shakespeare, *Hustler* as well as *Hamlet*.

Seen through this lens, even the more extreme manifestations of the "culture industry" are not a sign of modern man's decadence, as cultural pessimists claim. Nor are they simply the ideological reflection of an unfree society, a kind of secular counterpart (or successor) to the drug of religion, as many orthodox Marxists would have it. To assume this is to believe that there could ever be a social order without such forms of sublimation and surrogate satisfaction—as if one could make fire under water. Rather, they constitute an *alternative* to the socially more harmful expressions of man's propensity for barbarity.

To say this is not to fall victim to the Blochian fallacy that popular culture expresses an anthropologically based potential for social emancipation. For Bloch, popular culture (just as, in his view, literature, art, philosophy, religion, and various other cultural phenomena) is similar to daydreams in that it provides illuminations of a better life: in spite of all the commercialism and ideological distortion, it gives voice to man's yearning for "something perfect which the world has not yet seen" (POH, 14). This view is seriously mistaken for at least two reasons. First, daydreams are not primarily social. They are mostly about the individual dreamer, about *me*, not about the community; and the (usually sexual and destructive) things the dreamer likes to imagine tend not to be very social either. To make daydreams the anthropological foundation of a philosophy of humanity's desire for social perfection is therefore entirely unconvincing. Second, barring a small number of exceptions (such as hardcore pornography) the various instances of popular culture are not like daydreams. Daydreams are forms of sublimation because they retain the flow of libidinal energy before its destructive nature spills over into society. Popular culture represents a significantly higher stage of sublimation at which libidinal energy is transformed into contents that are themselves social in nature. The visions of perfection it expresses are therefore culturally and historically specific, and there is no reason to assume they are in any way more fundamental or "deeper" than the other (realistic, conformist, reformist, dystopian, etc.) views of society they embody. They are certainly not more fundamental or "deeper" than the libidinal energy on which they feed. Bloch's cultural *Vollkommenheits-symbole* (symbols of perfection) represent specific sociopolitical projects, or specific sociopolitical hopes, not a universal human longing for "a happiness . . . that only Marxism can initiate" (*PoH*, 16, translation modified).

XI

Is all this really enough? What about "true" heroism? Nietzscheans need not worry. For genuine heroes, too, there is more than enough room. Our liberal-democratic, bourgeois-capitalist society offers innumerable opportunities for "genuine" heroism: professions such as policeman, bodyguard, or firefighter, for instance. And we may safely assume that crime, terrorism, social unrest, and environmental problems will be with us until the end of time. Seen from this perspective, even the imperfections of our society are part of its strength.

So maybe the combination of liberal democracy and market capitalism characteristic of the West is not so bad after all. And as the French proverb goes that Hegel cites in the *Philosophy of Right*: "Le plus grand ennemi du bien c'est le mieux."[40] Perhaps this is what philosophy should learn: not to strive for utopia, but to leave well enough alone.

Notes

1   Ernst Bloch, *PoH*, 3. The German original [*Es kommt darauf an, das Hoffen zu lernen*] in all likelihood establishes a rhetorical link with the second part of Marx's Eleventh Thesis on Feuerbach [*es kommt darauf an, sie zu verändern*].

2   "Dreams of a Better Life" is the title Bloch originally envisaged for *The Principle of Hope*.

3   "Life does not live" is the opening epigram of *Minima Moralia*. See Theodor W. Adorno, *Minima Moralia: Reflections on a Damaged Life*, trans. E. F. N. Jephcott (London: Verso, 2005), 19.

4   In the same period that Heidegger became enamored with Hitler, Bloch turned to Stalin as one of the "true leaders guiding us toward happiness, inspiring love, trust, and revolutionary adoration" [*wirkliche Führer ins Glück, Richtgestalten der Liebe, des Vertrauens, der revolutionären Verehrung*]; his blindness culminated in a staunch defense of the Moscow show trials of 1936–37. See Arno Münster, *Ernst Bloch: Eine politische Biographie* (Berlin: Philo, 2004) and Peter Zudeick, *Der Hintern des Teufels: Ernst Bloch—Leben und Werk* (Moos: Elster, 1987).

5   The phrase *retour de l'Homme à l'animalité* comes from Alexandre Kojève, who manages to reduce even Nazism to a stage in this process. On Kojève's *konvergenztheoretisch* view of capitalism and communism, see Henk de Berg, *Das Ende der Geschichte und der bürgerliche Rechtsstaat: Hegel—Kojève—Fukuyama* (Tübingen: Francke, 2007) and "Bonjour Tristesse: Alexandre Kojève's Reading of Françoise Sagan," in *Phrasis: Studies in Language and Literature* 50, no. 1 (2009): 3–20.

6   On the phrases "lonely crowd" and "other-directedness," see David Riesman, *The Lonely Crowd: A Study of the Changing American Character* (New Haven, CT: Yale University Press, 1950).

7   This refers to the population of the Western world. The inhabitants of the so-called Third World are seen as still being exploited in the "traditional" manner. The distinction between "true needs" and "false needs" comes from Herbert Marcuse, *One-Dimensional Man: Studies in the Ideology of Advanced Industrial Society* (London: Routledge and Kegan Paul, 1964). The phrase "false consciousness" goes back to Friedrich Engels; see his letter to Franz Mehring of 14 July 1893, in Karl Marx and Frederick Engels, *Collected Works* (London: Lawrence and Wishart, 2004), 50:164.

8   *Gespräche mit Ernst Bloch*, 2nd ed., ed. Rainer Traub and Harald Wieser (Frankfurt: Suhrkamp, 1977), 126–27, my translation.

9   Bloch uses this phrase—*das Dunkel des gelebten Augenblicks*—throughout his work; for one instance among many, see *POH*, 12.

10 In what follows, I shall be leaning heavily on the ideas developed by the Ritter School of German philosophy (after Joachim Ritter, 1903–74), whose most important representatives are Hermann Lübbe and Odo Marquard. Specific references are given below. On the Ritter School in general, see Jens Hacke, *Philosophie der Bürgerlichkeit: Die liberalkonservative Begründung der Bundesrepublik* (Göttingen: Vandenhoeck und Ruprecht, 2006) and Odo Marquard's afterword to the new, revised edition of Joachim Ritter, *Metaphysik und Politik: Studien zu Aristoteles und Hegel* (Frankfurt: Suhrkamp, 2003), 442–56.

11 A good description of this process can be found in Jürgen Habermas, *Die Neue Unübersichtlichkeit: Kleine Politische Schriften V* (Frankfurt: Suhrkamp, 1985), 67–68.

12   G. W .F. Hegel, *Elements of the Philosophy of Right*, ed. Allen W. Wood, trans. H. B. Nisbet (Cambridge: Cambridge University Press, 1991), 229, addition; cf. 266.

13   This is something Marxists have never come to grips with. A good example is Wolfgang Fritz Haug's classic "critique of commodity esthetics": his adoption of the distinction between use value and exchange value merely manages to transform the complexity of human desire—with its mimetic, competitive, and selfishly lustful aspects—into a simplistic dichotomy of authentic and artificial needs. See Wolfgang Fritz Haug, *Kritik der Warenästhetik: Gefolgt von Warenästhetik im High-Tech-Kapitalismus* (Frankfurt: Suhrkamp, 2009), which is the fully revised, updated, and significantly extended edition of the original study published in 1971.

14   Contrary to what one might suspect, this argument, which integrates a critique of capitalism and consumerism with what Paul Virilio has termed a "dromological perspective," is by no means of recent origin. Nietzsche, for example, in a passage prefiguring contemporary anti-Americanism, already castigates *"modern restlessness.—The farther West one goes, the greater modern agitation becomes; so that to Americans the inhabitants of Europe appear to be relaxing and enjoying the good life, whereas in fact the Europeans are buzzing around like flies. This agitation is becoming so great that the fruits of higher culture no longer ripen; it is as if the seasons were following too quickly on one another. From lack of rest, our civilization is ending in a new barbarism."* Friedrich Nietzsche, *Human, All Too Human*, trans. Marion Faber and Stephen Lehmann (London: Penguin, 2004), 171–72, translation modified.

15   The complex relationship between time and freedom is central to the work of Hermann Lübbe, on which my second thesis is based. See Hermann Lübbe, *Zeit-Verhältnisse: Zur Kulturphilosophie des Fortschritts* (Graz: Styria, 1983); *Im Zug der Zeit: Verkürzter Aufenthalt in der Gegenwart*, 2nd ed. (Berlin: Springer, 1994); *Die Zivilisationsökumene: Globalisierung kulturell, technisch, und politisch* (Munich: Fink, 2005).

16   Hegel, *Elements of the Philosophy of Right*, 233. The following reflections draw on the works by Lübbe mentioned in note 15.

17   Cf. Niklas Luhmann, "Risiko und Gefahr," in *Soziologische Aufklärung 5: Konstruktivistische Perspektiven* (Opladen: Westdeutscher, 1995), 131–69.

18   Leo Rauch, *Hegel and the Human Spirit: A Translation of the Jena Lectures on the Philosophy of Spirit (1805–6) with Commentary* (Detroit: Wayne State University Press, 1983), 179.

19   Edward Shils, *The Intellectuals and the Powers and Other Essays* (Chicago: University of Chicago Press, 1972), 263.

20   Immanuel Kant, *Perpetual Peace and Other Essays*, trans. Ted Humphrey (Indianapolis: Hackett, 1983), 34. The translation of this phrase is Isaiah Berlin's; see Isaiah Berlin, *The Crooked Timber of Humanity: Chapters in the History of Ideas*, ed. Henry Hardy (New York: Vintage, 1992).

21   Thus it does not require (or at least ought not to require) an especially conservative disposition to be worried about the political consequences of a philosophy that

defines "ideals, corrected and aligned by utopian function," as "those of a self- and world-content developed in terms adequate to man" and *variations of the basic content: highest good"* and then propounds: "Ideals relate to this supreme hope-content, possible world-content, as means to an end; there is therefore a hierarchy of ideals, and a lower one can be sacrificed to a higher one, because it is resurrected anyway in the realization of the higher one. For example, the supreme variation of the highest good in the socio-political sphere is the classless society; consequently, ideals like freedom and also equality act as means to this end, and derive their value-content (one which in the case of freedom has been particularly ambiguous) from the highest good in socio-political terms. In such a way that it does not merely determine the content of the ideals as means, but also varies them according to the requirements of the supreme end-content, and where necessary temporarily justifies the deviations" (*PoH*, 173).

22   For the following see Odo Marquard, *Skepsis und Zustimmung: Philosophische Studien* (Stuttgart: Reclam, 1994), 38–39 and 105–7.

23   As Marquard puts it: "Die Entlastung vom Negativen . . . verführt zur Negativierung des Entlastenden": *Skepsis und Zustimmung*, 38 and 106.

24   This is not a bad thing in itself. After all, the solutions that constitute cultural progress do tend to generate problems of their own. What I am referring to is the necessity to retain perspective—the ability to distinguish, for instance, between the fact that liberal democracy has problems and the false conclusion that liberal democracy is the problem.

25   Adorno's famous inversion of Hegel's "The true is the whole" can be found in *Minima Moralia*, 50.

26   Cf. Fritz Stern's classic study *The Politics of Cultural Despair: A Study in the Rise of the Germanic Ideology* (Berkeley: University of California Press, 1989; first published 1961). The study's German translation is aptly called *Kulturpessimismus als politische Gefahr* [Cultural pessimism as a political danger].

27   This criticism explains why Bloch's philosophy only "works" if one adopts his Marxist perspective.

28   For the following, see Francis Fukuyama, *The Great Disruption: Human Nature and the Reconstruction of Social Order* (London: Profile Books, 2000). Fukuyama himself does not mention Hegel but instead bases his reconstitution thesis on biological, anthropological, and sociological studies.

29   For a fuller account, see my article "Utopia and the End of History," in *Utopia: Social Theory and the Future*, ed. Michael Hviid Jacobson and Keith Tester (London: Ashgate, 2012), 7–31.

30   Hegel, *Elements of the Philosophy of Right*, 232–33.

31   The best example is the European Coal and Steel Community, which gave rise to the European Economic Community, which in its turn became the European Community, which then morphed into the European Union. Other obvious examples include the WTO, the IMF, and the Kyoto Treaty, but similar forms of coordination and cooperation can be found on national, regional, and local levels.

32   The famous phrase from *The Communist Manifesto*, "All that is solid melts into air,"
      however poetic it may be, is but a poor translation of the German, "Alles Ständische
      und Stehende verdampft." The adjective *ständisch* (here used as a noun) refers to the
      division of society into *Stände*, estates, and evokes all that goes with it ("natural" hier-
      archies, people's "station" in life, and so forth). See Karl Marx and Frederick Engels,
      Collected Works, ed. Richard Dixon et al. (London: Lawrence and Wishart, 1975–
      2005), 6:487.

33   Cf. *The Communist Manifesto*: "All fixed, fast-frozen relations, with their train of an-
      cient and venerable prejudices and opinions, are swept away, all new-formed ones
      become antiquated before they can ossify." In other words, even if capitalism "colo-
      nizes the life-world," as Habermas puts it, it also continuously undoes the reifications
      it effects. The phrase *decolonization of the citizen*, which seems to have been coined by
      H. J. A. Hofland, is used in the context of Dutch history to describe the end of the
      system of *verzuiling* (the "pillarization," or social division, of the Netherlands along
      ideological, above all religious, lines). See Maarten van Rossem, Ed Jonker, and Luuc
      Kooijmans, *Een tevreden natie: Nederland van 1945 tot nu* (Baarn: Tirion, 1993) 104–5.

34   Friedrich Nietzsche, *Thus Spoke Zarathustra: A Book for All and None*, trans. Walter
      Kaufmann (New York: Viking Press, 1961), 17.

35   Nietsche, *Thus Spoke Zarathustra*, 16.

36   I use the word *revolutionary* in the general sense of "aimed at radical change" (with
      regard to society, individuals, or both).

37   Nietzsche's other, equally empty exhortations include the need for man to "plant the
      seed of his highest hope" and "shoot the arrow of his longing beyond man." *Thus
      Spoke Zarathustra*, 16.

38   As Hegel already observed: consumerism entails both "the need for . . . equality,
      together with *imitation* as the process whereby people make themselves like others"
      and "the need for *particularity* . . . , the need to assert oneself through some distinctive
      quality." Hegel, *Elements of the Philosophy of Right*, 230, translation modified.

39   This is one of the central insights of Hegel's philosophy. See above all the *Elements of
      the Philosophy of Right*; for example 73, addition: "The rational aspect [*Das Vernünf-
      tige*] of property is to be found not in the satisfaction of needs but in the superseding
      of mere subjectivity of personality" [*sondern darin, daß sich die bloße Subjektivität der
      Persönlichkeit aufhebt*].

40   Hegel, *Elements of the Philosophy of Right*, 248.

Francesca Vidal and

Welf Schröter

Translated by Nick Hodgin

13

Can We Hope to Walk Tall in a Computerized World of Work?

Daydreams

People evolve as a result of their experiences. Similarly, desires, which are closely bound to memories, develop into wishes. Stuck in the "facticity of life" [*Dass des Lebens*] the ability to look beyond immediate existence, to transcend it, begins first as an indistinct urge and becomes a yearning as it begins to look outward (PH, 65–77). The urge develops into a certain and purposeful drive. People's desires are bound up with fantasy, for they are able to envision the object of their desire. There is a moment between awareness of desire and its fulfillment when we are able to summon up the very image of our desire. For this reason, we not only desire, we also allow our desires to become wishes; the fulfillment of these wishes we imagine in daydreams, which may occur when we are thinking about quite unrelated personal, social, scientific, or artistic questions.

Daydreams are for Sigmund Freud a first stage toward (night)dreams. But for the philosopher Ernst Bloch, they are the anticipation of imagination. He stresses that daydreams do not seek meaning in the way that dreams do, but wish to be transformed into reality. In his masterpiece, *The Principle of Hope*, Bloch describes daydreams according to four distinct characteristics.[1] The first of these concerns what he terms the "dream's free roam," which is to say that the dreamer is not overwhelmed by the images of the dream, since these are summoned by her.

The dreamer directs the course of the dream. Second, the dreamer does not become detached from the conscious, waking world, regardless of how unconventional the dream's content may be. In the daydream, the ego remains unchanged, even if the "castles in the air" are blissfully built without recourse to the usual moral censor. The third stage concerns the important relationship to other people. Daydreams urge communication. The daydreamer seeks to improve the world and is better able to share her (day)dreams since this is easier with general wishful images than it is with (night)dreams. The dreamer is inspired by a distant goal and projects her desires onto dream images that can activate the expansive dreams [*Ausfabelung*] of some utopian design. Thus fantasies may anticipate art or scientific or sociopolitical projections. The fourth characteristic of the daydream is its need for fulfillment, its drive to realization, for the daydream is always concerned with objectives that it hopes to achieve; the daydreamer is mesmerized by conceivably tangible wishes. Wishes, which are passive in nature, are distinguishable from active wanting, but such wanting is always driven by the wish. Daydreams, then, are not an alternative to reality, but rather the anticipation of productive action and a new reality. Wishful images reflect our relationship to the world—the actual, existing relationship as much as the possible future one. If they aim only to reproduce in miniature the resolution of desires within the secret confines of private happiness, then they are likely to become kitsch. If that should be the case, then people are concerned only with finding a place in the world as it really is. In a world based on the principles of commodity exchange, it seems as though improving one's existing life is only possible in the private sphere. The wishful image fuses with those desires generated through advertising. These debased wishful images are then so tied to their social framework that they can easily be steered by the interests of the market. In kitsch, beauty becomes compliant, feelings become sentimental. Even if in kitsch the desire for a harmonious and happy world finds expression, it is unable to escape from the private idyll. The world will stay as it is. These private wish fulfillments limit themselves to notions that can only be communicated though kitsch. Ernst Bloch refers, by way of example, to the imagined "happy bourgeois family life" and of sentimental love that hopes to transcend all social strictures and problems without ever questioning them. He reproaches the desire to appear pleasant in order to achieve a better position in contemporary society. This wishful image, which focuses only on externalities, is facilitated by people's desire to become cheap commodities themselves. This is why, in the desire to fit in, every possible criticism directed at the structures of society must be suppressed. The wishful images are thus those of "desirable good conduct, of fruitless appearance" (PH, 341).

But Bloch is in no way condemning the reasons for kitsch's appeal. He recognizes that the hope for a better world remains intact even in private desire; and in this, perhaps, he offers us the tools with which to focus on these private hopes. Given global problems, is it not legitimate to draw on private hopes and to shape these according to our own individual needs? Is there such a thing as critical maturity [Mündigkeit, after Adorno] within the sphere of seemingly private wishful thinking?

Work as the Daydreamer's Site of Utopian Dreams

This question needs to be addressed specifically in the context of the working environment. That said, we acknowledge that all private dreams at first seem to focus on things beyond this environment. The social scientist Wolfram Burisch added to his essay "On the Discrimination of Emancipatory Work" the ironic title "Life Is Leisure."[2] As a result of interactive media, and because flexible work environments may now also be the same as leisure sites, leisure time is no longer a private sphere. Leisure time is now for those who have worked to enjoy it and who need it in order to return to work, and for those people who acquire social recognition through their work and thus have a right to leisure. These are in contrast to those increasingly large numbers of people "released" from work who must endure protracted redundancy. Leisure time once signified the place to which we sought to give some meaning and for which we needed secure work. On the one hand, one might view such striving as directed by external forces; the world beyond the working environment as a chimera. On the other hand, this flight into leisure time prompted the question whether work was no longer the activity of the autonomous individual but in fact a pretext. According to this interpretation, finding happiness within work is ruled out per se; so, too, is the working environment as even a site of wishful thinking. The wish therefore limits itself simply to wanting a job, even if the work involved is degrading.

Given how far developed automation is, we might be tempted to ask whether leisure really has become the one area into which the authorities cannot intrude, but we already know the answer. On the one hand, work increasingly intrudes into our free time; on the other, it is the one place where individuals should increasingly be able to improve their capacity to work. And yet, despite this aggravation, some claim that work is once again a place where the individual can be creative, even having some influence on future work because it is increasingly a question of individual activity. In other words, work is said to be a place that values autonomous individuals and is for that reason a place that offers meaningful action.

So should we be asking once again about the workplace as a site of opposition and struggle, and can this be seen in the demands for meaningful work? It is precisely because of work's increased intrusion on daily life that one has to ask whether the significance that the individual attributes to the working environment has the potential to challenge and expose the contradictions of this world. Are the individual's choices, which are focused on the formation of their workplace, evidence of a new Eros that will help to shape the future?

For the philosopher Ernst Bloch, work plays a decisive role as a factor in the workings of the world toward *Heimat*.[3] Work is a timeless notion since the interrelationship between man and nature is inevitably bound up with work. And of course the different forms of work can only be seen in dialectical relationship to social configurations. Since the relationship between shifting social relations and the corresponding expectations of work are changing, both the working environment and the idea of work will undergo some transformation. What this currently means is that it is even more unclear what we mean by work, not least because products are increasingly ambiguous now that information represents both a factor of production as well as a commodity. Given that digitization, virtualization, and dematerialization have fundamentally changed the nature of work, is it still relevant to discuss the desire to become "upright individuals" and to ask how this is manifested in the working environment.

If we follow Bloch's reasoning, this means we must question the objective and subjective conditions which are today undoubtedly connected to the development of a globalization that has rapidly accelerated due to technological advances. The type of work will not be transformed simply by technical innovations, but digitization and networking are already accelerating existing socioeconomic developments in a globalized world.[4] These developments coincide with the virtualization of work, the separation of work from traditional places of work, the dematerialization of production processes, the development of new relationship paradigms, and the shift from company structures. New modes of work will evolve which will seek new ways of overcoming traditional organizational, spatial, and temporal boundaries. But precisely this will call into question the function of the working environment as a site for effective productivity for both employer and employee. The prognosis is that stable work relationships through which we develop personal and social identities will become fewer and that attitudes toward work, thoughts about careers, and modes of education will therefore also change.[5]

Walking Upright in a Computerized Working Environment?

As well as the increased flexibility of new working arrangements, the subjectivization of the working environment that allows the individual greater room for creativity is constantly being advocated. This is a requirement of the transformation, since computerization can only be achieved through the individual's activity. Technologically speaking, computerization first means an increase in the use of information and communication technology. Such increased usage is due not to the wider reception of the new medium but to the competitive pressures of a globalized market. This increasingly networked market, which is facilitated by the media, influences all social areas. The technology, however, disappears from view, since the gadgets and equipment are becoming smaller and multifunctional, and the access to them is greater and easier. We accept the media as a natural feature of our world without ever questioning the increasing sensors and communication interfaces that feature in our environment. Every social phenomenon is affected. Transformations within the working environment are symbolic of a changing society; the hopes and creative intent with which we encounter the working environment will become the decisive question regarding the direction in which society should be steered. Looking at this development's general trends gives rise to a rather dismal prognosis—an increased service sector, a fall in the number of jobs available as a result of automation, rising unemployment, a growing gap between highly qualified jobs and precarious working conditions, and atypical employer/employee relationships—even if all of these correspond with people's wishes.[6] It is a question, then, of the hopes people have for their lives, especially their private dreams, and a question, too, of how far the potential for resistance to increasing alienation can be maintained. Globalization is a process that will alter existing cultural structures. Since this will lead to widespread uncertainty, it will depend on whether people can communicate their dreams in such a way that they can challenge and inform the construction of new social arrangements. Is there any hope of managing the integration of new technology into today's work so that the working environment actually accords with the hopes of those who work in it?

The individual assumes a more significant role in the working environment because communicative activity has developed greater relevance in the course of networked productivity and organizational processes. And it is precisely because the production and organizational structures have become more complex that those working with them must not be made to feel as if they are mere operators but that they are responsible actors. The individual should become so essential that the business is dependent on her willingness to cooperate.[7] People will be granted more responsibility; their social competence and their creativity will be a valuable resource for the business. But this will not occur altruistically and represent greater recognition of the individual. Employees today are expected to master an uncertain market, and external demands are passed directly down to them. This does not mean that management will disappear, only that it will be less direct. If, however, the working sphere forms the individual, then their expectations become calculable, and it will simply be a question of how she adapts to demands, for example, to what extent she seeks to meet the criteria of employability. If, however, this assumption suggests that the individual's subjectivity is challenged, then we must ask to what extent there is the potential to recognize and to challenge contradictions. The sociologist Rudi Schmiede critically evaluates the new demands on subjectivity thus: "Highly complex production and organization processes are extremely sensitive to disturbance and therefore require the engaged and motivated participation of those working in them; the increasing significance of information and communication processes requires the individual, who thinks, speaks and acts, to be a central participant. The various capital sums involved require the optimal involvement of a cooperative subjectivity in order to lure or force independent subjectivity to co-operate."[8]

Those who have secured and hope to maintain a job can feel pressured because they must constantly train—professionally, methodically, and socially—in order to meet various demands. The question, then, is whether during this lifelong education and training there is ever the potential not just to meet the professional demands but also to realize one's own dreams with a view to becoming capable of changing the working environment? This in turn gives rise to a new challenge of how best to acquire such structural competence.

In order to arrive at some possible answer to this question, we wish to hypothesize a project that engages with this theme.

VIW—Virtual Institute of Work, Philosophy, and Communication

The working environment and its forms of communication are undergoing far-reaching changes. But a new, deeper dialogue between philosophy and the working environment is needed in order to achieve the necessary structural competence. The Bloch Academy,[9] which had been engaged in a project titled "Working Environment Meets Philosophy—Philosophy Meets Working Environment," responded to this need for such development by proposing to establish a VIW—a Virtual Institute of Work, Philosophy, and Communication.[10] This is intended to initiate, structure, and document the process of discourse and is based on five assumptions:

1. The dialectic of work under the contradictory conditions of the expanding Internet economy has resulted in new modes of traffic and new working infrastructures. These lead to a more flexible type of work as well as increased measures to greater flexibility in working relations. The model of a socially equipped/standardized (normal) employer-employee relationship developed for the industrial society

will no longer constitute the dominant or paradigmatic pattern in an IT-based company. In addition to (autonomous) employment, individual and/or individualized independence will gain considerably in influence.

2. The transition from industrial society to an IT-based production and service economy as well as a community of "knowledge workers" affects not only the dynamic of value creation but, alongside the modular production of material and immaterial goods, also gives extended character to the social relations of value creation. This new type of virtual economics polarizes the character and the definition of work within the context of a globalized market relationship. The constantly expanding integration processes of e-working produces atomized "Net Hermits" in the Taylorist sense. On the other hand, it forces the creation of networked individuals who are accustomed to integration and emancipated independence. The extension of the relations of value creation accelerates the process of the total economization of work while increasing the potential for self-determination through "Knowledge Working."

3. A society based on the knowledge economy and IT applications will experience a new dialectic of alienation and at the same time create the potential means of countering such alienation. Judged in terms of the material nature of industrial production, work in the context of virtual value creation is increasingly characterized by abstraction, objectification, and alienation. Digitization, understood as disembodiment, intensifies the separation of the creative human from their product as much as it increases the pace of the economization of individual time by forcing economic considerations into all areas of life. Industrial work, which is traditionally restricted by spatiotemporal considerations, is confronted by a more flexible understanding of place and time in its transition to online worlds. Employees suffer from deterritorialization and detemporalization as additional characteristics of alienation. However, the "Knowledge Worker" is given new options for a reformulation and constitution of self-directed autonomy through human-centered, virtual, space-time integration as well as through the reformulation of liberated space and time.

4. The concrete utopia that works for the liberation of labor, which Ernst Bloch himself envisaged in the workers liberating themselves

from wage labor, no longer adequately describes the process of social hope. The working environment of the present and of the near future will change not only at the level of appearances within a commodity producing society but also structurally. The emancipatory origin of a liberating dialectic of work will come to nothing if the individual acting as part of the collective is construed as the sum of traditional wage labor conditions. If the Blochian framework for emancipation is to maintain some relevance to the working world, it must also be imagined and given priority beyond the confines of wage labor. The diversification of working environments goes hand in hand with the diversification of emancipated workers as well as the diversification of both the routes and goals of the process of emancipation

5. In the future, communication, communication skills, and the integration of interactive media rhetoric [*Rhetorizität*] in communicative practices will determine the ability to work and the employability of those employed. Knowledge-based work environments follow the architecture of communication. Communication follows the structures of knowledge-based work. It is necessary to work out this relationship as well as its potential for emancipation and to focus on the possibility of a future in which labor has become fully liberated.

Hence some further developed theses for future VIW discussions.[11]

I. The industrial working environment of material production and services is increasingly pervaded by virtual working environments. Material and virtual working environments are merging into a new reality, into a tense relationship.[12]

II. This new reality results, among other things, from the fact that the real determines the virtual and the virtual determines the real in a dialectical relationship. Neither is able to function for long without the other. Work of an industrial nature is being gradually replaced by one that combines the material and the virtual. The permeability of the spaces shapes the perception of space as nonstable.

III. The triple unity of place, time, and organization within the traditional industrial workplace has been displaced by a *permanent fourth constant*; namely, the asynchronous reality of work in the knowledge economy in the form of a *nonsynchronous* appearance of place, time, and organization. The work environments of an information and knowledge society are based, among other things, on nonsynchronicity [*Ungleich-zeitigkeit*] between the real and the virtual. Such nonsynchronicity demands a structurally different strategy of emancipation. It includes emancipation with help from the virtual and—especially—within (!) the virtual.

iv. This operational nonsynchronicity of process-related work demands of the subject and of the individual that they see the nonsynchronism[13] of cultural experience and changing consciousness not as a temporary phenomenon but to recognize it as a lasting identity/nonidentity.

v. The power of traditional income-related labor to shape individual identity is beginning to recede. The significance of income-related labor is diminishing while other identity-building factors are increasing. These include the power of communication, urbanity, the aesthetic power of the virtual, and the pull of the ephemeral and the fleeting.

vi. The path of emancipation through the objectification of work is intersected by the path of dematerialization, which allows nonmaterial activity to become a challenge to our sense of individual development.

The Privatization of Hope

What is it that connects our concern for the future of the working environment with the concept of the "privatization of hope"? The answer lies in the Blochian idea that it is in our dreams that the hope for a better world shines forth. The desire/hope for a better world for all arises from the dissatisfaction with existence as well as the uncertainties in individual lives. In this sense, Bloch teaches us to look at the social figurations that determine the lives of individuals. It is quite possible that this may result in kitschy (sentimental) dreams that aspire to and are intended to pander to an entirely personal happiness and that can be readily realized through adjustment to the "given." This danger is especially prevalent in the working environment. But it is also the evolving working environment that makes it clear that only the democratized empowerment of work processes can lead to the improvements that we dream of, that are developed and shared in the workplace, and that serve as a basis for the promotion of the active participation of those involved.

The atomization of workers and their unfair one-sided submission to the needs of the market and capital isolate individual hope. The Taylorization of daydreams, their fragmentation in reified everyday life, threatens to turn dreams and hopes into the lone activity of online-hermits. But the dialectic of the liberation of work as a social hope for emancipation introduces cracks, contradictions, something indelible. At their edges and points of contact the hope of becoming more than ourselves begins to take shape. Various new requirements for and processes of emancipation develop through networks, communities, open source organizations, and the like. It is a question of recognizing them, making structural use of them, and allowing them to become the starting point of activity. Abolishing alienation continues to be a public daydream in postindustrial societies. The new round of discussion between philosophy and the working environment has begun.

Notes

1   Ernst Bloch, "Fundamental Distinction of Daydreams from Night-Dreams: Concealed and Old Wish-Fulfillment in Night-Dreams, Fabulously Inventive and Anticipatory Wish-Fulfillment in Daylight Fantasies" (*PH*, 77–113).

2   Wolfram Burisch, "Das Leben ist Freizeit—Über die Diskriminierung emanzipatorischer Arbeit," *VorSchein* 8 (1987): 17–25.

3   On the question of whether *Heimat* can be a goal in a modern, virtualized world, see *Heimat in vernetzten Welten*, Jahrbuch der Ernst-Bloch-Gesellschaft 2006, ed. Francesca Vidal and Irene Scherer (Mössingen: Talheimer, 2006). The term *Heimat* here has special significance in that it is the word with which Bloch concludes *The Principle of Hope*. It means "home" or "homeland," but Bloch uses it to describe a place we all know from our childhood but we have never visited. This proleptically imagined nostalgic place will only be the outcome of the process of the "laboring and creating human being" and cannot simply be rediscovered.

4   For more on this theme discussed from the perspective of Blochian philosophy, see *Philosophie und Arbeitswelt*, Jahrbuch der Ernst-Bloch-Gesellschaft 2003, ed. Francesca Vidal (Mössingen: Talheimer, 2003). On the relationship between man, nature, and work, see *Naturallianz—Von der Physik zur Politik*, Jahrbuch der Ernst-Bloch-Gesellschaft 2004, ed. Francesca Vidal (Mössingen: Talheimer, 2004).

5   See, for example, Welf Schröter, *Wie wir morgen arbeiten werden: Eine Einführung in die Berufswelt der Informationsgesellschaft* (Mössingen: Talheimer, 2004); Jürgen Kocka and Claus Offe, eds., *Geschichte und Zukunft der Arbeit* (Frankfurt: Campus, 2000).

6   See Christian Fuchs and Wolfgang Hofkirchner, "Die Dialektik der Globalisierung in Technik, Politik, Ökonomie und Kultur," Beitrag beim Jubiläumskongress der Öster-

reichischen Gesellschaft für Soziologie, Vienna, 21–23 September 2000. Available at http://igw.tuwien.ac.at/christian/infogestechn/glob.html.

7 See Rudi Schmiede, "Informartisierung und Subjektivität," in *Wissen und Arbeit: Neue Konturen von Wissensarbeit*, ed. Wilfried Konrad and Wilhelm Schumm (Münster: Westf. Dampfboot, 1999), 134–51.

8 Rudi Schmiede, "Informatisierung und Subjektivität," 10.

9 See www.bloch-akademie.de and www.talheimer.de/presse/20050729.html.

10 Irene Scherer, Welf Schröter, and Francesca Vidal, "via—Virtuelles Institut Arbeit, Philosophie und Kommunikation," in *Träume von besserer Bildung*, Jahrbuch der Ernst-Bloch-Gesellschaft 2007, ed. Francesca Vidal and Irene Scherer (Mössingen: Talheimer, 2007).

11 Welf Schröter, "Wachsende Entfremdung oder Rückkehr einer emanzipativen Antithese? Über Virtualisierung und Entgegenständlichung von Arbeit," in *Heimat in vernetzten Welten*. Jahrbuch der Ernst-Bloch-Gesellschaft 2006, ed. Francesca Vidal and Irene Scherer (Mössingen: Talheimer, 2006).

12 Jutta Rump, Dirk Balfanz, Anatol Porak, and Welf Schröter, eds., *Electronic Mobility—Mobile Arbeitswelten und Soziale Gestaltung: Thesen und Empfehlungen* (Mössingen: Talheimer, 2005).

13 Welf Schröter, "Ungleichzeitigkeiten auf dem Weg in die Informationsgesellschaft—Prozesse der Virtualisierung menschlichen Arbeitens," in *Jahrbuch der Ernst-Bloch-Gesellschaft 1995/96*, ed. Francesca Vidal (Mössingen: Talheimer, 1996), 114: "Entering the virtual forms of work can significantly exacerbate the perception and subjective experience of cultural dislocation, isolation, helplessness, and need for orientation. A supposed security provided by the early phase of Taylorized work processes seems to weigh more heavily as the chances of humanizing both the workplace and the path to the workplace. The political implications of a backwards looking hope for stability are obvious. They are based on social conditions, but are increasingly influenced by social discontinuities. The fracture of the traditional work concept follows the fracture of social stability. Given this scenario, the Blochian category of nonsimultaneity and the approach of thinking in nonsimultaneous contradictions assume a new and important relevance."

Contributors

ROLAND BOER is a researcher at the University of Newcastle, Australia. He writes in the area of Marxism and religion and has published many works, including *Criticism of Earth: On Marx, Engels, and Theology* (2012) and *Nick Cave: Love, Death, and Apocalypse* (2012).

FRANCES DALY is writing a book on Ernst Bloch. Her research interests are in modern and contemporary European philosophy, aesthetics, and cultural theory. She is a Humanities Fellow in the Department of Philosophy, School of Humanities at the Australian National University. She has published works on messianism, the Renaissance, contemporary French thought, and European modernism.

HENK DE BERG is professor of German at the University of Sheffield, UK. His most recent books are *Modern German Thought from Kant to Habermas: An Annotated German Language Reader* (edited with Duncan Large, 2012), *Das Ende der Geschichte und der bürgerliche Rechtsstaat: Hegel—Kojève—Fukuyama* (2007), and *Freud's Theory and Its Use in Literary and Cultural Studies* (2003), which received a CHOICE Outstanding Academic Title Award and has been translated into three European languages as well as Chinese.

VINCENT GEOGHEGAN is professor of political theory at Queen's University in Belfast. He is the author of *Reason and Eros: The Social Theory of Herbert Marcuse* (1981), *Utopianism and Marxism* (1987), *Ernst Bloch* (1996), and *Socialism and Religion: Roads to Common Wealth* (2011). His current research interests are in utopian social theory, postsecularism, and the history of modern British and Irish political thought.

WAYNE HUDSON is Visiting Professor at the University of Tasmania and Adjunct Professor at Charles Sturt University, Canberra. His books include the first standard work on Bloch in English, *The Marxist Philosophy of Ernst Bloch* (1982), and *The English Deists* (2008). He has published eighteen books and sixty-six articles and chapters on related topics.

RUTH LEVITAS is professor of sociology at the University of Bristol. Her books include *The Concept of Utopia* (1990; reissued in 2010), a special issue of *Utopian Studies* on music and utopia (edited with Tom Moylan, 2010), and *Utopia as Method: The Imaginary Reconstitution of Society* (2013).

DAVID MILLER completed his doctoral work at the Bakhtin Centre of the University of Sheffield and was a research fellow at the Institute for Advanced Studies in the Humanities, University of Edinburgh. Working on the relationship of poetry, memory, and trauma, he is showing the continued and crucial relevance of the work of Adorno and Bloch for contemporary literary studies. He is the founding editor of the *Journal of Literature and Trauma Studies* and a lecturer in English literature at Manchester Metropolitan University. His most recent research is a monograph on poetry, trauma, and modernity.

CATHERINE MOIR was awarded her doctorate on the contemporaneity of Ernst Bloch's speculative materialism at the University of Sheffield's Centre for Ernst Bloch Studies in 2013. She is currently a lecturer in German intellectual history at the University of Cambridge and coeditor of the *Bloch Bibliothek* series.

CAITRÍONA NÍ DHÚILL is the author of *Sex in Imagined Spaces: Gender and Utopia from More to Bloch* (2010). Recent and forthcoming publications include articles and essays on Hugo von Hofmannsthal, Ingeborg Bachmann, Frank Wedekind, Ilija Trojanow, and Ingmar Bergman. A graduate of Trinity College Dublin, she has taught at the universities of St Andrews and Vienna and was a full-time researcher at the Ludwig Boltzmann Institute in Vienna. She is currently a lecturer in German at the School of Modern Languages and Cultures, Durham University, and holds a fellowship of the Institute of Advanced Study, Durham.

WELF SCHRÖTER is on the executive board of the Ernst-Bloch-Gesellschaft, is co-head of Thalheimer-Verlag, and is the author and coeditor of many books, including *Karola Bloch: Architektin, Sozialistin, Freundin* and *Lieber Genosse Bloch: Briefe Rudi Dutschke an Ernst and Karola Bloch*.

JOHAN SIEBERS is senior lecturer in the School of Language, Literature, and International Studies of the University of Central Lancashire and Associated Fellow of the Institute of Germanic and Romance Studies, School of Advanced Study, University of London. He is vice president of the Ernst-Bloch-Gesellschaft. His main research interests are in the history of German post-Kantian philosophy, and he has published widely on the thought of Ernst Bloch.

PETER THOMPSON is reader in German history, thought, and politics at the University of Sheffield and director of the Centre for Ernst Bloch Studies. He published *The Crisis of the German Left* in 2005 and has written numerous articles on Ernst Bloch and related subjects. He is currently working on the monographs *Does Marx Still Matter?* for Zero books and *The Metaphysics of Contingency* for Upper West Side Philosophers.

FRANCESCA VIDAL teaches philosophy and rhetoric at the University Koblenz-Landau. Publications include *Rhetorik des Virtuellen: Die Bedeutung rhetorischen Arbeitsvermögens in der Kultur der konkreten Virtualität* (2010) and *Kunst als Vermittlung von Welterfahrung: Zur Rekonstruktion der Ästhetik von Ernst Bloch* (1994). She is president of the international Ernst-Bloch-Gesellschaft and editor of the Yearbook of the Ernst-Bloch-Gesellschaft.

RAINER E. ZIMMERMANN is professor of philosophy at the General Studies Faculty of the University of Applied Sciences in Munich and works primarily on metaphysics and the philosophy of nature, including the philosophy of science. He is co-founder, scientific director, and chairman of the executive board of the Institute for Design Science in Munich. He is author of about 350 publications, among them 24 books.

SLAVOJ ŽIŽEK was born, writes books, and will die.

Index